The Handbook
of Hospital Admitting
Management

Contributors

Kevin D. Blanchet

Edsel A. Cotter

William A. Giwertz

Donald D. Hamilton

Donald E. Hancock

Ollivene Hickman

Lynn Howard

John E. Jacoby

Dale J. Konrad

A. Laurie Laughner

Lucile LePert

Michael H. Littmann

Patricia A. Long

James M. Perez

Betty Powell

Murray Rimmer

Miriam Ross

Marion P. Tanner

Annette L. Valenta

George E. Woodham

Editorial Advisory Panel

The Handbook
of Hospital Admitting
Management

Edited by

Kevin D. Blanchet

Sister Mary Margaret Switlik

AN ASPEN PUBLICATION®
Aspen Systems Corporation

1985

Rockville, Maryland
Royal Tunbridge Wells

Library of Congress Cataloging in Publication Data
Main entry under title:

The handbook of hospital admitting management.

"An Aspen publication."
Includes index.
1. Hospitals—Admission and discharge. 2. Hospitals—Administration.
3. Health Facilities—Administration. I. Blanchet, Kevin D. II. Switlik,
Mary Margaret. [DNLM: 1. Hospital Departments—organization &
Administration. WX 158 H236]
RA971.8.H273   1985   362.1'1'0685   85-7433
ISBN: 0-87189-121-2

Editorial Services: Ruth Bloom

Library of Congress Catalog Card Number: 85-7433
ISBN: 0-87189-121-2

Printed in the United States of America

1 2 3 4 5

Table of Contents

Preface

The growth of health care in this country has been dramatic over the past several decades. As a result, a variety of specialized areas in the delivery of health care have increased their body of knowledge to such an extent that their evolution into recognized professions has become a reality. One of these areas worthy of professional recognition is the field of hospital admitting management.

The development of admitting management into a professional discipline is analogous to that of the field of medical records, which has enjoyed its professional status for a number of years. Admitting managers have their own national association and regional organizations. They have annual conventions, continuing educational opportunities, and their own professional journal. Admitting managers can experience professional development by receiving the accredited admitting manager designation. Thus the entire field of hospital admitting management has been brought to the forefront as a recognized specialization within the field of hospital administration.

Nevertheless, fields such as medical records administration have had one other dimension to their professional stature that admitting did not have. For example, the field of medical records has practically been defined by Huffman's *Manual for Medical Record Librarians*. However, it has only been in the past several years that scholarly research has produced management literature inherent to the field of hospital admitting management. The profession has never had a definitive handbook covering all of the specialty areas encompassed by the admitting department.

With the publication of *The Handbook of Hospital Admitting Management* another milestone is being added to the development of hospital admitting management as a professional discipline. Produced to fulfill this basic need, this handbook has been expressly designed to provide a central source of knowledge about admitting management and its philosophy, theory, and practice.

Among the authors are representatives of some of the finest health care institutions in the country. All are noted for their particular specialty within the field of admitting management. Many are the true pioneers of the profession. They have seen the field grow from a simple clerical function into a highly complex task within the modern-day hospital.

Although the more traditional aspects of hospital admitting management are included, newer areas are addressed as well. These include quality assurance, computer applications, governmental regulations, and the professional admitting manager. This handbook also provides the reader with the latest techniques in the innovative areas of public relations, marketing, and statistical analysis. Some inconsistency and duplication may be encountered, but this is to be expected given the interdisciplinary nature of the field and each author's perspective on the subject matter.

This handbook is designed for admitting managers and others who find themselves faced with managing an admitting department. As such, it is also designed for senior-level administrators who may have the admitting department under their administrative auspices. Most administrators have not been made aware of just how vital the admitting department is to the entire hospital. It is our hope that administrators may be educated to this realization by reading this handbook. Although throughout the text hospitals are used as a reference, the management techniques described can be applied to any situation in which people must be processed in a medical environment, such as a nursing home, urgent care center, clinic, health maintenance organization, or medical group practice.

It is hoped that this text will provide a solid and central source of admitting management knowledge to be used, applied, and adapted to fit the ever-changing needs of hospital admitting departments. We would like to think that it creates a firm case for the importance of hospital admitting as an integral department and for why the admitting department can be the hospital's front line defense in this age of competition.

We wish to acknowledge Sister Nora Phelan, who previewed the original manuscript, and Gail Takacs, who provided assistance with specific illustrations. Finally, we wish to thank all those who provided their moral and professional support to this project. You know who you are.

Kevin D. Blanchet
Sister Mary Margaret Switlik

Chapter 1

The Nature of Admitting

Murray Rimmer

Of all the services available to the American consumer, the one that almost every individual will use at some time is health care services. One may never obtain life insurance, retain an attorney, or consult a stockbroker. However, inevitably, virtually everyone becomes a user of the health care system, with a significantly large number using hospital inpatient services. In addition, the overwhelming number of patients who enter a hospital will have contact with the admitting department.

Considering the frequency and nature of this interaction, the admitting department must be structured to maximize its effectiveness and its efficiency through excellent management. The basic policies relating to patient admissions generally stem from the governing board, based on recommendations from the administrator and the medical staff. The role and functions of admitting departments vary from institution to institution. Some are narrow in focus, while others encompass a broad scope of duties.

Admitting departments may be responsible for or involved in all or some of the following:

- preadmission registration
- preadmission testing
- advanced admission booking
- operating room scheduling
- financial interviewing
- birth certificate preparation
- death certificate preparation
- patient admission
- bed assignment
- patient escorting

- maintenance of liaison with physicians' offices
- generation of information to other hospital departments
- emergency department and outpatient registration functions
- processing of consent forms for treatment and special procedures
- preparation of daily census and other reports
- review of hospital admission designations
- review of length of stay
- acceptance of hospital deposits for patients without insurance
- preparation of identification bracelets

In addition, in some cases, total financial involvement in the patient admission from the point at which the reservation is made until monies for the period of hospitalization are collected from the third party payer is the responsibility of the admitting department.

Because of the complex nature of admitting, it is difficult to establish a uniform definition of the term that would apply in every situation. To better understand the nature of admitting, a simple working definition might be "the process of intake in which an individual becomes a hospital inpatient." The varied and complicated subsystems that relate to the implementation of this process are reflected more accurately not in a definition of the term but in a description of the functions that the admitting department performs.

Effecting a smooth transition for the patient and directing a department in which there are extensive requirements are just two functions of the hospital admitting manager. As such, the manager requires knowledge and skills unique to this highly specialized hospital function. The person charged with the responsibility of managing this department must be multitalented and extensively trained. Increasingly, hospital revenue is dependent on the skill of the admitting manager in maximizing occupancy. The changing regulatory scene, whether the result of legislation or requirements established by accrediting bodies or governmental agencies, makes necessary the requirement that admitting department managers keep abreast of changes that affect the department. Recognizing and dealing with the psychological needs of patients and their families is vital. There are only limited opportunities available to acquire information and for continuing education since this basic hospital service has yet to be afforded the recognition of a hospital vocation. The relatively recent emergence of admitting as a hospital specialty has underscored the need for an educated leadership in this pivotal hospital department.

The supervisory and managerial know-how is critical in an operation that, in most facilities, functions 7 days a week, 24 hours a day, and 365 days a year. There is a scarcity of specific information available in the hospital literature, and the numbers of educational programs available are minimal. Only as recently as

1973 did a small group organize an association of admitting managers dedicated to enhancing the role of admitting in the health care field. The availability of educational opportunities since that time has expanded. Despite this concentrated activity, there is much to be done to prepare future managers for the responsibilities they will assume and to maintain state-of-the-art intelligence.

HISTORICAL OVERVIEW OF ADMITTING

A review of the literature on the method of admitting patients to the hospital is remarkable in that practically no information is available. Various localities throughout the country have seen numerous systems employed to register patients. Not only has the information being sought by the patient differed, but the employee who was responsible for obtaining the data also changed as a reflection of the needs of individual hospitals. In the absence of written information about the history of the admitting department, oral recollections have been relied on to offer insights into the way admitting was done in the past.

In a significant number of hospitals, nurses would record basic patient data, which became the medical record and the hospital's record of the admission of the patient. Since nurses were already on duty during the day, evening, and night hours, it appeared to be logical that since they were readily available, they could obtain the data necessary to effect the patient's admission. In some institutions, this tradition continues. Today, professional nurses combine clinical skill with admitting management proficiency and serve most effectively as managers of the admitting department. There are some facilities in which the admitting department does not operate 24 hours a day. In these cases, a professional nurse assigned either to the department of nursing or the emergency department will record basic patient information and create an admission to be completed by the admitting department staff on the next shift.

Prior to the introduction of sophisticated techniques, and at a point when the knowledge base of the admitting interviewer was not as extensive, clerical employees and information desk staff were called on to serve as admitting interviewers. Social workers, too, were once members of the admitting team. In an earlier time, many governmental institutions used the intake process not only as the means by which to admit patients to the hospital but also to perform a social and family assessment as well as a financial interview. Today, in some psychiatric hospitals, the admitting department is supervised and/or staffed by professional social workers so that a multifaceted interview can be conducted. Prior to the establishment of medical records as a discrete discipline, medical records personnel were among those whose responsibilities included patient admissions.

In the past the responsibility for patient admissions rested with a variety of hospital personnel, ranging from those workers who would obtain the most basic information to professionals who would combine the knowledge of their individual disciplines with the registration of the patient into the system. Undoubt-edly, the simplicity of the hospital system allowed for personnel from a variety of departments to participate in the enrollment of patients into the institution. Today, many persons whose orientation to hospital structure goes back in time may be heard referring to the "admitting room." This designation of one room that housed the admitting activities is a reflection of the minor scope of its role. It is inconceivable to imagine today that the business of hospital admissions could be conducted in such a small physical space other than in hospitals with a small bed size. The notion of a "room" rather than a department refers to the position the function occupied in the organization. As the system has become more complex, the need for a vastly expanded knowledge base has grown and the requirements for admitting patients have changed dramatically.

MYTHS AND STEREOTYPES

The image of the admitting department as reflected in the movies or on television is consistently negative. An aggressive clerk who delights in badgering a patient who is bleeding or in agonizing pain is often seen demanding that a Blue Cross identification card be produced. The concern of staff seems to center around money. Admitting personnel are portrayed as lacking in compassion and under-standing. They perform their jobs routinely, asking questions as if they were robots programmed to perform a specific task.

In addition to being depicted as insensitive persons who require patients to hand over their assets in order to be assigned a hospital bed, admitting staff have been portrayed as stupid, smiling fools whose "do-gooder" behavior borders on ridiculousness. This role of greeter does a disservice to the efficient, knowledge-able interviewers and receptionists who staff admitting departments. The media has presented the impression to the public that admitting personnel are rude and uncaring, since that representation provides for more humorous situations than would exist if they were characterized more realistically.

The perception of the admitting department staff within the hospital community often is negative as well. This may be due in part to the fact that it is the admitting department that generates work for many other hospital departments. The patient who is admitted in the late afternoon, for example, imposes an additional work-load on the house staff, the nursing staff, laboratories, radiology, dietary services, medical records, and all other departments that must establish a record for the patient being in the hospital or must deliver a service to the patient. Often the nursing staff, in particular, has a strained relationship with the admitting depart-ment. In order to perform their responsibilities and use available beds maximally, the admitting department staff must transfer patients or make bed assignments, which creates additional work for the nursing staff. When one recognizes the need for the admitting staff to protect the income of the hospital by making use of available beds, and realizes that admitting personnel must work to make certain the operating room schedule is maintained, these transfers become vital to hospital operations despite the inconvenience they may cause. This can create negative feelings between the admitting and the nursing staffs. The nursing staff may have to assist the patient in recovering from a poorly conducted admitting interview. The effect on the patient of the admitting department experience will extend beyond the admitting encounter, and nurses will certainly view negatively any psychological trauma to the patient prior to the arrival on the unit.

The physician stereotypes the admitting department as well. Admitting may be perceived as the barrier that stands in the way of the patient being hospitalized. In hospitals with high occupancy, the admitting staff may be viewed with distrust and be suspected of favoritism in the selection of patients to be admitted. Situations do arise when admitting staff, for reasons of personal gain or to meet their own psychological needs, show partiality toward members of the medical staff whose patients are given an undeserved high priority for admission. The admitting manager must initiate systems to monitor the flow of patients to ensure the fairness of the bed assignment process. If ever it can be determined that pressure from certain physicians or other means to subvert queuing are employed, the damage to the reputation of the department and its manager can be irreparable. Disgruntled physicians may create the myth that the department may be corrupt even when no partiality is shown.

Staff who work in a variety of hospital departments may receive work inaccurately prepared in the admitting department. If errors are made frequently, additional and unnecessary work is created for other hospital staff members. Significantly frequent errors generated in the admitting department result in negative feelings, and the work of admitting is characterized as careless and negligent. Poor communication results, and unhealthy interdepartmental rivalries occur. The smooth workings of the hospital's operating machinery is compromised, and despite efforts to improve the situation, the resulting inefficiency takes much time to correct.

The administrator's view of the admitting manager varies among institutions. There is a high correlation between the broadness in scope of the manager's role and how that person is viewed within the organization. The admitting manager's performance is the benchmark of how administration perceives the role of admitting, and that is how stereotypes form. The individual's ability to direct others toward the institutional goals and to meet the needs of the organization becomes the critical areas of measurement. As a result, generalizations cannot be made regarding myths and stereotypes administrators may have about the department and its personnel. With the exception of certain clinical areas, the stress in the admitting department is unrivaled in the institution. In a facility where the demand for beds exceeds the supply, pressure is generated by patients, medical staff, administration, and others within the institution. In every setting, requirements are made on the admitting department, some of which are imposed solely because no other nonclinical area operates around the clock. Assignments may be made to admitting for work unrelated to its function simply because the tasks do not fit into the traditional roles of any other hospital department. The admitting manager who reacts inappropriately to these stresses and reacts with untoward, unprofessional behavior creates a stereotypical image that generations of successors cannot overcome.

EXPANSION AND DEVELOPMENT OF ADMITTING

Maintaining the fiscal integrity of the institution and its income picture is a vital contribution the admitting department must make. In preparing the hospital's operating budget for the coming year, revenue estimates are based largely on anticipated occupancy. Occupancy projection, although primarily historical in nature, is modified by changes that can be anticipated during the coming period.

Maximizing bed occupancy, while being aware of the internal and external audit procedures relative to lengths of stay, is a critical element in the day-to-day management of the admitting department. Ensuring that beds are used effectively is not only a function of the creative utilization of beds as they become vacant but also requires positive communication with the physicians who admit patients to the hospital whether they are house staff, full-time faculty, or voluntary attending staff. Successful admitting management is dependent on the development and maintenance of effective relationships with other hospital departments, principally the nursing department. The high degree of interaction between these two key functions must be optimal if the census projections are to be achieved. As an integral part of the hospital team, the admitting manager must recognize the existence of formal and informal organization, knowing how to use each when required to do so.

The information gathering process, which is the keystone of the clerical activity taking place in the admitting department, must be done accurately and the date disseminated with equal accuracy to those departments within the institution who rely on this information. The breadth of admitting knowledge is wide, and its components are diverse. Medical terminology, insurance coverages, clerical skills, systems analysis, work simplification methods, and task orientation must all be included in the armamentarium of knowledge the manager must possess. In dealing with a staff that in many institutions functions around the clock, knowledge of personnel management techniques is essential. The admitting manager should possess demonstrated ability in recruiting and selecting staff, scheduling work hours, appraising and evaluating job performance, disciplining employees, providing counseling, and developing inservice training.

Automated systems in the admitting department require the individual in charge to be knowledgeable in the language and application of computers as they affect reservation systems, preadmission data collection, bed assignment, and, in some instances, integration of admission date with operating room scheduling. Today's admitting department head must be aware of architectural and environmental needs in order to deliver an effective service. The integration of same-day preadmission testing with the hospital admission procedure provides the department head with the opportunity to demonstrate knowledge of how space can be used creatively.

In many instances, the admitting department has responsibility for involvement in medical-legal matters, and it is essential that the manager have knowledge of the laws as they apply to consent for treatment, recording and reporting births and deaths, and other issues that are specific to individual admitting departments.

It is of paramount importance to effect the transition from the state of nonpatient to patient in the most positive and calming manner. The psychology of hospitalization and the behavior this evokes in patients and families, as seen in Appendix 1–A, must be thoroughly known to the admitting manager. Admitting department employees must be attuned to the patient's needs at this sensitive time and their behavior must be understanding and supportive while at the same time obtaining all of the information necessary to prevent any billing or data collection error.

This often neglected aspect of the admitting operation deserves emphasis. The attention placed on the collection of financially related information from the patient results in inattention to the importance of effecting a smooth transition from the status of nonpatient to patient. It is essential for admitting department personnel to understand that the element of fear surrounds each admission. The patient and family are concerned about outcome, pain, disability, disfigurement, and even death. They are afraid the hospital stay will bankrupt them emotionally as well as financially. The hospital is an awesome place, and the mystique surrounding the activities that take place behind the doors creates abject terror for those who enter the system. The level of anxiety is at a high point when the patient and accompanying family or friends are waiting for the admitting interview to occur. The loss of independence and the potential for depersonalization may very well begin in the admitting department. The interviewer must treat the patient warmly and with dignity. The well-trained admitting staff can do much to allay fears and to make the patient feel comforted and reassured. No one expects the admitting personnel to be therapists. However, these employees must have an understanding of basic human behavior, recognizing how vulnerable the patient is at this time. Having the patient arrive at the nursing station calm and at ease has a positive effect on the hospital stay.

The picture of the admitting field that emerges shows a professional in charge whose body of knowledge is different from any other member of the hospital staff.

The elements that have been described form a composite of the relatively new discipline in the hospital field: admitting office management. In contrast to the practice in past decades in which the manager's position was given as the reward to the clerk with the longest period of service to the department, the need now exists for managers who are experienced and educated.

AN EMERGING PROFESSION

In this new profession, the knowledge required is extensive. The manager of the admitting department should possess a college degree, preferably in the social sciences, and should have direct admitting experience. The qualified individual is someone who personally has accepted reservations from physicians, admitted patients to the hospital, and negotiated patient transfers with the nursing staff. Not only will the education leading to the degree provide the manager with concrete information and training in critical analysis, but the skills associated with communication, organization of ideas, and research that are developed and enhanced in the learning process are of inestimable value. A prime reason for the employment of an individual with no less than a baccalaureate degree is the necessity for this principal department to be led by a manager who is viewed by the rest of the hospital staff on somewhat the same level. The hospital hierarchy is replete with staff members who have had years of formal preparation for their responsibilities and have earned degrees at a high level. In today's hospital environment the admitting manager without a formal education will not be perceived as a professional in the light of all those whose positions require degrees, and this ultimately will be deleterious to the impact and effect admitting must have in the institution. In addition to the knowledge requirement in the many subject areas in which admitting is involved, the person in this important job classification must have specific personality qualities. The manager should be creative, assertive, intelligent, dynamic, articulate, and well organized. The list of characteristics is virtually infinite. This person must fulfill all of the requirements to be a leader and at the same time be concerned about the human condition. The department head must be a role model, instilling in the staff the philosophy that "the patient comes first," and demonstrating this credo by the individual's own belief in the worth and dignity of each person who enters the admitting department. The manager has a challenging and often frustrating occupation and cannot always satisfy everyone.

Admitting department personnel must be selected not only for their ability to handle a responsibility that is detailed and requires thoroughness and accuracy but also for specific personality traits. The interviewer must be patient, caring, and vivacious, asking the required questions as if they had never before been asked. The long list of personal qualities that each employee can develop should conclude with "closed mouthed." The data available to admitting staff are confidential and must be treated accordingly. Personal data, diagnostic information, and the operative procedures being considered are among those items of information that staff members must recognize fall within the patient's right to privacy, and this right must be respected.

The ability to remain current is a challenge to those managers who recognize the essential need to update their knowledge in order to perform optimally in a system that is ever changing. Opportunities for acquiring the tools of this new discipline are becoming widely available. Educational institutions have developed curricula specifically designed to enhance or introduce skills in admitting office management. Seminars and workshops under for-profit and not-for-profit auspices are available on a regular basis. In 1974 the National Association of Hospital Admitting Managers was created to provide an organization of professionals whose primary concern was to ensure high-quality patient care. This association has set out to serve as an educational medium for those in the field and has developed a mechanism for certification and for continuing education. Regional organizations throughout the country provide a forum for professional interchange between individuals whose job functions are essentially identical. The calendar of educational programs in the admitting discipline on a nationwide basis is evidence of the need for and the interest in continuing education opportunities.

There is much to be done to educate administrators in how important the admitting manager is as a member of the hospital team. Those in the field have the responsibility to educate the hospital community in what the requisites are for the professional admitting manager. It is only after such education takes place that administrators will recruit or promote qualified individuals into the management position within the admitting department. There is a parallel between the history of this discipline and that of registered record administrators. Medical records administrators have been successful in developing degree programs, levels of certification, and accreditation that created the status these professionals now enjoy. With the same type of effort, admitting managers will be afforded the same status and recognition their medical records colleagues have achieved.

HOSPITAL ADMITTING: TODAY AND TOMORROW

There is no question that the admitting function has made major strides in recent years in being accepted as one of the major nonclinical hospital departments. From its earliest beginnings as the place where patients merely gave their name, address, and next of kin to a staff member to the era of sophisticated computer setups, the admitting department has been the place where the individual makes the transition from outsider to hospital patient. Its continued importance or its passage into extinction is dependent on those who manage these departments across the country. Forward-thinking, assertive, educated managers who understand the health care delivery system and the place of the admitting department within that system will shape the future. This is not the time for passivity. Within the next few years, innovative methods of reimbursement and delivery will be implemented, at the core of which will inevitably have to be the admission of the patient to the hospital. To secure a future for admitting, today's managers must be identified as the experts in developing methodologies to monitor patient flow, physician access to the hospital, length of stay, and the multitude of related activities in which they are already involved.

All indicators for the future point to the development or expansion of mechanisms in which lengths of stay and appropriateness of admissions will be criteria for reimbursement. The entry point for the system will be the admitting department. It is likely that more and more emphasis will be placed on projecting lengths of stay and determining the effective use of hospital resources. The dynamic state of health care spending creates infinite opportunities for admitting to be in the forefront of change. The admitting manager will have greater responsibility than ever before. The next decade will see hospital closings throughout the country. Those institutions that will survive are those that will have developed rational plans for serving the community. The admitting manager will have to be involved in examining population shifts, aging trends, utilization patterns, and other data to assist administration in making decisions about the resources to be made available. Case mix by diagnosis and payer must be analyzed as relevant factors in determining the future direction of each individual hospital. The admitting manager must be thoroughly skilled in analyzing the data available in order to build for the future.

Computerization will affect greater numbers of hospitals, and more admitting tasks will become automated. Despite advances in technology, it is likely, and essential, that people, rather than machines, will continue to admit people to the hospital. The admitting manager must oppose vigorously any attempt to further dehumanize any aspect of hospitalization. The future of admitting management is tied to whom the person reports. Many believe that the admitting function is primarily financial in nature since it does have the responsibility of obtaining complete and accurate information regarding billing and is reflective of a credit and collection function. As a result, it is this philosophy that results in the admitting manager's responsibility directly or indirectly to the fiscal arm of the institution.

A small minority view admitting as an extension of patient care that can be found on the table of organization reporting to nursing services or some other clinical department. More frequent, however, is the situation in which the manager of the admitting department reports to a member of the administrative staff. Those who support this approach see the admitting function as broad in scope and related to a more generic set of responsibilities than either of the two previously described situations. There are other reporting relationships in individual institutions based either on historical or pragmatic rationales. In admitting circles, arguments are heard often regarding the advisability of the department reporting to the finance department as opposed to administration and vice versa. This philosophical debate provides for intellectually stimulating conversation when admitting managers gather. In today's hospital, the structure of the organization, the goals of the institution, the needs of the community and the staff, and many other considerations must be borne in mind when a decision is made regarding the place of admitting within the hospital's organization. Despite disagreement regarding administrative reporting lines, the admitting manager should be at the same level as other department managers and should have responsibilities and benefits equivalent to those at the middle management level.

CONCLUSION

Each hospital operates with unique policies and procedures. The admitting department functions in a different way as one looks from hospital to hospital. Although the tasks that are performed vary from institution to institution, and the manner in which these are executed are subject to individual approach, there is, overall, a sense of unity in the admitting functions and in meeting the goals of an effectively managed department. Each hospital in the United States provides access to inpatient care through an admitting function. There may be great variation in the extent of the role the department and the manager may play. There is no way in which a patient can end up in a bed without some involvement on the part of the admitting department.

The government-sponsored institutions (federal, state or local), the proprietary institutions, and the voluntary hospitals, whether under religious auspices or not, have all developed a system through which individuals are processed for subsequent inpatient care. Emergency patients whose critical condition precludes a stop in the admitting department enroute to the intensive care unit will have their names communicated to the admitting department even as John or Jane Doe if identification is unavailable. Patients planning elective procedures whose reservations may have been placed three months in advance and are asked to report to the admitting department at a specific time will personally experience the components of the admitting system. A vast number of persons seeking in-hospital care, for the delivery of a newborn, for the treatment of a terminal illness, for elective care, and for emergency care, will all have contact with admitting department personnel.

The hospital admitting department must present its face to the community, a community that consists of potential patients, physicians, and employees. For most, it is the patient's first impression of the institution. It is the storehouse for information on large numbers of patients, and its manager must be highly competent and trained in many dimensions in order for the department to function effectively.

Appendix 1–A

Open Letter to Hospital Employees

I am your patient . . .

You've seen me a hundred times . . . with many faces . . . many forms . . . many reasons for being in your care.

I am the frightened, middle-aged woman waiting at your admitting desk, nervously opening and closing my purse.

I am the impersonal, sheet-covered form you see through the partly opened door as you patrol your hallway.

I am the shuffling, stoop-shouldered figure in faded flannel you encounter at every corner as you go about your daily work.

I am the starry-eyed girl who has become a mother for the first time, longing to hold the miracle I have produced.

Everything is new and strange to me. Yesterday I was in familiar surroundings and was happy planning my tomorrow. Today I am in an alien world, trying hard to adjust. The little familiar things of my own world seem to take on great importance. I may complain to you. I may rebel against the strangeness. You see, I don't want to be in the hospital. I want to go home.

From the moment I walk into the admitting office I am a mass of fears. I am fearful of the unknown. I am alarmed over the prospect of pain, disfigurement . . . even death. I fear financial distress or catastrophe. More than anything else, I am lonely.

If I tell you my coffee is cold, it may be because coffee is more than a breakfast drink to me. It has a deep symbolic meaning. Through years of experience, I have come to associate it with congeniality, friendship, the warmth and security of home. And just as hot coffee symbolizes these good things to me, cold coffee reminds me that I am among strangers, antiseptic, and somehow frightening strangers.

When I object to early morning awakening, I often mean that I am insecure.

When I report that my nurse is indifferent, I often mean I feel forsaken.

Source: Reprinted from "I Am Your Patient," Pamphlet Number 50–452 by Gordon F. Lee with permission of Blue Cross of California.

Please understand that often in my complaints about little things, I am trying to tell you of far deeper needs.

Will I lose my identity? Will I be exposed to all sorts of indignities? I'm afraid that I'll be treated not as a housewife . . . father . . . plumber . . . farmer . . . banker . . . but as a fascinating gallbladder . . . an interesting thyroid . . . a stubborn kidney.

I appear normal, but I have left normality outside your door. Though I am mature, I have suddenly become a child, frightened of the long, dark nights.

And . . . oh, how I want you to be warm and friendly! I want you to know that I bring with me a personality, not just another problem in surgery or internal medicine. I want you to know I am much more than a name typed on the band welded around my wrist.

I am suddenly hypersensitive.

In spite of your modern equipment, your electric call boards, your sophisticated systems, I can be devastated by a blunt word from the admitting staff.

Admitting procedures may be routine, but I've never been exposed to them before. In three minutes, the admitting interviewer can wipe me out as an intelligent person, can strip me of privacy, turn me into an impersonalized case history, build an animosity from which I will never recover.

It may be that my sensitivity is exaggerated. But when I show the admitting interviewer my hospital insurance identification card, make me feel welcome. Let me know you're glad I've come to your hospital. Tell me by your attitude that you respect me as an individual.

You may tell me what I expect is impossible, that some "discomforts," some "fears" are part of any hospital stay. I will tell you that I understand this perfectly when I am not a patient, but from the minute I enter your hospital as a patient, my outlook changes. Minor things take on abnormal importance.

Much of my fright as a fledgling patient comes from lack of understanding on my part. All too often you take for granted that I know these things and I'm left to grope for my answers alone.

How can hospital personnel help me through this twilight period?

Warn me about such things as the postoperative depression that is so likely to torment me. Assure me that this is normal and temporary.

Help me bridge my initial feelings of embarrassment. Assure me that the bedpan is only temporary and that as I improve I'll be able to look after myself to a greater degree.

Assure me that I am never alone or abandoned, even on the busiest hospital day. Reassure me that my struggle is not a private one . . . that my feelings, frustrations, resentments and emotions are simply a part of being a patient.

Never forget, you've been a symbol to people like me ever since the Samaritan traveled the road between Jerusalem and Jericho two thousand years ago.

The equipment and the methods have changed. But the concept continues unchanged. You're the benevolent healer, you cannot . . . you dare not . . . change!

Chapter 2

Organizational Aspects of Admitting

Lynn Howard

Admitting departments throughout the country have demonstrated great flexibility in meeting their organizational needs. The various styles of organizing an admitting department, from the centralized, decentralized, and the mini-department concepts, have developed from ten years of experimentation coupled with keen involvement and understanding of client and administrative concerns.

A variety of factors need to be considered when organizing an admitting department. These factors include the size of the facility, the mission and philosophy statements, the physician and departmental needs, and the patient type served by the facility. Important to any organized admitting department are job descriptions for the specific duties and responsibilities in the department in order to back up administrative, corporate, and board policy.

The admitting department is a key element in the coordination of hospital departmental activity that begins with patient registration. This is accomplished by conveying an image to the patient of a sensitive and caring health care provider of quality care. It is also accomplished by providing complete and accurate registration information so that personnel in other departments in the hospital can efficiently process the paperwork and care for the patient. Since the activities of other departments are contingent on those of the admitting department, organization of the department itself is a prime consideration of the admitting manager.

LINES OF AUTHORITY

An Identity Problem

Lines of authority for admitting departments are as varied as the types of admitting departments. In many hospitals the admitting department is positioned under the financial section of the organizational chart. One may also see a hospital

14

admitting department situated under a support function such as medical records or social services. In other hospitals admitting may be under the direct control of nursing. Finally, it may be felt that the only position for the admitting department to operate from is under administration directly. Although the decision as to where one should place the admitting department within the organizational chart comes from upper administration, it is not uncommon to shift this position more than once in an attempt at experimentation.

Reporting Relationships

Pyramid structures in hospital organizations are still the most common, with the admitting manager reporting to a specific director or officer under the administrator. With administrators taking on more responsibilities in an effort toward cost containment, admitting department personnel must become more involved in intradepartmental matters. Providing information and assisting with systems development enhances the admitting manager's role in the health care profession and the ability to deliver quality patient care.

The organizational structure of each health care institution identifies the number and reporting format for departments under its governing body. Similar or related functions are often aligned under the same director or officer to promote greater coordination and communications, thereby maximizing the use of time.

Many hospital administrators break down the main functions of their facility by dividing departments into four major groups: (1) financial, (2) support, (3) professional, and (4) administrative. The admitting department manager most often reports to the administrative or financial officer. However, interaction with all divisions is critical and assistant administrators who have responsibilities for other support departments related to admitting may provide additional support to provide the necessary communication between departments.

Crossing All Lines

A chief function of admitting department personnel is to initiate and collect patient information for which medical records is responsible to keep on file and to subject it to accreditation review. The admitting department also interacts with the patient accounts department. The accounting staff must bill and collect on accounts from the information supplied them by the admitting staff. The nature of admitting dictates the functions of conveying first impressions in patients, collecting data, and disseminating that same data. These functions indicate that admitting crosses all lines to effect coordination and communication on the patients' behalf. Organizational charts showing a hospital admitting department under lines of authority from finance, support services, and nursing are presented in Figures 2–1 through 2–3.

Figure 2–1 Organizational Chart with Admitting under Finance

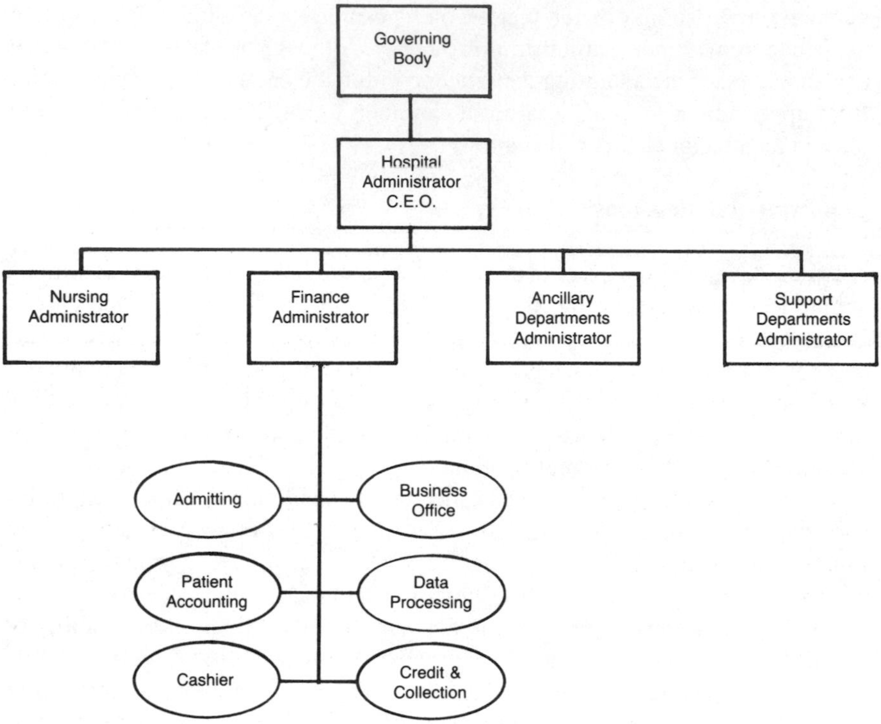

Internal Structure

Within the hospital admitting department, a smaller organizational structure exists. The lines of authority should be clearly identified here, too, with proper labeling of staff and management in the department. The organizational chart of a typical admitting department depends on the size of the institution and the volume of admissions. Positions within the structure of an admitting department may include the following:

- receptionists
- schedulers
- aides
- volunteers
- admission clerks

Figure 2–2 Organizational Chart with Admitting under Support Services

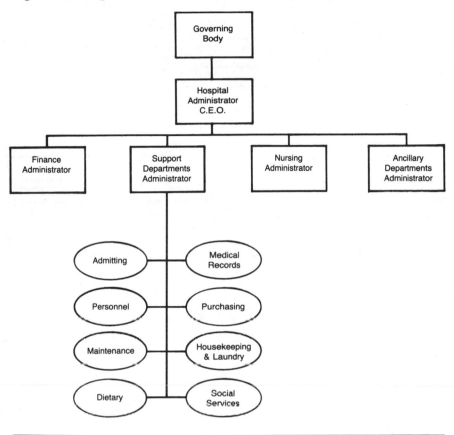

- bed controllers
- escorts
- preadmission clerks
- switch board operators
- outpatient registrars
- cashiers
- emergency department registrars

The organizational chart used for the hospital can be used as a guideline in setting up lines of authority and avenues of communication within the admitting department. An example of an organizational chart for a hospital admitting department can be seen in Figure 2–4.

Figure 2–3 Organizational Chart with Admitting under Nursing

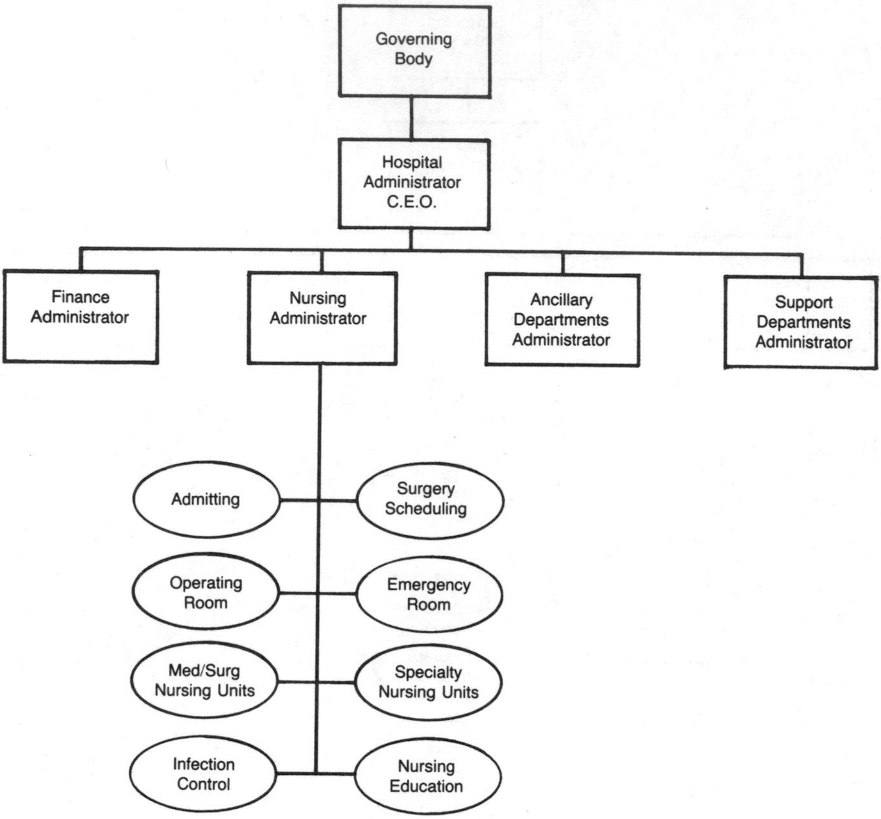

```
                    ┌─────────────┐
                    │  Governing  │
                    │    Body     │
                    └─────────────┘
                           │
                    ┌─────────────┐
                    │  Hospital   │
                    │Administrator│
                    │   C.E.O.    │
                    └─────────────┘
```

| Finance Administrator | Nursing Administrator | Ancillary Departments Administrator | Support Departments Administrator |

Under Nursing Administrator:

- Admitting
- Surgery Scheduling
- Operating Room
- Emergency Room
- Med/Surg Nursing Units
- Specialty Nursing Units
- Infection Control
- Nursing Education

THE ORGANIZATION OF FUNCTIONS

Key Elements

The position a hospital admitting department occupies on the organizational chart is not the only factor that plays a major role in how an admitting department functions. Basic elements of management must also be adhered to in the process. Leadership, staffing, and work functions are just some of the key elements in setting up a department to ensure its successful meeting of day-to-day responsibilities.

Figure 2–4 Organizational Chart for Admitting

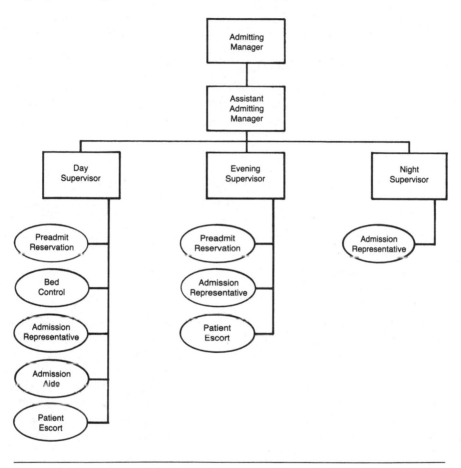

Leadership and Supervision

Capable effective supervision and direction of a hospital admitting department requires the ability to perform the following:

- plan—looking ahead and providing for the future
- organize—structuring the department within the hospital
- staff—scheduling, hiring, and training personnel
- direct—accomplishing mission through the staff
- control—reacting to or improving the above four areas

Staffing

The volume of work dictates the amount of staffing needed to cover all shifts on the days the department is open. Staffing involves the following:

- adequate coverage for the volume of work
- adequate management levels used in the departmental structure to ensure proper supervision each hour the department is open
- shift supervision used or available for each shift

Work Functions

Work functions should be properly aligned so that staff members can make the best use of their time. Ways to accomplish this are as follows:

- separate distinct functions for each responsibility (e.g., verifiers versus admitters)
- let the type of patient determine the location of responsibilities (e.g., emergency department versus outpatient)

Staff members must be held accountable for doing their jobs in a productive manner and completing those items that are a part of their positions. Productivity management standards are often used today that dictate the amount of staff needed for varying levels of activity. Yearly plans coupled with goals and objectives help establish what is expected in productivity, quality, and improvements. A good line of communication is needed to keep the staff informed as to management's expectation of employee performance and to provide the necessary feedback if the department manager is to best use the abilities of the staff.

The Communication Function

Within the department, an often overlooked or underestimated factor is the facet of communication. Often, the typical lines of communication are provided that are necessary for important information. One tends to overlook the needed communication lines within the department for the minor changes such as procedural items that, on the surface, do not seem too important. Yet, over a period of time, these will create major problems. The method of communicating these changes can take place in the form of meetings, reports, or a communication log that is read daily. Whatever form is used, it must be a consistent and ongoing requirement that everyone in the department participates in the meetings or reads the communication log before starting work on the shift.

The communication log is a very flexible system in that any staff member can make comments in the book for those on the oncoming shift that may alert them to difficulties just encountered on the previous shift or that may be coming up for future shifts. A distinct advantage of this system is in the form of the employee just returning from a significant absence (e.g., vacation). In just a few minutes, the returning employee can become familiar with what has occurred during the absence. This will reduce mistakes and the excuse usually made about not knowing a change was made in the department. Everyone benefits from the system.

Job Descriptions

Job descriptions for each category of positions will assist the admitting manager in identifying responsibilities and will more equally distribute the workload. Each job description developed must be read and understood by any applicant to avoid costly misunderstandings in hiring. In departments where there is more than one job description the manager should encourage all employees to be familiar with each one. Cross training to provide for better coverage is effective when duties are clearly understood by all. Employee morale is strengthened when staff members in each area of the department are equally busy or are able to assist those in an area experiencing a high workload. Teamwork and cooperation in the admitting department can be reinforced by clear job descriptions and a spirit of "what can I do to help."

Job descriptions are also useful when developing performance by objective forms for employee evaluation. Using the job description and then noting performance levels next to the function allows the employee to be evaluated in a consistent manner emphasizing equality. Areas of strength and weakness can be discussed with the employee and a counseling plan developed if necessary. An example of a job description for the common position of an admitting clerk is given in Appendix 2–A. An example of a job description for another common position in the admitting department, the bed control clerk, is given in Appendix 2–B.

The Nursing and Infection Control Function

Nurses have been a part of the admitting department scene for many years. Duties of nurses in admitting range from bed placement, physician order taking, and preadmission testing to discharge planning. Whether or not nurses are formally a part of admitting, they play a great role in contributing their judgments to the admission process. In facilities where nurses are not part of the admitting staff, their judgments are critically important to patient placement. Staffs of physicians' offices who call to arrange admission are often without pertinent information to effect placement. Smoking status, room preference, actual condition of the patient at the time of arrival, infections, telemetry requirements, and available nursing staff all present valid concerns when placing a patient in a hospital bed or nursing unit.

Infection control has become a prime concern for admitting managers. Infection control nurse coordinators assist in this process and recognize the fact that the admitting department representative is the first contact by the patient with the health care facility. It is recommended that the admitting department manager be on the infection control committee since this enables admissions to gain firsthand information that will assist the department. These are just a few examples of how important intradepartmental communications and relationships are within a modern hospital. The admitting department personnel must depend on employees in many other departments and on physicians and their staffs as they, in turn, rely on the admitting department personnel.

THE CASE FOR PLACING ADMITTING UNDER FINANCE

The Business of Admitting

In many hospitals the admitting department is placed under the finance division of administration. The business of a hospital is to provide quality health care to the patient. This requires that the hospital be responsible to the community, both financially and regarding employment. Hospitals are caught between the state of being both financially sound and responsive to employee needs and that of providing care that is sensitive to the patient's medical condition. They must also generate sufficient cash flow to meet future needs in equipment and personnel, and maintain an adequate cash flow to meet salaries and supplies on a daily basis. Hence, the reasons for the admitting department to be under the finance department are many.

The admitting department has a very important role in the success or failure of a hospital accounting department. It helps collections by providing complete and accurate information in three areas for the patient accounts department:

1. general background information
2. third party payer information
3. credit information

It also assures good public relations with patients by being responsive to questions about financial policies at the time of admission. Finally, admitting personnel promote good interdepartmental relations and attitudes by supporting all departments in the presence of the patient.

The Bottom Line

Proper collection of patient social and financial data will ensure that the business office can receive payment. This usually consists of completing or clearing each patient account to a paid or zero balance. However, not all accounts are paid in full. Some accounts are charged off to charity, to assistance programs, or as bad debt. A decision as to what can be done with each patient account is impossible without complete and accurate registration information.

Missing information not obtained at the time of admission can delay both the time it takes to get reimbursement and the process of sending the statement. This missing information also hinders the verification of insurances and makes collecting self-pay accounts difficult or virtually impossible. Each day of delay is costly, both in terms of interest lost on the income and the salaries spent in the business office on follow-up procedures to get the needed patient financial data.

Other Reasons

There are still other reasons why the admitting department should come under the finance department. One of these reasons is cash collection. Cash collection at the time of admission and discharge is rapidly gaining favor in hospitals. By aggressive preadmission and good collection of information, an admitting department can be instrumental in maximizing cash inflow prior to admission or on discharge.

Another area in which the admitting department is of assistance is in providing information on policies for private rooms. Today it is often requested that the patient pay the additional amount charged for the private room on dismissal since most insurance plans will not pay for private rooms granted as a patient request.

Verification of insurance benefits is still another good reason. This is usually a full-time position in most hospitals, and it soon pays for itself in identification of potential payment problems prior to admission. Occasionally patients choose not to be admitted after learning that no coverage is available for their elective surgery or that the coverage is not as good as they thought.

Finally, the admission area has also come under the diagnostic related group (DRG) concept. This is a recent plan that affects the Medicare admissions and discharges, including transfers of Medicare patients. The biggest contribution admissions makes here is an accurate admission diagnosis and proper documentation on dismissal of the patient as to where the patient was discharged, such as a rehabilitation hospital, a nursing home, or a transfer to another medical facility. All of these areas have their own guidelines as to the DRG regulations. Some admitting areas code the admissions with the ICD-9 coding that is used for DRG systems.

THE CASE FOR PLACING ADMITTING UNDER ADMINISTRATION

Regulation of Admissions

There are many hospitals in which it is preferred that the admitting manager report to a senior member of the administrative team. Once again, there are many reasons for support of this position. One of the reasons is the impact on admitting regarding governing board policies concerning admissions. County or community hospitals may be in the position to accept any patient regardless of ability to pay as dictated by their board. Private and specialized facilities, on the other hand, may only be able to obtain payment prior to or at the time of service and turn away those who cannot pay. Health maintenance organization (HMO) subscribers must obtain service at designated facilities and from designated physicians. Legal and moral responsibilities must be well documented in the admitting department, and personnel must be aware of admission policy changes on a timely basis. The administration and governing body of each institution are concerned and aware of the trends in health care. In the future, more attention will be paid to the admission policy of hospitals and changes will affect the admitting department directly.

Reductions in Staffing

In addition to offering new or specialized services and developing outpatient processing, administration will also be responding to decreasing census by cutting down on staff. Statistics related to volume and time must be measured against institutional expectations of admitting. Productivity studies and other methods of relating work to staffing can be useful when justifying personnel budgets to administrators. The concern for cost containment within admitting requires admitting managers to be creative and innovative when responding to cutbacks. The challenge has been extended to admitting managers to direct their departments with fiscal integrity and yet to keep standards high in patient interactions and data collection efforts.

Legal Issues and Risk Management

Another reason for placing admitting under administration stems from the popularity of risk management programs and the legal issues facing administration. Consent policies are now regarded as a critical part of patient care. State and federal laws have mandated the use of the consent form by requiring certain information to be relayed to every patient. Combining authorization for care, release of medical information, Medicare certification, release for valuables, and the financial requirements has guided this into prominence.

An example of risk management in admitting would be documenting a patient's fall as the patient enters the building, objectively explaining the circumstance in written form, and forwarding the document to the risk manager. Also, any variation in the norm for the admitting department would justify a variance report. As these reports are accumulated, patterns emerge that might not otherwise be apparent in daily activity. Safety in the admitting department is as important for the employee as it is for the patient. Admitting managers should be aware of any risks presented in their department and be prepared to act on any risk identified in their department.

There are two other areas of importance to administration that involve the admitting department. One of these is the safekeeping of valuables. The responsibility for proper documentation and the obtaining of proper signatures falls to the admitting staff person assigned to this duty. An administrative concern relating to valuables procedures is the release of valuables to other individuals besides the patient. Administrators need to be aware of problems and concerns with respect to valuables since the implications for litigation and angry customers are ever present.

Administrators have also realized the importance of customer and physician relations within the admitting department. Patients have a perception of being at the mercy of the hospital. Likewise, physicians understand that their referrals keep hospital doors open. Administrators want an admitting department organized to respond to perceptions so that impressions can be enhanced and business promoted. A positive admitting department reflects well on the administration as to how much admitting can offer to the community.

TYPES OF ADMITTING DEPARTMENTS

Much variation exists in establishing the type of admitting department in each facility. Two popular types are centralized (one area) and decentralized (two or more areas). Because of the logistics within the department, much of the decision making is largely due to layout. A facility in which the admitting department was planned as an afterthought rather than as a key to access must have personnel who are prepared to deal with ensuing problems. However, many innovative ideas have resulted from this. Benefits from each type (centralized and decentralized) must be weighed with reference to meeting customer expectations and departmental requirements and cost.

The Centralized Admitting Department

Centralized admitting departments combine inpatient and outpatient admission functions into one area. The ability to cross train, cover for vacations and illness, and maintain a view of the total picture can be most advantageous. The workload is also easier to control if all entities are within a short distance, offering the supervisor visual access to the total department. Systems for receiving patients have been developed that allow separate waiting rooms for inpatients and outpatients so as not to confuse their perception of service. Reception areas often will have a check-in system identifying the patient status, so the admitting personnel can process patients more efficiently. Inpatients are most often ill or anticipating surgery and expect to be dealt with in a more urgent fashion. Outpatients often require tests or treatments or elective surgery and demonstrate less anxiety on admission. Separating the waiting areas can reduce the problem of an outpatient feeling left out when an inpatient was served first. Each patient, whether an inpatient or an outpatient, expects first-class treatment on arrival at the admitting department.

The Decentralized Admitting Department

Decentralized admitting departments are more varied in the ways to process patients. Some will have a separate outpatient unit to handle outpatients only. This method of admission often has a specific access door to the outside of the building to further specialize the service. Depending on the volume of patients and their inpatient or outpatient status, this method can be useful in reducing large numbers of patients in waiting areas. If outpatient volume is very high, a preadmission system for routine tests can be very beneficial. Assigning times for patients can help reduce waits and will allow other department managers to project staffing needs as a side benefit.

The Mini-Admitting Department

The mini-department concept provides a separate self-contained admitting department on each unit of a health care facility. The admissions representative located on each nursing unit produces the mini-department concept for each nursing floor. This has several advantages for the nursing unit and the physician. With admitting staff on each floor, the nursing unit and the physician get personalized attention. This permits direct admission to each nursing unit. The admitting staff can get follow-up information and forms signed as the patient is able to do so. Emergency admissions do not present the problems here that they do with a centralized admissions concept since the admissions staff can work with the family or patient in the nursing environment. Often there is a greater rapport and respect for each other's work responsibilities and difficulties that are a very real part of daily jobs. Nursing and physicians like this approach to admitting.

On the other hand, the increased administrative responsibilities and higher costs associated with the mini-department concept may not be acceptable to a hospital.

Coordination of staff is difficult and requires a higher concentration of admitting supervisors to ensure that the paperwork from each unit is complete. Staffing schedules may become complex, and a larger staff is required since several small admitting departments are needed. Each of these smaller departments has its own demands and becomes very specialized in the work of its own nursing unit. A considerable amount of cross training is required if the staffs are to work on other nursing units. With the additional amount of supervision required, one can see that costs of running this type of department are higher. This concept is more applicable to smaller hospitals in which less complex communication channels are needed. In larger hospitals, it is more efficient and productive to centralize the admitting staff and enjoy the economies of scale that happen when common equipment, staff, and work areas are used.

The Right Choice

A review of current organizational structure, alignment of departments, and location of hospital entrances is in order before one selects which admitting department concept will work best for the hospital. Difficulties may be encountered if centralized admissions are desired and if there are many entrances to the hospital that encourage inpatients to enter at one location and outpatients to enter at another location. Whatever the size or organizational makeup of the hospital, the admitting department can be organized in an efficient and effective manner that will meet the administrative needs. The long history of flexibility within the admissions area has proven this.

The Patient Services Representative

Another type of admitting department has its main difference contained in the functional roles of the personnel working in it. Admitting managers have recognized the need to meet financial as well as social needs of patients by introducing patient services representatives to their staff. These individuals are trained primarily in two different ways. First, they serve as a combination of admitting clerk, billing clerk, and collection clerk. This combines the functions of the business office and the admission process to offer patients personalized financial services. One person admits the patient, processes the claim, and collects any balances. The intent here is to reduce patient frustration. Also, the increased knowledge base of the patient services representative has had a positive impact in hospitals around the nation.

The second type of patient services representative is trained to function in a slightly different manner. The difference here is that these persons do not function as collection clerks. Instead, they combine the admission function and patient representative function. They handle inquiries regarding patient concerns or compliments regarding their insurance, the staff, or physicians. They investigate and document this and may submit written reports to the department concerned. They must be very familiar with their hospital's policies and will refer the patient to the social services department in cases where direct patient care or legal issues come up. Their goal is to promote excellent relationships between the patient and the hospital staff.

CONCLUSION

Within each organization there are people with their own sense of responsibilities. The most important requirement of an admitting manager in organizing a department is the ability to interrelate with each type of individual in an effective and cooperative manner. Understanding the people involved can offer perspective in day-to-day operations as well as for future planning for the admitting department. By never losing sight of the most important responsibility—the patient—the admitting manager can use intelligence and compassion in striving to make the best of this area of responsibility. The admitting department organization may seem simple by design as viewed on an organizational chart. It is much more complicated, however, than many people realize. Dealing with and providing information for so many entities will enhance the professional role in health care as well as develop the admitting manager as a human being. The role of an admitting manager may seem minor to an outsider. A smoothly functioning department is the best reward there is. The administrator should be informed as to the admitting manager's part in the daily activity in the hospital. A simple board that posts census figures daily often draws the administrator into the admitting department to check occupancy as well as interact with personnel. Thus admitting managers can demonstrate and market their capabilities to those who control the hospital, the organizational structure, and the operating funds.

Many organizational structures have been used in admitting and have been successful, thus offering hope to the admitting manager looking into alternatives. The cooperation among admitting managers is high, and questions and interactions are welcomed by all who manage admitting departments. This is a means of enhancing professionalism within the field of admitting. A hospital's first impression often starts with the admitting department and is imparted by the way staff members have treated the patient or conducted the admission process. The service and impressions left are also left with those in other hospital departments by way of an accurate registration process that demonstrates the quality of the admitting department's organization, supervision, and staff.

Appendix 2–A

Typical Job Description for Admitting Clerk Position

JOB TITLE: Admitting Clerk

SUPERVISED BY: Admitting Supervisor (or Manager)

STAFF SUPERVISED: None

JOB SUMMARY:

Interviews incoming patients or their representatives. Is responsible for information that is accurate and complete. Must maintain a positive public image to patients, hospital, or medical staff. Prepares admission form and obtains signatures as required. Answers patients' questions on admission policies. Informs patients of hospital policies regarding valuables or room charges. Is responsible for maintaining confidentiality of the patient admission information.

Duties:
1. Welcomes all new patients or relatives in a courteous prompt manner
2. Obtains social, financial, and personal data from patient
3. Obtains insurance forms and/or copies of insurance cards
4. Explains hospital policies regarding admission
5. Determines nursing floor to be used, room preference of patient and makes bed assignment (may give this information to bed control clerk for bed assignment if bed control clerks are used)
6. Obtains required signatures
7. Completes the admission, legal, financial, or medical forms as required
8. Prepares the admission form, copies as required

Source: Courtesy of Poudre Valley Hospital, Ft. Collins, Colorado.

9. Prepares ID bracelet and other related items as required (PBX or visitor information cards)
10. Verifies that preadmitting tests are completed and routes patient to proper department for tests as ordered by physician
11. Prepares admission chart that will accompany patient to floor
12. Introduces patient to patient escort with instructions as to the location the patient is to be taken, such as laboratory for testing, the nursing floor, etc.
13. Distributes the remaining admission forms to appropriate areas
14. Follows up on incomplete information or makes arrangements to obtain
15. Preadmits patients, explains policies, etc., in same detail that is required for admissions
16. Answers phone, assists with other jobs in department as requested
17. Attends department meetings, training sessions
18. Performs related duties as assigned

Specifications:

High school education. Must follow oral and written instructions. Able to use good grammar and spell correctly. Be able to type 45 WPM minimum. Have had a course in medical terminology or is willing to take a class within six months of starting. Course in cardiopulmonary resuscitation helpful. Able to handle wheelchair with heavy patient. Able to operate under pressure of demands on time for short periods of time. Must have a friendly personality, tact, patient empathy, and a helpful yet professional attitude.

Personal Contacts:

Hospital employees, medical staff, visitors, and patients both by phone and in person.

Working Conditions:

Work includes using typewriter, computer terminal, copy machine, card embosser, and imprinting equipment. Patients may be escorted or transported by wheelchair to nursing units or ancillary areas. Work also involves walking to appropriate areas with forms.

Promotion From:

No formal line of promotion—possible transfers from related clerical positions within the hospital.

Promotion to:

Admitting supervisor.

Appendix 2–B

Typical Job Description for Bed Control Clerk Position

JOB TITLE: Bed control clerk

SUPERVISED BY: Admitting Supervisor

WORKERS SUPERVISED: None

JOB SUMMARY:

Provides a bed control and information center for admissions, hospital staff, and outside agencies on all inpatient bed information. Continually updates bed control panels and daily census figures. Answers phone to disseminate information as requested. Reserves rooms and takes information on new admissions. Assigns rooms in accordance with hospital policies regarding the appropriate nursing units. Coordinates physicians, patients, and nursing bed or room requests with the available beds and approved procedures. Coordinates nursing and patient room transfer requests in a timely manner.

Duties:

1. Remains at control desk during entire shift, unless properly relieved
2. Scheduling

   - records physician requests for admission on admission request log
   - assigns rooms to requested admissions at beginning of shift
   - works with nursing units in assignments if unusual; otherwise follows approved patient room assignment nursing guidelines

Source: Courtesy of Poudre Valley Hospital, Ft. Collins, Colorado.

31

3. Bed assignments

- coordinates patient's request for room, smoking status, sex, and diagnosis with the available beds and assigns patient preference when possible
- assigns beds in accordance with placement guidelines of each nursing unit
- coordinates bed assignments with nursing units and nursing supervisor when a patient must be admitted to an inappropriate unit

4. Transfers

- records all requests for transfer on transfer request log
- makes necessary arrangements to transfer patients as requested by medical staff or hospital staff
- arranges transfer of patients to accommodate patients' requests for type of room, semi or private
- arranges transfers within the priority of transfer guidelines

5. Bed control panel

- at beginning of shift verifies all admissions, transfers, discharges agree with bed control panel
- continually updates bed control panel with current admissions, transfers, and discharges
- contacts nursing units for information on planned discharges, and records this on bed control panel to allow planning for use of these beds for incoming patients
- verifies accuracy of bed control panel with nursing units each shift
- works with medical records in assuring accuracy of daily census statistics

6. Answers phone to give information on patients, admission room policies as requested
7. Assists hospital departments with patient location information
8. Works with nursing units in determining numbers of planned admissions for the next shift as a factor in planning for staffing required on the nursing unit
9. Works with related hospital departments such as nursing supervisor if difficulties arise in placement of patient, census high, unclear physician orders, or need to open or close nursing units

10. Works with infection control officer as required
11. Verifies accuracy of daily census figures
12. Attends department meetings, training sessions
13. Performs related duties as assigned

Specifications:

High school education preferred with one year of experience as admitting clerk. Must be able to follow oral and written instructions. Able to pass a typing test of 45 WPM, use good grammar and spell correctly, have had a course in medical terminology. Course in CPR helpful. Ability to operate under pressure of demands on time for short periods, ability to make accurate timely decisions within the area of departmental and hospital policies.

Chapter 3

Architectural Design Principles for Admitting

Annette L. Valenta

In the interim since the research herein was reported, I have worked as a consultant with many admitting managers on the design of their admitting departments. In this process, two significant issues have emerged:

1. Admitting managers do not have available the research conclusions needed to support design alternatives that may better meet their needs but result in more expense.
2. Admitting managers frequently want to replicate another hospital's design solution, not realizing that the layout requested cannot be duplicated due to structural barriers and may not meet the behavioral needs generated in their admitting milieu.

This chapter has been written to respond to these observations. It provides an in-depth, scientific review of pertinent literature and reports the results of a project specifically developed to evolve guidelines for the design of admitting departments. It should be noted that research continues in the field of office design on an international scale. Its evolution is providing increasingly sophisticated data on which to base design responses.

It is my hope that those reading this chapter will digest the philosophy of design needs and will follow the guidelines in order to develop an admitting department design that accurately reflects each department's unique administrative and structural setting, while meeting the universal behavioral needs of the admissions environment. It is my belief that understanding the basic design needs of a particular hospital is more important than replicating design solutions arrived at by other hospitals.

The discussion and conclusions in this excerpt are derived from information emanating from a two-part study that served as the basis for a 1981 doctoral dissertation entitled ''Architectural Implications of Human Behavioral Needs in

Hospital Admissions Management.'' An introductory pilot study involved research in four Chicago and Milwaukee hospitals. The main study expanded that research project to 22 more hospitals in the same regions.

The project focused on developing design principles for use in hospital admitting departments by interviewing staff members about acceptable and unacceptable physical design features of the sample admitting departments and substantiating their positive impressions and/or uncovering different examples of appropriate design responses in the literature available in the field of environmental psychology.

It was apparent during the research interviews that regardless of the final layout of a new department, those admitting staff who had participated in the design process considered the physical space more successful. Sloan has shown that office workers who have been actively involved in decision making are more satisfied with, or more tolerant of, their work environment, even in its faulty aspects.[1] This guide is intended for use by both groups involved in design decisions—architects/planners and hospital personnel (especially admitting staff). Workers want honest and meaningful participation. It was found that those workers who reported ''slight participation'' in the space design and furniture selection process expressed the most dissatisfaction. Although this guide outlines the general considerations necessary in the responsive design of an admitting space, the nuances disclosed in admitting duties and responsibilities among hospitals make it necessary that those individuals most familiar with the ''wrinkles'' of their job participate to ensure the best incorporation of the design responses discussed.

SPECIAL DESIGN NEEDS

Early in each interview during the hospital survey, questions were asked regarding the presence or absence of certain programs and physical spaces. It was postulated that inclusion of these elements would change the needs of the department. Some spaces, such as discharge waiting areas and playrooms, were not found in any of the hospitals. There appeared to be no particular need for a separate ''patient escort'' waiting area. The occurrence of pretesting facilities in departments was so low (2 in the sample of 26) that it was difficult to determine any special needs other than those covered by regulations for laboratory spaces. It was found that the physical responses to psychological needs do not differ among the various stages of admission. Confidentiality (privacy) in the interview area was affected by the same architectural elements as confidentiality in the preadmissions area. As a result of these findings, the design principles have been developed for use throughout the entire department, not just for use in certain spaces within the department.

The second issue that was examined was similarity of architectural needs/ responses across cultural groups. Hospitals had been selected to represent a wide range of patient populations; however, the interview responses were similar regardless of site. There appeared to be no specific architectural elements dependent on the patient population (socioeconomic conditions) served. It could be that the research instrument was not sensitive enough to these cultural design codes; for example, it did not examine whether seating patterns were different among different patient populations, only whether seating was flexible. It could also be that the identified behavioral needs in one group are affected by the same architectural responses as these needs in another group; for example, confidentiality (privacy) among blue collar workers is supported by private offices as it is among white collar workers. For the time being, however, it was found that responses were the same across all institutions, regardless of the population served.

DESIGN PRINCIPLES

During the research, it became apparent that staff needs, in order of urgency, were communication, stress reduction, confidentiality, and safety/security. For patients, confidentiality was most urgent, followed by communication, safety/ security, and stress reduction. The environmental elements most often mentioned during the course of the study focused on the many forms of privacy. The environmental design receiving the poorest ratings overall for privacy in all its forms was the open plan office. The classification used to describe the variety of open plan offices available was developed by the Buffalo (New York) Organization for Social and Technological Innovation (BOSTI).[2] This classification recognizes three arrangements for open plan offices and a fourth arrangement called a private office:

1. bullpen—in this open plan the only office walls are the exterior structural walls or a single set of partitions enclosing a group of desks.
2. screen—this open plan incorporates either purchased or built in-house partitions separating desk tops. This arrangement usually has a long counter top with partitions, creating cubicles.
3. system—this open plan arrangement requires the purchase of an entire office unit including partitions, desks, storage bins, and so on from a manufacturer.
4. private—this is the only alternative to the open plans. It has offices enclosed by solid walls, incorporating a door and perhaps a window.

This dissatisfaction with open plans led to an inquiry as to the cause. Were open plan offices inevitably unsatisfactory, or were there remedial design responses possible? An explanatory article written by Howard revealed several possible reasons for the apparent failure of this design scheme.[3]

The original theory of the Quickborner Team (the German management consulting company who introduced the concept to the United States in 1964) was that an open office, carefully arranged, minimized the time lost in transporting people and paper throughout the office. It was not automatically more efficient, however. Comprehensive planning was mandatory, not optional.

When its cost effectiveness was questioned (time was needed to understand the workings of a firm's management to design an office landscape properly), the concept was marketed on the merits of increased flexibility over dry wall construction, permitting rapid changes in management policies. Launched as a management concept, however, office landscaping was never intended to depend on landscape furniture design because its flexibility then depends on whatever is the least flexible furniture element. Without flexible lighting fixtures or a flexible electrical outlet system, the landscape is no more movable than conventional offices.[4] In fact, Planas of the Quickborner Team questioned efforts by landscape furniture designers in the early 1970s. He believed the systems were too primitive and too piecemeal to make a landscaped office work.

The Quickborner Team found that the absence of walls in open plans facilitates communication (and, indeed, several managers during the survey for this research believed their open plans increased staff communication). In an office where mechanical chores have been computerized, this increased ability was supposed to stimulate thought and increase productivity. Since this communication depends on the physical environment, it was the next chosen selling point for landscaping. Unfortunately, increased communication has meant increased distraction, and there is no evidence that an increase in communication increases productivity.[5]

In research completed on open plan offices by Sundstrom and colleagues practically no relationship at all was found between architectural accessibility and social interaction among co-workers.[6] The authors suggest that this finding results from the fact that those employees in the study had already worked in the environment for six months, and perhaps moving into an open plan office increases interaction for only a short period. Employees may then revert to earlier habits of interaction as they adapt to the less private conditions and develop ways of regulating social contact. It may also be that as individuals communicate more by means of computer, the landscape's "enhanced communication and interaction" may be less needed.[7]

Open plans do decrease the amount of circulation (corridor) space required per employee. The Quickborner Team found a 30 percent savings in the number of cubic feet per worker.[8] Since spaces used for corridors in conventional office arrangements can be enlisted as work space in landscaped offices, more people can be fit in, which can reduce initial costs. The trade-off here is as density increases, so does clutter, while privacy declines.[9] Crowding together of work spaces can be detrimental to productivity.[10] Overcrowding is a phenomenon that can occur easily in a work organization that makes space layout calculations based on purely mechanistic notions of the amount of space taken up by bodies and movement. Crowding is in large part a psychological and social phenomenon, not an engineering measure. Whether a layout seems crowded will depend on the norms and needs of the workers who use it.[11]

It is said that an open office can be provided with acoustical and visual privacy.[12] Ranger Farrell Associates, an acoustical consultant, has proposed that it is the distance between work spaces that is the second most important noise control factor for a landscaped office. (First, is the loudness of the employees' voices.) Another office design consultant believes that if open plans are to work— if one wants open interaction while still providing privacy—each employee actually needs more space than in a traditional office, not less.[13] Within this admitting study the most successful open plans were those with dispersed layouts providing plenty of open space. The use of sophisticated and expensive acoustical treatments (acoustical fiberglass ceilings, sound-absorbing partitions, and masking sound systems) will help reduce the din, but only at the cost of raising initial expenses.[14]

Employers have been unwilling to make the initial expenditures for such sound-proofing systems in the past. Brill believes such "economizing" might backfire because employers "think they're saving money and space, but they may be losing productivity." That cost is much greater than the initial expense of furniture and space. "The real cost of running an office is the people," says Brill. "The facilities cost 2 percent; the energy and cleaning costs are 6 percent. But the people cost 92 percent. If you change the facility, that 2 percent area, the relative cost is tiny, but the payoff could be immense."[15]

Thus, landscaping must be bought in concept, not piecemeal, which means proper space planning, acoustics, lighting, electrical wiring, duct work, and so on.[16] Its space efficiency is highly questionable. It is a "money is in the details" concept,[17] which may make landscaping more expensive than erecting dry walls.[18] Perhaps the actual expense of a well-planned, well-executed office landscape is the cause of failure of this option within the admitting environment. To remain within the budget, corners are cut in landscape design. Inadequate space is provided between interview areas; the perception of crowding increases along with the perception of noise and loss of privacy. There may be nothing inherently wrong with open plan designs; the problem may be that so far office workers have seen only half-hearted attempts to create open offices.[19]

Communication

When admitting staff members were asked during the survey for this research whether the present physical design of their admitting department supported the need for staff communication, overall the present designs were most successful. Centralization of staff spaces seemed to be key; however, centralization of work means centralization of noise and its concomitant disruption of communication. As a result these same spaces were rated as unsupportive of patient communication. Since the perception of confidentiality (privacy) is closely linked, these spaces were also unacceptable in supporting that patient need. Only private office plans fared well in supporting patient confidentiality and communication.

Sommer has examined extensively how space affects the effectiveness of communication.[20] He established that people prefer a face-to-face orientation during informal conversation rather than a side-by-side position, until beyond a separation of chairs of three feet, six inches. Then, the side-by-side seating arrangement, although judged to be more spatially intimate, is preferred. Mehrabian and Diamond replicated Sommer's work, using college students, and found most conversation occurred when chairs were angled at 90 degrees rather than 30 degrees or 180 degrees.[21] Self-disclosure seems to reach a maximum within a particular range of interpersonal distance. Outside of this range, with both increased or decreased proximity, disclosure probably begins falling off.[22]

Besides the availability of personal space affecting communication within an office, the location of the desk alone bears on communication. Formal interactions occur where discussions are carried out over a desk top, with the occupant seated in a private zone and the visitors seated in a public zone. When seating is side-by-side, there is not the same formal interaction, and although during interviews and discussions the occupant may still remain in a private zone, there is no clear physical barrier separating the two. Whether or not the desk forms a barrier between occupant and visitor communicates what sort of interaction is desired.[23]

In a study in which physicians wanted to reduce patient tension, physician offices were designed so that patients sat by the doctor's side to talk rather than across the desk.[24] During the research interviews, however, some admitting staff members felt that patients got too close and encroached too far into staff personal space. This was generally the case in smaller offices that barely held the registrar and the patient let alone registrar, patient, family members, and luggage. In another study of furniture arrangement in offices, desks were arranged so that occupants could see both windows and doors when seated. It appeared to be more important to be able to see who was coming into the room and to be instantly prepared for them than to be able to glance out the window. Whether or not the occupant sits facing the door communicates readiness for interaction.[25]

Perhaps environments should be arranged so that when people are in them they will not be locked rigidly into personal space relationships. Office chairs that have fixed positions may be too rigid. An alternative would be offices with optional configurations—chairs on opposite sides of the desk, at the corner of the desk, on the same side of the desk. In this way the personal space of occupant and visitor are adjustable.[26] (Flexible furniture arrangements are not common in the admitting environment. Of the 21 hospitals observed, only four waiting areas had furniture that permitted flexible seating patterns to suit the various conversational groupings of patients and families. Generally, there is no way to adjust personal space infringement except to get up and move.)

Confidentiality

Unfortunately, the better the health centers are organized and designed to facilitate communication between their occupants, the greater the risk that confidences will be shared. Because communications are more difficult to control in a larger group, there is a greater chance that neighbors and workmates will be present and able to make damaging inferences from what they see and hear through accidental disclosure.[27] Perceived control of privacy is lowest in places used by the largest number of people,[28] and the main lobby of a hospital is probably the most heavily used space by the widest range of people in the entire facility.

Off this lobby, there is usually a single entrance that leads to admitting. The interview cubicles there often consist of no more than a long counter with several reception stations, all of them overlooked on one side by a large, open office and on the other by a larger waiting area. The response to increase privacy has been a variety of screen designs on or near the big counter and installations for calling patients from the big waiting rooms. Sometimes screens like those used in polling booths give partial privacy between adjacent queues at the reception area. Patients may be called by any of a bewildering variety of combinations of names, numbers, buzzers, loudspeakers, lights, and signs. The variety only serves to suggest that an unsolved problem remains.[29] Although this is a description of registration areas found in health centers established under Great Britain's National Health Service, it is, sadly, quite descriptive of some newly opened admitting facilities surveyed for this research.

In completing a nationwide survey to quantify the effect of the office's physical environment on productivity and job satisfaction, the BOSTI study identified five factors within the issue of privacy: (1) speech confidentiality, (2) visibility by others, (3) personal accessibility, (4) noise distractions, and (5) visual distractions.[30] They learned that more than 50 percent of those interviewed need at least one confidential conversation per day; 81 percent find it very difficult to have a confidential conversation in their work space. The percentage of response by office type for three different parameters examined is shown in Table 3–1. The results are not at all surprising. Since people need confidentiality and need personal control over accessibility, the more one can be seen, the more one is dissatisfied. The majority of people want private work spaces. In another study of the correlation of office privacy and job performance, the results gave a limited indication of a positive correlation of privacy and performance, even among employees with the least complex jobs.[31]

Table 3–1 Percentage of Response of Workers within Different Office Settings

Office Setting	Parameter Examined		
	Confidentiality Difficult*	Workspace Satisfying†	Accessibility Controlled‡
Bullpen	90	26	8
Screen	91	21	8
System	91	47	6
Private	36	56	66

*Percentage of respondents experiencing difficulty in having a confidential conversation in this work space.
†Percentage of respondents satisfied with this work space.
‡Percentage of respondents able to control access to the work space.

Source: Design of the Work Place by M. Brill. Paper presented at the Twelfth International Conference of the Environmental Design Research Association, Ames, Iowa, April 1981.

The admitting interviews replicated these results. The strongest negative commentary centered on open plans and poor adjacencies (interview areas next to waiting areas or equipment rooms). There was little perceived control over accessibility in the open plan office space in admitting or in private offices adjacent to the main lobby. Control is supposed to be highest at the individual's primary work place.[32] Goodrich found in his study of open plans that those employees experiencing the greatest problems with confidentiality especially of people overhearing what they should not—were located in areas where frequent movement occurred and where there were a number of employees working in the immediate vicinity.[33]

Therefore, privacy is related to various features of the physical environment such as amount and type of enclosure a person has, the distance between fellow workers, and the location of a work space in the larger environment. These features also govern the control of access that workers have over who comes into their own work spaces. This invasion can take place either bodily (the person walks into the space) or sensorily (the person looks into or listens to what is going on in the space).

The difficulties in open plan offices are that the conditions of privacy and communication are required and exist simultaneously in the same place,[34] and they often lack the features found related to workers' satisfaction with their spaces, especially features that limit visibility and audibility, such as partitions and buffer zones.[35]

Three distinct zones can be recognized in the admitting setting: (1) the public— the patients en masse on arrival are usually confined to a limited zone, clearly signposted, furnished with chairs, magazines, and so on; (2) the staff, who usually enter the building by a different door from the public, carry out their administrative duties in a backstage zone out of bounds to patients, so that there is little risk that the confidential messages and reports they are handling will be seen or heard by patients; and (3) interactions between the two categories where the public become individual patients with problems and staff members become individuals trying to solve them. It is there, in the joint-use zone, that most of the confidential material is generated.[36]

When staff zoning is fragmented or a separate route between the staff and joint-use zones is lacking, areas carry mixed traffic. There are few places where confidential documents are not at risk of exposure. In the research survey, admitting personnel particularly appreciated a "staff only" working area because it increased the perception of confidentiality; outsiders could not overhear conversations.

If the territory is subdivided by a major public route and the joint-use zone is separated from the administrative part of the staff zone, information must somehow traverse this area without being intercepted. In one admitting facility confidences could be shared when discussions continued as the manager walked out of the interview area and into the waiting room on the way back to the administrative office.

The experience of enclosure, which increases perceived privacy, can be mediated through design. The organization and characteristics of vertical elements (walls) distinguish an undifferentiated, open area from a confined, articulated enclosed space. As walls appear nearer and taller, the perception of enclosure increases regardless of actual scale of space.[37]

Baum and colleagues have noted that partitions can increase psychological comfort in spaces otherwise overloaded.[38] The negative effects of invasion of privacy may be decreased through the use of partitions. The fewer individuals an occupant can see, the better the person's perception of privacy, with one or two persons being an optimum design goal in open area offices.[39] One can use partitions to form individual work station modules to block occupants' views of each other.

In one successful open plan admitting facility, the system offices were staggered in arrangement so occupants of one office could not see into the office opposite. The partitions were about 60 inches tall. The perception of privacy was quite high. Another open admitting plan suffered a great lack of perceived privacy, although the partitions were well above the head of a seated person. The partitions, however, were glass. While this feature increased surveillance and gave a feeling of increased size of the department, its contribution to privacy was practically nil. When people are shown silent films of an office situation, they correctly identify the friendliness of the situation by body language alone.[40] Hence, there is cause for concern about the extent of visual privacy afforded by partitioning. This concern may represent in part the reason for the move back to more enclosed space—more screens and partitions, for some work stations.[41]

Concern for privacy was greatest in those admitting department open plans in which there was circulation directly behind the registrar and patient with no intervening enclosure. Workers need a much stronger definition of the boundary of their primary work place if it opens directly onto an aisle used by many people than if it opens onto an aisle used by only a group of 2 to 12 and a few visitors.[42] One can use partitions to form individual work station modules to inhibit "flow-through circulation" in the work areas. Since proximity to circulation paths has an impact on privacy, these paths should be short dead ends that are screened from the actual work stations, with any major circulation at least ten feet away.

Probably the main way to achieve privacy control, however, is to have separate office rooms with doors because that layout involves the enclosure of two or more people as participants of an interview, excluding all others.[43] The overwhelming design response mentioned to increase confidentiality (privacy) for both patients and staff was the private office. The hazard to confidentiality in this situation is overhearing.[44] An unplastered wall of single-brick thickness is known to be inadequate in preventing transmissions of speech between adjacent rooms.[45] A door, especially one having a keyhole, is difficult to soundproof. The psychological effect of doors on patients promotes some anxiety about unknown others lurking on the other side.

The adjacency of admitting interview spaces to patient waiting areas was very unpopular in the research survey. This situation was thought to greatly decrease the patient's perception of confidentiality. Overhearing through the entrance door to an interview room can be prevented by maintaining sufficient distance between the door and potential listeners.[46] Providing distance between waiting and interview areas would also reduce the stress felt by both patient and staff owing to a lack of visual privacy. Patients became very upset if the registrars were not "busy" with patients; registrars felt as though they were working in a "goldfish bowl."

As for administrative confidentiality (the confidential interstaff discussions that have nothing to do with any particular patient but may yet need confidentiality in the sense of the exclusion of others—staff as well as public), managers valued their private offices highly. Some administrators have to discuss the pay, promotion, even the dismissal of their staff in fully glazed offices visible to the rest of the clerical personnel or even to the main waiting area.[47] Some admitting facilities had no space for such discussions except the public corridor or cafeteria.

Whether the department is an open plan or a private office design, there are some areas that may still need some "tricks" to increase the perception of privacy (e.g., patient waiting areas). "Planting" for privacy control is secluding an area from its surrounding for special use.[48] At one hospital with a bullpen open plan, the only thing separating the interview desks was a row of tall (about five feet) plants. There were no complaints about privacy in this (possibly the most open) open plan. The plants gave the impression of privacy since they blocked the view.

The degree of seclusion of plantings varies from complete blockage of sight and sound to the ephemeral, diaphanous, suggestive veiling of a curtain. The direction, amount, and source of privacy infringement are prime determinants of form, size, type, and location of privacy control elements. Waist-high plants provide partial privacy. Chest-high plants provide privacy while sitting. Plants extending above eye level provide full privacy. The density of the individual plants and their spacing determines how opaque or translucent the privacy barrier will be.

Finally, to reduce the possibility of accidental disclosure within a private or open plan work space, an area should be provided to allow a staff member to put something aside for a few minutes until it can be worked on again. One hospital staff member felt it was the lack of patient file folder space that threatened patient confidentiality. Often within individual interview areas, there is barely enough space on the desk top to spread out the paper work (let alone to provide an adequate writing surface for the patient to sign the necessary forms). The situation is exacerbated when bulky computer hardware is brought into the space. It usually takes up whole sections of the desk top. Thus, shelves on partitions or carrel units on desk tops should be provided.[49] Such office amenities would reduce the chronic lack of storage described by Heath and Green and noticed during observation of the admitting facilities.[50]

Safety and Security

The admitting department is a 24-hour operation, and staffing patterns, duties, and perceptions change drastically between shifts; therefore, spatial requirements change thoroughout the day. The architectural design for this area must attempt to support the heavy volume of work during the day shift yet support equally the task performance and security of the skeletal night staff.

When asked to rate the supportiveness of the present physical design of their department for safety/security, staff members felt the design did not support staff needs but did support patients' needs. Safety/security was rated a less urgent issue for both staff and patients. The trend of the interview comments for staff was security and for patients, safety. The safety comments usually centered on furniture designs that proved unsafe and on hazardous storage situations.

In general, furniture choice in the hospital environment has been quite poor in the past, especially that chosen for patient's use. Chairs whose cushions are too soft, that topple easily when moved, and that lack sturdy arm supports should not be used. Unfortunately, well-designed chairs are expensive and, therefore, are frequently eliminated from the budget or substituted with lesser priced chairs that usually are not designed as thoughtfully. For those interested in more information on the topic, Bennett[51] and Lozar and Porter[52] provide a good basic discussion on general considerations necessary in choosing furniture for this area.

Interestingly, a number of comments in discussions of patient safety focused on the issue of accessibility of the interview area. Of 21 hospitals observed in the research, only nine interview areas were accessible to a wheelchair. Of those nine, there were two in which the wheelchair could not approach the desk closely enough for the patient to use it as a writing surface. As a result of this inaccessibility, the area became so cramped, safe movement became difficult and tripping often occurred.

The problem of providing adequate space for wheelchair maneuverability is supposedly being resolved by incorporating the accessibility standards into new designs; however, some of the departments surveyed that had this difficulty were new. It appears that in an effort to provide enough interview spaces, those spaces are cut to a minimal size, too small for wheelchairs, family members, and luggage. As with noise attention, increased space allotments for the interview areas are a solution. To require a registrar repeatedly to move patient chairs out of an office to permit a patient in a wheelchair to enter is tiring for the registrar, embarrassing for the patient, and with more considerate design responses should become unnecessary.

The remainder of this section is devoted to those architectural elements that increase the perception of security, whether a situation actually is harmful or is only perceived as harmful. There were a number of situations described during the research interviews by staff members that dealt more with the perception of harm than with actual harm. For example, the requirement that night staff go down to a large, lower level locker room was disliked intensely. In another example, having one's back to a solid wall with a door either to the right or left meant the staff person could be further into the room than the patient. While from this position one can see all that is going on in the room and is able to face other people directly when they are entering the room or are in the room, the patient could be closer to the door. Some incoming patients are very unstable. The fear of staff is that of being locked in their own office by one of these patients during an admitting interview. In reality, the registrar would not necessarily be alone when admitting this type of patient, but the fear is still present.

There are four models that have been developed to describe methods of increasing security. Each model is increasingly dependent on physical design for its success.

1. urban village. This model emphasizes human interaction as the approach to crime prevention through the mechanisms of recognition, neighboring, and mutual protection. Crime is in part the result of the breakdown of close social mechanisms resulting from the socially heterogeneous neighborhoods common today.[53]

2. urban fortress. This model places sole reliance on securing buildings and areas so outsiders cannot gain access without approval.[54]
3. defensible space. This model promotes the concept that the design of the physical environment has the capacity either to deter or to facilitate crime by enhancing the occupants' ability to monitor and control their own environment. It presents a design-oriented approach for allowing the social interaction of the urban village.[55]
4. environmental security. This concept incorporates architectural design with crime prevention theories. In this model the structure of the physical environment influences how and by whom the environment is being used and, therefore, influences the resulting use and possible conflict within the environment. Competition of use may inadvertently encourage crime opportunities.[56]

It is evident that there are two levels of security measures possible within physical design. Basic security emphasizes the occupants' ability to control their own environment, given a supportive physical design. Enhanced security is intended to provide additional security measures with less reliance on the individual. It demands a more structured organization of manpower and security devices such as security patrols and electronic monitoring equipment. Enhanced security can be characterized by more obtrusive design solutions.[57]

The supportive physical design necessary to provide basic security is dependent on three theories relating crime and the physical environment: (1) access control, (2) territoriality, and (3) surveillance. Access control is the most obvious means through which the environment affects criminal behavior.[58] It works simply by limiting entry to territories that are defined by physical or psychological barriers. Symbolic access points are physical structures that indicate an entrance but that do not physically prevent intrusion (such as a reception desk). Actual access points physically prevent access until some predetermined condition is met, such as unlocking a door.

The success of symbolic versus real barriers in restricting entry hinges on four conditions:[59] (1) the capacity of the intruder to read the symbols for their intended meaning; (2) the evident capacity of the inhabitants of the internally defined space to maintain controls and reinforce symbolic space definition through surveillance; (3) the capacity of the internally defined space to require that the intruder make obvious his or her intentions, that is, the space must have a low tolerance for ambiguous use; and (4) the capacity of the inhabitants to challenge the presence of the intruder and to take subsequent action if need be.

By restricting access only to those with a legitimate purpose, the opportunity for crime to occur should be reduced. At night the hospital entrance is usually secured. These entrances are generally enclosed with break-resistant glazing. Another element of basic security seen at some facilities is the entry intercom/door lock release system for the department entry. To prevent unwanted access at night, the entrance to the department is locked. Selective control of access is accomplished by a visitor-announcing system (buzzer or bell) and an occupant lock release. Other items seen were intrusion alarms or emergency call lights.[60]

Territoriality is the most widely recognized theory relating crime and the physical environment. In its simplest form territoriality involves three conditions:[61]

1. The occupant feels a proprietary interest and responsibility over areas beyond the front door, a responsibility shared by the neighboring occupants.
2. The occupant perceives when this territory is potentially threatened by the intrusion of strangers and is willing to act on that perception.
3. A potential offender perceives that he or she is intruding and, therefore, is more likely to be deterred from criminal behavior.

An environmental setting that facilitates the ability of primary users to exercise control and encourages them to exercise this control appears to discourage crime. To increase the sense of territoriality, there should be clear separations between public and private spaces.[62] One should provide symbolic markers to indicate such separations by changes in pavement, paint, floor covering, color, or texture,[63] or by any other interruptions in the sequence of movement along an access path that creates perceptible zones of transition from public to private space.[64] Territoriality is achieved also through graphics and through effective utilization of the space to promote opportunities for casual surveillance and to deter loitering.[65]

The concept of surveillance is concerned with an occupant's ability to observe the environment. Observation reduces opportunities for undetected crime or escape. Physical elements that contribute to surveillance must either provide new locations from which surveillance can occur or increase the effectiveness of existing surveillance points. Surveillance can be direct (direct viewing) or indirect (electronic monitoring).

Direct surveillance would be promoted by the installment of windows, good lighting, and observation mirrors in appropriate places.[66] There should be clear sight lines to vulnerable areas from adjacent high-use areas.[67] One generally wants to scan the terrain before using it.[68]

Indirect surveillance would occur if a particular problem needed additional security. The basic strategy might be enhanced by a trained security detail and closed-circuit television monitored by a central security station. This enhancement will have a greater effect on an occupant's perceptions than design features that increase sense of territoriality; however, security patrols or video surveillance requires training, salaries, equipment repair, and parts inventories. Enhanced security requires budget priorities.[69]

The comments made by staff on architectural elements affecting staff safety/ security fell into two groups: (1) those relating to increasing access control and (2) those increasing surveillance possibilities. These are all "hands-on" methods of protecting oneself. No comments were made related to territory here; however, when asked about architectural misfits several examples of territorial invasion were mentioned as decreasing security. In one facility the reception desk of admitting was within a few feet of the main door of the hospital. This close juxtaposition made staff very uncomfortable since everyone entering the hospital had to walk by the space. Furthermore, since the department was within the main lobby, anyone could come in to use the public restrooms or the telephones, which made the staff even more concerned. The second set of comments related to the interview area itself. If there was only one exit to the space or if the patient sat nearest the door, there was a perception that something unpleasant could occur. Their space was simply being invaded.

Quite obviously, all three of these theories—access control, territoriality, and surveillance—are interrelated. If territories are clearly defined and anonymity reduced, undesirable people and situations will be more obvious during surveillance. Points of access are required for all territories. Surveillance is an integral part of access control. To the extent that access is monitored at control points, surveillance is enhanced.[70]

Stress Reduction

Stress reduction was described as a very strong behavioral need by those staff members surveyed during the research interviews. The issue for environmental planning, however, is not to create environments in which stress is entirely absent but rather to attempt to limit the amount and types of stress the user of an environment must experience.[71] It is generally believed that there is an optimal level of arousal for performance of a particular task. Performance increases with increments in arousal up to that optimal point and decreases as the arousal level increases above that point.[72] Environments should not exceed the human ability to cope and adapt.[73]

Wayfinding

When completion of goal-directed activity is frustrated by the environment, a basic stress-provoking situation results.[74,75] This kind of frustration may be experienced by patients confronted with a layout so confusing that they cannot find the department they want or by the staff person who is assigned a post near the entrance and as a result spends a good part of the time giving directions to strangers who wander in rather than completing an assigned task. In the Heath and Green study there were frequent complaints about the entrance to one new hospital.[76] It was considered "difficult to find—just a hole in the wall."

Unfortunately, the study of direction finding in a natural or created environment is at an early stage of development. There is no unified theory of cognitive perception, that is, how individuals become aware of their surroundings.[77] Research has been more oriented toward spoken rather than visual images.[78] There is evidence that people under stress have a smaller attentional capacity.[79] Regan notes that patients constrict their search strategy just when they need most to broaden it.[80] They fixate upon one or another set of clues that may or may not be relevant.

A discussion of the three general types of orientation aids used by people in wayfinding follows.

Architectural and Spatial Elements. Architectural and spatial elements arise from the "built" form itself and the uses to which the internal spaces are put. It is hypothesized that the ability to see through or out of a setting, the extent to which one location looks "different" from another, and the overall plan or layout of a setting may all influence wayfinding behavior. Weisman found there was a strong correlation between judged simplicity of an architectural plan and frequency of disorientation; that is, the simpler the building was, the less likely one was to get lost.[81]

Hospital architecture constrains the orientation efforts of visitors through the physical association of several differently built forms—especially old versus new; the relationship between parking structures and the hospital; the problem of choosing an entrance close to one's intended destination; the problem of adapting to ongoing construction and hospital activity; frequently changing patterns of circulation, and physically separate service providers.[82] During the surveys for this research, problems with wayfinding were experienced that related to each of these constraints.

Orientation Aids and Systems. Orientation aids and systems include such items as signs, maps, and directions provided by staff. Mowafy commented that a color system may serve to orient people by way of its link to edge perception, its ability to establish focal points, and its affective meaning.[83]

Basically, the points to consider in evaluating a specific visual display are the degree to which the display stands out from the background, the size of the display, and the length of time one views the display.[84,85] While this advice is straightforward, the situations surrounding the implementation of a sign system can destroy its simplicity. The following description adapted from Regan shows how the committee preferred symbols, but it was too expensive; they investigated color coding, but 10 percent of the male population is color blind; and they attempted to link exterior signs and parking lot cues with internal aids but were thwarted by separate regulations governing them.[86] Consultants were brought in but provided very unsatisfactory solutions; therefore, in-house staff devised their own solution without any tested methodology to examine orientation difficulties.

The list of wayfinding difficulties surrounding orientation systems includes the following:

- lack of integration among the various aids to orientation used throughout the health care center
- signs that may be difficult to read because of lighting
- several "generations" of signs with widely varying colors, sizes, and lettering styles
- signs found at many levels and in many locations
- outdated signs and maps
- lack of a single, agreed-on name for some departments and the common use of acronyms referring to many parts of the hospital
- lack of orientation systems that can address fully the needs of a bilingual urban population
- difficulties of finding simple amenities such as restrooms, telephones, and drinking fountains
- need for full-time personnel in large medical institutions to coordinate existing systems and to update orientation aids

Data from the research survey substantiates these difficulties; a few examples will suffice. Of the 21 exterior sign systems observed, none were bilingual; of the interior sign systems, 3 were bilingual. Within one search for an admitting facility, the name of the department changed several times (outpatient/patient registration, admitting). In only 7 of 21 hospitals were the restrooms visible from patient waiting areas. In the other facilities signs were generally so poor that the only way to find the restroom was to ask directions.

Behavior of Other Visitors. The behavior of other visitors refers to what the visitor can learn through observation of other visitors. Unfortunately, visitors to the hospital may be limited by physical weaknesses from disease. They may be elderly or carrying children. They may follow someone who is equally disoriented. This does not lead to very satisfactory wayfinding.

The ways in which visual/spatial features of an architectural setting contribute to or help to resolve problems of wayfinding are little understood. This brief description of the problems encountered by those in the hospital environment only served to show the extent of the problem. However, environments do not have to promote frustration; they can actually provide psychic security.

Provision of Private and Communal Areas

Goffman suggests that social systems maintain stability and that members carry out their "performances" by having settings that are separated into "front-stage" areas where contact with the public takes place (the admitting interview area) and "back-stage" areas that are generally reserved for insiders only (the staff work room).[87] These latter areas provide a setting where role performers can from time to time step out of their assigned social roles and reduce tension. When the setting is structured so that it is difficult to separate front- and back-stage areas, the protective function is unreliable and tensions are higher. Over time, the costs of this locked-in feeling may be considerable in terms of both reduced efficiency and the psychic energy used to push down uncomfortable feelings of being intruded upon.[88]

Altman believes architects should design responsive environments that permit easy alternation between a state of separateness and a state of togetherness.[89] Even if the space is open plan, there should be a completely enclosed area to work in when one really needs to concentrate, especially since private offices fare much better in reducing staff stress.[90] In admitting, such a private room could be used for deceased patient discharge procedures by those departments with this responsibility. (At present any available space is used.) As important as private space are communal rooms where a number of workers participate in a communal activity from which others are excluded—staff in meetings, coffee breaks, and so on.[91] There should be shared spaces where workers can gather.[92] Saegert believes quiet retreats and busy places must be provided as available options rather than alternative possibilities of a particular area, since employees under stress are less likely to use space innovatively.[93]

During the admitting interviews staff members spoke highly of a lounge when one had been provided. Often, the staff work room was the only place to calm down after a particularly distressing admitting interview.

Provision of an Aesthetic Environment

Perhaps the aesthetic quality of environments and its potential for stress reduction deserves to be taken more seriously.[94] Berlyne has suggested that reduction in size and complexity of a space, the use of cool colors, and the use of familiarity achieved by redundant design elements may all lower stress levels.[95] In the BOSTI study, office workers had a preference for cool, pastel colors and wood and fabrics.[96] Admitting staff members felt similarly. A postoccupancy evaluation of hospital waiting spaces in 1975 showed that there seems to be no visitor preference between traditional or modern furniture and decorating styles. They value carpets and patterned wallpapers in preference to tile floors and walls, smooth plaster walls, or solid color vinyl wall coverings.[97]

The ambiance provided by plants and artwork was much appreciated by those interviewed for this research. Several admitting interviewers made it a point to mention that their personal memorabilia in their offices reduced patient tension because family photographs provided a common topic of conversation.

In 1978, Spector and Sistrunk completed a study to determine if the mere presence of other people in a room reduces anxiety levels in people.[98] The findings were somewhat ambiguous. The presence of others appears not necessarily to reduce anxiety. One may be able to lessen the arousal of having other people in a designed space by providing visual foci such as windows or artwork that permit occupants to avert their eyes from other people in the room[99] or by painting rooms light colors to increase apparent size.[100] In a study of students in a high-rise dormitory, it appeared that lightness (sunlight availability) was correlated with perceived room size.[101]

The issue of color preference, as with wayfinding, has not been adequately researched. Most research in the past has been based on measurement of biologic response through electrocardiography and electroencephalography or on more subjective studies (personal experience, case studies).[102] It is going to take some time before adequate numbers of studies uncover, for example, which wavelengths produce which physiologic responses. Some are discussed in this report.[103,104] As more of these objective measures are uncovered, there will be a more solid research base on which to choose color. For the time being it appears that light, pale, warm colors; medium-sized, quiet patterns; and textures with strong tactile appeal are much preferred over large involved patterns and highly saturated colors for use in health care facilities.[105]

Effects of Noise, Temperature and Humidity, and Illumination

Another group of physical environmental factors contributing to the general impression of a particular room are noise, temperature and humidity, and illumination.[106]

Noise. In his review of office literature, Thorne makes quite obvious the neglect of the whole topic of office acoustics.[107] Furthermore, the present complaints about noise levels are not due merely to the shift to open landscaping. Manning, in 1965, when office landscaping in Great Britain was the exception, cites studies to illustrate that noise already was a problem.[108] Prior to air conditioning, the major problem was street noise, but internal noise was a problem in large clerical areas and in typing and machine rooms. Manning also provides examples of noise spectra from a number of office designs with a variety of surface finishes. These and his final description of one large open plan office that possessed good acoustic treatment but still experienced noise levels of 50 to 55 decibels measured on the A-scale (dBA) indicate that acoustic treatment of the basic interior shell is a necessity.[109] In another study, Langdon and Keighly found that sound transmission loss was quite inadequate through lightweight curtain walls (similar to those found in private office construction).[110]

Ideally, the acoustic environment in an office should satisfy three conditions:[111]

1. allow face-to-face and telephone conversations to be clearly understood by the people involved (speech communication)
2. allow private conversations to be carried out without their being understood by people who are not part of them (confidential speech privacy)
3. provide reasonable freedom from distracting sound (normal acceptable speech privacy)

The degree of speech privacy or communication is determined by the intelligibility of the speech concerned, which in turn depends on the proportion of spoken sounds that lie above the level of the general background noise. Where speech can be heard clearly above the level of background noise, its intelligibility is high and conversation can easily occur. A great reduction of intelligibility, whether by increasing background noise or reducing speech level, makes it increasingly difficult to communicate, yet increases privacy.

For open plans one index that has gained acceptance in evaluating conditions of speech and communication is called the articulation index. Of the factors affecting this index, two are related to physical design: the speaker-to-listener distance and the presence of screens. The third, background noise, is subject to some design manipulation.

The factor of speaker-to-listener distance depends for its success on the physics of the sound wave in air. This principle is generally called normal attenuation of sound and has been described by Moore.[112] As the sound travels over a distance, it is absorbed partially by the air and partially by the ground. Each time the distance from a source is doubled, there is a reduction of six decibels. In the case of multiple sound sources, the rate of reduction in overall sound levels will be less.

The introduction of elements between the sound source and the receiver that absorb, deflect, reflect, and refract sound waves is known as excess attenuation.[113] Absorption takes place when an element receives the sound waves and entraps or absorbs them, converting the sound into other energy forms and, ultimately, heat. This type of absorption is the source of sound reduction of cloth-covered panels. Deflection is accomplished by introducing an element that causes the noise to be bounced away from a recipient into an area or direction less offensive to the hearer. Reflection causes the sound to be reflected toward its source, thus shielding the receptor from offense. Refraction occurs when acoustical energy is dissipated, diffused, or dispersed by striking a rough surface.

The third factor, background noise, is not actually a form of attenuation. The noises used are of the broadband, continuous variety, which are themselves lower-level, information-bearing sounds that would cause annoyance.[114] These systems can be purchased, but air-handling systems, which are designed to a fixed noise level, do produce a certain amount of background noise. These levels may differ from the design standard by plus or minus six decibels, however, which can change a situation of acoustic privacy to one of communication.[115]

Leonard points out that there is a difference between "masking" and "white" sound systems.[116] White sound is not shaped to conform to the optimum masking characteristics. Thus, masking is actually an unobtrusive sound, while white sound is obtrusive. The drawback of white noise is that it works by raising the general level of background noise. In an open plan situation this noise replaces the acoustic attenuation provided by walls in a private office. It is, however, only acoustic masking: it will neither isolate nor insulate sound.[117] It is not superior to isolation or insulation. Bennett likens white noise or music to "throwing sawdust on the floor to hide the dirt.[118] White sound only masks noise; it is no solution.

Two areas of consideration exist for minimizing noise producing speech interference and the corresponding annoyance: noise from outside the space as well as noise from inside the space must be controlled.[119] When sound hits a solid wall, if little energy is absorbed and much is reflected, two effects will be noticed: (1) intermittent sounds will be mixed together and (2) steady sounds will accumulate into a reverberent field, making the space "noisy." Conversely, if much energy is absorbed and little reflected, the room will sound quiet to speech. Absence of reflection prevents the speaker from gauging proper voice levels and tends to cause excessive effort or shouting. Thus, proper design of a room for speech is a compromise between the need for some reflection and the desire to minimize reflection to preserve intelligibility.[120]

Sound transmission between spaces can be discussed in terms of airborne sound, which originates in a space with any sound-producing source, and structure-borne sound, which is generally understood as direct impact caused by a vibrating or impacting source directly contacting the structure. Machines cause noise by vibration or impacting.

Vibration reduction takes on two forms: (1) damping and (2) isolation. Damping is accomplished by rigidly coupling the vibrating source to a large mass. Isolation is accomplished by supporting the vibrating mass on resilient supports. Large machines can be supported on special commercial "sandwiches" of asbestos, lead, cork, and other strong resilient materials. Impact vibration can be reduced by cushioning the impact using floor tiles of vinyl, rubber, cork, or carpeting on pads (in ascending order of impact insulation). Although it is quite obvious that these principles evolved from industry, even in an office situation vibration of equipment can be just as annoying. Typewriters and other office equipment can be made quieter simply by slipping an acoustical pad underneath. This issue is especially significant since centralized work areas are important to staff communication. If this is the case, acoustical treatment is even more crucial to prevent the concomitant reduction of patient communication in adjacent interview spaces.

Unlike structure-borne sound, airborne sound in an office situation (especially in open plans) may be very difficult to control. Absorption by room contents and wall coverings controls noise levels within a space. The structure itself controls noise transmission between spaces, and isolation of sound requires hard, dense, heavy structural materials such as blank walls (no windows) or solid masonry or concrete walls. Since sound transmission requires that the barrier be set into vibration by the sound energy, the more massive a wall is, the more it will reduce sound transmission. Gaps in doors, windows, and electrical boxes can undermine transmission loss.[121]

Although it appears that noise levels in open plan offices are very close to being within acceptable standards (discussed later), in a study by Nemecek and Grandjean, 46 percent of the workers found conversation disturbing; 25 percent identified office machines as disturbing; 19 percent were disturbed by telephones; 7 percent, by movement back and forth; and 3 percent, by miscellaneous noise of traffic and industry.[122] Moreover, it was not so much the loudness of the conversation as its content that disturbed them. Langdon and Keighley found that clerical staff were annoyed by fluctuation in noise levels.[123] Open plan partitions keep office workers visually blind to much of the environment around them, and they become much more sensitive to sound because the sounds in many instances are unexpected and because their sense of hearing is sensitized with the reduction of visual stimuli.[124]

The use of sound-attenuating screens and carpets in open plan offices is not noise control. These items will not isolate sound but will insulate it. The best that can be accomplished with acoustic room treatment is elimination of reverberent field, that is, to make the intensity at the room boundaries what it would have been in free space. The transmission loss of acoustic material itself is very low.[125]

Acoustic privacy in open plan offices depends on a high rate of speech reduction with distance. Speech levels continue to fall off as the distance from the speaker increases through normal attenuation. The two open plans receiving the fewest complaints about noise during the interview were large, airy spaces. One hospital, a bull pen plan, had four interview "offices" in a space of 690 square feet.

If all the surfaces in an office were totally absorbent, the rate of speech attenuation would be the same as in open air, that is six decibels with distance doubling. In practice, this situation does not occur, and a five decibel fall-off with distance doubling is the maximum achievable rate. If, however, the surfaces are not highly absorbent, a four decibel or less fall-off with distance doubling may occur.[126] Thus, the acoustic absorption of any surface finishes should be high. The absorption capability of partitions is not always proportional to thickness but depends on the type of material being used and the method of installation, which is reflected in their cost.[127] The ceiling should provide a high degree of sound absorption. Floors should be carpeted.[128]

The expected level of noise reduction due to any screen depends on the path length difference it provides plus the extent and mass of the barrier. To be effective, a barrier should be positioned as close as possible to either the source of the noise or the receiver in order to maximize the path length difference for a given barrier height.[129] In the Steelcase survey done by Louis Harris & Associates, intelligibility of speech from neighboring open plan offices decreased with increasing height of the partitions.[130] In general, barriers must be long and continuous or, alternatively, wrapped around the area to be protected to prevent sound from passing around the ends. To provide the maximum decrease in noise level, the barrier must be solid, without holes, gaps, or openings.[131] Partitions should go all the way to the floor.[132] Thus, to be its most effective, a screen should cast a large acoustic shadow; that is, it should be high, wide, and near the speaker, with the listener being well within the shadow boundaries. Since people move about, however, effective acoustical shadows are reduced.[133]

In analyzing a noise problem, one must consider that sound from a source can travel by more than one path to the point at which it becomes objectionable. The solution is to determine during schematic design which paths carry the most sound energy and then select appropriate methods of obtaining the desired reduction along those paths.[134] Storage areas and circulation paths (hallways) can serve as buffers.[135] Draw simple "lines of sound" from the various work stations, and place absorbent-faced sound-blocking screens to suit. Where hard surfaces cannot be avoided, use the fundamental principle of angle of incidence equaling angle of reflectance to determine the travel path of the sound, taking into account the slight "bending" that occurs around a barrier.[136] (Sound can bend over the top and under the bottom of partitions if there is a gap, so it is actually amplified as it focuses on the opposite side of the partition.)

Besides the difficulties of sound transmission experienced in open plan offices, both these and private offices experience problems when the internal noise levels are so high that speech (communication) is interrupted. The internal background noise level must not be too low or external noises will cause distractions and/or internal conversations will get out. If it is too high, the noise itself is distracting. In a small private office the proximity of the walls and other reflecting surfaces causes the speech level to remain constant throughout the room. Even in a private office, intelligibility can be low if sound reflects back to the source off the wall. The solution is to use sound-absorbing internal surface finishes and "quiet" office equipment.[137]

Typewriters and terminal printers are noisy. Hinged screens or other acoustical housings for covering platens and typing elements are available. For maximum reduction of typing noise, these systems should be augmented by acoustic screening and provision of absorptive surfaces to prevent reflection of sound from the immediate area of the typists or the printers. Telephone ringing caused frequent disturbances in the admitting areas surveyed. Systems are available permitting quiet buzzing or even blinking lights instead of a loud ring. Admitting interviews were often interrupted by poorly timed telephone calls. Some phone systems automatically transfer calls to a switchboard or to another telephone, or the transfer can be achieved with manual switching if necessary.

Furniture designs having "hard against hard" surfaces (e.g., metal against metal) at the closing point of all drawers and doors should be avoided. Closure impact should be well dampened to eliminate this noise source.[138]

Windows in an office have already been mentioned for their contribution to stress reduction. They are highly desired items; however, if conventional windows are placed in a blank wall, the attenuation of sound produced by the wall/window combination is considerably reduced since glazing attenuates sound poorly. To avoid this possibility, the face glazing and openings should be carefully designed. Methods of obtaining such attenuation from a window are to seal standard windows in the building facade, reduce window size, increase the glass thickness, and use double- or triple-glazed windows with the appropriate width of air space between panels.[139]

Indoor noise is likely to become annoying at sound levels exceeding 30 dBA in conference rooms, 40 dBA in private offices, and 50 dBA in large offices.[140] In general, criteria suggest that acceptable background noise levels in open plan offices should be in the region of 55 to 60 dBA. In a private office, however, the background noise should be only 40 to 50 dBA. For a more detailed discussion of speech intelligibility/interference, general office noise, and the maximum desirable decibel level for various room uses, the reader is referred to the work of Piesse[141] and Beranek.[142]

Temperature and Humidity. The next factor influencing the environment that caused much discomfort to admitting staff was temperature. Over half of the hospitals surveyed had difficulties controlling heat, ventilation and air conditioning systems. The most common complaint was excessive heating. The complexity of mechanical systems in general and the specificity of engineering adjustments at each facility in particular prohibit any analysis of causation in this report (there was often a great increase in thermal load when departments introduced computers); therefore, this section on the thermal environment is intended to do the following:

- draw attention for those involved in the mechanical engineering decisions that, on the whole, the thermal environment is not as carefully controlled here as in other areas of the hospital. It cannot be denied that the thermal environment in admitting does not have the life and death consequences as in, for example, the premature infant nursery. As with noise distraction, however, thermal discomfort reduces the quality of the environment. Enough workers were uncomfortable in 11 of 20 hospitals to comment on the heat. There is some cause for concern.

- introduce this topic, in general, to those using this guide who may have little or no background in mechanical engineering yet as decision makers need access to some basic information

Most basic textbooks on mechanical engineering list factors that can be controlled by air conditioning systems as temperature of the surrounding air, mean radiant temperature of the surrounding surfaces, relative humidity of the air, motion of the air, odors, and dust.[143] The textbooks go on to state the first four, relating to the thermal environment, should be adjusted so that occupants of conditioned space can experience a thermal equilibrium by which bodily heat loss is adjusted to the heat generated by the level of activity in the space.

Although, ideally, buildings should be designed to provide indoor thermal environments that would not require corrective action by the human body, this concept is not practical. There is a range of thermal environments to which the response of the body is not thermal discomfort. In terms of air temperature the width of this range is eight to ten degrees Fahrenheit. It is therefore possible to satisfy the majority of people engaged in similar activities, dressed in clothing of similar insulating value, and remaining indoors for sufficiently long periods (about one hour) to eliminate possible effects of previous environments and activities. With these restrictions the preferred thermal environment is defined primarily by air temperature and velocity.[144]

At present, research has not discovered the particular sort of environment people prefer; warmth, not comfort, is the research variable almost exclusively examined. It is clear that any difference in preferred temperatures between sexes, if real, is too small to be of practical significance; therefore, at the present state of knowledge it is reasonable to treat groups of people as homogeneous for the purpose of determining suitable thermal environments.[145] It is fairly safe to say that anything above 75 degrees will be generally considered too warm,[146] although increasing air velocity may reduce the thermal discomfort caused by higher temperatures.[147] (There was evidence of this effect noted from the frequent presence of portable fans within the admitting area.)

There does not appear to be any case for thermal boredom in the literature. Griffiths and McIntyre found subjects preferred low rates of change or no change in temperature to larger rates of change.[148] If people were to dislike the lack of stimulation produced by invariant thermal conditions, they would presumably prefer the control conditions of larger rates of change to smaller rates of change. Unfortunately, both radiant and convective heating and cooling systems more often lead to nonuniformity than to uniformity of temperature in a room. Hot air rises, leading to vertical gradients in air temperature. Radiant heat sources tend to be relatively small in relation to the surface area of the enclosure, and nonheated surfaces are imperfect reflectors of thermal radiation.

There is no subjective differentiation in studies between heating or cooling that is predominantly convective and that which is predominantly radiant.[149] Interior building surface temperatures should be at the same temperature as air to avoid excessive local radiant effects, but in reality little is known of the effects of nonuniformity in air temperature.[150] People seem to be quite tolerant of radiant nonuniformity. Large surfaces such as ceilings and walls can probably be allowed to reach temperatures 10 degrees higher than their surroundings.[151]

One of the claims of open plan spaces is that heating and cooling costs are lower because the whole floor can be treated as one space rather than regulating individual offices.[152] Interestingly, the most complaints during the admitting surveys came from those workers in open plan spaces. Although some private offices suffered nonuniformity as a result of outside wall temperature differentials, it seemed that thermal discomfort was more common in the open plan.

The design aim for indoor environments should be to maintain relative humidity within the range of 25 to 70 percent.[153] As far as the effect of humidity on warmth is concerned, there is little effect in the region of comfortable air temperatures, but in warmer temperatures (above 82 degrees Fahrenheit) a change in relative humidity from 20 to 75 percent could be equivalent subjectively to raising the temperature by 2.7 degrees Fahrenheit. At moderate air temperatures (73 degrees Fahrenheit) a moderate humidity of about 50 percent is preferred.[154] For those interested in a fuller treatment of how to arrive at a suitable temperature for a group of people at a given level of activity in given clothing, see the article by Fanger.[155] McIntyre provides a briefer version of that work.[156]

Illumination. The final factor considered during the research surveys for this report was presence and quality of lighting within admitting. The observation data on lighting and views show that, on the whole, most hospitals had some natural lighting and had a view out the window in the patient waiting area. During the interviews, windows were mentioned as a factor reducing staff and patient stress, yet few hospitals had windows in their interview areas.

Adding a window not only provides contact with the exterior but also admits daylight.[157] Windows, like thermal comfort, affect environmental quality and have to do with the visual escape and distraction from the properties of a room.[158] It has been said that a view to the outside is most important to workers who have minimal work station furnishings.[159]

People appear to prefer daylight to be dominant in offices.[160] Daylight, which is light scattered in the atmosphere, is more desirable than sunlight, which is light direct from the sun. It appears that more extreme illumination is acceptable from windows before they are described as glaring than is the case for artificial light sources, provided the level of discomfort is not too high.[161] In one study almost nine of ten people felt it was important to see outside the building regardless of the quality of artificial light and, it appears, regardless of the view.[162] A pleasant view is not as necessary as just the chance to look out.[163]

In a study to determine which of a pair of views subjects would prefer for their home and how much extra rent they were prepared to pay for it, very few of the 75 subjects expressed a willingness to pay more for views.[164] For the elderly and housebound a view with an element of activity in it is desired for its interest, but for other groups the preferred view is one that reflects their status in society.[165] In a study to determine window size preference Ne'eman and Hopkinson found that the main determinant of the critical window size was the amount of visual information provided by the view.[166] Windows that gave views of close objects needed larger widths to be acceptable than those that revealed distant views.

Keighley examined people's reactions to windows to determine the effects of decreasing window size and of dividing the glazed area into different patterns of apertures.[167] It was found that the most frequently preferred condition was a central horizontal aperture with the elevation being determined by the skyline of the view. In another study examining window area, Keighley found the most preferred situation was one in which a large horizontal aperture was used, occupying 25 to 30 percent of the window/wall area. Above about 30 percent window/wall area satisfaction was high and remained so up to the 65 percent maximum area used. Thus, windows arranged in a symmetrical pattern that occupy at least 25 percent of the wall area are desired by people.[168] Since excessive heat is already a fairly common complaint in the admitting department and since daylight is usually associated with summer overheating and solar glare, natural lighting should probably be provided in moderation.[169]

Artificial lighting within the admitting environment on the whole was quite adequate in the interview areas. As for the waiting areas, however, in 9 of the 21 hospitals (43 percent) lighting levels were too low for a young person with good vision to read comfortably. Generally, these areas were lit with some form of decorative lighting that gave nonuniform illumination. Many people read while waiting; others watch televison. Still others talk to pass time or bring handwork, office work, or schoolwork. Soft or warm lighting is most desirable, with brighter lights for reading. Harsh fluorescent ceiling lights were often turned off in waiting areas where people were most anxious.[170] In the study by Flynn and co-workers it was discovered that more pleasant lighting consisted of combinations of different lighting systems.[171] Best was the combination of overhead diffuse and downlighting and peripheral lighting. In their study of conference rooms, those interiors with lighting only over the table and those of low illumination were considered to be cramped, but the presense of wall lighting alone, the addition of wall lighting, or an increase in illumination on the table alone made the interior seem spacious, which could help reduce stress levels.

In any case, to use lighting appropriately in an interior such as an office is a difficult exercise. People face in various directions and sit, stand, and walk about. What is visually more or visually less important must be determined, and there must be built-in flexibility because office layouts are subject to frequent change. Flexibility is difficult for two reasons: (1) lamps have to be connected to the electrical supply, so moving them is apt to be laborious and expensive, and (2) directional lighting, which is necessary to achieve pattern, is too hard if it comes from a small source and too glaring if it comes from a low angle.[172]

Boyce suggests that for most two-dimensional tasks with a large visual component, the main features influencing performance are illumination levels and presence of disability glare (that is, when one's ability to see is reduced by a light source having sufficient illumination and being sufficiently close to the direction in which one is looking).[173] For good vision there should be high contrast between the task (e.g., printing on forms or magazines) and its background (e.g., paper). Between the background (paper) and the immediate surround (the desk top or a reading table) the contrast should be low. Between the immediate surround (the desk top or reading table) and the entire field of view (the interview or waiting room) the contrast should also be low. Since the task of reading was high reflectance, the desk top should be light to ensure equal reflectance. If the desk top is light, the room should be light. Recessed (usually fluorescent) ceiling fixtures usually violate this rule of contrasts since no light falls on the ceiling surrounding the fixture. It is too sharp a contrast between light and dark.

One final consideration in lighting is the effect of room furnishings on illumination levels. If lighter surfaces are used (ceilings, walls, floors, furniture), they will reflect more light, and the room will be brighter. If dark wood or fabrics or furniture are used in places where important vision is required, either more light will have to be provided, or there will be a risk of poor vision.[174]

DESIGN PRINCIPLES SUMMARIZED

Designing To Increase Communication

Research Findings

Communication was rated the most urgent need for staff members and the second most urgent need for patients. Flexibility in furniture placement to facilitate communication is not at all common in the admitting environment. Centralization of staff work spaces seems key; however, it brings with it a concomitant reduction in patients' communication and confidentiality. Sound transmission from adjacent spaces (lobby/waiting area, equipment room/work area) decreased both patients' and staff communication. The private interview office was the overwhelming architectural element increasing patients' communication.

Discussion of Design Principle

Office type (private versus open plan), environmental stress (noise), symbolism in the environment (staff having better chairs than patients), or a poor seating arrangement (office visitors placed too distant from the office desk) can distort or destroy communication. Whether an occupant sits facing the door communicates readiness for interaction. Whether a desk forms a barrier between the occupant and the visitor communicates what sort of interaction is desired. Formal interactions occur when discussions are carried out over a desk top, with the occupant seated in a private zone and the visitor seated in a public zone. Informal interactions can occur when seating is side by side. Unfortunately, the better the facilities are designed to foster communication, the greater the risk that confidences will be overheard.

Examples for Specific Design Responses

- Provide a centralized plan in which the central "staff only" work area is adjacent to or surrounded by the patients' areas, recognizing the need for proper acoustical treatment.
- Provide private interview offices whenever possible. Or, at the very least, ensure that open plan offices are well planned and well executed spatially and acoustically. These provisions will be expensive, but economizing precludes satisfactory office landscaping.
- Provide office arrangements in which the personal space of occupant and visitor is adjustable. Office chairs having a fixed position may be too rigid. Stronger verbal responses occur in a face-to-face rather than a side-by-side position until beyond a separation of chairs of three feet, six inches. Most informal conversations occur when chairs are angled at 90 degrees rather than at 30 degrees or 180 degrees.

Designing To Increase Confidentiality (Privacy)

Research Findings

Privacy/confidentiality was rated as the most urgent need for patients and the third most urgent need for staff members. The open plan office received the poorest ratings overall for privacy in all its forms. Only private offices fared well in promoting patients' and staff confidentiality. Interview areas next to waiting areas and equipment rooms were strongly disliked.

Discussion of Design Principle

There are five forms of privacy of concern to those in the admitting environment: (1) speech confidentiality, (2) visibility by others, (3) personal accessibility,

(4) noise distraction, and (5) visual distraction. Each of these forms is controlled in part by psychological privacy, the sense of control over access to oneself or one's group, and in part by architectural privacy, the visual and acoustic isolation supplied by the environment either by symbolic or real barriers. In an office, privacy is related to various features of the physical environment, such as amount and type of enclosure a person has, the distance between fellow workers, and the location of a work space in the larger environment. Environments should permit different degrees of control over contact with others.

Examples for Specific Design Responses

- Separating (e.g., buffering by distance) staff work areas, patients' waiting areas, and interview areas increases the perception of confidentiality by reducing the intrusion of noise and onlookers and by limiting overhearing. A high rate of speech reduction with distance increases acoustical privacy. Buffering should not fragment staff, patient, and staff/patient zones, however. In that case, corridors carry mixed traffic and an accidental leak of information can occur.
- Department managers should have a private office. Even in open plan design, at least one office should be provided for use during private conversations.
- Partitions can increase privacy by blocking views and by rerouting circulation paths away from the work station. The fewer individuals office occupants can see, the better their perception of privacy, with one or two persons being an optimum design goal in open area offices. When rerouting circulation paths, ensure that major circulation areas are at least ten feet away from the office entry.
- Recent research suggests that high panels provide more effective enclosure in open plan offices.[175] There must be a minimum of three sides. If low panels are used, partially enclosing the fourth side will enhance privacy.
- Planting for privacy control secludes an area from its surrounding. The direction, amount, and source of privacy infringement are prime determinants of the form, size, type, and location of privacy plantings.
- Storage space should be provided for papers within an office to reduce accidental disclosure of information and, in the interview office, to increase writing space at the desk. Incorporating shelves on partitions or carrel units on desks increases storage capacity.

Designing To Increase Safety/Security

Research Findings

Safety/security was rated as the third most urgent behavioral need for patients and the least urgent need for staff. Staff responses centered more on security needs; those for patients, on safety needs. Architectural elements described by staff as misfits affected their sense of territory; fits concerned improved access control (lockable department/lobby, purse/coat lockers) and surveillance (security personnel nearby). The safety comments usually centered on furniture designs that proved unsafe and on hazardous storage situations. There were a number of comments about the cramped and, therefore, unsafe conditions found in interview spaces that were barely accessible to wheelchairs. The present physical designs did not appear to satisfy the need for staff security, although they did support patients' safety needs.

Discussion of Design Principle

The admitting department is a 24-hour operation, and staffing patterns, duties, and perceptions change drastically between shifts; therefore, spatial requirements change throughout the day. Security is dependent on three theories relating crime and the physical environment: (1) access control, which works simply by limiting entry to territories that are defined by physical or psychological barriers; (2) territoriality, which involves the perception of ownership of a physical space and the consequential defense of that space; and (3) surveillance, which is concerned with an occupant's ability to observe the environment either through direct viewing or through electronic monitoring. There are two levels of security measures possible within the physical design. Basic security emphasizes the occupants' ability to control their environment, given a supportive physical design. Enhanced security is intended to provide additional security measures with less reliance on the individual. It is characterized by more obtrusive design solutions that can have a greater impact than subtle design changes.

Examples for Specific Design Responses

- Provide a buffer zone between the admitting department and the front entrance of the hospital to reduce the possibility of undesirable intrusion.
- Provide a clear separation between public and private spaces, perhaps with graphics and paint or with changes in pavement, floor covering, or surface textures to increase sense of territory.
- Reduce to a minimum the number of entry points to the department to increase surveillance capabilities.
- Ensure that any open plan or private office design has security entrance doors for the department that can be locked when necessary.
- Provide opportunities for casual surveillance using direct sight lines or observation mirrors to deter loitering.

- Consider inclusion of staff purse and/or coat lockers in the department to reduce both theft and the need for night staff to leave the perceived safety of the department.
- Ensure that the size of the interview space permits use by wheelchair patients while providing safe movement around the wheelchair.
- Ensure staff safety regarding confrontations with patients in the interview room by providing interior designs that place personnel, not patients, nearer the door. Preferably, interview rooms should be provided with two doors: one for staff, one for patients.
- Avoid using chairs whose cushions are too soft, that topple easily when moved, and lack sturdy arm supports.

Designing To Decrease Stress

Research Findings

Stress reduction was rated the second most urgent need for staff members and the least urgent for patients. Wayfinding for patients was almost always a problem within the sample facilities. Noise levels within hospital admitting departments are often at the upper end of the decibel spectrum normally found in offices. In over half of the hospitals, staff complained of excessive heating. Windows were mentioned as a factor reducing stress. Most hospitals had some natural lighting and a window in the patient waiting areas; however, few hospitals had windows in their interview areas. Artificial lighting in the waiting area was often too low for reading. A pleasant ambiance (e.g., artwork, plantings) seemed important in the reduction of patients' stress. Staff members spoke highly of lounges or conference rooms when provided. The private office plan contributed significantly to the reduction of staff stress.

Discussion of Design Principle

The issue for environmental planning is not to create environments in which stress is entirely absent but rather to attempt to limit the amount and types of stress the user of an environment must experience. Physiological needs are represented in the work environment by shelter factors of sufficient intensities of light, sound, air, and heating and observance of the principles of anthropometrics and ergonomics. Noise levels become annoying above 30 dBA in conference rooms, 40 dBA in private offices, and 50 dBA in large offices. The use of sound-attenuating screens and carpets in open plan offices is not noise control. These items do not isolate sound but only insulate it. The structure itself controls noise transmission between spaces. Isolation of sound requires hard, dense, heavy structural materials such as blank walls or solid masonry or concrete walls. Lightweight curtain walls do not stop sound transmission as well as heavier walls. Preferred thermal environment is defined primarily by air temperature and humidity. People prefer no change or low rates of change to greater change in temperatures. Visual acuity is affected by the task (paper), the visual field immediately surrounding the task (desk top), and the entire field (room); thus, fixture type, furniture choice, and room color can affect vision. Skimping on the quality and choice of colors, finishes, and furnishings may have a higher psychic cost than initial cost. Environments should permit easy alternation between a state of separateness and a state of togetherness. Quiet retreats and busy places should be available options rather than alternative possibilities of a particular space. Wayfinding depends in part on architectural and spatial elements (the simpler the built form, the less likely one gets lost) and in part on orientation aids and systems.

Examples for Specific Design Responses

- In evaluating visual displays for wayfinding, determine the degree to which the display stands out from the background, the size of the display, and the length of time one views the display.
- Reduction of stress levels may occur by reduction in the size and complexity of a space and in the use of familiarity achieved by redundant design elements.
- Use of visual foci like plants, artwork, and windows or painting rooms light colors increases the apparent room size to help reduce the arousal of having other people in the room.
- If windows are to be installed, windows that give views of close subjects need larger widths to be acceptable than those that reveal distant views. Large horizontal apertures, symmetrically arranged, that occupy at least 25 percent of the wall area are desired.
- Light, pale colors; medium-sized, quiet patterns; textures with strong tactile appeal; and wallpaper, fabrics, and wood should be used for interior design.
- Private offices are very important in reducing stress. At least one completely enclosed area should be provided to work in when one really needs to concentrate, even in open plans.
- A ''back-stage'' area (lounge, conference room, work room) in which personnel can unwind away from the public is needed. People need a communal place to gather.
- During schematic design, which paths carry the most sound energy should be determined and then appropriate methods of obtaining the desired reduction along these paths are selected. By locating noise sources during design, one can more effectively plan their control.

- Distance can be used as a noise barrier in open plans since doubling the distance from a noise reduces loudness by nearly half. This is one of the most important noise control factors in open plan designs.
- Installation of sound masking (not white noise) systems can be planned from the outset in an open plan office design. Carrying through with its installation is a necessity to ensure normal speech privacy.
- The ceiling should provide a high degree of sound absorption. Floors should be carpeted.
- Acoustical barriers (partitions) should be high, opaque, and solid (without holes, gaps, or openings) and should go all the way to the floor. They should be placed either close to the source of the noise or close to the receiver of the noise.
- Quality sound-absorbing surfaces should be used even in private offices or the sounds will accumulate into a reverberant field, making the space noisy. Use care, however, since overuse of such surfaces may make the room "dead" and make it difficult to gauge voice levels.
- One must be aware of sound attenuation principles for glazing in window installations.
- Use of techniques of damping and isolation prevents disturbing structure-borne noise from equipment vibration. An example in an office is placing an acoustical pad under a typewriter.
- "Quiet" office equipment (e.g., typewriters with acoustical housings) can be used, even in private offices. Telephones with quiet buzzing, blinking lights, or "on-off" switches can be introduced, if necessary. Furniture designs having "hard against hard" (metal against metal) surfaces at the closing point of all drawers and doors should be avoided.
- When choosing lighting, soft or warm lighting is preferred, with brighter lights for reading. A combination of overhead diffuse and downlighting and peripheral lighting is best.
- Groups of people must be treated as homogeneous for the purpose of determining suitable thermal environments.

NOTES

1. Sloan, cited in "The Pros and Cons and Future Prospects of Open Landscaping," *American Institute of Architects Journal* 66(1977), no. 7:46–47, 82.

2. M. Brill, "Design of the Work Place" (Paper presented at the Twelfth International Conference of the Environmental Design Research Association, Ames, Iowa, April 1981).

3. P. Howard, "Office Landscaping Revisited," *Design and Environment* 3(1972), no. 3:41–46.

4. "Pros and Cons," 46–47.

5. Howard, "Office Landscaping Revisited," 41–46.

6. E. Sundstrom, R.E. Hall, and D. Kamp, "Privacy at Work: Architectural Correlates of Job Satisfaction and Job Performance," *Academy of Management Journal* 23(1980):101–117.

7. Lerner, cited in "Pros and Cons," 46–47.

8. Howard, "Office Landscaping Revisited," 41–46.

9. "Pros and Cons," 46–47.

10. Howard, "Office Landscaping Revisited," 41–46.

11. F.I. Steele, *Physical Settings and Organization Development* (Reading, Mass.: Addison-Wesley, 1973).

12. Howard, "Office Landscaping Revisited," 41–46.

13. Lee, cited in S. Seliger, "Are Cubicles the Answer, or Just an Open Invitation to a Hard Day at the Office?" *Chicago Tribune*, August 9, 1979, sec. 2, 1;4.

14. "Pros and Cons," pp. 46–47.

15. Brill, cited in Seliger, "Are Cubicles the Answer," 4.

16. Slepicka, cited in "Pros and Cons," 46–47.

17. Howard, "Office Landscaping Revisited," 41–46.

18. "Pros and Cons," 46–47.

19. Brill, cited in Seliger, "Are Cubicles the Answer," 1;4.

20. R. Sommer, *Personal Space: The Behavioral Basis of Design* (Englewood Cliffs, N.J.: Prentice-Hall, 1969).

21. A. Mehrabian and S.G. Diamond, "Effects of Furniture Arrangement, Props and Personality on Social Interaction," *Journal of Personality and Social Psychology* 20(1971):18–30.

22. S.M. Jourard and R. Friedman, "Experimenter-Subject Distance and Self-disclosure," *Journal of Personality and Social Psychology* 15(1970):278–282.

23. D. Joiner, "Social Ritual and Architectural Space," *Architectural Research and Teaching* 1(1971), no. 2:11–22.

24. "The Doctor's Dilemma: A Report on Group Practice Surgery," *The Architect's Journal* (May 14, 1969):1279–1281.

25. Joiner, "Social Ritual," 11–22.

26. I. Altman, *The Environment and Social Behavior* (Monterey, Calif.: Brooks/Cole, 1975).

27. R. Cammock, "Confidentiality in Health Centres and Group Practices: The Implications for Design," *Journal of Architectural Research* 4(1975):5–17.

28. G. Davis and I. Altman, "Territories at the Work-place: Theory into Design Guidelines," *Man-Environment Systems* 6(1976):46–53.

29. Cammock, "Confidentiality in Health Centres," 5–17.

30. Brill, *Design of the Work Place.*

31. Sundstrom, Hall, and Kamp, *Privacy at Work*, 101–117.

32. Davis and Altman, "Territories at the Work Place," 46–53.

33. "Office Environment Post-occupancy Evaluation: A Dialogue with Ronald Goodrich," *Man-Environment Systems* 8(1978):175–190.

34. P.T. Lewis and P.E. O'Sullivan, "Acoustic Privacy in Office Design," *Journal of Architectural Research* 3(1974):48–51.

35. Sundstrom, Hall, and Kamp, "Privacy at Work," 101-117.

36. Cammock, "Confidentiality in Health Centres," 5–17.

37. S.C. Hayward and S.S. Franklin, "Perceived Openness—Enclosure of Architectural Space," *Environment and Behavior* 6(1974):37–52.

38. A. Baum, M. Reiss, and J. O'Hara, "Architectural Variants of Reaction to Spatial Invasion," *Environment and Behavior* 6(1974):91–100.

39. C.C. Lozar and R.L. Porter, *Developing Habitability Information for the Design of Office Environments*, technical report no. E-142 (Champaign, Ill.: U.S. Army Corps of Engineers, Construction Engineering Research Laboratory, 1979).

40. T. Burns, "Nonverbal Communication," *Discovery* 25(1974), no. 10:31–35.

41. Brinkman, cited in "Pros and Cons," 46–47;82.

42. Davis and Altman, "Territories at the Work-place," 46–53.

43. Lozar and Porter, *Developing Habitability Information*.

44. Cammock, "Confidentiality in Health Centres."

45. Scottish Home and Health Department, *Design Guide: Health Centres in Scotland* (London: Her Majesty's Stationery Office, 1973).

46. Cammock, "Confidentiality in Health Centres," 5–17.

47. Ibid.

48. G.O. Robinette, *Plants/People and Environmental Quality: A Study of Plants and Their Environmental Functions* (Washington, D.C.: U.S. Government Printing Office, 1972).

49. Lozar and Porter, *Developing Habitability Information*.

50. M. Heath and J.R.B. Green, *Information Usage in Health Facility Planning and Design: The State of the Art* (Sydney: University of New South Wales, School of Health Administration, 1976).

51. C. Bennett, *Spaces for People: Human Factors in Design* (Englewood Cliffs, N.J.: Prentice-Hall, 1977).

52. Lozar and Porter, *Developing Habitability Information*.

53. H. Gans, *The Urban Villagers* (New York: Free Press of Glencoe, 1962).

54. R.A. Gardiner, *Design for Safe Neighborhoods: The Environmental Security Planning and Design Process* (Washington, D.C.: U.S. Government Printing Office, 1978).

55. O. Newman, *Defensible Space: Crime Prevention Through Urban Design* (New York: Collier Books, 1973).

56. Gardiner, *Design for Safe Neighborhoods*.

57. Arthur Young & Company, *Public Housing Security Planning Manual and Catalog* (Chicago: Author, 1980).

58. J. Merrill, "Environmental-Behavior Research in the Service of Crime Prevention," *Man-Environment Systems* 7(1977):364-365.

59. Newman, *Defensible Space*.

60. Arthur Young & Company, *Public Housing Security Planning Manual*.

61. Gardiner, *Design for Safe Neighborhoods*.

62. Merrill, "Environment-Behavior Research," 363–364.

63. C.M. Zimring, G.W. Evans, and E.H. Zube, "Dynamic Space: Proxemic Research and the Design of Supportive Environment," in *Design for Communality and Privacy*, eds. A.H. Esser and B.B. Greenbie (New York: Plenum Press, 1978).

64. Newman, *Defensible Space*.

65. Arthur Young & Company, *Public Housing Security Planning Manual*.

66. Ibid.

67. Merrill, "Environment-Behavior Research," 364–365.

68. Newman, *Defensible Space*.

69. Arthur Young & Company, *Public Housing Security Planning Manual*.

70. Ibid.

71. S. Saegert, "Stress Inducing and Reducing Qualities of Environments," in *Environmental Psychology: People and Their Physical Settings*, 2nd ed., eds. H.M. Proshansky, W.H. Ittelson, and L.G. Rivlin (New York: Holt, Rinehart and Winston, 1976).

72. E.C. Poulton, *Environment and Human Efficiency* (Springfield, Ill.: Charles C Thomas, 1970).

73. Saegert, "Stress Inducing and Reducing Qualities."

74. M. Arnold, "Stress and Emotion," in *Psychological Stress*, eds. M.H. Appley and R. Trumbull (New York: Appleton-Century-Crofts, 1967).

75. R.S. Lazarus, "Cognitive and Personality Factors Underlying Threat and Coping," in *Psychological Stress*, eds. M.H. Appley and R. Trumbull (New York: Appleton-Century-Crofts, 1967).

76. Heath and Green, *Information Usage in Health Facility Planning*.

77. F.H. Allport, *Theories of Perception and Concept of Structure* (New York: Wiley, 1955).

78. J.J. Souder et al., "A Conceptual Framework for Hospital Planning, in *Environmental Psychology: Man and His Physical Setting*, eds. H.M. Proshansky, W.H. Ittelson, and L.G. Rivlin (New York: Holt, Rinehart and Winston, 1970).

79. S. Cohen, "Environmental Load and the Allocation of Attention" (University of Oregon, 1975).

80. T. Regan, *Wayfinding in Hospital Environments: An Overview* (Los Angeles: University of California, School of Architecture and Urban Planning, n.d.).

81. J. Weisman, "Evaluating Architectural Legibility: Way-finding in the Built Environment," *Environment and Behavior* 13(1981):189–204.

82. Regan, "Wayfinding."

83. M. Mowafy, "Color as an Orientation Cue" (Paper presented at the Twelfth International Conference of the Environmental Design Research Association, Ames, Iowa, April 1981).

84. K. Ellis, "Methods of Scanning a Large Visual Display," *Occupational Psychology* 42(1968):181–188.

85. J.M. Rolfe, "Evaluation of Visual Displays," *Occupational Psychology* 41(1967):49–56.

86. Regan, "Wayfinding."

87. E. Goffman, *The Presentation of Self in Everyday Life* (Garden City, N.Y.: Doubleday Anchor, 1959).

88. Steele, *Physical Settings*.

89. Altman, *Environment and Social Behavior*.

90. Brill, cited in Seliger, "Are Cubicles the Answer," 1;4.

91. Cammock, "Confidentiality in Health Centres," 5–17.

92. Brill, cited in Seliger, "Are Cubicles the Answer," 1;4.

93. Saegert, "Stress Inducing and Reducing Qualities."

94. S. Langer, *Mind: An Essay on Human Feelings* (Baltimore: Johns Hopkins Press, 1967).

95. D.E. Berlyne, *Aesthetics and Psychology* (New York: Appleton-Century-Crofts, 1971).

96. Brill, *Design of the Work Place*.

97. "Post-occupancy Evaluation of Hospitals," *American Institute of Architects Journal*, 1975, *63*(1), 30–34.

98. P.E. Spector and F. Sistrunk, "Does the Presence of Others Reduce Anxiety?" *Journal of Social Psychology* 105(1978):301–302.

99. R.G. Coss, "The Perceptual Aspects of Eye-Spot Patterns and Their Relevance to Gaze Behavior," in *Behavior Studies in Psychiatry*, eds. S. Hutt and C. Hutt (New York: Pergamon Press, 1970).

100. A. Baum and G.E. Davis, "Spatial and Social Aspects of Crowding Perception," unpublished manuscript.

101. D.R. Mandel, R.M. Baron, and J.D. Fisher, "Room Utilization and Dimensions of Density: Effects of Height and View," *Environment and Behavior* 12(1980):308–319.

102. A.F. Styne, "Lighting and Color in Health Care Facilities from a Designer's Viewpoint," in *Color in the Health Care Environment*, NBS special publication no. 516, ed. B.C. Pierman (Washington, D.C.: U.S. Government Printing Office, 1978).

103. J.E. Flynn et al., "Interim Study of Procedures for Investigating the Effect of Light on Impression and Behavior," *Journal of the Illuminating Engineering Society* 68(1973):87–94.

104. R.M. Neer et al., "Stimulation by Artificial Lighting of Calcium Absorption in Elderly Human Subjects," *Nature* 229 (1971):255–257.

105. Styne, "Lighting and Color."

106. D. Canter, "Heat, Noise, Light and User Satisfaction," in *A Short Course in Architectural Psychology*, ed. D. Canter (Sydney: University of Sydney, Architectural Psychology Research Unit, 1974).

107. R. Thorne, "The Inappropriateness of User and Satisfaction Studies for the Designer, as Demonstrated through Problems of Noise in Office Environments," in *Proceedings of the Twelfth International Conference of the Environmental Design Research Association* (Washington, D.C.: Environmental Design Research Association, 1981):326–337.

108. P. Manning, *Office Design: A Study of Environment* (Liverpool: University of Liverpool, Department of Building Science, 1965).

109. Ibid.

110. F.J. Langdon, E.C. Keighley, "User Research in Office Design," *Architects Journal*, February 5, 1964.

111. Lewis and O'Sullivan, "Acoustic Privacy," 48–51.

112. J.E. Moore, *Design for Noise Reduction* (London: Architectural Press, 1966).

113. Robinette, *Plants/People/and Environmental Quality*.

114. W.J. McGuiness, B. Stein, and J.S. Reynolds, *Mechanical and Electrical Equipment for Buildings*, 6th ed. (New York: Wiley, 1980).

115. Lewis and O'Sullivan, "Acoustic Privacy," 48–51.

116. M. Thomas, "Achieve Speech Privacy with Sound Masking Systems," *Facilities Design and Management* (July/August 1984):78–81.

117. J. Ollswang, personal communication, April 1981.

118. Bennett, *Spaces for People*.

119. Ibid.

120. McGuiness, Stein, and Reynolds, *Mechanical and Electrical Equipment*.

121. Ibid.

122. J. Nemecek and E. Grandjean, "Results of an Ergonomic Investigation of Large-space Offices," *Human Factors* 15(1973):111–124.

123. Langdon and Keighley, "User Research."

124. "Office Environment Post-occupancy Evaluation," 175–190.

125. McGuiness, Stein, and Reynolds, *Mechanical and Electrical Equipment*.

126. Lewis and O'Sullivan, "Acoustic Privacy," 48–51.

127. McGuiness, Stein, and Reynolds, *Mechanical and Electrical Equipment*.

128. Lewis and O'Sullivan, "Acoustic Privacy," 48–51.

129. J. Manuel, "Sound, Site Design, and Structure: Aspects of Land-use Planning," in *Noise in the Human Environment*, Vol. 1, ed. H.W. Jones (Edmonton: Environmental Council of Alberta, 1979).

130. Louis Harris & Associates, *The Steelcase National Study of Office Environments: Do They Work?* (Grand Rapids: Steelcase, 1978).

131. Manuel, "Sound, Site Design, and Structure."

132. Brill, cited in Seliger, "Are Cubicles the Answer," 1;4.

133. Lewis and O'Sullivan, "Acoustic Privacy," 48–51.

134. V.H. Hill, "Control of Noise Exposure," in *The Industrial Environment: Its Evaluation and Control* (Washington, D.C.: National Institute for Occupational Safety and Health, 1973).

135. McGuiness, Stein, and Reynolds, *Mechanical and Electrical Equipment*.

136. Thorne, "Inappropriateness of User and Satisfaction Studies," 326–337.

137. Lewis and O'Sullivan, "Acoustic Privacy," 48–51.

138. Thorne, "Inappropriateness of User and Satisfaction Studies," 326–337.

139. Manuel, "Sound, Site Design, and Structure."

140. J.H. Botsford, "Noise Measurement and Acceptability Criteria," in *The Industrial Environment: Its Evaluation and Control* (Washington, D.C., National Institute for Occupational Safety and Health, 1973).

141. R.A. Piesse, "Noise Criteria," *Australian Building Science and Technology* 6(1966):19–26.

142. L.L. Beranek, *Noise Reduction* (New York: McGraw-Hill, 1960).

143. McGuiness, Stein, and Reynolds, *Mechanical and Electrical Equipment*.

144. J.J. Kowalczewski, "Thermal Comfort in Buildings," in *A Short Course in Architectural Psychology*, ed. D. Canter (Sydney: University of Sydney, Architectural Psychology Research Unit, 1974).

145. I.D. Griffiths, "The Thermal Environment," in *Environmental Interaction: Psychological Approaches to our Physical Surroundings*, eds. D. Canter and P. Stringer (New York: International Universities Press, 1975).

146. N.W. Heimstra and L.H. McFarling, *Environmental Psychology* (Monterey, Calif.: Brooks/Cole, 1974).

147. Burton and Deakin, cited in Kowalczewski, "Thermal Comfort in Buildings."

148. I.D. Griffiths and D.A. McIntyre, "Sensitivity to Temporal Variations in Thermal Conditions," *Ergonomics* 17(1974):499–507.

149. Griffiths, "The Thermal Environment."

150. Kowalczewski, "Thermal Comfort in Buildings."

151. Griffiths, "The Thermal Environment."

152. "Pros and Cons," 46–47; 82.

153. Kowalczewski, "Thermal Comfort in Buildings."

154. Griffiths, "The Thermal Environment."

155. P.O. Fanger, "Improvement of Human Comfort and Resulting Effects on Working Capacity," *Biometeorology* 5(1972), no. 2:31–41.

156. D.A. McIntyne, "A Guide to Thermal Comfort," *Applied Ergonomics* 4(1973), no. 2:66–72.

157. P.R. Boyce, "The Luminous Environment," in *Environmental Interaction: Psychological Approaches to our Physical Surroundings*, eds. D. Canter and P. Stringer (New York: International Universities Press, 1975).

158. Mandel, Baron, and Fisher, "Room Utilization," 308–319.

159. Lozar and Porter, *Developing Habitability Information.*

160. Markus, cited in Boyce, "The Luminous Environment."

161. Ibid.

162. Heimstra and McFarling, *Environmental Psychology.*

163. Manning, *Office Design.*

164. S. Van Der Ryn and W.E. Boie, *Value Measurement and Visual Factors in the Urban Environment* (Berkeley: University of California, College of Environmental Design, 1963).

165. P.E. Clamp, "Approach to the Visual Environment," *Architectural Research and Teaching* 2(1973):153–160.

166. E. Ne'eman and R.G. Hopkinson, "Critical Minimum Acceptable Window Size: A Study of Window Design and Provision of View," *Lighting Research and Technology* 2(1970):17–27.

167. E.C. Keighley, "Visual Requirements and Reduced Fenestration in Office Buildings in a Study of Window Shape," *Building Science* 8(1973):311–320.

168. E.C. Keighley, "Visual Requirements and Reduced Fenestration in Offices in a Study of Multiple Apertures and Window Area," *Building Science* 8(1973):321–331.

169. Boyce, "The Luminous Environment."

170. "Post-occupancy Evaluation of Hospitals," *American Institute of Architects Journal* 63(1975):30–34.

171. Flynn et al., "Interim Study of Procedures," 87–94.

172. S.D. Lay, "The Building as a Filter: Lighting," in *A Short Course in Architectural Psychology*, ed. D. Canter (Sydney: University of Sydney, Architectural Psychology Research Unit, 1974).

173. Boyce, "The Luminous Environment."

174. Bennett, *Spaces for People.*

175. R. Korman, "Where the BOSTI Study Defies Design Wisdom," *Facilities Design and Management* (July/August 1984):70–73.

Chapter 4

Staffing the Department

Ollivene Hickman

Admitting managers of the future will need to define clearly two abilities. The first is marketing ability to face the challenges of competition. The other ability centers around departmental staffing and strategies. Admitting managers will find that the challenge of personal flexibility must be faced. Also, they must be able to motivate their staff and to disseminate change so as to achieve the desired results with a minimal amount of effort. This will have to be done with the least amount of change noted on the part of the admitting manager's staff.

Staff development and continuing education within the department are important factors in accomplishing the above objective and meeting the exciting changes of the future. Both of these will provide a means for effective overall utilization of employees while establishing a foundation to build and maintain a staff at the highest competency level.

While important, staff development and continuing education are not the only two factors necessary to accommodate change in future admitting departments. Adjustments in the operating schedules of departments will have to be made as conditions warrant. Along the same lines, manpower issues will be addressed to ensure continuity of service. Finally, thorough orientation and training of new employees will be necessary so that the basic foundations are built for future training and education. Admitting departments, like any other hospital department, are team efforts. The staff and the manager must work together to accomplish the many requests that will be made tomorrow.

OPERATING SCHEDULE

There are no set rules regarding just when admitting departments should be open. Although they are a necessary and integral department for hospital operations on a daily basis, they need not be open on a 24-hour basis in every hospital.

One of the reasons for having an admitting department not assume a continuous operating schedule is the availability of personnel in emergency services registration. One of the more frequent options available to a hospital is to have the main admitting department open between the hours of 7 A.M. and 11 P.M. The emergency services department would then assume responsibility for any admitting functions during the night shift. Some hospitals prefer to close their admitting departments even earlier, such as at 6 P.M. or 7 P.M., with the emergency services department again taking over. Some even prefer to see their admitting department closed on Saturday with the emergency department handling both unexpected admissions and any outpatients.

Preadmitting Hours

Within the admitting office, certain functions may be limited to certain specified hours. One of these functions is preadmitting. Actual admission of a patient has assumed a logical correct time of the afternoon in order for an adequate number of beds to be freed up by morning discharges. Many admitting departments have found that mornings present the ideal time to coordinate and book preadmitting procedures on patients. A typical admitting department may decide to preadmit patients from 8 A.M. to 11 A.M. By this time, which is the usual discharge time for patients, the department is in a good position to begin admitting patients. Admitting of patients can then take place until 7 P.M. or even later, with the bulk of patients arriving in the mid afternoon hours. During the morning hours of preadmission, the emergency services department would admit patients. By providing patients with specific times for arrival into the admitting office and limiting the amount of call-ins on any given day, the admitting office can operate on a limited time schedule. Properly staffed emergency services departments can also provide successful limited operating hours for the admitting department.

Shift Monitoring

If an admitting department elects to be open on a limited-hour basis, the manager of such a department needs to have experienced personnel at work during the hours when the office is closed. Equally important is to understand the behaviors of individuals who work evenings and nights. One of the primary objectives is to make certain a continuity exists between the functions of the main admitting office and the emergency services department. An adequate understanding of the work performed during the day will provide a basis for analysis of the work performed at off hours. By the same token, differences will exist between personnel on both shifts. One should find employees in the emergency department more adept at patient handling and skilled at adapting the workload to the pace of action in the department. The only difficulty with late night employees centers around attendance at inservice education meetings held during the day. Admitting managers should make every effort to come in during these hours and present individualized instruction to these employees. Late night personnel are difficult to obtain and should be treated with respect and consideration so both departments maintain continuous operation as if they were one.

Staffing Patterns

Most admitting offices find themselves the busiest between the hours of 11 A.M. and 4 P.M. It is advantageous then to have maximum staffing patterns in place at this time. Skeleton crews seem adequate on Fridays and Saturdays for those hospitals electing to have their emergency departments take over the admitting function from 11 P.M. to 7 A.M. during the week and through Saturday until Sunday at 7 A.M. Emergency departments can usually handle room admits, private outpatients, and routine admissions if staffed with two employees plus a supervisor. This is an ideal working relationship for those institutions finding themselves registering 150 to 200 patients in a 24-hour period. These institutions are large 1,200-bed facilities. If half of these patients are registered in a 24-hour period, one person per shift would be adequate. If it takes ten interviewers to admit 150 to 200 patients Sunday through Thursday, then three interviewers should be adequate for admitting up to 75 patients and six interviewers should be needed to handle the admission of 75 to 100 patients.

Benefits of Adequate Staffing

Adequate staffing allows for a variety of increased services provided by an admitting department. Certainly, adequate staff enables the department to handle patients in a variety of ways, each unique to that patient's situation. The admitting interviewer should be a leader in the first impression concept for the patient. This individual should be allowed adequate time to admit the patient but also to perform other functions that can facilitate the patient's admission. Escorting the patient to the room, assisting with safekeeping of valuables, finding desired accommodations, locating out-of-town bank funds, discussing past due balances, or even just helping the patient to relax are all within the realm of admitting the patient. If adequate staffing is present, interviewers will not be hassled to speed this process up unnecessarily.

Adequate staffing in preadmission can also help in the efficient operations of the department. If all of the background information on the patient has been obtained by the preadmission interviewing team prior to the patient's arrival, the admission interviewing team can provide personal attention and get that patient into a room faster. This can also allow the patient to avoid the business office at the time of discharge. Patients want to have the admitting interviewer ready with adequate forms, complete information, and the time to answer pertinent questions. Finally, patients simply want to have the quickest route to their room available.

The Emergency Services Department

A different story exists for those individuals working in emergency services registration and admitting. There is simply no time available to spend with patients in order for the admitting function to be done in the same fashion as in the main department. Staff in this department often must quell fears of patients, dispel anger, and recognize acute illness and injury when present. These individuals know when to simply allow the patient to sign and obtain information later when the patient is in a more stable condition. These decisions as to when to perform a complete interview or simply obtain basic facts and signatures are made every day by personnel working in this department. This, too, can be appreciated as much as the extended treatment performed in the main admitting department.

STAFFING PHILOSOPHY

Strong Definitions

Admitting has become justified by its impact on the marketing capabilities of a given hospital. Whereas the admitting department of the past was often viewed as the clerical department that assisted the treatment team in the preparation of essential paperwork, today's admitting department is perceived as the first step in the initial treatment of the patient. If attention is not given to initial hiring practices within the department, this current view can be in significant trouble. Strong and clearly defined roles must be in place within the department in order for employees to understand their particular responsibilities within the team concept. The admitting manager must also have a strong grasp of the responsibilities and duties that accompany each position when entertaining a hiring decision.

Strong Management

It is appropriate for the admitting manager to select and be held accountable for the employees brought into the department. Equally so, the hospital has a responsibility to bring into the department a well-informed, competent, and qualified admitting manager to be in charge of this vital hospital operation. The admitting director should be responsible for the well-organized, properly directed department staffed with an adequate number of qualified employees integrated with other hospital units and departments. The admitting director shall review the quality of appropriateness of staff services performed and take necessary action. Administration should emphasize the admitting manager's ability to assume a state of flexibility, particularly in regard to staffing requirements. This is especially evident today. Admitting managers should be able to reduce successfully the number of required staff without a reduction in the quality of service provided by the department and without any morale problems. The challenge that proceeds from this is the ability to add services amid reductions in staffing.

Strong Supervision

Regardless of the size of the hospital, an overall standard of required supervision is an average of 10 to 15 employees per supervisor. Supervisory staff is not an area in which cutbacks should occur if at all possible. As changes in the department take place, the functions of the admitting supervisor will also change to accommodate the given situation. In many instances, the admitting supervisor will assume tasks usually assigned to the employees. Nevertheless, it will be important to continue these supervisory roles in light of new marketing approaches provided by the department. Adjustments required by the reduction in staff must be allowed to occur with the added responsibilities so that no detriment to the overall effectiveness of the employee takes place.

Strong Role Models

Admitting managers must have strong leadership skills coupled with a natural ability to motivate and to accomplish task-oriented skills. The manager must be the role model admitting personnel desire to become. A strong and effective planner, the admitting manager must consistently monitor results for effectiveness and completeness. This must be accomplished within the context of the manager's own duties and responsibilities. Finally, a harmonious attitude of working together must take place between the admitting manager, the patients, and the physicians. This environment is conducive to the byproduct of staff development. Morale will increase on the part of the staff, and turnover will decrease. Absenteeism will decrease, reducing expenses and allowing the department to operate in a much more cost-effective manner.

Strong Considerations

Above all else, the admitting manager has to understand the specific personalities of the employees in the department. Cross training and flexibility works only up to the point of individual differences. Not all employees can work in the emergency services department. Discovering what each employee is capable of and what that individual enjoys can do much to match employee with the ideal position in the department.

A similar situation exists with regard to personalities. By understanding the employee's personality, an effective role can be discovered for that individual. Mild-mannered individuals would probably do well in the preadmitting function. Aggressive types would serve the department well in resolving patient financial problems. Placing the right employee in the right position is essential, is efficient, and, in the long run, is good management.

ORIENTATION AND TRAINING

Training is a key issue in the development of a new employee. It is a good idea to use a formal checklist when training a new employee. An example of such a checklist is given in Appendix 4–A. Prior to training, reviewing standards of performance can help guarantee the effectiveness of an employee. The applicant can then see in writing what is expected for that particular position.

The Trainer

Each admitting department should have at least one training and development individual to provide adequate orientation and frequent inservice educational programs for all employees. Having one individual to train new employees assists in achieving continuity in the training methods used in the department. A good trainer candidate would be an individual with a good knowledge of departmental function and hospitalwide activity. This individual does not have to be a supervisor, although a senior-level employee would be a logical choice. The individual should have a good attitude, enjoy the work, and display loyalty to the institution. If the trainer sets good examples on how to treat fellow employees, the new employee will get along much better with the trainer and fellow subordinates.

Skill Development

During the training of a new employee an emphasis should be placed on technical skill development. This helps the employee perform the daily tasks essential to be successful in the position. One of the first technical skills that needs to be developed is typing. Typing has become increasingly important with the advent of computerized admitting systems. The trainer should strive to achieve complete understanding by the employee of all forms and equipment used during the admissions process. A sound understanding of public relations technqiues needs to be gathered by the employee in order to make decisions during the admitting interview. A good example of this is in the area of collections. Admission is the most effective time for discussing finances and collecting deposits. The same holds true for preadmitting personnel who must discuss this aspect of hospitalization over the telephone. Overall individualized training is necessary to develop the fullest potential within each employee.

Inservice Education

A good inservice education program for admitting department staff should include a class at least once a month. Continuing education classes foster continued growth of the department and also maintain interest on the part of the staff in each major position and function. Nursing involvement at various inservice meetings helps the employee understand the condition of the patient and thus helps eliminate potential medical emergencies in the admitting areas. Other departments that should also be included in these meetings include data processing, dietary services, housekeeping, and the business office.

Throughout the year, major emphasis should also be placed on inservice education in the technical aspects of the admission process. At least one inservice class should be dedicated to the personal needs of departmental members. Topics could include such items as effective time management, improving self-esteem, and individual growth and goal setting.

New Employee Evaluation

After hiring the new employee, the admitting manager should not wait until a 90-day period has elapsed before a first evaluation takes place. A weekly evaluation should be conducted using a checklist similar to the one mentioned earlier. A 30-day evaluation should then be done in writing. Finally, the 90-day evaluation should be performed with earlier evaluations attached and ready for review at this time. An extension of 30 days can be added to the probation time if uncertainty still exists.

Training, education, and staff development include orientation, on-the-job training, department inservice workshops, outside job-related workshops, and related courses. All new employees are orientated to general hospital policies and procedures. Following this, there should be a departmental orientation, which covers all items on the checklist and other specific department policies and procedures.

Preservice Training

Preservice training and education begin on employment and end when the employee assumes full responsibility for on-the-job activities. This training is conducted within the department. During this time the new admitting employee is made aware of what is expected and taught initial skills.

Inservice Training

The inservice on-the-job training begins when new employees assumes their duties. This training should be carefully planned, with expected results spelled out fully. The performance should always be evaluated and documented in writing. Inservice ongoing training continues for the entire department with inhouse classes, workshops, off-site seminars, and job-related courses. The continuing education of an employee is vitally important as more changes in the role of the admitting department occur.

CONCLUSION

The real key to the success of any admitting department is leadership. The admitting manager should have the ability to inspire and motivate others with the desire to cooperate. Individuals must be happy with their work schedule, their environment, and the challenges of their position. How persons are led is important, but how they are nourished is critical.

Appendix 4–A

Employee Evaluation Checklist

EMPLOYEE: EMPLOYMENT DATE:

JOB TITLE: SHIFT:

QUALIFICATIONS	YES	NO	COMMENTS
Peripheral Capabilities			
1. ADMITTING INTERVIEWERS:			
A. Typing CRT			
B. Patients' signatures on admitting form			
C. Plates and armbands			
D. Know hospital's policies and procedures			
E. Obtain medical record numbers from terminals/microfiche			
F. Collect deposits and write receipts			
G. Log patients' arrivals and obtain room preference			
H. An awareness of patients' conditions and act in accordance			
I. Communicate with foreign patients			
J. Assist the general public and patients requiring directions and information			
K. Maintain constant flow of patients into offices and to assigned rooms			

Source: Courtesy of St. Luke's Episcopal Hospital, Houston, Texas.

	YES	NO	COMMENTS

2. ADDRESSOGRAPH:

   A. Maintain printer and embosser
   B. Keep daily admission sheets
       filed
   C. Plates and corrections on plates

3. CONTROL:

   A. Room census
   B. Room assignments
   C. Transfer of patients to rooms
       and ICU's
   D. Central patient information
   E. Information concerning foreign
       patients
   F. Assist doctors and residents in
       locating patients

4. PREADMITTING:

   A. Obtain admitting information
   B. Use CRT for medical record
       numbers/microfiche
   C. Type and complete all preadmits
   D. Check reservation list
   E. Ensure that all preadmits are
       completed and on the CRT

5. TERMINALS:

   A. Make census report
   B. Enter inpatient discharges,
       transfers, and admissions
   C. Discharge for all inpatient
       preadmits who did not show
   D. Enter inpatient preadmits
   E. Work cashier report

6. NURSE ADMITTING:

   A. Vital signs
   B. Transpose orders
   C. Stamp charts

	YES	NO	COMMENTS

7. RESERVATIONS:

  A. Take all doctors' calls for reservations in the hospital

  B. Book reservations on CRT

  C. Handle compensation and attorney cases with verifiers

  D. Handle clinic reservations

8. OUTPATIENT REGISTRATION:

  A. Register all patients for treatment

  B. Obtain medical record numbers on CRT/microfiche

  C. Type laboratory and x-ray slips if not done

  D. Price and code

9. EMERGENCY DEPARTMENT ADMITTING:

  A. Register ED patients for treatment

  B. Admit on inpatient basis

  C. Assign rooms when Control is closed

  D. Collect fees for services and write receipts

  E. Work cashier report

10. ESCORTS:

  A. Assist patients to room

  B. Take stat papers to floors or care units

  C. Assist in putting together various admitting forms

11. OTHER:

  A. Order supplies for department

Chapter 5

The Admitting Manager

Donald D. Hamilton

Admitting managers answer to many titles depending on the institution. Some may be called admitting or admissions manager. Others may go by director of admitting or admitting director. Still others may have titles such as admitting supervisor, registration supervisor, or central registration coordinator. Regardless of what title is used, admitting managers must have a multitude of skills at their command in order to control one of the main departments in the hospital. The field of admitting management is still relatively new, and managers of these departments find themselves assuming a variety of roles. These contradictory roles can make admitting management difficult to define and difficult to practice.

Patients come to the hospital ill, or at least anxious and uneasy. The admitting staff are often the first hospital professionals these patients meet who are able to convey a feeling that the patient is welcome, in safe hands, and will be given good care. In this sense, the admitting staff and the admitting manager provide a primary introduction to the health care team. This role can be described as one of nurturing and presents a corporate image that conveys the idea that the hospital is a good place to be. More often than not admitting managers find themselves serving as social workers, planners, systems analysts, counselors, and politicans, as well as fulfilling a host of other roles. They must be ready to adjust to any situation and be able to adapt to any new technology. In addition, they must be ready to solve the problems that accompany such changes in their field.

RESPONSIBILITIES

Probably the most important responsibility any admitting manager has is to carry out the role of leader in the department. Without respected leadership ability, the admitting manager will be unable to function in a department that is always busy. Efficient running of an admitting department requires the unified actions of every member of the admitting team in a knowledgeable manner. Staff knowledge can only come about by having the admitting manager fulfill the obligations of the role as leader of the department. Other responsibilities of the admitting manager can then be carried out in a professional and workable way.

The Responsibility of Information Gathering

The principal responsibility of an admitting department is to secure patient information. Thus, the admitting manager is responsible for the registration of patients and the dissemination of the information gathered at the time of the initial interview to other hospital departments. At the same time, the admitting manager is responsible for assessing the financial condition of each patient and making tentative decisions concerning the patient's ability to pay. This requires routine but sometimes intrusive questioning, which might be difficult at any time but is especially unwelcome in the face of illness or injury. This role is typically administrative and has little to do with the patient's medical or emotional needs. Controlling the elective admission load and using the bed complement in an efficient manner so as to maintain a high census without delays in admissions are two more responsibilities of an admitting manager.

The Responsibility of Information Reporting

Reports are a vital part of the responsibility of the admitting department, and it is the admitting manager's responsibility to see that all reports are done in a timely and accurate manner. After they are completed, the manager must review them and have these reports sent to the proper areas of the hospital. Some reports are more important than others. One report with special significance to the admitting manager is the hospital census. A good hospital census report is really the lifeline of the hospital and, therefore, must always be accurate.

Another important report for the admitting manager and administration is the departmental budget. The manager is concerned with all budgetary processes and decisions within the admitting department's realm. Budgetary allowances must be available for plans or changes taking place in the department. During this time of uncertainty in the health care field, this task of the admitting manager is not an easy one. All decisions made in connection with the budgetary process must be weighed both in necessity and in cost. The admitting manager must make sure that every process in the department is cost justified.

The Responsibility of Information Sharing

Admitting managers, given their frequent communication with other major departments in the hospital, are often asked to serve on hospital committees. Other department heads find they need the expertise and judgment a good admitting manager can provide in solving hospitalwide problems. Four of the committees admitting managers frequently find themselves serving on are (1) utilization, (2) communications, (3) forms, and (4) nursing. Whether the committees have been longstanding ones or ones created to serve a short-term goal, admitting managers always find themselves involved in a variety of meetings to discuss the ever-changing complexity of the health care field today.

Admitting managers must also share their knowledge intimately with their subordinates in the form of training. Training new employees and providing continuous inservice education for their veteran employees is usually done by the departmental supervisors under the direction of the admitting manager. Nevertheless, the manager must be certain the supervisors have adequate knowledge of the department. Equally important, the manager must allow freedom for these supervisors to perform the training in a clear and precise manner.

The Responsibility of Information Updating

The development of admitting department policy and procedure along with consistent updating can prove to be a critical function of any admitting manager. Very few managers ever have the pleasure of setting up their own department. Most, if not all admitting managers have either been hired or promoted into the position in an already existing and fully running department. One of the first activities to be undertaken by any new admitting manager is to read thoroughly and critically the department's policy and procedure manual. Once this has been accomplished, the manager should check out daily activity to see if it corresponds to what is given in the manual. If changes have been made, these should also be included as updates to the procedure manual. Periodic reviewing and updating of this manual along with the creation of new policy and procedure for a new departmental activity is something admitting managers should be concerned with all the time.

A similar function is in the area of job descriptions. The admitting manager is responsible for the development of all new job descriptions as well as for the updating of current ones. Job descriptions should always reflect the employee's responsibilities within the specific position. Since employee salaries are based on the magnitude of their job descriptions, updating these documents becomes a matter of necessity and good employee relations. Of course, admitting managers should not neglect their own job description, since a well-written one will assist them in their own promotional desires. A sample job description for an admitting manager position is seen in Appendix 5–A.

Admitting managers also have responsibilities of a more ongoing nature. They establish and monitor departmental goals. They help to foster a positive public relations image. Also, managers must be certain that the confidentiality of all patient records is upheld.

The Personnel Function

Admitting managers are responsible for interviewing, hiring, training, disciplining, and sometimes terminating employees. As any departmental manager knows, these are not easy tasks. Most admitting managers find it difficult to perform many of the above functions.

Interviews to hire a new employee can be especially awkward. Since the prospective candidate and the admitting manager both present their best characteristics, it is difficult for the admitting manager to see the real person behind the many shields candidates put up during an interview. The skill of going beyond the surface during an interview is something an admitting manager develops with time, experience, and proper education in the area of the psychology of the interviewing process. During the selection of a new employee, the admitting manager should work with the personnel department in deciding on the best candidate.

Another difficult interview situation for the admitting manager is the process of disciplining employees. The manager should have all the pertinent facts available during the session so that no surprises take place. It is important to approach the employee with honesty and to assure the person that together the problem can be overcome. An employee should not be disciplined for revenge or punishment. Rather, an attempt should be made to achieve a positive reaction with the hope that the person will become a better and more knowledgeable employee.

There are those circumstances in which an employee has not improved and is causing the same problems as before. Here termination may be the only answer but only after other options have thoroughly been exhausted. Once again, the use of honesty and sincerity is the best approach, with all reasons being given to the employee, including a reminder of all other times the person has been spoken to regarding the same problem. All department heads share the frustration, stress, and insecurity that is associated with these important, yet sometimes unpleasant tasks.

The Planning Function

A large responsibility of admitting managers is that of planning. Planning is vital in the admitting department since this department interrelates with all other areas of the hospital. A variety of planning functions are under the jurisdiction of the admitting manager. The development of an efficient and productive staff working in a good environment are two issues that take a lot of planning effort. The implementation and development of an information system in the department along with integration of hospital policies and those of the department in order to reach the same goals are two more planning functions. The admitting manager must develop plans that are cost effective and cost efficient. In order to accomplish this, the manager must be capable of measuring the productivity within the department. Productivity measurement is the only tool by which an admitting manager can determine if the department is operating in an efficient and productive manner.

Developing a Productivity Model

The first step in developing a productivity model is to conduct a time study on all of the functions performed in the department. These functions include such activities as taking reservations, assigning beds, performing preadmission telephone interviews, preparing forms, and performing on-site interviewing. If the department is responsible for inpatient, referred outpatient, and emergency department registrations, then possibly a separate time unit may be developed for each of the interviews. If the length of time for each interview is relatively equal, then only one unit of measurement need apply. Another area needing a time measurement is the amount of time spent on the telephone and any other type of work each specific department does.

The next step is to determine the amount of fixed time. This is the amount of time spent on activities not dependent on the volume of registration. This refers to the duties performed by members of the department regardless of the number of patients. This could also include the duties of bed control, department management, reservations, night shift, telephone, patient escort, addressograph, and so on. A formula for the development of this time unit is shown in Exhibit 5–1.

The next unit is the variable hours required to accomplish the activity, whether it be outpatient registrations or inpatient registrations. This unit of measurement is acquired by taking the number of registrations times the hours required per registration. This is depicted in Exhibit 5–2. One then adds the total variable hours to the total fixed hours to receive the total hours required. Dividing the required hours by the number of worked hours will give the percentage of productivity. One should always strive for a productivity level of 80 percent or more.

PROFILE OF AN ADMITTING MANAGER*

Research has demonstrated that admitting managers, when compared by personality type to a group composed of young adults represent type distributions that are significantly different from the general population. This research was based on the Myers-Briggs Type Indicator (MBTI) and involved 297 subjects from across the United States and Canada.

---

*Material on pages 89–93 and Exhibits 5–1 through 5–6 are original research contributed by Warren Althaus, A.A.M., Director of Admitting, St. Joseph Hospital, Tacoma, Washington.

Exhibit 5–1 Calculation of Fixed Activity Time

QUALITY MEASUREMENT
STANDARDS SUMMARY SHEET

COST CENTER: _____   DATE: _____

FIXED COMPONENT (Activities not dependent on volume):

Position or Activity	Hours per Month	×	% Dedicated to Fixed Activity	=	Fixed Monthly Hours
Bed Control	364.0		75%		273
Department Management	346.7		90%		312
Reservations	173.3		90%		156
Night Shift	173.3		60%		104
Others: prepare and schedule same day testing, phone, escort patients, make new plates and armbands	182.0		100%		182
				TOTAL	1,027

VARIABLE COMPONENT (Activities dependent on volume):

Activity or Workload Indicator	Source of Activity Count	Hours Required Per Unit
Registrations	Admissions lists Outpatient Logs	0.167

Goals for Ratio of Required to Worked Hours: __80_ %

Source: Courtesy of Deaconess Hospital, Cleveland, Ohio.

The MBTI describes an individual's personality in process terms, looking at individual preferences and methods of making decisions. These preferences are grouped into eight categories:

1. extrovert—prefers to be with others at work and play
2. introvert—prefers to work and relax alone
3. sensing—prefers to deal with known facts
4. intuition—wants to deal with possibilities
5. thinking—makes decisions from a logical perspective

Exhibit 5–2 Calculation of Variable Activity Time

QUANTITY MEASUREMENT
SAMPLE MONTHLY REPORT CALCULATIONS

COST CENTER: _____   PERIOD ENDING: _____

Activity	Number of Units	$\times$	Hours Required per Unit	$=$	Variable Hours Required
Registrations	3,600		0.167		601.2

Total Variable Hours: 601.2
+ Total Fixed Hours: 1,200.3
Total Hours Required: 1,801.5

Ratio of Required to Worked Hours: $\dfrac{\text{Required Hours}}{\text{Worked Hours}}$ = 80.3 %
(2,242.75)

Source: Courtesy of Deaconess Hospital, Cleveland, Ohio.

6. feeling—makes decisions based on emotion
7. judging—prefers to be well organized
8. perceiving—takes life as it comes

By combining these type traits, one finds 16 personality types described by the MBTI. The study showed that all 16 types were found in the study group of admitting managers but that some types were overrepresented while others were less numerous than expected, as seen in Exhibits 5–3 through 5–5.

The traits most frequently found were the sensing, thinking, judging types. This indicates that the typical manager is interested in known facts, makes logical decisions, and prefers to be well organized.

This research, while being restricted to admitting managers, leads one to suspect that admitting specialists also fit unique profiles when viewed from a psychological perspective, although no such research presently exists. The study correlated the type of information to demographic traits such as age, sex, education, salary, job title, and so on, so that it is possible to make general assumptions about an applicant without having to do psychological testing. A portrait of a typical admitting manager is given in Exhibit 5–6. This new skill may prove to be the basis for a new facet of personnel selection and utilization with regard to the hiring of admitting managers and staff.

Exhibit 5–3 Admitting Manager Type—Male*

E = Extrovert		T = Thinking	
I = Introvert		F = Feeling	
S = Sensing		J = Judging	
N = Intuitive		P = Perceiving	
ISTJ	*ISFJ*	*INFJ*	*INTJ*
14.89%	8.51%	0.00%	6.38%
(7)	(4)	(0)	(3)
ISTP	*ISFP*	*INFP*	*INTP*
4.25%	4.25%	2.12%	2.12%
(2)	(2)	(1)	(1)
ESTP	*ESFP*	*ENFP*	*ENTP*
6.38%	0.00%	0.00%	4.25%
(3)	(0)	(0)	(2)
ESTJ	*ESFJ*	*ENFJ*	*ENTJ*
21.27%	10.6%	4.25%	10.63%
(10)	(5)	(2)	(5)

*Forty-seven men were studied; the numbers with each combination of personality type are given in parentheses.

Exhibit 5–4 Admitting Manager Type—Female*

E = Extrovert		T = Thinking	
I = Introvert		F = Feeling	
S = Sensing		J = Judging	
N = Intuitive		P = Perceiving	
ISTJ	*ISFJ*	*INFJ*	*INTJ*
13.30%	9.27%	3.22%	2.41%
(33)	(23)	(8)	(6)
ISTP	*ISFP*	*INFP*	*INTP*
4.43%	3.22%	4.03%	4.43%
(11)	(8)	(10)	(11)
ESTP	*ESFP*	*ENFP*	*ENTP*
2.41%	4.03%	6.04%	4.43%
(6)	(10)	(15)	(11)
ESTJ	*ESFJ*	*ENFJ*	*ENTJ*
19.35%	12.50%	3.22%	3.62%
(48)	(31)	(8)	(9)

*Two hundred forty-eight women were studied; the numbers with each combination of personality type are given in parentheses.

Exhibit 5–5 Admitting Manager Type—Total Sample*

E = Extrovert		T = Thinking	
I = Introvert		F = Feeling	
S = Sensing		J = Judging	
N = Intuitive		P = Perceiving	

ISTJ	*ISFJ*	*INFJ*	*INTJ*
13.56%	9.15%	2.71%	3.05%
(40)	(27)	(8)	(9)
ISTP	*ISFP*	*INFP*	*INTP*
4.41%	3.39%	3.73%	4.07%
(13)	(10)	(11)	(12)
ESTP	*ESFP*	*ENFP*	*ENTP*
3.05%	3.39%	5.08%	4.41%
(9)	(10)	(15)	(13)
ESTJ	*ESFJ*	*ENFJ*	*ENTJ*
19.66%	12.20%	3.39%	4.75%
(58)	(36)	(10)	(14)

*Two hundred ninety-five managers were studied; the numbers with each combination of personality type are given in parentheses.

REPORTING RELATIONSHIPS

The way the manager approaches the job is affected by the way that position is seen in the organizational hierarchy. Some degree of confusion can develop because of an unclear job title or functional relationships. Individuals may share a similar job title and have very different roles. This perhaps becomes more understandable when there are two individuals with the same position title and one is a full-time administrative officer in a university hospital setting while the other is the head clerk in a two-person office with additional duties of information desk clerk and telephone operator.

Admitting managers report to a variety of administrative staff members. These may include the president, vice president, chief administrator, controller, chief financial officer, administrator of nursing, or medical director. There are many reasons for this, and each in its own way can provide for a convincing case. Many believe admitting managers should report to a top administrative officer such as the president, vice president, or medical director. This allows the admitting manager to work consistently toward the goals of the entire hospital and not for the fiscal or nursing functions of the hospital. Admitting has the ability to make or break a

Exhibit 5–6 Portrait of a Typical Admitting Manager

Age: 36 to 50
Sex: Female
Religion: Protestant
Education: less than college degree
Geographic area: Midwest and East
Job title: Director of Admitting
Salary: greater than $20,000 (1982)
Supervisor: fiscal branch of hospital
Goal: leave the admitting field
Other characteristics:

- has identified long-term goals
- attends meetings of regional professional organization
- is nonaccredited
- is not eligible to sit for accreditation examination
- works in hospital owned by public agency
- supervises fewer than four nonadmitting functions
- processes admissions
- is married (no marital change in previous five years)
- has no reported physical problems
- does not perceive herself as a member of a minority group
- lives in city of less than 100,000 population
- works in hospital with fewer than 300 beds

hospital. Therefore, the admitting manager should always be answerable to top administrative officers. Each hospital must make its own choice with regard to reporting relationships, but the admitting manager should always be involved in such decision-making processes.

ADMINISTRATIVE EXPECTATIONS

The admitting manager needs to balance the relative priorities of the nurturing, public relations, and administrative aspects of the position. It is understandable that admitting managers will differ in the way they deal with these necessary but sometimes conflicting role expectations held by each manager's superior.

Administration looks to the admitting manager for providing professionalism in the handling of all patients entering the hospital. This is done through the training process of all admitting personnel. Admitting must be the mirror of the hospital, and thus the admitting manager must always be knowledgeable of all regulations (i.e., local to federal).

Patients entering the health care process sometimes are overwhelmed at the redundance and amount of information they must supply. They begin to look for someone or something to complain about, and that usually ends up being the admitting department. The admitting staff may not have done anything wrong but will take the blame and try to correct the situation by passing along the concern of the patient to the next level of care being given. This is a responsibility of the entire department that must be second nature to all personnel.

Another administrative expectation more important in today's world of cost cutting in health care is the economical operation of the department. Every process must be studied, timed, and given a standard cost. This can then be checked on a monthly basis to evaluate the total costs of operating the department. By knowing this, the admitting manager can do some creative staffing to either increase or decrease the staff to handle an increase or decrease in registrations. Without this knowledge, the department would run at full force at all times and be a very costly operation.

The other expectation is for the admitting manager to have a scheduling process that allows for the maintenance of the highest possible census at all times. The most costly thing for a hospital is to have an occupancy of 90 percent one day and 70 percent the next. This is very difficult to do, but with a good relationship between the admitting manager and the medical staff and the keeping of exact statistics, it can be accomplished. Cost-effective productivity must remain in the mind of every admitting manager at all times.

EDUCATION AND TRAINING

Admitting managers working in hospitals in today's world have come from a wide variety of backgrounds in education and experience. However, this is coming to an end. Admitting managers are now being required to have an undergraduate degree or better and 3 to 5 years of experience as a manager in a hospital or health care facility. Also, promotion from within the department or the hospital is no longer in wide practice. Most managers are now being brought in from the outside with the above-mentioned education and experience. Managers with 10 to 15 years of experience are usually able to qualify without having the educational background. The manager should have a thorough knowledge of the operation of a hospital and should have at least 2 years of admitting officer experience. A hospital is so different from industry that just having business office experience is not enough to qualify for this position. A good admitting manager is always respected by the administrative staff of the hospital.

Promotion to Administration

It is a natural tendency to hire individuals who share common philosophy and goals. MBTI research found that there is no predictable relationship between health administrators and admitting managers. In this situation, it is very likely that an individual who is hired as an admitting manager based on similarity to traits held in common by hospital administrators may not be successful in the position. This relationship becomes understandable when one remembers that the administrator is largely insulated from contact with people, being concerned with the larger issue of running the hospital from the corporate level, while the admitting manager deals with patients every day and is attuned to the needs of individuals but may have difficulty seeing the hospital at the corporate level. Also, owing to their unique personality types, admitting managers might not be good candidates for promotion into the upper levels of hospital administration.

Degree and Course Requirements

Today there are many colleges and universities offering a wide range of business management courses with specific interest in health care. It would be advisable to select the bachelor level work or graduate level work along these lines. Some of the courses that should be included in the educational background of an admitting manager are listed in Exhibit 5–7.

Certain types of hospitals require different levels of education and experience. The university-based hospital will usually always require at least a bachelor's if

---

Exhibit 5–7 College Courses Recommended for Admitting Managers

Business Communications
Principles of Hospital Accounting
Principles of Management
Labor Relations
Administrative Systems
The Legal Environment of Health Care
Budgetary Control
Current Issues in Health Services Management
Business and Professional Speaking
Organizational Behavior and Leadership
Marketing
Principles of Sociology
Economic Analysis of Health Services
Business Decision Making
Systems Analysis
Professional Writing Skills

not a graduate degree. One or both degrees must be in business management. The large urban hospital of approximately 800 beds or more usually requires a bachelor's degree but will hire admitting managers with five to ten years of experience in medium- to large-sized hospitals. A hospital of 150 to 800 beds would require an admitting manager with a bachelor's degree or with two to five years of experience. Hospitals with fewer than 150 beds have requirements of anywhere from a high school diploma to a bachelor's degree with several years of previous experience in either the admitting department or another department within the hospital. Quite often hospitals of this size have one person to manage both the admitting department and the business office.

Professional Associations

Admitting managers must involve themselves in several professional associations. Depending on their responsibilities, admitting managers can belong to the following four associations:

1. National Association of Hospital Admitting Managers, 1101 Connecticut Avenue, N.W., Suite 700, Washington, DC 20036
2. Local admitting manager associations. Many states have two or more local associations.
3. Hospital Financial Managers Association, 666 North Lakeshore Drive, Suite 245, Chicago, IL 60611
4. American Guild of Patient Account Managers, Linn Street North, Boone, IA 50036

The most vital association is the National Association of Hospital Admitting Managers (NAHAM). This professional association is dedicated to the continuing education and professionalism of the admitting manager. NAHAM is currently in its tenth year and has grown from a group of ten admitting managers to an association of over 1,600 members with headquarters in Washington, D.C. NAHAM publishes *The Journal for Hospital Admitting Management* on a quarterly basis. It also holds educational conferences each spring in different sections of the country.

THE NURSE AS ADMITTING MANAGER*

Some facilities have found it advantageous to have a registered nurse in the capacity of admitting manager. The role of the nurse in admitting has as many

*This section was contributed by Dorothy Gale, A.A.M., Admitting Manager, Presbyterian Inter-Community Hospital, Whittier, California.

variations as there are hospitals with admitting nurses. The role of the nurse as manager also varies from institution to institution, but this is true of any admitting manager. However, there are certain advantages that a nurse manager can bring to the department, and primary among them is the establishment of a patient-oriented approach to the admitting process.

The nurse's professional knowledge adds greatly to the role of manager. The knowledge of disease and of disease processes, the needs of patients with particular diseases, and the compatibility of roommates as patients with certain diseases are all vital to accurate placement. Medical terminology is also familiar and readily understood.

The ability to evaluate the patient's condition, to know the difference between an emergent, urgent, or routine admission, or to know when to take the patient directly to a bed or to an emergency holding area are all important aspects of patient-oriented admissions. It could be very detrimental to the patient if none of the admitting personnel has these skills.

The nurse takes orders from the physician for the entire gamut of the patient's admission and treatment. With priorities set and tests completed before the patient goes to the room, results are on the chart by the time the physician makes rounds in the evening after admission. This enables treatment to be started in a more timely manner.

Patients feel at once comforted and reassured by the presence of a registered nurse. Having developed a trust over the years in nurses as well as physicians, patients feel that, should anything happen, the nurse could take care of them and get them the help they require.

The professional interaction of nurse to nurse, or nurse to physician, is an asset. By having the professional-to-professional conference, the credibility of the department is enhanced. Head nurses or unit supervisors are more apt to discuss the merits of admitting patients to their particular nursing stations with a nurse manager. Difficult placements are resolved on a more valid basis when the discussion is between nurses.

Physicians have long been accustomed to discussing freely with the nurse the problem and prognosis of their patients. Since they may believe it is a breach of ethics to discuss some of these topics with anyone else, some placement problems can be averted by physician-to-nurse and then nurse-to-nurse discussions.

The nurse manager can more easily direct the physician toward the acceptance of restricted admitting diagnoses, of changing admission times, and of changing from inpatient to outpatient or same-day surgery than the manager who has not had the professional relationship with the physician that years of nursing tradition has built.

The nurse manager also has a direct liaison with the nursing office. Whether the nurse reports to nursing services or to the finance department, the nurse has an equality of position with other nursing managers.

The nurse manager has the background for establishing such programs as preadmission testing with all the ramifications of such a program, that is, selling the program to the physician's office staff as well as the physician and acting as liaison between the physician, the patient, and the various departments within the hospital that provide the services the patient requires.

Nurses come into the position of admitting manager after many years of similar experience and tasks, usually spent as a manager of their own nursing stations. The problems on the floors are basically the same as those of managers anywhere else. Administrative functions of the job must be attended to in a timely manner. Along with all the planning, forecasting, establishing of goals and objectives, scheduling, budgeting, and the developing of policies and procedures, time is required to develop and maintain the personal relationships with all the employees in the department. Even much of the financial information has been a part of the daily routine on the floors, since diagnosis and length of stay are a part of this planning, too.

The disadvantages of the nurse as admitting manager must be noted. The nurse can be so involved with the patient–physician–nurse relationships that the nurse does not keep up with some of the other aspects of the job. There are only so many hours in which to accomplish the task of administration of the department. It stands to reason that all the time spent on nursing will take away some of the time others spend managing their departments. Priorities must be set and maintained. Many of the committees that admitting managers sit on are interesting and time consuming but are not productive for the admitting department. It takes a strong commitment to the department to say to the manager's boss that some committees do not actually use the manager's expertise and that the time spent at the meeting could be better spent in the admitting department. It is important to be selective in committee participation and to be active on the committees in which admitting can be influential or on those that try to influence admitting.

As with any manager, the nurse manager must delegate those tasks that can be effectively accomplished by others. The nurse must keep abreast of all the developments that seem to occur daily and that affect the financial security of the institution. The nurse manager must manage the admitting department but must remember why there is an admitting department in the first place—for the welfare of the patient.

ACCREDITATION AND CONTINUING EDUCATION

The National Association of Hospital Admitting Managers (NAHAM) has developed an accreditation examination that is given in different sections of the country. Successful passing of this examination, which is given each fall and also during the annual conference, earns the admitting manager the recognition of being an accredited admitting manager. The criteria to sit for this examination are available through the accreditation chairperson of the association. These criteria include education, experience, work background, supervisory background, and several other areas of professional development. All these criteria have been assigned point values. One hundred points is required for approval to write the examination for those admitting managers who have entered the field on or after January 2, 1977. For those who entered the admitting profession prior to this date, 50 total points are required. It would take an admitting manager just entering the field two to three years to acquire the necessary points to take the examination depending on the amount of formal education the manager has acquired. Information regarding the accreditation process may be obtained from NAHAM's national office.

After obtaining the status of accredited admitting manager, NAHAM has an accreditation maintenance program. This program is required to maintain the manager's accreditation status. Those managers becoming accredited after January 1, 1982, enter a three-year cycle beginning on the first day of January following their accreditation. During each three-year cycle, a specific number of educational points are required to maintain the accreditation. Since the point requirements change periodically, those interested should obtain current information from the national office.

Owing to the changes in government and accrediting agency regulations, medical and computer technology, health care industry needs, consumer education and public attitudes, the job responsibility of the admitting manager has expanded. There is a need for an assurance that the health care professional is indeed competent in the field of hospital admissions. A primary means of keeping managers up to date on changes and innovations in their field of endeavor has been continuing education. It is therefore necessary that a maintenance program be followed and minimum requirements be set.

Continuing education can be accomplished through a mixture of the following six components:

1. formal education in a college or university setting leading to a degree
2. college courses taken as a separate entity
3. seminars offered by National Association of Hospital Admitting Managers (NAHAM), American Guild of Patient Account Managers (AGPAM), Hospital Financial Managers Association (HFMA), or other organizations throughout the country
4. video-cassette programs offered through the American Hospital Association and other health care educational facilities
5. correspondence courses offered by several universities and colleges
6. management seminars offered by each manager's hospital

It is necessary to always search out and obtain information regarding courses or seminars that are offered that will both be beneficial and aid in obtaining career goals. The more knowledge and education that are obtained, the greater is the chance for advancement of the manager into higher levels of responsibility in the health care industry. Admitting managers with the proper education and background can move up the ladder within their hospital or other hospitals and health care facilities. Some of those advancements could include assistant administrator, director of patient services, or the administrative responsibility for a multitude of departments, including admitting, mailroom, transportation, and communications.

CONCLUSION

Admitting managers are individuals with a vast amount of knowledge of hospitals. Today, the admitting manager's position is competitive and not an easy position to fill. The educational requirement is more important than ever before. The knowledge of hospitals and how they operate is also an important requirement.

Admitting managers have an important role in the operation of a hospital and have many responsibilities assigned by the administrative staff. Administration realizes that the admitting department can "make or break" the hospital.

For admitting managers to stay on top of the rapid new developments in their field, they must belong to professional organizations. They should also strive to obtain the professional designation of accredited admitting manager.

The admitting manager's position is a very rewarding career to enter in hospitals if one does not want hands-on care but still wants to work in the health care field. The challenge is there for those who seek it.

Appendix 5–A

Job Description for Hospital Admitting Manager

JOB TITLE: Admitting Manager

REPORTS TO: Administration

JOB SUMMARY:

- has overall responsibility of all registration functions, including inpatient, outpatient, and possibly the emergency department
- coordinates with physicians, nursing divisions, clinical and support services, and patients in executing a total public relations effort
- responsible for developing and maintaining the emotional tension associated with the admission process as well as ensuring the efficient acquisition and dissemination of patient information
- responsible for ensuring that the employees are empathetic to the needs of the patient and family yet efficient in meeting the administrative needs for the hospital

DUTIES:

- prepares, justifies, and monitors the department budget
- develops departmental goals that help to achieve the primary goals of the hospital
- designs and implements a productivity program that will help to both predict and monitor the workload in the department
- develops the staffing needs and arranges the scheduling to meet those needs
- communicates regularly with the medical staff office to determine which physicians have admitting privileges

- develops contingency staffing plans for employee illnesses or disaster situations
- reviews all work performed in the department for accuracy and timeliness
- schedules department meetings to discuss any changes or new procedures within the department or the hospital
- interviews, hires, disciplines, and terminates employees as necessary
- schedules and provides the training for new employees or in-house transfers to the department
- plans working environment, designs new forms, and develops new policies and procedures
- performs evaluations on all admitting department staff
- counsels employees according to above evaluation results
- maintains good communications with other departments to ensure all policies and procedures are working well
- works on any special projects assigned

QUALIFICATIONS:

Education and Certificates:

- Graduation from a four-year college or university is preferred but not required. Coursework should include psychology, sociology, business administration, and personnel.
- An accredited admitting manager is preferred.

Experience and Training:

- at least two years of experience in an accredited hospital or social agency
- one year of admitting supervisory experience

Other Skills and Aptitudes:

- ability to communicate effectively with patients, doctors, and hospital staff members, while exercising a high degree of tact and poise and occasionally overcoming a language barrier
- understanding and ability to apply medical terminology
- clerical ability to recognize pertinent detail in reports and to identify errors in omissions or calculations when reviewing admittance records
- preference for business contacts to deal with patients, their families, medical personnel, and hospital employees

- temperament for directing all activities relating to admitting patients, and dealing with them, as well as physicians, hospital staff members, and others involved with the admitting department
- independent thinking to exercise own judgment in determining actions in emergency situations and in maintaining control of room occupancy
- analytical skills to evaluate other information from established criteria, such as interpreting policies and issuing information on room rates and hospital regulations

ADVANCEMENT:

- can assume responsibilities for other departments and promotion to next level of hospital management

Chapter 6

Computers in Admitting

Michael H. Littmann

More and more admitting departments have reached the stage at which they have outgrown their long-existing manual systems. It is at this point that the admitting manager must begin to look at computerized admitting systems. It is inevitable that with the constant growth and expansion of the functions performed by the admitting department the use of computers is only a natural development and an essential fact of hospital life. This chapter serves as a guide to computerization of the admitting department.

As the admitting manager considers computerization, an important understanding must be present. Computers are primarily methods of communication. They are communication for the department and the various areas within the hospital that use the data on file. It is essential that the entry or accessing of information be done in a simple and logical manner.

SELECTING A SYSTEM

Basically, there are two methods of computerization. The first method is the purchase of an existing set of programs. Another method is the creation of a system to match the specific needs of the admitting department and the hospital. The decisions regarding the best type of system for a given institution are usually made by higher levels of administration. This does not mean that the admitting manager has no say in the matter. Recommendations and input from the admitting manager often become important considerations before any choice is made. The admitting manager should be in the position of knowing the advantages and disadvantages of each type of system.

Purchasing an Existing Package

There are many advantages to the purchase of an existing package of programs. One advantage comes from the research already done by the computer company marketing an admissions package system. This company has already researched the needs of the admitting function and has programmed the various elements required to perform these functions. Some of these elements might be question-naires containing demographics, fiscal data, physician service data, and so on. Since this research has already been performed, the company has worked out the terminology and logic needed to perform the admitting tasks.

Nevertheless, there are problems for the potential buyer of this type of system. Several significant problems to take into consideration are the following:

- being locked into an inflexible (difficult to change) system
- being forced to use terminology that, although the same as or similar to what may presently be in use, may have a different meaning
- having a system that requires extensive periods of time to accomplish change or improvement
- having a system that was not designed for the special needs of a specific department

Creating a System

The development of a comprehensive admitting system requires knowledgeable people, talented programmers experienced in the hospital field, and a significant investment of time and energy on the part of the admitting manager. It must be done one step at a time and one program at a time. The integration process must be slow and extremely careful. This method may require years to complete and to implement fully.

However, the benefits of developing a system are very real. They include several advantages:

- a system that exactly fits the department's needs
- a system easily upgraded and that lends itself to modification relatively inexpensively
- the ready availability of on-site programmers

When developing a computerized system, it is also important to identify the areas that the prospective system is to address. Clearly the most vital programs that must first be developed are admissions, discharges, and transfers. Each of these are important enough to be examined on an individual basis. These are areas that should be addressed in any package of existing programs as well.

PROGRAMS FOR ADMITTING DEPARTMENTS

The Admissions Program

The admissions program is essentially the merging of specific event data (e.g., admitting physician, service, diagnosis) with the registration data. In any admitting system, it should also be mentioned that concurrent access to the medical records data base is infinitely better than attempting to establish a data base from scratch. It is hoped that the existing medical records data base will have been entered so that the admitting department has access to this information. If it is decided, however, that it is too costly to contract out to enter their old files, new registration will have to be the method of establishing the patient data base.

Four elements should be part of the admissions program:

1. demographic information: this includes such items as name, sex, date of birth, address, zip code (from a built-in dictionary), parents/spouse information, marital status, and religion
2. next-of-kin information: name (two persons if possible), address, telephone, relationship to patient
3. reimbursement data: occupation, employer, insurance data, Medicare/Medicaid information
4. clinical data: doctor, service, date and time of admission, room number, location, admitting diagnosis, surgical data

Once fields for these basic data have been established, there may be other information one may wish to collect. Examples of additional facts are as follows:

- special relationship of patient to hospital (e.g., employees, trustees, staff physicians, major donors, celebrities)
- patient tracking questions such as source of admission (e.g., health maintenance organization, private doctors, transfers from other facilities)
- patients' habits such as smoking or nonsmoking
- medical and surgical team assignments
- primary nurse relationships
- referring physicians
- special program relationships, such as oncology patients or home hemodialysis patients

The more detailed data that are collected, the more information can be retrieved at a later date.

The Discharge Program

The admissions program is designed to transfer a patient into inpatient status. Conversely, the discharge program is simply a way of maintaining the current state of the inpatient file by transferring the inpatient to a non-inpatient status, or to discharge status.

This type of program may be broadened by being able to record various types of discharges. Examples of these types of discharges are as follows:

- discharged home
- discharged to an extended care facility
- discharged to another acute care hospital
- discharged against medical advice
- discharged due to death

This phase can be further expanded by selecting specific categories within each discharge type. For example, after the discharge type has been identified as discharged to an extended care facility or hospital, the next item to be answered might be the name of the facility as listed in the dictionary of codes for the department. Similarly, for a patient who died, information might also be entered as to the time of death and whether an autopsy will be performed. This potential for data collection and/or reporting capabilities is limited only to the admitting manager's imagination.

The Transfer Program

Whereas the purpose of the admissions and discharge programs is to enter and remove patients from the inpatient file, the transfer program is designed to maintain the inpatient file while allowing freedom of movement during the hospitalization. Simply stated, this program would allow changing the room and/ or nursing station. The computer programmers, in designing this program, have already entered (or loaded) the room numbers and nursing stations that relate to those room numbers. Changing rooms will be recognized by the computer as being either a room-to-room, bed-to-bed, or nursing station-to-nursing station move.

It is also possible to expand the transfer program to allow for additional changes. Examples of these changes are service or doctor changes and surgical or medical team changes. It is even possible to send an order to the computer to generate new forms and/or plastic charge plates should the system be able to perform such tasks.

It is the admission-discharge-transfer (ADT) system that all other programs depend on for their success. Therefore, having complete and flexible ADT programs will make expansion into other areas easier.

Data Lists and Changes

It has been mentioned earlier about established lists of data or dictionaries as sources of answers for data questions in the various computer programs during data entry. The admitting manager may want to establish a variety of reports at a later date about the patients admitted from outside the department. One of the best ways to establish these profiles on patient admissions is to categorize the patients into specific groups. If the programs call for the data entry in the form of free fields (write-in or typed-in alphabetical words), it may be extremely difficult to access these fields owing to the different ways in which admitting clerks may answer such questions during data entry.

In order to avoid problems connected with accessing patient information that is written in on free fields, predetermined answer lists are developed from which the admitting clerk can select an appropriate answer. Two lists that may be used in this manner are those of marital status and religious preference. These lists may look like the following:

Marital status:	Religion:
1. Married	1. Catholic
2. Divorced	2. Episcopalian
3. Single	3. Hebrew
4. Widowed	4. Baptist
5. Separated	5. Jehovah's Witness

Change or correction of existing information on a file should be a relatively simple task. Virtually all systems allow for such editing of data both in the entry mode (when re-registering a patient already in the system, changes can be made on what appears on the screen) and by directly entering a patient's file and selecting specific data to change in an edit program specifically designed for such changes. Some systems will keep records of which changes were made, what the changes were, and, if the system has a security key entry restriction, who made the changes.

OTHER ADMITTING PROGRAMS

The Cancel Program

In conjunction with the admission–discharge–transfer programs, it is important for the systems to recognize the problems of the admitting department. There will be times when admissions and discharges will be cancelled after the transactions have been entered. Therefore, programs that cancel such entries and restore the patient to a previous status and location are vital. One does not want a system that is so inflexible as to require a readmission of a mistakenly discharged patient in order to restore one to inpatient status or to discharge a patient to remove someone who should not have been admitted. These solutions are not only cumbersome and time consuming, but they generate inaccurate statistics and may even result in unnecessary patient charges.

The ADT Report Program

Once the ADT system is in place, the next logical programs to develop are the ADT reports (assuming these reports will be printed and distributed somewhere within the facility). These reports can be as simple or as complex as each facility demands.

The Admission Report

An admission report usually consists of the patient's name, identifying records numbers (medical record/billing number), and room number. It can also include such data as patient's sex, age, admitting service, physician, and ultimate location if different from the admission location, such as a transfer to intensive care. Other information could include the admission type taken from a possible list of seven categories:

1. elective
2. waiting list
3. direct emergency
4. emergency department emergency
5. ambulatory surgery admission
6. other ambulatory area emergency
7. same-day admission

Finally, other information such as the time of admission, the patient–physician relationship, such as private or clinic, and the financial code indicating the reimbursement status of the patient (e.g., Blue Cross, Medicare, self-pay) can also be included in these reports. Typical printout headings for an admissions list that is computer generated can be found in Exhibit 6–1.

The Discharge List

The discharge list usually consists of a simple alphabetical listing of all patients discharged for a given day. This report includes all or most of the data on the admissions list. It could also list the date of admission, and, if indicated, note death and time of death. Representative headings for a computer-generated discharge list can be seen in Exhibit 6–2.

Exhibit 6-1 Computerized Admission Listing

BETH ISRAEL HOSPITAL ADMISSIONS SYSTEM
ADMISSION LIST FOR: OCT. 19, 1984 RUN: SAT. OCT. 20, 1984 2:03 A.M. PAGE: 1

UNIT #	NAME	FISCAL #	ROOM	SERV	HOUR	A-T	PPR	FC	
439765	ABEL, CHARLES	1155926 3	865	MED	2316	1	1	H	LATER TRANS. TO: 805
398423	BABCOCK, VERONICA	1155837 9	CCU	MED	1447	4	1	M	
549241	CALLIHAN, DOROTHY	1155792 1	561	ORTHO	0117	7	2	S	LATER TRANS. TO: DIS
717332	DAWSON, CARL	1155956 5	685	PSYCH	1827	3	1	M	
832916	EDWARDS, BARBARA	1155796 7	425	GYN	1216	1	2	B	

Key: A-T, admission type; PPR, patient–physician relationship; FC, financial code.

Source: Courtesy of Beth Israel Hospital, Boston, Massachusetts.

Exhibit 6–2 Computerized Discharge List

BETH ISRAEL HOSPITAL ADMISSIONS SYSTEM
DISCHARGE LIST FOR: OCT. 19, 1984 RUN: SAT. OCT. 20, 1984 2:06 A.M. PAGE: 1

UNIT #	NAME	FISCAL #	ROOM	SERV	A-T	PPR	FC	ADMITTED	EXP	TIME
832878	ALLEN, JEFFREY	1155490 4	1265	PSURG	1	1	I	10/14		
661572	BARKER, WILMA	1155714 7	686	CSURG	1	1	M	09/06	Y	0945
832931	COHEN, STEPHEN	1152953 4	776	GU	4	2	W	10/17		
716048	DONAHUE, FRANK	1155386 4	519	SURG	4	1	B	10/06		
591779	EDMONDSON, PAULA	1155450 8	817	MED	4	1	H	09/30		

Key: A-T, admission type; PPR, patient–physician relationship; FC, financial code.

Source: Courtesy of Beth Israel Hospital, Boston, Massachusetts.

The Transfer List

The last computer-generated report in the ADT report program should be the transfer listing. This listing is an alphabetical report of all patient transfers for a 24-hour period. This should include room changes and doctor service changes. An example of the format used for this report can be found in Exhibit 6–3.

It should also be mentioned that any of these lists could include the admitting diagnosis. However, it is important to be acutely sensitive of the possibilities of violating the patients' rights of privacy.

The Admission Form

A direct result of the admissions program is the admission form. The facility might choose to design its own or to adapt to an independently designed one. Whichever is chosen, the system should generate a form immediately following the completion of the admission entry. One should also be able to generate a form independent of the admission process should that ever be necessary.

In addition, if the facility should have a computerized plate-embossing unit, the creation of that plate should be triggered by the completion of the form. Again, the plate should be able to be called individually or, if desirable, batched and run for defined groups of admissions, such as elective patients, future obstetrical admissions, and day-care patients.

COMPUTERS AND CONFIDENTIALITY

Computers are primarily communication tools, and as such, the issue of protecting the confidentiality of patients should be addressed. There are several mechanisms available to the admissions manager for effecting such safeguards.

The computer system can, by use of restricted keys, allow limited access to file data. For example, an entry-level employee can only access demographic information. Medical records personnel may be additionally allowed access to diagnostic and procedural data. Physicians would be allowed into the clinical information on file, such as laboratory and radiologic data. Such a system does require departmental and supervisory control over these keys and what the employees are allowed to accomplish.

Some prefer to use departmental restrictions on computer data and retrieval. In this particular case, the admitting department (or other specific areas), along with the individuals employed there, is permitted to see and do only specifically defined procedures in connection with the computer system. Finally, one may also opt for absolutely no controls in place. Regardless of the method employed, there should be a clearly established hospital policy concerning this vital issue from the very beginning that the system is in place within the respective departments.

Exhibit 6–3 Computerized Transfer Listing

BETH ISRAEL HOSPITAL ADMISSIONS SYSTEM
TRANSFER REPORT FOR: 10/19/84 RUN: SAT. OCT. 20, 1984 2:04 A.M.

UNIT #	NAME	FISCAL #	ROOM FROM	ROOM TO	DOCTOR FROM	DOCTOR TO	P-T SERVICE FROM	P-T SERVICE TO
676775	ADAMS, THERESA	1155842 6			COX, MARK	DEAN, MARTIN	MED	CSURG
750059	BOYLE, CATHERINE	1155608 1	CCU	1178				
816355	COOK, KENNETH	1155925 9	866	876				
832878	DAY, SAMUEL	1155776 6	674	MIC			SURG	MED
793624	ELDRIDGE, MARY	1155723 8	MIC	576				

Source: Courtesy of Beth Israel Hospital, Boston, Massachusetts.

OPTIONAL ADMITTING PROGRAMS

In addition to the basic ADT functions, there are many other programs available to the admitting office. They include the following:

- patient scheduling
- pre-registration
- inquiry/information options
- reporting programs

Patient Scheduling Program

The patient scheduling and booking system allows the admitting department to establish patients in future dated admission files. In simple terms, it is a mini-registration process allowing admitting officers to enter as little (or as much) demographic data as they wish. The admitting physician, service, date of admission, date of and name of procedure to be done during the admission, and so on, can also be entered. From this system, many other programs are possible. Examples of three potential programs are (1) daily lists of scheduled admissions, (2) communication with other departments regarding future admissions (e.g., quality assurance), and (3) patient notification programs (e.g., letters).

Pre-registration Program

Most admitting departments pre-register patients scheduled for future admission. This program allows complete entry of all the data contained in the admissions program except for the elements that finalize the admission, such as the fiscal charge number, the room number, and the admission time. Therefore, patients who have been pre-registered only need minimal interviewing at the time of admission. This is especially useful for hospitals with active obstetrical departments.

Inquiry/Information Options Program

In keeping with the premise that computers are communications tools, it is essential that speedy access to data be available throughout the hospital. Programs that allow the viewer to determine quickly bed availability, census information, transaction history, patient demographics, clinical data, and fiscal information are extremely valuable. Such programs are always in great demand and are heavily used.

Report Option Programs

The importance of generating reports and statistical information from the admitting system cannot be overstressed. Virtually all statistics used in developing plans for future hospital needs emanate from the inpatient admitting programs. Facts such as the following can be gleaned from the admitting department:

- admission volume by service
- admission lists by physician with patient-days and average length of stay
- referral data (patient source)
- geographical source of patients
- patient-days
- average daily census by service
- census information
- nursing station activity
- patient profiles (e.g., marital status, employment information, payer class, religious affiliation)
- physician/service activity
- emergency department activity
- admissions by type (e.g., elective, emergency)
- admission/discharge trends
- lengths of stay

This list could go on indefinitely. However, the importance of gathering, sorting, and printing the information entered by the admitting department cannot be overstated. The variety of reports is literally limitless. If the system can be expanded easily, it is necessary to pay attention to the needs of the administration. The reports can be designed to be as informative and as useful as possible. Computer sort time may be at a premium—it should be used to the greatest possible advantage.

SYSTEM IMPLEMENTATION

Equipment Needs

At this point, the selection process has been completed and it is time to implement the new system. The needs of the department must be evaluated. There must be enough terminals so that the problems of sharing equipment or overburdening the areas with terminals in order to compensate for too few work stations with CRTs will not occur. One terminal per work station is the standard.

If forms and/or reports are going to be printed, it is important to have enough printers. Good, moderately high performance printers are relatively inexpensive. Too few printers will result in a severe handicap.

Training Needs

The actual conversion onto computers will take significant investments of time and energy. Training of personnel starts at the top with the admitting manager and the supervisors. In all likelihood, many of the employees, especially long-term older individuals, will be suspicious and/or frightened by the prospects of the computer. They do not understand computers and cannot accept what is wrong with their "tried and true" ways. They may resist change and be less than cooperative. It is up to the admitting manager and departmental supervisors to train and convince them of the benefits to them as well as to the hospital.

In order to accomplish this, the admitting manager and the supervisors should learn and know the system before installation begins. They should always be at least one step ahead of the conversion stage. Employees should be able to go to their supervisors for answers and support instead of having to rely on the inservice education provided by the installing computer personnel. The employees trust and rely on their supervisors. They know the supervisor and if the supervisor cannot help them or get them prompt reliable answers, the employees will lose faith in the system even before it has a chance to perform in the department.

The admitting manager should be prepared to spend large amounts of time with all the employees in the department. This will mean spending evenings, nights, and weekends with these various employees. The time investment will pay rich dividends, and losses in this area will hamper successful implementation.

The Process

Usually implementation begins with loading or entering into the computer all the necessary files to accept patients, such as nursing stations and room numbers. This means that each nursing station will have all of its room numbers entered, each room categorized as to the number of beds, and the appropriate room rates assigned. Once these files have been established, admitting can then begin to enter admissions.

For a predetermined time, dual systems will be used. This means that the old, existing manual method and the new computerized system will be used together. All admissions will be compared until all those involved are satisfied that the computer-generated admissions are at least as effective and as accurate as the present system, and that the inevitable problems with entry questions and techniques have been solved. It is not recommended that conversion to a new computerized admitting form should take place during these initial stages. Programs should be phased in gradually. Too many programs, implemented simultaneously, will prove costly in terms of frayed nerves, seemingly endless insurmountable problems, and inefficient use of the system.

At the end of this predetermined time frame it will be necessary to make certain that all the inpatients who were admitted prior to the onset of the conversion have been entered. From this point, each new program should be gradually introduced to the department with careful checking and rechecking for possible flaws. It is not absolutely necessary to be locked into a time schedule for final completion. It is infinitely better to pace the process to the ability of the employees to learn and get used to this new process.

Feedback from employees is essential in gaining a smooth-running system. If, after repeated admission and entry work, they state that they are having difficulties, their concerns should be addressed immediately. If there are problems with the system, they will not vanish by themselves. The problem may be in the way the employees are using the equipment or in the programs themselves. The admitting staff may be able to suggest better or alternative ways of doing things. The admitting manager should talk with the programmers and computer personnel and insist that they be available at all times.

In implementing the system it is vital to remember that computers are electronic aids and that like any electrically operated system there will be inevitable times when the system will be inoperable. Most systems require planned periods of nonoperation or ''dump'' times. During such ''down'' periods, back-up systems will have to be used that must later be integrated once the computers return to on-line status. Therefore, these back-up systems are absolutely necessary to the continual smooth operation of the department.

CONCLUSION

It is suggested that a great deal of time and care be taken in building and implementing a computer system for an admitting department. Once a system is in place and operational the admitting manager will not be able to make whole-scale changes without significant and costly efforts. Good planning and careful study can make the computerized admitting department efficient and the admitting manager's life much simpler.

Chapter 7

Reservations and Preadmissions

Lucile LePert and Patricia A. Long

Reservations and preadmissions are among the most vital functions of all hospital admitting departments. All the information obtained from the patient during the preadmitting interview is used for the final collection of money. Ninety-five percent of all hospital charges are paid for by the collection of money from third party payers, such as government programs. Since this area is such a vital function, continuous education and training are required for all individuals working with securing patient information. This education is necessary owing to new and changing laws, reimbursement programs, and management concepts. Some of the laws and reimbursement programs affecting changes in hospital procedures and preadmitting include the following:

- uniform billing 82 (UB-82)
- diagnostic related groups (DRGs)
- professional standards review organizations (PSROs)
- revision of Medicare precertification
- county programs
- preferred provider organizations (PPOs)

In addition, a variety of alternative health care delivery techniques affect the reservations department. Some of these are the following:

- child birth centers
- mobile testing units
- walk-in storefront clinics
- business services for patients

- same-day surgery programs
- postoperative outpatient surgery

The latter is having minor surgery performed in the hospital outpatient facility prior to being admitted to the hospital with a fixed fee per surgery. All of these programs, with the exception of a walk-in storefront clinic, require prior notification of a patient's reservation.

RESERVATIONS

Definition and Source

The definition of a reservation is the engagement, in advance, of an accommodation or service. It also can mean a promise, guarantee, or record of such an engagement. Reservations are generated from a variety of sources, with a principal one being staff physicians. Other sources common in large specialty hospitals are resident physicians, physician offices, and emergency departments.

Identification and Verification

An important aspect of accepting a reservation from a physician centers around the medical status of the physician in question. Most reservations will come from either active or associate staff physicians. Other categories of physicians who may deal with admitting departments are courtesy and visiting staff and honorary staff. *Courtesy staff* is defined as physicians who have received administrative approval to either admit and treat a particular patient or to assist team physicians on a particular procedure such as a heart transplant. *Visiting staff* physicians cannot admit a patient or chart on any patient. They may visit patients in the hospital. *Honorary staff* are usually physicians who have retired from serving on the active staff for their hospital.

Also, at the time the reservation is made, verification is made against the medical roster provided by medical records to determine that the physician's admitting privileges are current. A suspension of privileges usually occurs when the physician is delinquent in completing medical records. If a physician's admitting privileges are suspended because of delinquent charts, a notification is issued by the medical records department to the physician. Reservations personnel in admitting who are taking that physician's reservation remind the physician of this notification and inform the physician that the reservation cannot be taken. A physician's privileges remain suspended until the admitting department receives notification of change in status from the medical records department.

Room Assignment

The reservations procedure, along with the preadmission interview, enables the admitting department to prepare in advance, as much as possible, a patient's arrival into the hospital. It also assists in providing the patient with the appropriate room accommodations as well as making entry of the patient into the system run smoothly, comfortably, and efficiently by obtaining all needed personal and financial information in advance.

Through the team efforts of administration, physicians, and nursing personnel, certain areas of the hospital are designated for specific types of illnesses. Within these designated areas there are generally several different types of accommodations such as private, semiprivate, and wards. The determination concerning disposition of patient room assignments is determined by physician's orders and/or patient preference.

By the time the patient arrives at the hospital for admission, the room has been assigned and made ready for the patient's use. Generally the patient is escorted to the room after a brief stop in the admitting department.

PATIENT ADMISSION CATEGORIES

The Need for Categories

The hospital's medical staff is responsible for developing the criteria that define the category of the patients to be admitted. The three most frequent categories of admission are (1) emergency, (2) urgent, and (3) elective. Categorizing patient admissions enables the reservations and bed control departments to monitor the proper distribution of beds. It also enables the department to make all the necessary arrangements for immediate bed placement of any emergency and urgent patient admissions. Reservations for any elective admissions can then be handled by another area of the admitting department that coordinates planned admissions with the preadmission area. By doing this, bed control personnel are freed up for urgent reservations. This function is accomplished by publishing different telephone numbers made available to physicians and their office staffs for their use when calling in the different types of patient admissions.

The Emergency Admission

An emergency admission involves a situation in which there is an immediate threat to the life or limb of a person. All measures are taken to ensure the immediate admission of this patient. This might include the displacement and/or discharge of another less ill patient. An emergency admission is considered a high priority admission.

The Urgent Admission

A reservation by a physician of an impending admission in which an undue or prolonged delay could be harmful to a patient's life is considered an urgent admission. Since this patient is usually admitted through the emergency department, a copy of the reservation is then forwarded to that department.

The Elective Admission

When the health of a patient is not in jeopardy, the admission is considered to be elective or prescheduled. It can be booked anywhere from one day to two months prior to the date of the admission. The reservations department should try to accommodate both the admitting physician and the patient as far as the date of admission and type of accommodations. This is an ideal candidate for the pre-admission program and preadmission testing program. If necessary, this type of patient's admission can be deferred on criteria established by the hospital and physician. Reservations taken on all types of admissions must be coordinated with the bed control department.

THE RESERVATIONS PROCESS

Recording the Reservation

A reservation can be made in one of several ways. It can be typed directly into a computer terminal if the system is equipped with an admission–discharge–transfer (ADT) program. The reservation can also be written by hand or typed. The same information can be obtained by using any one of these three systems. Generally, a reservation form can be used for adequate information recording. An example of an effective reservation form is seen in Exhibit 7–1.

Significant information to be collected by the reservations department should include the following items:

- room number or suggested hospital area
- admission date
- admitting physician (attending and/or associates)
- admitting physician code number
- type of service

Exhibit 7-1 Reservation Information Form

ST. JOSEPH'S
HOSPITAL AND MEDICAL CENTER

Post Office Box 2071
Phoenix, Arizona 85001-2071
285-3000 (Area 602)

DATE TAKEN _____ ROOM # _____ ADMISSION DATE _____

DOCTOR _____ DR. # _____

REFERRING DOCTOR _____ DR. # _____

TYPE _____
SERVICE _____

PATIENT _____ LAST _____ FIRST _____ MIDDLE _____ SEX _____ AGE _____ BUS. _____ PHN. — HOME _____

ADDRESS _____ STREET _____ CITY _____ STATE _____ ZIP _____

RELATIVE OR SPOUSE _____ ADDRESS _____

PATIENT # _____ ACCOMODATION _____ READY — YES _____ NO _____ SMOKE — YES _____ NO _____ TEACH — YES _____ NO _____

DIAGNOSIS _____ DIAG. CODE _____

PROCEDURE _____ DAYS CERT _____

MEDICARE — YES ☐ NO ☐ CERT # _____

SOURCE OF ADMISSION CODES

TYPE OF ADM.

ADULT AND PEDIATRICS

☐ X EMERGENCY ☐ RP PHYS. REF. ☐ TM HMO/AHCCCS REF. ☐ INFORMATION NOT AVAIL.

☐ U URGENT ☐ OU CLINIC REF. ☐ TR TRANS. FROM HEALTH FAC.

☐ R ELECTIVE ☐ TE TRANS. FROM SKILLED FAC. ☐ EO EMERGENCY ROOM

NEWBORNS

☐ N NEWBORN ☐ TA TRANS. FROM HOSP ☐ TL COURT/LAW ENFORCEMENT ☐ NE EXTRAMURAL BIRTH

AHCCCS — YES ☐ NO ☐ PLAN _____ CCS — YES ☐ NO ☐ ACC. _____ AUTO _____ OTHER _____

☐ PRE-ADMIT ☐ FILE ☐ PRE-MAIL ☐ DIRECT ☐ HOME ☐ OFFICE ☐ Y/PRE ☐ N/PRE

REMARKS _____ INITIALS _____

ADMIT-1 (REV. 2/85)

ADMITTING RESERVATION SLIP

Source: Courtesy of St. Joseph's Hospital and Medical Center, Phoenix, Arizona.

- patient's name
- patient's sex
- patient's age
- patient's home and business telephone numbers
- patient's hospital number
- type of accommodation desired
- readiness of bed
- smoker or nonsmoker
- is patient a teaching case?
- diagnosis
- diagnosis code
- number of days certified
- location of patient origin: home, doctor's office, emergency department
- type of admission (emergency, urgent, elective)
- financial classification
- initials of person taking reservation

The reservations clerk may also want to inform the admitting physician about the hospital's participation or nonparticipation in any special group health contracts. If the patient is a transfer from another hospital, bed control does not assign a bed until all insurance benefits are verified and the physician is notified of their approval.

Recording Systems

As mentioned earlier, the admitting reservations form is an excellent method of recording a reservation of a patient. This form is usually in triplicate with each copy a different color. The first copy will be sent to the patient receiving section for admission of the patient. Bed control can keep the second copy as a record of the reservation. The third copy can be sent to the emergency department if the patient enters by way of this route. The form can also be inserted into an imprinter recording the month, day, and time the reservation was taken.

Also useful for the reservations function is what is known as a day book. All reservations for a particular day are typed into this book, which lists basic information on every patient reservation, such as name, physician, and diagnosis. The only patients not listed in the book are maternity patients. The book serves as a handy reference by listing all admissions for every day of the year. It becomes a re-source for interns, residents, infection control nurses, and staff personnel. Each book is usually maintained for one month, with previous books being filed by the date of admission and retained for one year. Sheets within the book can be color coded in order to indicate adult patients, pediatric patients, and so on. The back of the book is used for listing the deaths that occurred that day. A day book also has a use in statistical reporting.

Benefits of a Defined System

Many benefits can be derived from having and using a well-defined hospital reservations system. One of these benefits is having prior knowledge of a patient's diagnosis to facilitate proper bed assignment. In the case of an infectious disease, it ensures the safety of all patients by proper assignment of beds. Patients can then be assigned accommodations within the proper service area (e.g., surgical patients to the surgical wing) where the nursing personnel are specially trained to care for these types of patients.

A good system allows for the consideration of patient preference in room assignments. This includes whether or not the patient prefers a private, semi-private, or ward bed. It also allows for smoking and nonsmoking patients to be placed together. Finally, a variety of other specific preferences such as a room with a view or a room in the new wing, for example, can be taken into consideration for the patient's comfort and satisfaction.

An additional advantage to reservations in advance is that the patient is assigned a specific time to enter the hospital. This regulates the flow of traffic, both patient and visitor, in the admitting department. It also helps ancillary services schedule their examinations and tests. For hospitals that have an admitting nurse, physician's orders can be received and dispersed to the units and ancillary services prior to the patient's admission. This enables the proper medications to be on the unit as well as radiographs, laboratory studies, electrocardiograms, and other tests to be scheduled while relieving staff nurses of this responsibility.

An effective reservations system allows patients to be told where to park their car, what door to enter, and how to get to the admitting department. Similar instructions are given to the patient if testing prior to admission is ordered by the physician. This procedure is enormously helpful in relieving patient anxiety.

Staffing patterns within the admitting department can be adjusted according to the number and type of admissions coming in for any given day. This allows for cost-effective measures to be implemented. More staff can be assigned during the peak admission times in order to process the patients through the system effectively and efficiently. At other times, less staff would be required. A final cost-effective outcome of a good working system is the advanced verification of all insurance benefits. These can be performed on all preadmitted patients, intrahospital transfer patients, and psychiatric patients.

PREADMISSION

Advantages of Preadmission

A well-planned preadmission program improves productivity and allows for an efficient use of resources by regulating the work flow and improving the quality of patient information. This type of program usually applies to elective admissions and, under certain circumstances, urgent admissions. Any size or type (manual or computerized) facility can implement this program. A major advantage of the preadmission system is that it enables cash flow projections to be made in advance.

The Prescheduling Process

A reservation can be booked anywhere from one day to two months in advance. The preadmission information obtained should be the same as that for a same-day admission from a physician. A prescheduling section of admitting can be designed to receive all reservations on these pre-patients. Members of physician office staffs can call this section directly and give information similar to that for reservations discussed earlier. An admitting reservation slip can also be used for this purpose. In this particular case, the first copy of the form can be given to the preadmitting section for follow-up, with the second copy being kept in the prescheduling section filed under admission date. The final copy can be given to the admitting orders nurse.

The Prescheduling Board

A good device to use with the concept of prescheduling is the prescheduling board. All reservations can be written on this board, which is divided into the various services. Allotments are created for each service and each day, with Sunday and Monday receiving the most admission bookings. This board listing is balanced each evening against the actual reservation slips and with the admitting orders nurse as a quality control mechanism. The same system can be used with a computer terminal using the same methods of information gathering and quality control. Conference calls can also be set up between the physician and the surgery department if a surgical date needs to be assigned along with the actual admission date.

Cancellations and subsequent rescheduling of patient admissions can be accomplished by using another specialized form (Exhibit 7–2). Copies of this form can then go to preadmission, prescheduling, and the admitting orders nurse, with a corresponding change on the prescheduling board.

A prescheduling board does have advantages over a reservations book in that all admissions can be examined at a glance for a complete two–month period. Physicians' offices can also check on the entrance dates of their patients.

Exhibit 7–2 Reservation Change Form

```
┌─────────────────────────────────────────────────────────────────┐
│                                    DATE_____            │
│                                                                    │
│  DR._____    ROOM_____           │
│                                                                    │
│  PATIENT_____    SEX_____  AGE_____        │
│                                                                    │
│  DIAGNOSIS_____        │
│                                                                    │
│  _____  ___     │
│                                                                    │
│  SCHED.                                                            │
│  DATE   _____   REMARKS_____         │
│                                                                    │
│  TRANSFERRED TO NEW DATE_____FROM PRESENT DATE_____   │
│                                                                    │
│  ☐ CANCELLATION    ☐ TRANSFER SLIP    ☐ RESERVATIONS SLIP          │
│                                                                    │
│  ADMIT - 15                                                        │
│    Source: Courtesy of St. Joseph's Hospital and Medical Center, Phoenix, Arizona. │
└─────────────────────────────────────────────────────────────────┘
```

PREADMISSION INFORMATION

After reservations are received, each admission can be categorized into one of two categories. These two groups are "to mail" and "to call." Both these groups refer to the method used to obtain information from the patient prior to the actual admission date. If a reservation is received within two to three weeks from the date of the admission, a preadmission packet can then be mailed to the patient. A good preadmission packet should contain the following items:

- one copy of the hospital admission form (Exhibit 7–3)
- an information brochure on the hospital
- a patient instructions brochure indicating what items to bring on the date of admission
- a financial policy information sheet
- a sheet with directions for parking and finding the hospital entrance

After receiving the hospital admission form from the patient, the admission packet can be completed and insurance information verified.

If an admission is ten days or less away from the date of the reservation, there is not enough time to use a mailing system. In this particular case, a designated admitting representative will telephone the patient and obtain the needed informa-

Exhibit 7-3 Hospital Admission Form

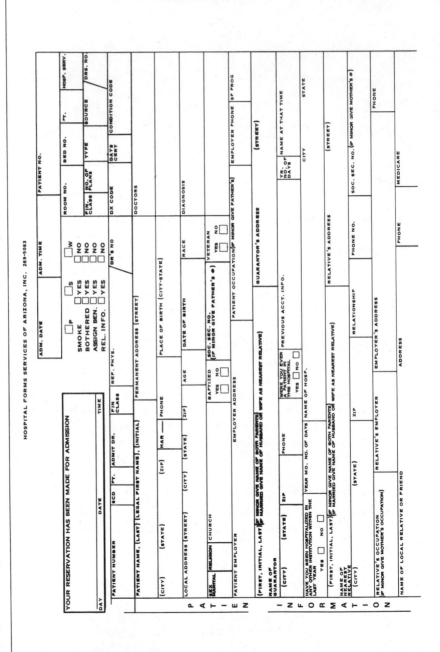

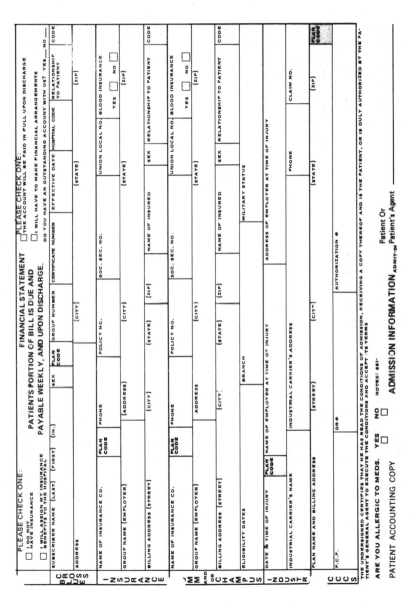

Source: Courtesy of St. Joseph's Hospital and Medical Center, Phoenix, Arizona.

tion. Instructions can then be given to the patient at this time. The admission packet is completed in this manner, and the information concerning insurance is verified.

Obtaining accurate information in a minimal period of time requires the interviewer to both ask questions and to listen to the responses. An interview with the patient has the advantage of making the process more personal and allows the patient to ask questions. It can be more time consuming for the admitting staff.

Information obtained from both the personal telephone call and the mailed-in hospital admissions form is filed by the date of the patient's admission. A copy of this information should also be forwarded to the insurance verification department. This information can then be retrieved to complete the admission packet prior to the patient's actual day of admission. For computerized systems, this information is stored in the appropriate program and can be retrieved by both preadmission personnel and insurance verifiers prior to the patient's actual admission for completion.

PREADMISSION TESTING

Preadmission testing is the performing of diagnostic tests and procedures on an outpatient basis before the patient's admission. The reception and processing of patients can be greatly enhanced by this type of program. When a patient is finally admitted, the patient can then be taken directly to the room. This saves the patient the time and trouble of going through testing at this time, which makes the admission much easier for the patient as well as for the hospital staff.

The Preadmission Testing Process

The admitting department is notified by the physician's office of the impending patient admission and the required tests. If the physician does not have standing orders or fails to give orders at the time of the booking, the physician is then called by the admitting orders nurse to obtain such orders.

Once all orders have been issued, the patient is then called by the preadmitting department and all pertinent information is obtained. Directions can be issued to the patient by the preadmitting personnel or admitting orders nurse regarding the time of such testing and where to go. The patient can also be counseled about any prior preparations, such as fasting before taking the test. Each patient is told approximately how long each test will take and whether or not the patient needs someone in attendance. Patients are then prepared for the day of their preadmission tests.

Routine questions about the program are usually answered by a brochure given to the patient in the physician's office. Physicians also receive a brochure describing the program (Exhibit 7–4). Insurance information can then be obtained at the

Exhibit 7–4 Physician Preadmission Brochure

Here is detailed information about this service, provided by   for the benefit of physicians and patients:

PURPOSE

To provide a means of assuring that physician's orders are at the nursing station in time for the patient's arrival, and particularly of assuring that medications ordered for the patient are immediately available. This service also provides a means of individualizing your patient's orders, thereby eliminating unnecessary routine testing.

PROCEDURE

1. At the time that arrangements are made for the patient's admission (or at any time thereafter before his or her scheduled arrival). the physician or physician's office calls the   admitting orders nurse and gives the physician's orders.

2. The admitting orders nurse records the physician's orders on a four-part form.

3. Early on the day of the scheduled admission, the admitting orders nurse forwards the Pharmacy (white) sheet of the four-part form to the Pharmacy so that any medications that have been ordered can be delivered to the nursing station before the patient's arrival.

   The physician's copy of the order form (blue) and the medication nurse's copy (pink) are sent to the nursing station as part of the admitting package on the patient's admission date. (The fourth copy of the four-part order form is retained by the admitting orders nurse.)

PHYSICIANS PLEASE NOTE:

In the interest of saving time and assuring efficiency, it is requested that the physician, or member of his or her office staff, have all necessary information immediately at hand when placing orders. On medications, for example, not only the name of the medication but also the strength and frequency. (Please lift up this page to see the sample of the form used by the admitting orders nurse in recording physician's orders.)

In accordance with JCAH rules, when physician's orders have been given by telephone, the patient's chart must be signed by the physician within 24 hours of the patient's admission time.

HOURS OF SERVICE

The regular hours of the Admitting Orders Nurse Office are 9:00 a.m. to 5:00 p.m., Monday through Friday. Physicians' orders may be called in for recording on a message device in the office when the admitting orders nurse is not on duty.

TELEPHONE

The telephone number of the Admitting Orders Nurse Office is . . .

ALTERNATIVE PROCEDURE FOR PRE-ADMIT PHYSICIAN'S ORDERS

Physicians may also use a drop-box in the physicians' lounge to transmit pre-admit orders to the admitting orders nurse: standard physician's order forms are available at the drop-box. The procedure for handling and distributing such orders is similar to the procedure prescribed above.

Pickup hours from the physician's lounge drop-box are 11:00 a.m. and 4:00 p.m., Monday through Friday. Please note that orders pertaining to same-day admissions must be deposited in the drop-box before 11:00 a.m.

FOR FURTHER INFORMATION

Call or visit the
ADMITTING ORDERS NURSE OFFICE
Admitting Department
Admissions Building, Second Floor
Tel:

Exhibit 7–4 continued

DATE ORDERED	ADMITTING DIAGNOSIS

AMBULATION: _____ AD LIB _____ WALK _____ CHAIR _____ BRP _____ BED REST

_____ H & P DICTATED

NURSING: V.S.q _____ _____ I & O _____ DAILY WEIGHT

OPERATION PERMIT
(SPECIFY PROCEDURE & DATE)

_____ PRE-OP ORDERS PER: (DR/GROUP) _____

_____ OTHER _____

DIET: _____

LABORATORY: (Initial indicates sample collected)

_____ CBC & DIFFERENTIAL _____   _____ SMAC 20 _____   _____ OTHER: _____

_____ ROUTINE UA _____   _____ COAGULATION PROFILE _____   _____

_____ TYPE & SCREEN _____   _____ CHEMISTRY PANEL _____   _____

_____ TYPE & CROSS_____ UNIT(S) _____   _____ POTASSIUM ONLY _____   _____ VDRL _____

RADIOLOGY: _____ CHEST X-RAY (P-A & LATERAL) _____
(Initial when completed)   _____ OTHER _____   _____

OTHER DIAGNOSTIC STUDIES: _____ EKG _____   _____ OTHER _____   _____
(Initial when completed)

ALLERGIES TO MEDICATIONS: _____

MEDICATIONS: _____

_____ M.D.

PHYSICIAN'S SIGNATURE

NOTED BY

MR-245   **PRE-ADMIT PHYSICIAN'S ORDERS**

Source: Courtesy of St. Joseph's Hospital and Medical Center, Phoenix, Arizona.

same time, thus enabling the insurance verifiers to screen financially and to ensure a smooth entry into the hospital system at the time of admitting. Much of the anxiety and apprehension of the patient can be greatly reduced through this process. It can set the stage for the patient's entire hospital stay.

The Advantages of Preadmission Testing

Preadmission testing eliminates the delay at the time of admission and ensures that test results are available to the physician when the patient is admitted. Hospitals that have a preadmission testing program have proven that the patient's length of stay can be shortened at least from one to two days. Should any test results be abnormal, it provides the physician ample time to evaluate the patient and determine if the admission and surgery dates need to be cancelled or rescheduled.

From the patient standpoint, it saves the patient unnecessary hospitalization and money. In the case of surgical patients, physicians, surgeons, and anesthetists have the test results available to them prior to the patient's admission. The admitting department correlates the patient information and the test results with the physician's orders and financial information so that the time of the patient's actual admission is decreased.

CONCLUSION

In this era of significant changes in the health care field, the reservations and preadmission areas of the admitting department will also be challenged to change as well. Some suggestions for the future include the following:

- complete computerization of all functions
- more active involvement in marketing
- development of preadmission testing programs
- employment of an admitting orders nurse to take physician orders, triage patients, and make assessments

Another consideration for the future might be the development of an on-line computer system with physicians' offices. Reservations would then be transmitted from the physician's office to the reservations department via a computer.

This is an exciting and innovative time for the reservations and preadmission departments. It is imperative that a concentrated effort be made to upgrade the skill level of the staff serving these areas. This should be prioritized as a necessary goal and objective if the personnel are to continue performing their tasks efficiently, effectively, and, above all, compassionately.

Chapter 8

Bed Assignment and Control

A. Laurie Laughner

One of the key responsibilities of admitting departments is bed assignment and control. Although specific policies and procedures vary from institution to institution, the general concepts and techniques for bed assignment and control are similar for all. The bed control function is the major patient trafficking mechanism of the hospital, channeling patients into, around, and out of patient beds. As such, it is vital to the efficient operation of the hospital and must provide for tracking the availability of beds, permitting strategies for appropriate placement of patients, and verifying and accurately recording the location of the patient population.

With the current emphasis on cost effectiveness in hospitals, bed assignment and control has become an even more important issue. Beds cannot be assigned taking into consideration only the "normal" issues of sex, service, acuity, and availability. They must now be assigned by taking into account the least costly bed (e.g., nurse unit, physician staffing) and a host of in-hospital matters related to containing costs.

Balancing the needs of the hospital requires a great deal of skill and knowledge about the policies, procedures, and desires of many departments within the hospital, as well as a clear understanding of diagnosis and its implications. Because this process demands a rather "neutral" third party to be effective, the admitting department has become the principal site for bed assignment and control. The admitting department has proven effective in balancing the various needs—financial, nursing, medical, and those of the patient. Its communication with the many departments lends itself to a wider, more sensitive understanding of the institution as a whole.

Each hospital is unique, however, in its design and requires tailormade policies and procedures. The bed management function of a psychiatric hospital will probably be different from a general, acute care hospital, and different again from a children's hospital. To be truly effective, the assignment and control of beds must have customized guidelines in the form of standard hospital policies and procedures. In addition, strong administrative support in enforcing the guidelines is necessary to achieve continuity, effectiveness, and avoidance of problems.

With this type of support in place, bed assignment and control can begin. There is little equipment needed to accomplish this process other than a *bed index* used to record patient and empty bed location. The process demands more abstract needs, such as communicative skills, integrative thinking, quick memory recall, and stategic orientation.

Although new computerized "bed control" systems do exist, to date they are limited in their actual "bed management" features. Some can assist in the process with up to the minute reporting of patient locations, and in a few of the more sophisticated systems, some can forecast the number of new patients the hospital can expect and absorb in a day.

The reasons computers fall down in their ability to manage bed assignments is because they discriminate only between "yes" and "no" questions in a mathematical sense. They do not deal with the medium of situational responses that are not mathematical.

One example of this would be the emotional dynamics involved in placing patients. The perception of stress of a nursing unit or a family request not to have a patient assigned to a room because a close relative had died there are not quantifiable elements. However, they may make the difference in whether or not a bed plan for a particular day is successful.

Establishment of a basic framework flexible enough to accommodate the highly communicative "people skills" and unusual medical situations not found in ordinary businesses is the key element. This framework consists of the previously described hospital policy guidelines and administrative support; provision of proper equipment (bed index and computer support if possible); an outline of patient placement criteria, infection control, discharge, and transfer rules; and a cooperative plan of the hospital strategy on bed control management, both long and short term.

Each of these areas are topics that need further explanation to appreciate fully the relationship in bed assignment and control.

THE BED INDEX

The bed index is the main tool used for aiding bed assignment and control. As its name implies, it is a recording device for all available beds. It may be in the form of a bed board, Cardex file (Vertiflex), chart, or a computer file. Generally, the bed index notes patient beds by nursing unit, the type of accommodation (private, semiprivate, ward), and any other special limitations hospitals consider important, such as isolation.

As patients are admitted, the bed index is adjusted to reflect visually the fact that the bed is occupied. In most cases, a minimum notation of the patient's name and sex are recorded. In many systems, age, service, physician, and diagnosis are also noted. When a patient is transferred, discharged, or admitted, the bed index is adjusted so that at any given time, if requested, an accurate visual record of occupied and unoccupied beds is available. This visual record assists the admitting bed coordinator in bed assignment and planning.

The bed coordinator from the admitting department records or flags the bed index with other information needed to place patients. For larger and/or tertiary institutions, nursing units are usually separated into service specialties. Flags on the bed index may include specialized equipment (e.g., telemetry monitoring, Balken frame), restrictions (e.g., disoriented, precautions, repair), and patient gender. The individual bed coordinator also develops a method of recording special needs and "shorthand notes" for such things as holding a bed for a transfer out of an intensive care unit, pending admission, pending discharge, anticipated late discharge time, or a special patient problem.

The actual method of recording is less important than providing the bed coordinator with a visual representation of the patient population, so that where and at what time beds are available for patient occupancy can be ascertained. Chances are, the bigger the hospital, the more specialized the recording system. Bed systems currently in use can be seen in Table 8–1.

The bed board is one of the oldest forms of a bed index and is still popular in many hospitals. It may be mounted on a wall or scaled down to a portable paper model. All beds—licensed, overflow, swing, and float*—have a slot on the bed board for insertion of a card or ticket with the patient's name, sex, and age, and any other criteria the individual hospital requires. When a patient is admitted, the card is simply inserted into the slot representing the room and bed number. If the patient is transferred while in the hospital, the card is moved to the corresponding slot. When the patient is finally discharged, the card is removed from the bed board.

Bed boards are advantageous for smaller hospitals because vacant beds can be spotted quickly. However, they lack space for pertinent patient data, become cumbersome in hospitals over 300 beds, and limit access to information needed for arranging patient transfers. For some of the smaller institutions and/or highly specialized institutions such as psychiatric hospitals, the bed board may be the preferred bed index since it is easy to use, it is highly visual, and patients' data are more likely to be committed to memory or be easily accessible in another file.

---

*For purposes of clarity in this instance, the types of beds are defined as follows:

- licensed—the number of beds for which the hospital has state licensure
- overflow—"extra" beds not part of the licensed bed complement. These beds may be "corridor" beds or beds set up in expandable rooms when all licensed beds are exhausted.
- float—acute care licensed beds used temporarily as chronic care cases

The most popular bed index is the Cardex or Vertiflex file. Plastic pockets that hold index-type cards are placed vertically upon one another, exposing only the top or bottom line of the cards showing the patient name. Rows of the cards are arranged by nursing unit and can be mounted on a wall, arranged in a page-like fashion on a stand (so one can "flip" through the pages of nursing units), or put in drawers. The Cardex allows easy access for visual or informational inquiries about bed availability on nursing units and data needed to place patients. Again, as in the previously described system, cards are added, moved, or removed to reflect the actual whereabouts of patients. The major benefit of this bed index is the accessibility it provides to patient information needed for transfer and inquiries.

Computerized bed indexes are now available on most automated admitting systems. The "bed management" function on "real time" computer systems maintains a picture of what is currently happening in the hospital. When a patient is admitted, discharged, or transferred and the information keyed into the system, the patient immediately appears in the appropriate bed. Inquiries can be made into each nursing unit to locate beds; however, most admitting systems are not truly "bed management systems" so that the tentative assignment to a bed is not visible. Some computerized admitting systems do list or record "vacant beds only," which can be printed out to aid in strategy for bed placement. Furthermore, although inquiries can be made on the system to obtain information needed for placement or transfer, usually only one patient record is available at a time and cannot be viewed simultaneously while viewing the nursing unit. For this reason, when computerized admitting systems are used, it is not unusual to also have a manual bed index or a vacant bed worksheet for planning bed assignments. However, many developments can be expected in this area in the future, including split-screen viewings, iconographic touch-screen tracking, ties to and from integrated accounting systems, and the development of comprehensive hospital management and information systems.

CRITERIA FOR PATIENT PLACEMENT

The patient placement criteria of any hospital establishes the individual hospital's priorities and guidelines for assigning patient beds. Examples of these criteria include type of admission (i.e., elective, urgent, or emergency), sex, service, age, diagnosis, level of care, special equipment needs, mental status, compatibility of diagnoses, infection control rules, and governmental mandates (e.g., definition of true pediatric cases and where they may or may not be housed). Establishing priorities for bed assignment must be done by individual hospitals. A comprehensive administrative guide in this area is crucial.

Larger institutions tend to have individual nursing units with restricted admission service specialties (i.e., beds designated to a particular service, such as

Table 8–1 Comparison of Bed Indexes

	Bed Board	Cardex File Vertiflex	Chart	Computer Bed File*
Major Features	Large wall-mounted bed index uses tickets with patient names to show where patients are housed by nursing unit.	Pockets holding patient information are vertically displayed in rows by nursing units. It can be wall mounted, on a stand, or in drawer form. All patients' cards are viewed by "flipping" the index.	Patient names pencilled (or tickets inserted) on/into a paper or cardboard chart.	Computerized file by nursing unit has access to the most current information on occupied and unoccupied beds for areas that have CRTs with appropriate security level "sign-on's" or "keys."
Hospital Best Served	Hospitals under 300 beds; hospitals with low in-house patient transfers; specialized hospitals	All	All	All
Advantages	Highly visual representation of bed occupancy is provided. In small institutions patient name tickets are easy to move around when planning beds.	Visual and easy access to patient information is provided. The three types of files make the tool adaptable to most work areas (and bed coordinator preference). Patients' names are confidentially listed. Pending discharges, transfers, and admissions are easy to flag.	It requires little space, is portable, and is highly visible.	Operator can query the system in a number of ways to retrieve patient location, occupied beds, and limited information on other patients on the same nursing unit. Some systems list vacant beds. Information is timely. Most systems have the capability of printing the bed file on demand.

Disadvantages	Large amount of wall space is needed. There may be a problem with patient confidentiality. It is visually confusing in large institutions. Patient transfer information is not easily accessible. Tickets fall out. It is cumbersome for hospitals over 300 beds.	Entire hospital bed situation cannot be seen at a glance (must turn pages to see all units).	Very limited patient information is available. Pencil version can be messy and requires frequent re-writing of hospital census by hand. Discharges, transfers, and admissions are hard to flag.	*Most systems are such that a bed board, Cardex, or chart to plan strategies are also needed for planning beds. Most systems do not allow viewing of the entire hospital bed picture on one screen. Usually both the nursing unit and enough information to plan transfers simultaneously cannot be viewed. Most systems' bed file works with only those patients who are admitted; it cannot key in room transfers to test the bed plan for the day because financial charges may be affected.*

*Computerized admitting and bed management systems vary significantly. Individual features therefore should be researched on a system by system basis.

orthopedics or neurology). This practice facilitates teaching in hospitals with residency programs or concentrations of specialized nursing skills. However, it will limit the ability to achieve maximum occupancies if exceptions are not allowed. Almost all hospitals do have some type of service designation on nursing units but without absolute exclusivity. This admitting department must know the patient's sex, date of birth or age, diagnosis (primary and secondary), mental status, and special needs such as equipment, medical precautions, or nursing care. This information is used to access compatibility with other patients, appropriateness of accommodations, and compliance with infection control regulations. (See Infection Control section.)

After this basic patient information is received and evaluated, several further factors are assessed:

- the urgency of the admission (emergency, urgent, or elective)
- the availability of vacant beds
- the timing of when the call to admit is received
- the expected arrival time of the patient
- the degree to which admission service specialties are restricted on nursing units
- the hospital's individual priorities relative to bed assignment

For the most part, the latter factors determine the assignment of a patient to a specific bed. (See Strategies in Bed Control Management.) In hospitals where a high census is maintained, these issues are critical. However, in hospitals whose census runs low, they may never be apparent to anyone other than the admitting bed coordinator.

Highly specialized and restricted nursing units such as intensive care units, pediatrics, obstetrics, nursery, and psychiatry will have further criteria limiting placement. The criteria may involve a triage screening of patients by medical staff with notification to the admitting department of acceptance or nonacceptance to the nursing unit.

The issue of manipulating the census to produce a more cost-effective method of assigning patient beds has become more prominent recently and can be expected to become ever more so. This method gives greater weight to management concerns. An example of this is placing patients so as to maximize the use of nurses, thereby achieving better productivity and decreased use of overtime.

INFECTION CONTROL

Infection control, the process whereby the spread of infection is limited through precautionary measures, is a major concern of hospitals. The specific techniques for the control of infection vary depending on the type of infection. Sterilization of equipment and instruments, washing of hands, isolation of patients having certain communicable diseases, and wearing masks and gowns are examples of infection control techniques.

Infection control liabilities can be minimized through a coordinated effort and by close communication among physicians, nursing staff, the surgical recovery room, the emergency department, epidemiology, and the admitting department. Guidelines to identify and classify patients on admission (and thereafter) ensure that susceptible and infected patients can be placed in the safest possible environments.

The role of the admitting department is important in the process of identifying susceptible patients as both a screening and referral body. Such guidelines are fairly routine, and it is not difficult to spot and place infected and susceptible patients appropriately as they enter the hospital. *The Centers for Disease Control (CDC) Guideline for Isolation Precautions in Hospitals* outlines two systems of isolation hospitals can use for infection control:[1]

1. system A—a category-specific system that groups diseases into various related methods of transmission
2. system B—a disease-specific method of identifying infected or potentially infective patients

System A is the more common method of isolation classification mainly because it is easier to use and requires less training than system B. Its main disadvantage is that patients are isolated more frequently than need be because the categories do not allow for adapting to each specific illness or infection.

System B is disease specific (i.e., each disease or infection has a specified method of infection control). Fewer patients will require isolation under this system. However, it is more difficult to use and therefore requires more training of the staff.*

Either system is acceptable if uniformly applied. The hospital must, therefore, choose a system and provide the appropriate guidelines for the staff.

Each hospital admitting department should identify the system selected for providing infection control through the infection control or epidemiology department. Admitting department infection control guidelines can then be developed in cooperation with infection control. Only the categories relating to admitting need be included.

---

*Specific regulations on identification and handling of communicable diseases and precaution cases may vary from state to state. Further information can be obtained through the individual hospital's department of epidemiology or infection control.

Generally, the following would be included in an admitting department procedure on infection control:

- identification of the CDC infection control system selected for use in the hospital—a broad overview
- identification of the diseases and/or grouping that may require isolation or precaution
- room assignment criteria
- patient compatibility criteria
- hospital communications system for if/when departments need to be notified of suspected infective patients

Examples of one hospital's admitting department infection control policy can be seen in Exhibits 8–1 through 8–3.

Exhibit 8–1 Procedure on Infection Control

SAMPLE ADMITTING OFFICE INFECTION CONTROL PROCEDURE
PATIENT SERVICES

STANDARD INTRAOFFICE PROCEDURE

Procedure No.: 2–22

Subject: Communicable Diseases   Effective Date: May 1, 1978*
            and/or Precaution Cases   *revised Dec. 14, 1981
            (Infection Control)   *reviewed Mar. 1, 1983
                                                 *revised Mar. 1, 1984

Scope: Admitting   Issued by: Laurie Laughner

                                           Approved by: Martin E. O'Toole

----

I. The purpose of this procedure is to ensure that all communicable disease admissions plus any admission having a diagnosis falling into the categories needing precautions are referred immediately to the epidemiologist.

II. All admissions falling into the previously mentioned categories (see guidelines attached) will be admitted as per instructions of Infection Control Committee, and the epidemiologist will be notified as soon as possible.

Source: Courtesy of St. Elizabeth's Hospital, Boston, Massachusetts.

Exhibit 8–2 Guidelines for Patient Placement

SAMPLE INTERDEPARTMENTAL (INFECTION CONTROL-ADMITTING OFFICE)
STATEMENT OF GUIDELINES FOR PATIENT PLACEMENT

PATIENT SERVICES

STANDARD INTRAOFFICE PROCEDURE

Procedure No.: 2–22

Guidelines for Patient Placement

Purpose: To place susceptible patients in the safest possible environment and to remove infected patients from the pathways open to the spread of infection.

Method: By identifying and classifying on admission and thereafter each patient in the appropriate category according to diagnosis, current surgical procedures, and underlying conditions.

To achieve this, coordinated efforts and close communication must be maintained at all times among physicians, nursing staff, intensive care unit, surgical recovery room, emergency department, and nurse epidemiologist.

Responsibilities:

If an exception is to be made, one of the following must be consulted:

- nurse epidemiologist
- chief of infectious disease
- chairman, infection control committee
- chief of service

Source: Courtesy of St. Elizabeth's Hospital, Boston, Massachusetts.

Exhibit 8–1 shows a sample admitting department standard intraoffice procedure on infection control developed to aid the admitting department in placing infection control patients.

Exhibit 8–2 is a sample statement of the combined infection control–admitting department guideline for patient placement. It contains the agreed-upon interdepartmental purpose, method of handling infection control patients, and the personnel responsible for carrying out the procedure.

Exhibit 8–3 is a sample chart from the admitting department intraoffice procedure. It incorporates the CDC system A infection control classification with those categories most important to admitting highlighted, an adaptation used again to facilitate identification and placement of applicable patients.

Exhibit 8–3 Infection Control Chart

SAMPLE INFECTION CONTROL CHART DESIGNED FOR ADMITTING OFFICE INTERNAL USE
STANDARD INTRAOFFICE PROCEDURE

Infection Control Classification for Patient Placement (System A)
Surgical Wound Classification

Classification	Definition	Examples	Can Place WithiIn*	Do Not Place WithiIn
Clean Surgical	Nontraumatic, uninfected operative wound; elective, primarily closed, and undrained wounds *not* located in respiratory, alimentary, or genitourinary tracts nor oropharyngeal cavities	Cardiac Eye surgery Reconstructive orthopedic Vascular	Another clean surgery High risk Other nonsurgical patients Clean contaminated surgical	Any infected patients
Clean Contaminated	Open wounds into respiratory, alimentary, or genitourinary tract without contamination	Appendectomy Bowel resection (without spillage to peritoneal cavity) Bladder Cholecystectomy Dental Hemorrhoidectomy Hysterectomy Lung Nose Throat	Another clean contaminated surgery Clean surgery High risk Nonsurgical	Contaminated surgery Dirty surgery Any patient with draining wounds
Contaminated Surgery	Open, fresh traumatic wounds, operations with major break in sterile techniques (e.g., cardiac massage), and incisions encountering acute, non-purulent inflammation	Fresh and closure colostomy Gunshot wound (not bowel) Acute cholecystitis Acute appendicitis Rectal surgery Trans-Urethral Resection (T.U.R.)	Another contaminated surgery Nonsurgical	High risk All other surgical (postoperative)

Classification	Definition	Examples		
Dirty Surgery	Dirty and infected wounds †(old traumatic wounds and clinical infection or perforated viscera)	Vaginal or cesarean section with Premature Rupture of Membranes (PROM) 24 hr. Self-explanatory	Another dirty surgery Nonsurgical patients	Other surgical patients (postoperative) High risk
Suspect	A patient who may spread infection	*Nonsurgical Classification* Bedsores Fresh conjunctivitis, draining Diarrhea (?contagious) Pneumonia	See specific disease category	Isolate all patients suspected of having transmissable disease according to the appropriate disease Any other patient
Communicable Disease and Infected	A patient with a confirmed or suspected contagious disease	Tuberculosis Meningococcal disease All other communicable diseases Purulent, open draining wounds	Private room or appropriate isolation If respiratory tract is involved, use strict or protective isolation (private room with proper air flow)	
High Risk	Patient with a greater than normal susceptibility	Burns Minor cancer Advanced on anticancer or leukemia drugs Dermatitis Severe diabetes, out of control Hemodialysis patients	Uninfected medical Another high-risk patient Clean surgical Clean contaminated surgical	Suspect patients Infected patients Contagious patients Major burn cases require protective isolation Any other patient when physician instructs isolation

*Many patients with like illnesses may be placed together. Consult with the infection control department for clarification.

†Organisms were present in operative field prior to surgery.

Source: Courtesy of St. Elizabeth's Hospital, Boston, Massachusetts.

TRANSFER OF PATIENTS

Due to medical necessity, case mix, sex distribution, personal preferences of patients and physicians, and a host of other factors, transfers within a hospital occur often. The two pieces of information needed to begin to establish the criteria for prioritizing transfers are (1) the source of the request and (2) the reason for the request.

There are seven major sources of transfer requests: (1) the patient, (2) the patient's family, (3) the physician, (4) the nursing unit, (5) epidemiology (infection control), (6) administrative, and (7) admitting. Patients and their families often have transfer requests for placement into preferred rooms such as private rooms or a room in a newer section of the hospital. Physicians also may have preferred nursing units where they will request to have their patients transferred. The preference may stem from medical necessity, favoritism of one nursing unit over another, desire for the particular medical expertise of staff on a nursing unit (e.g., an orientation to the care of neurological problems), convenience, or change of medical service.

Nursing unit and epidemiology transfer requests tend to focus around patient care issues. These would include incompatibility of patients sharing a room, the need for or release from medical precautions, the need to have a patient near the nursing station desk, or the need for equipment only located in particular rooms (or that only fits in certain rooms).

Admitting transfer requests generally concern creating bed spaces. The bed space opened may be needed in order to accommodate new patient arrivals who must be housed in specialized rooms and nursing units or to place a patient of a certain gender. They may also need simply to open up enough beds in appropriate locations to house new patient arrivals, especially when the hospital occupancy is high.

For the most part, administrative transfer requests are very limited. They usually concern closure of a patient room for renovation or mechanical or equipment problems that would cut off necessary services (e.g., repair of pipes or electricity in a patient room), and in some instances to accommodate those with VIP status.

Hospital admitting procedures for controlling the transfer process usually address who is authorized to request transfers, what are legitimate reasons for requests, and what type of requests take precedence over others. Furthermore, the general bed assignment priorities must consider transfers when assigning new patients to beds.

Authorization for transferring a patient to a room on the same nursing unit (intrafloor) is probably limited more by the reason a patient needs to be transferred than the particular individual making the request. All seven of the formerly described sources can probably generate a request in this situation. Interfloor transfers, transfers from one nursing unit to a new nursing unit, are usually much more restricted owing to the disruption in continuity of care of the patient.

For this reason, interfloor transfer requests are usually limited to physician requests, patient requests approved by their respective physicians, nursing requests on the supervisory or above level, and epidemiology, the admitting department, and administration requests. However, although requests are submitted, they may not be processed immediately because priorities are usually assigned to determine who is moved first.

The prioritizing of transfer requests establishes the "pecking order" for bed placement. Transfer priorities are integrated in the general priorities for bed assignment of the hospital. (See Strategies in Bed Control Management and the Admission System Cycle.) The priority for bed assignments is a function of each hospital's philosophy and can be quite variable from institution to institution.

Transfers also present a number of problems for hospitals and patients. For the hospital, the timing of moving patients may be critical, especially if the hospital is experiencing a high census. Available staff must be located to move the patients and their belongings. Housekeeping must be available to prepare new beds for the patients and then prepare the beds vacated by the move.

If an interfloor transfer occurs, the number of problems are even greater. Nursing reports must be given from one nursing unit to another and medical records (charts) relocated. The medical staff must become familiar with the new patient's routine medical and social needs.

Patients also experience new stresses related to transfers. They must leave familiar surroundings and routines if an interfloor transfer is needed. They must deal with unfamiliar personnel. They may worry about family and friends finding the new location. And, in most instances, they must adjust to a new roommate.

DISCHARGE AND DISCHARGE FORECASTING

An order written by a physician triggers the discharge process on a nursing unit. Once started, there are several ways the admitting department can be notified, including by telephone, discharge slip, hand-carried notices, or computer message. Although the notification of discharge usually takes place on the day of discharge, prior notification of anticipated discharge is becoming increasingly popular. In long-term facilities where knowledge of a discharge is known well in advance of the actual date, a "discharge forecast" is the rule. The forecast is a combined listing of anticipated discharges. It is a valuable tool in planning the number of new patients the hospital can accept for future dates. Prior knowledge of the new incoming patient load allows more organized placement of patients, better staffing plans, and fewer "bed crises" in which the number of new patients booked to be admitted exceeds the number of available appropriate beds.

Discharge forecasting for general acute care hospitals is a more difficult job. Prior knowledge of discharges is not as readily available, and discharge orders are rarely written by the physician in advance. Medical patients, in particular, pose a further problem, since predicting when the patient will be well enough to leave is difficult.

The diagnosis related group (DRG) system may eventually enhance the ability to forecast as computer systems begin to link the DRG coding to the patient's length of stay. Estimating discharge dates promises to become a byproduct of the system.

Early morning discharge hours are preferred by most hospitals. They facilitate the cleaning of the patients' rooms prior to the arrival of new admissions. The hospital's success in this process depends on its relationship with the medical staff. Not developing a cooperative effort may cause a breakdown in the admission cycle.

Timely discharges at the proper hour help the admitting department coordinate the timing of new patient arrivals and avoid "people" traffic jams. They also facilitate the planning of beds for the day and the management of census fluctuations. When the discharge hour is not (generally) honored, the admitting cycle may become interrupted.

Coordinating requests for new beds with bed availability is highly important (unless the hospital is willing to accept a low occupancy rate). In fact, late discharging of patients can cause an inability to run a high occupancy. Since the bulk of new patient admissions occur between 11:30 A.M. and 3:00 P.M., bed assignments need to be planned early in the day. Delaying the discharge of patients makes appropriate and efficient placement difficult. Patients may end up in less than ideal locations, or a disproportionate number of new patients may be assigned to the same nursing units because the discharge notifications were received too late in the afternoon. Worse yet, an elective admission might be cancelled or postponed due to lack of beds only to find an empty bed unused! Enough incidences of this type can drop the average occupancy of the hospital.

Other inefficiencies occur with late discharge problems, such as underutilization of the nursing staff and other inefficient allocation of resources. One overtaxed nursing unit, staffed for the "average occupancy" on the floor, may have to float nursing personnel to its unit or hire overtime or agency staff to contend with the increased patient load, while another nursing unit may find itself with empty beds at the end of the day.

As can be seen, hospitals with chronic late discharge problems have decreased ability to maintain high occupancies. In addition, the hospital staff will begin to feel that there is no way to plan or manage their departments in an organized fashion. The admission process will be viewed as a chaotic and unmanageable system. Physicians who may well, in fact, be one of the sources of the problem, will probably be the first to complain of inefficient operation of the hospital, the poor accommodations for their patients, and the incompetence of a hospital that cancels their patient when empty beds exist.

On the contrary, hospitals with a more controlled discharge process will be afforded an opportunity to have a manageable and efficient admission system and the potential to run higher average occupancies. (See Strategies in Bed Control Management.) A timely, efficient discharge process will not increase the occupancy in or by itself. It can, however, set the stage to allow maximum utilization of the hospital's resources in a more effective way.

STRATEGIES IN BED CONTROL MANAGEMENT

Developing strategies in bed control management is an important part of effective use of hospital beds. These strategies will help determine how smoothly patients are introduced into and released from the overall hospital system. They will also reflect the hospital's ability to coordinate and integrate its own systems. Ultimately, strategies affect the capability of a hospital to maximize overall bed use and minimize inefficient bed use.

Effective bed control strategies incorporate the organization's goals and objectives. They must be structured enough to be operational and consistent but flexible enough to allow for the human elements of emotion and stress found in hospitals.

The dynamics of bed control are quite complex. This is due, for the most part, to the high degree of communication and personal interaction involved in bed control. Finding an empty bed for a new patient is not just a matter of "pick and choose" but an intricate pattern of decision making requiring evaluation of circumstances, persons, and general needs. In fact, if the decision-making tree for bed control were to be plotted and graphed in detail, it could easily cover a wall measuring eight feet by ten feet.

Staffing, power issues, disturbances in the ebb and flow of patients being admitted and discharged, and census fluctuations all play major roles in affecting bed control. Admitting policies that fit overall bed control strategies help to manage these issues in an organized fashion and keep balance in the system.

The balance in this case is reflected in an admission system cycle. Although the cycle technically begins with admission of a new patient and ends with discharge, it is a fluid and continuous process. Overlapping of many admissions with varying lengths of stay causes a net balance of patients housed in the hospital at midnight, producing the "occupancy" or "end census." Along with several other critical elements, such as timing of admissions and discharges, disturbances in the ability to admit patients, and bed placement priorities, it contributes to the turning of the admission system cycle.

To understand the cycle, it is first necessary to examine bed control issues and how they relate to the admission system.

BED CONTROL ISSUES

As previously stated, one of the main reasons for the complexity of bed control is the high degree of personal interaction and communication involved in the process of assigning beds. Personal interactions and communications require establishing relationships and methods of exchanging ideas and plans. In the case of bed control, these interactions cross departmental, divisional, and professional lines.

This type of communications relationship provides maximum flexibility within the organization. However, because so many personal exchanges take place, there is a greater risk of conflict, distractions, and slowing down completion of necessary tasks.

To prevent difficulties yet maintain the benefits of such a system, it is important to understand the "human" issues associated with bed control. There are four key issues:

1. the purpose and goals of bed control in the organization
2. the relationship of bed control to other areas or departments in the hospital
3. the political power issues over beds
4. the need for balance in the system

Understanding the issues, of course, does not guarantee successful bed control, just the ability to develop procedures and guidelines to facilitate the process in a reasonable, manageable way. If the system is truly "managed," it stands the greatest chance of being successful.

One measure of this success is the ability to meet the goals and objectives of bed control. For most hospitals, this means getting patients assigned and into beds without upsetting the routine within the hospital while still satisfying patient and physician desires.

Another goal of bed control would be to distribute patients in the most functional manner possible. By doing so, the hospital resources are more efficiently consumed. For example, it is *normally* more efficient to admit patients where the greatest number of beds are vacant and/or the least number of new patients and transfers have been assigned.

Keeping these goals in perspective, one can begin to think of bed control as a management tool. The tool is simply a system used to accomplish goals in an orderly manner. It sets up a framework of procedures and guidelines needed to achieve a predetermined result.

Like all systems, in order for this system to "live" it must be open and responsive to feedback from the other systems with which it interacts. This is important because when changes occur in areas outside or within bed control, they may cause changes in the hospital system as a whole. By monitoring the feedback (e.g., the number of complaints received) and making an effort to respond to it when necessary, the system continually betters itself. Failure to respond to changes in the hospital that ultimately affect bed control will result in a system that can no longer function operationally.

Bed control systems that are open and responsive also enable the hospital to maximize its occupancy. Because the system is designed to place patients efficiently, the beds used are well planned functionally and there is usually greater cooperation from the personnel involved with receiving new patients.

One should be cautioned at this point that although good bed control can maximize the ability to run a higher census, it *does not guarantee* a higher occupancy. That is a function of the numbers of patients admitted and their duration of stay.

The second major bed control issue is the relationship of bed control to other areas/departments of the hospital. This includes understanding how the bed control procedures affect those departments; knowing the organizational reporting system (hierarchy); and knowing who in the organization has authority to make decisions concerning bed control.

Authority and control over beds fall in the next major bed control issue—politics. The admitting department has frequently been an area over which nursing, fiscal services, and clinical services want control. Nursing and clinical services departments want "ownership" because of a desire to control how patients are placed. They believe since bed placement has such a direct effect on them, they should also have the greatest influence on the process.

Fiscal services also believes it needs to control the admitting department. However, its rationale is that information gathering and financial screening on admission is the most vital concern to the hospital. Recently, this emphasis has become stronger owing to the drive to reduce health care costs and maintain better cash flow.

Two new departments have now emerged in a bid to control the admitting department: medical records and utilization review. As a result of the DRG system, which shifts reimbursement concerns to accurate documentation and reporting on patient records, they have also come into a position of greater influence in hospitals.

Although fiscal, medical records, and utilization review desire authority over the admitting department, bed control is not usually their primary objective. Control of the gate into and out of the hospital is important to them. Bed control and patient placement is only secondary.

Unfortunately, it must be recognized that all of these departments at any specific time are correct. Actually, it might even be said they are all correct. Bed assignment and control does dramatically affect nursing and clinical services. "Gatekeeping" and accurate information gathering does dramatically affect fiscal, medical records, and utilization review.

However, these departments or services do not usually consider gatekeeping, information gathering, and bed control equally important to the hospital needs. There are of course exceptions to this rule, but since the focus of these areas is, reasonably so, directed to their specialty, behaving otherwise is extremely difficult.

Specialty focus is good. However, there is danger of a particular specialty having control over a department whose functions have dynamic interaction with and impact on other specialties. The specialty is favored. The department under its control will reflect (or eventually reflect) that interest. In this scenario, it is difficult to step back and have the perspective needed to weigh all of the needs. The decision making will ultimately center around the concerns of the specialty because there will be internal pressure to do so.

There is one additional danger—difficulty in adapting to changes that make another specialty's needs, in reality, more important. An example of this would be to look back to the switch from cost-based reimbursement to case-based reimbursement. Under cost-based reimbursement, patient charges were important. During the former period it might have been equally desirable for fiscal or nursing services to control the admitting department (fiscal for its reimbursement reasons and nursing because the encouraged high occupancies had such a dramatic effect on their workload). However, the new case-based reimbursement shifted the emphasis to stress shorter length-of-stay for patients, medical record documentation for DRG coding, and the importance of screening via utilization review.

It is easy to see in this example that a dramatic shift in the hierarchy of needs of these specialties took place. If, for instance, the nursing specialty controlled the admitting department and beds, adapting to the priorities of medical records may have been difficult.

To return for a moment to the major goals of the admitting department, the bed control system should put patients into the system in an expeditious manner without disrupting other departmental systems, satisfy patient and physician desires to the extent possible, and distribute patient room assignments in a functional manner so resources are efficiently consumed. Shifting to medical record's needs in an organization where the admitting department and bed control were not tagged to a particular specialty would have been much less difficult than the switch for nursing to medical record priorities. This is not to say the change was not possible, just more difficult.

Looking at bed management from a systems point of view, the best way for the integrative function of bed control to operate and adapt to the needs of more than one specialty is to remain a neutral party. As such, the system can respond by weighing hospital needs from a management perspective rather than a territorial view.

As the hospital's needs then shift priorities for individual departments or divisions they can also shift with respect to admitting and bed control. The conflict that would have been created within admitting and bed control if they were focused within a particular specialty is reduced.

Conflict over control of beds and the admitting department will probably never be avoided, especially when a shift in priorities takes place. When any change of this nature causes distress, however, the distress can be minimized. Many hospitals obviously have managed quite well with specialty divisions controlling admitting and bed control. Organizations having a matrix reporting system in which an individual manager may have more than one superior in different divisions may accomplish the same end (although this is a difficult method). Again there are hospitals, especially small ones, that truly work in a team effort. Others have particularly talented managers who can implement organizational or departmental behavioral changes with great diplomacy.

The most important point here is that the bed management system should be thought of as a management tool designed to accomplish a predetermined goal. Furthermore, its internal goals and objectives should be consistent with the organization's goals and objectives. Lastly, the optimal control over bed management rests in a direct administrative reporting system.

Understanding the political issues, the need for balance in the system, how bed control relates to other hospital departments, and the purpose and goals of bed control in the organization is only the first step in bed management. The second is understanding the process of bed assignment and control, which is known as the admission system cycle.

THE ADMISSION SYSTEM CYCLE

The admission system cycle is a system whereby patients are admitted into and discharged from the hospital. This complex system drives the occupancy level of the hospital. It also triggers many other hospital systems into action. Because it integrates with a large number of other hospital systems, it is subject to and can produce disturbances in those systems. This is manifested in the ease of introduction into and release of patients from the overall hospital system as well as determining the maximum level of bed use the hospital can achieve.

Admissions and discharges are the key factors of the admission system cycle. They are much like pushing the pedals on a bicycle. Imagine one pedal as the admission, the other as the discharge. As long as the cyclist pedals with both feet consistently, the bicycle continues to move. The admitting cycle also moves as long as admissions and discharges continue to occur. Pushing the bicycle pedals turns the gear (or gears) that interlock with the chain and propels the bicycle's other moving parts. Again, the admission and discharge from the admission cycle interlocks with the other systems of the hospital and propels those systems into motion.

It is necessary to look at the admission and discharge as one unit in the admission cycle because each patient admitted will eventually be discharged. However, the relationship of the expected number of patients discharged to the expected number of patients being admitted *on the same day* is important to the admission system cycle. If the relationship is more or less than one, the occupancy of the hospital will change that day.

$$\frac{\text{Expected no. of discharges}}{\text{No. of admissions expected}} = 1 \qquad = \text{Occupancy Remains the Same}$$

$$\frac{\text{Expected no. of discharges}}{\text{No. of admissions expected}} = >1 \qquad = \text{Decrease in Occupancy}$$

$$\frac{\text{Expected no. of discharges}}{\text{No. of admissions expected}} = <1 \qquad = \text{Increase in Occupancy}$$

This would only cause difficulties in the admission cycle if the hospital occupancy were high and the relationship of expected discharges and admissions were less than or equal to one.

The reason for disturbances at high census stems from the lack of flexibility in placing patients and coordinating patient discharge and arrival times. As the number of bed vacancies becomes small, allowances normally given for bed control issues are difficult to manage. The entire hospital is stressed to its limits.

This is particularly difficult for hospitals with high proportions of emergency admissions that cannot be deferred. Conversely, hospitals with a large proportion of elective patients will feel less stress simply because patient arrival times are more easily controlled and if needed, admissions can be deferred. Mathematically, of course, for every new patient needing admission only one vacant bed is needed. When calculating the "end census" and "occupancy" a fixed point in time is used. This unfortunately does not reflect the occupancy/vacancy picture within the hospital at critical points during the rest of the 24-hour period.

Bed placement and the admission system cycle are dependent on the available occupancy at the actual time a bed is needed. As hospital occupancy fluctuates periodically during the day, the upper peaks may "bump" or be near the maximum levels. An analogy would be to consider occupancy to be like a container filled with water. The container has an open top and a valve to release liquid. The water represents the patient population housed within the hospital system. There are a finite number of drops of water (patients) that can be poured into the system at any one time (maximum occupancy) without first releasing others (discharges). If one were to watch the container over a 24-hour period, the water level (occupancy) would rise and fall depending on how many new drops of water are added to or released from the container.

The timing of when drops enter or leave the cup is critical because there is only so much room to contain the liquid or the cup overflows. In addition, when the container is full, disturbances around the cup or in the cup affect it to a much greater extent than when the cup is less full.

The shift of emphasis from inpatient care to outpatient care to help reduce costs has actually aided some hospitals in relieving the stress of high occupancies. The change has caused shortened patient stays and removal of some inpatients from the system entirely. The result in many instances has been a decrease in average occupancy.

One of the other important elements in the admission system cycle is establishing bed placement priorities to determine which patients need to be assigned beds first. Each hospital needs to identify its priorities clearly to all staff involved with admitting and caring for patients to maintain consistency of policies and reduction in conflict. The priorities may also change over the years to reflect new hospital goals and objectives or adaptations in the hospital's internal systems.

In an acute care hospital this would involve ordering the priority placement of transfers (into and out of intensive care units, medical necessity transfers, physician requested, patient requested, nursing, others), emergency admissions, urgent admissions, and elective admissions. The decisions on placement priorities should be based on a strategy that is in the best interest of the hospital on the whole. There will be a need for cooperation between admitting, nursing, medical services, finance, and administration to develop a rationally based placement priority plan. The plan necessarily must be management oriented and consistent with the hospital's goals.

The need for cooperation and input into the plan from the various divisions is important. Frequently, this involves negotiations among groups who have very different views of the priorities. However, striking a compromise initially saves conflict under conditions that would prove to be highly emotional later.

With bed priorities agreed on and the hospital's goals for bed management defined, the admitting department (bed control) can finally develop a daily bed strategy. This strategy will vary with the circumstances presented each day. However, it should stay within the parameters of the hospital strategy for bed control. The elements being considered on a day-to-day basis would be the following:

- expected volume of new inpatients
- expected discharges
- transfer requests pending
- expected time beds will be vacated
- identifying problems that might interfere with use of beds (e.g., leaks in a patient room, staffing shortages or excesses, disruptive patients, identifying potential changes in scheduling of surgery)

As the daily bed plan develops, the total process is most easily viewed by referring to Figure 8–1. Beginning with the "placement" portion of the center circle (top), the "Bed Need Priorities Established" includes identification of priority elements for the day-to-day strategy of bed priorities and needs. A "test" plan is developed in this "subsystem" as the next step of the main cycle is considered.

Moving to the "Assign Beds" portion of the main cycle, the "Beds Assigned" subsystem begins. Here the needs of the patient, including physician and patient requests, are considered for the patients needing bed placement. The end product of the subsystem is the actual assignment of beds.

Pushing again into the main cycle and off to the "Communications" subsystem, the interaction of the admission cycle begins to trigger other depart-

Figure 8–1 The Admission Cycle

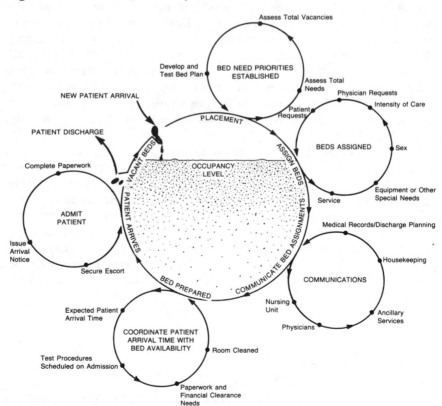

Source: Courtesy of St. Elizabeth's Hospital, Boston, Massachusetts.

mental systems. Notification of a pending admission or transfer patient to the nursing unit initiates preparation of nursing, house physicians, and housekeeping on the unit. Ancillary services personnel and medical records will also begin to prepare as the admitting department communicates the patient arrival.

The "Bed Prepared" section of the admission cycle swings the coordination efforts of the hospital personnel into motion in the next subsystem. The patient's arrival time must be coordinated with preparation of the patient's bed, testing schedule, and completion of the financial clearances.

Back in the main cycle, the patient arrives to be admitted. Paperwork is completed in the admitting department, notification of arrival is sent to numerous departments (e.g., patient information, operators) and the patient is escorted to a testing area or the nursing unit during the "Admit Patient" subsystem.

Unless the patient is transferred to another room the admission cycle is not affected until the patient is discharged from the hospital. The newly vacated bed created by the patient discharge allows the planning of arrival for the next patient as the admission cycle comes full circle.

The points on the subsystems may be quite involved despite their single-lined entries on the graph. The "Communications" and "Admit Patient" subsystems interlock with many nonadmitting systems and each other. In addition, all the systems are overshadowed by the issues discussed in the bed control issues section of this chapter.

Despite the complexity, the admission system cycle is manageable and is part of the bed management system tool. The products of this tool are measurable as admissions, patient-days, length-of-stay, occupancy, and other patient-related statistics (Table 8–2 and Figure 8–2). The statistics named above are extremely important because they describe the patterns and nature of the institution. This information is needed in planning overall bed management strategies for the hospital as well as hospital staffing needs, consumption of resources, indicating new trends of hospital use, and reporting statistical patient data to regulators.

This basic statistical knowledge allows managers to make decisions based on quantifiable data from the past and the predicted trends for the future. Bed management is highly dependent on the information because the admission cycle is affected and limited by it. Admissions and occupancy are the two most critical factors of bed assignment. For any one day the number of admissions is the measure of the volume of workload expected and the vacant beds needed. The occupancy of the hospital, however, limits the ability to accommodate the admissions into the hospital system. Furthermore, the patient-days and patient's length of stay determine what the occupancy will be for each day.

The occupancy of a hospital will fluctuate on a day-to-day basis in most instances. Large swings in the occupancy level are also not unusual. However, most hospital's monthly *average* occupancy level fluctuates in a pattern over the period of a year as does the number of admissions. These particular patterns will be

Table 8–2 Statistical Definitions Used in Bed Control

Statistic	Definition	Used to Plan/Calculate
Admissions	The total number of patients admitted to the hospital as inpatients	Departmental workloads related to new patient admissions
Patient-days	The number of midnights the patient has spent in the hospital as inpatient plus The number of patients admitted as inpatients and discharged on the same calendar day	Patient length of stay Consumption of supplies and services Nursing unit workloads Consumption of resources
Length of stay and Average length of stay	The total number of patient-days a patient accumulates on an inpatient stay in the hospital Average $=$ $\dfrac{\text{No. of all patient days}}{\text{No. of all admissions}}$	The cost of each admission Consumption of resources and goods Calculating expected numbers of discharges and potential vacant beds
Occupancy (expressed in percent)	$\dfrac{\text{No. of patients in hospital at midnight}}{\text{No. of licensed beds}}$	Projecting hospital utilization Projecting resource consumption Identifying the rise and fall pattern of use of the hospital services

repeated from year to year and can be used to plan staffing patterns, consumption of resources, and bed needs.

Average occupancies and number of admissions are particularly important in planning bed needs and admission policies for the admitting department. For example, during months of high occupancy, the admission of elective patients may need to be regulated to help ''level off'' the occupancy to a manageable point. By limiting the number of elective admissions each day, a hospital may be able to disperse the number of admissions over several days and maintain a more stable occupancy level. This is of course preferable to running the occupancy with large peaks and valleys over the same period. Large swings in the occupancy make scheduling of hospital staff extremely difficult and costly.

Another example of management planning for bed needs would be to schedule bed closures for renovation, remodeling, and major (nonemergency) repairs during the months with traditionally lower occupancies. Taking advantage of the

Figure 8–2 Projected Occupancy Graph

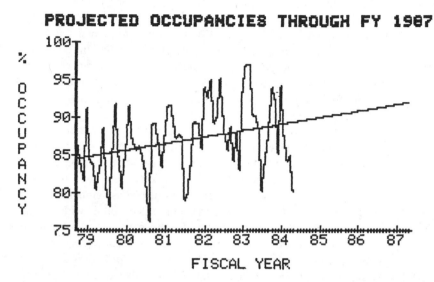

PROJECTED OCCUPANCIES THROUGH FY 1987

% OCCUPANCY

FISCAL YEAR

Note: Graphing the monthly average occupancies plots a visual pattern that is generally repetitive. This concept can be expanded to include predicting the future occupancies of the hospital through statistical analysis of the "trends" based on the historical data.

In this graph, the hospital's average monthly occupancies were plotted and the points connected to show the peaks and valleys over a period of five years. Using the actual data provided, the computer has plotted a straight line showing a trend of increasing average occupancy.

Source: Courtesy of St. Elizabeth's Hospital, Boston, Massachusetts

normal dip is then used wisely. If the dips and peaks of the occupancy are extremely erratic, the hospital may face a "crisis" form of management because personnel will never know how to plan for the next day, only how to react to the situation at present. Thus, they will be constantly "putting out these fires" because the occupancy or number of admissions is too high or too low.

There are three primary elements in dealing with occupancy or census fluctuations proactively. The first is the hospital's ability to understand the extrinsic factors (factors outside the hospital environment) and how they affect the occupancy of the institution. This would include new laws or regulations on health care, changes in the community that the hospital services, and changes in their market share for services they do or do not provide.

The second element is the ability to adapt to the extrinsic factors proactively. For the admitting department this would mean adapting policies and procedures to produce a positive reaction to changes in regulations or in the community that, in the long run, are beneficial to the hospital. An example of such an adaptation would be changing the criteria for admission of elective inpatients to meet the needs of the DRG system. Another would be to anticipate greater numbers of admissions to the hospital because of new building projects within the community and "gearing up" policies (or staff) to accommodate the larger influx of patients. Both of these examples would have an impact on the occupancy of the hospital.

The last element dealing with occupancy fluctuations is the ability to predict numbers of discharges expected on a daily and weekly basis. By "anticipating" the number of discharges on a particular day and for the week thereafter, the admitting department can plan to target numbers of admissions to be allowed into the system each day. The development of an admission–discharge–transfer (ADT) system entails compiling historical data on admissions, case mix and related length-of-stay, transfers, and establishing priorities of bed assignment.

Several computerized ADT systems are available for hospitals with real-time computer capabilities as well as manual systems for those without. Although these systems are relatively new and somewhat unrefined at present, a few have been successful in helping to stabilize hospital occupancies and providing some manageability to what was once thought to be an unpredictable situation. As hospital computerization and computers become more sophisticated and information from the DRG system is evaluated over a longer period of time, expectations and availability of ADT systems should improve. As such, they may add an important part to the puzzle of how to manage hospitals better with assistance from integrated computer systems.

CONCLUSION

Strategies in bed control management are an important part of the ability to use hospital beds effectively. With the use of systems and management techniques, strategies can facilitate patient placement and the introduction of new patients into the hospital.

Understanding and addressing bed control issues is necessary when developing bed control management strategies. These issues concern the "human" elements related to bed control. Because bed control is a process dependent on personal interaction, communication, and information, these critical elements should be dealt with in an organized proactive rather than reactive fashion. This management approach helps avoid "crisis"-oriented behavior and reduces the conflict often associated with bed control.

Only after bed control issues are understood and conflicts concerning them resolved can the admission system cycle function in a productive manner. Failure to do so hinders the transition from point to point within the cycle, slowing the system or creating conflict. The transitional ease is especially crucial given the integration of the admission system cycle with so many other departmental cycles.

The admission system cycle is composed of the logistical steps necessary to admit patients on a day-to-day basis. It is the management tool necessary to achieve bed control and patient admission to the hospital. Although sometimes thought otherwise, it is manageable on a day-to-day and long-range basis. It can also be used to manage hospital occupancy and provides the ability to maximize bed utilization.

The strategies in bed control management steer the admission system cycle to operate such that bed control management accomplishes bed control and hospital goals. Since hospital goals differ, bed control strategies will also differ to reflect the hospital's unique qualities. This may be especially evident with respect to setting of priorities. Complexity of the strategies may also vary significantly depending on the size, type, management style, and behavioral climate of the hospital. However, the ideas and concepts presented in this chapter will be applicable with few exceptions.

NOTE

1. Julia S. Garner and Bryan P. Simmons, *The Centers for Disease Control Guideline for Isolation Precautions in Hospitals*, U.S. Department of Public Health and Human Services publication no. (CDC) 83-8314 (Washington, D.C.: Government Printing Office, 1983).

Chapter 9

Admitting Policy and Procedure

George E. Woodham

The admitting department has undergone radical changes in the past few years. Increased federal regulations, precertification requirements regarding insurance coverage, preadmission testing programs, increases in ambulatory care services, and so on have all played a role in changing the scope and character of hospital admitting departments. Now, more than ever, it is vital to the smooth running of admitting departments and of the hospital that a workable and complete policy and procedure manual be a staple for progressive admitting departments. No longer can one rely on the memory of the admission staff to recall all the outside factors that affect the admissions and registration of patients to health care facilities. Admitting departments must have the resources necessary to make the patient's transition into the health care facility a smooth one. Therefore, a policy and procedure manual will allow the admitting staff to meet the challenge of today's changing health care world.

A policy and procedure manual for the admitting department fulfills several needs of the admitting manager and the admitting staff. Properly developed, policies and procedures will assist management staff and "on-line" staff to complete the daily activities. Policies give consistent guidelines to questions and situations that arise on a regular basis. Departmental policies, when developed in conjunction with the mission, goals, and objectives of the hospital, help to maintain consistency for the admitting department.

Procedures explain how to perform the many different functions and tasks that must be performed in today's fast-paced admitting department. Procedures help cut down duplication of effort and confusion related to who does what and provide a consistent tool for employee evaluation. Since procedures set down in writing the official protocol for established functions and tasks, a fair and concise evaluation for the admitting staff can take place. This will allow for a very objective evaluation by the admitting manager.

WHY A POLICY AND PROCEDURE MANUAL?

In order to ensure, within reason, that all admission situations are handled in a consistent and proper manner, written policy and procedure must be present. This allows the admitting manager the tool to train the staff in the major functions and tasks of their job duties. Without written protocol concerning the preadmission program, precertification, preadmission testing, the admissions interview, and all other admission factors, it is left to chance that all the areas of responsibility of the admitting department will be carried out in a logical and consistent manner.

COMPONENTS OF THE ADMISSION MANUAL

The hospital's first contact with the prospective patient is usually at the point, in the case of elective admissions, when the reservation or scheduled date of admission is made by the physician's office staff. Therefore, policies covering who is eligible to admit patients to the hospital must be established. These policies may cover delinquent charts of physicians and subsequent suspension of admitting privileges. Procedures will follow policies to ensure that a smooth admission will take place. Emergencies, while usually not considered reservations, fall under the same policies regarding physician eligibility to admit patients to the hospital; urgent or "subacute" admissions are also affected by these admission policies and procedures.

Once the reservation is made, a preadmission program is a vital ingredient to the success of the admitting department. In the past, a preadmitting program may have been thought of as merely a means to speed up the actual admission of patients once they arrived at the admitting department; it still is a benefit of the preadmission process. However, of greater importance and benefit to the hospital is the information gathered during the preadmission stage. Specifically, the financial responsibility and insurance areas of preadmission are of major importance to the reimbursement for hospital charges. Policies and procedures regarding responsibility for payment should and must be addressed. The diagnostic related group (DRG) era has caused commercial carriers to jump on board and they, too, along with the Medicare program, now have numerous precertification requirements regarding their role in reimbursement to the hospital. Special time and thought to preadmission must be given to ensure that the hospital receives adequate and accurate information regarding financial responsibility and hospital insurance coverage, if at all possible, prior to admission. Detailed procedures regarding preadmission and precertification must be a part of the policy and procedure manual for the admitting department.

When the patient arrives at the admitting department, so that the admission can be finalized, is by far the most important function of the admitting department.

The initial contact with the patient, to a large extent, will be the deciding factor as to the impression the patient has of the hospital. Too much emphasis cannot be given to ensure that all goes smoothly for the patient during the admission process.

The admitting department is responsibile for gathering all the information that will appear on the patient's chart. The medical record begins in admissions, and, because of this, all information obtained must be as accurate and complete as possible. Policies and procedures regarding all the variables of admission must be established. These variables include the following:

- eligibility of admitting physician based on hospital criteria
- type of admission (i.e., emergency, urgent, or elective)
- completion of all required information including demographic, financial, and in some cases, medical. ICD-9 coding is now becoming part of the admissions process. In addition, uniform billing (UB-82) requirements have broadened the scope of admission information to include onset of symptoms, chief complaint, and, as applicable, accident information
- room accommodation regarding medical necessity, medical specialty, patient convenience, or high occupancy
- obtaining deposit related to insurance deductible, room difference, or patient with no hospitalization coverage
- safeguarding patient valuables
- completion of physician orders (i.e., preadmission testing and/or preoperative tests including blood work, radiology, and cardiology procedures)

SPECIFIC TOPICS

Specific topics that should be included in the manual for the admitting department are listed below:

- types of admission (emergency, urgent, and elective)
- length of time, in advance, that elective admissions can be scheduled
- information required to constitute a scheduled admission
- circumstances that would cause an elective admission to be postponed or cancelled
- criteria to assess eligibility for admission
- emergency admissions
- urgent (subacute) admissions
- preadmission program
- amount of information needed to complete the preadmission process

- criteria for patient's financial responsibility
- preadmission deposits, insurance deductibles, and room differences
- precertification requirements regarding insurance verification on patient's hospital coverage
- job title responsible for obtaining precertification information
- job title responsible for informing patient that precertification is delayed or denied causing admission to be either postponed or cancelled
- length of time, prior to admission, that preadmission testing can be performed, both for medical reliability of tests and from a financial point of view
- listing of preadmission procedures that can be performed on a preadmission testing basis
- "on-line" computer admitting department
- criteria to control patient's arrival time for preadmission testing procedures
- level of importance related to patient room assignment
- criteria regarding assignment of rooms related to new admissions, in-house transfers, and specialty units
- information necessary to complete inpatient admission process
- provisions to obtain incomplete admission information
- protection of patient's valuables
- consents, if any, that are signed in the admitting department
- bedside admissions
- admissions of VIPs
- infection control cases
- inpatient room transfers
- interaction of hospital departments as related to patient transfers
- inpatient discharges and the role of the admitting department
- inpatient deaths and the role of the admitting department
- discharge planning and the role of the admitting department
- unique identification of each patient (i.e., patient identification armbands)
- unit number and/or account number (how they relate)

IMPLEMENTATION

Training is the key to implementing changes, additions, or a complete new policy and procedure manual for the admitting department. It is important to notify all personnel of any changes or additions that will affect them or their work routine. A general staff meeting or training session may be the approach to take, if feasible, to present the manual. The advantage to this is that all personnel can be given the same information and instructions at the same time, thus avoiding conflicting or erroneous information.

It is important in the training process that all personnel be made aware as to why the new policies and procedures are necessary. If the staff members have the background to the new additions and changes, they will more likely understand the importance of the changes and the consequences that may occur if the policies and procedures are not followed. Unless policies and procedures are followed, why have them?

ASSESSMENT

In order to determine the effectiveness of the policies and procedures, an on-going assessment process should take place. The astute manager should consistently check to ensure that the policies and procedures are being followed and are meeting the needs, goals, and objectives of the department and the hospital.

One method for determining the effectiveness of departmental policies and procedures is to ask the staff. This will give the manager some idea as to how the policies and procedures are working for those who must use them. Are the procedures clear and easy to follow? Are they meeting the needs of those who use them on a daily basis? Is the information contained in the procedures adequate to complete the particular task?

Another method for checking the effectiveness of the policies and procedures is to audit work that is produced in the admitting department. Is it consistent from employee to employee? Are there major differences between the approach used to interview patients by the admission staff? How does the personnel in the physician's office view the admitting department? When stating departmental policy and procedure to other departments and physicians and their staff, does the department appear organized and consistent? These methods for evaluating and assessing the department policy and procedure manual will afford valuable information concerning the efficient and effective flow of work in the admitting department. By the continuous monitoring of the quality of work that is produced, the admitting manager will be able to locate potential problem areas before they become major headaches.

CONCLUSION

No longer is a policy and procedure manual a luxury for the admitting manager—it is a necessity. A complete and workable policy and procedure manual can be a very important tool in the management function for the admitting manager. The admitting staff will come to depend on the information in the manual. What is important is to make the manual work for the department.

Chapter 10

Financial Aspects of Admitting

Betty Powell

The hospital admitting department has since its beginning been like a child born out of wedlock. It was or was not the child of the medical records department; it was or was not the child of the financial services department. It was, in fact, and is to this day a department serving a very useful function, which must know a little about a lot of things from business (i.e., financial aspects, statistical record keeping, data processing) to medical (i.e., diagnosis, treatment, isolation procedures, estimated length of stay) but continues to fall into its appointed place in the organizational charts, across town or across the nation in various places, as diversified as the physical appearance of the institutions. Because of this difference the total responsibility of the admitting department becomes distinct to its particular institution.

A conversation in a hospital personnel office went like this:

"I'm not sure which position I would fit into; could you tell me something about them?"

"There are openings in medical records, admitting, business office . . ."

"What does the admitting department do?"

"Oh, they find beds for patients."

In today's admitting department, patient placement combined with bed control is only one part of a complex system. Some admitting department managers have responsibility for the outpatient and emergency department admissions as well as the hospital's communications system and the information desk, while others have only a few of those responsibilities. The one thing that admitting managers are responsible for, whether or not it is in their job description, is the financial ingredient that is becoming inherently important in today's admissions office.

ADMITTING: A COMPLEX DEPARTMENT

The Five Divisions

Patient registration is the name of the various combined departments. Its decentralized registration locations are referred to as outpatient registration, inpatient registration, and emergency department patient registration. This department consists of five divisions of expertise:

1. preadmissions/insurance verification
2. scheduling/reservations
3. bed control/patient placement
4. patient registration
5. patient transportation

The individual functions of each of these divisions contribute to the total efficiency of the department, which subsequently contributes to the total efficiency of the hospital.

Preadmissions/Insurance Verification

The preadmissions/insurance verification division contributes by constantly striving to meet a goal of 100 percent preadmissions for all elective inpatients and scheduled outpatients each day. Insurance is verified with the individual insurance company or the industrial firm as a portion of the preadmission procedure, and patients are notified of deposit requirements, or of inadequate or insufficient insurance, prior to the day of admission. The preadmissions/insurance verification personnel have become experts in third party reimbursement. They know and comply with all requirements for reimbursement.

Scheduling/Reservations

The scheduling/reservations division contributes by operating a very effective central scheduling area where all but a few outpatient procedures are scheduled as well as inpatient reservations are taken. This most welcome system to busy physicians and their office staffs avails a multiple scheduling/reservations service by dialing *one* telephone number. The personnel in this area also have become experts in third party payer requirements.

Bed Control/Patient Placement

The bed control/patient placement division makes its contribution to departmental effectiveness by a very efficient method of *total* bed control. Once again, physicians or their office staff make one telephone call to request a bed in the intensive care, coronary care, transitional care, or neuroscience units, as well as any medical/surgical acute care bed because all of the beds are controlled entirely in one central area. The proper placement of patients contributes to the overall efficiency of the hospital. With specialty units and the geographic location of patients, the length of stay may be shortened considerably by placing patients in the proper specialty units. Because it is a point at which patients enter the system, bed control/patient placement must also exercise a special expertise in the third party payer requirements.

Patient Registration

The patient registrars' contribution is equally important because these are the individuals who help the patients and/or their family members make the transition from normal routine to hospital patient as easy and uncomplicated as possible. The registrar completes the registration process with information required by the hospital to meet all internal and external governing regulations, gets consent and financial responsibility documents signed, and explains hospital policy and routine. The personnel in the patient registrar division must have a good working knowledge of third party payer requirements but may rely on the expertise of bed control or insurance verification.

Patient Transportation

The patient transportation division contains a patient assessment section where patients are given an initial nursing assessment and priority is established for their registration, orders are initiated, and patients are transported to the ancillary departments and/or to the nursing units. Patients transported externally for specific treatments or tests and a courier service for sending specimens and reporting results are all included in patient transportation.

Of the above-listed division personnel, approximately 85% of these employees are cross trained to work in at least four of the five divisions. Some perform in five of five divisions effectively. Figure 10–1 is an organizational chart for this patient registration department.

It may be of special interest to acknowledge the fact that the hospital vice president, to whom the patient registration department reports, also has responsibility for nursing service activities. The financial services department reports to another vice president.

Figure 10–1 Organization Chart for Patient Registration Department

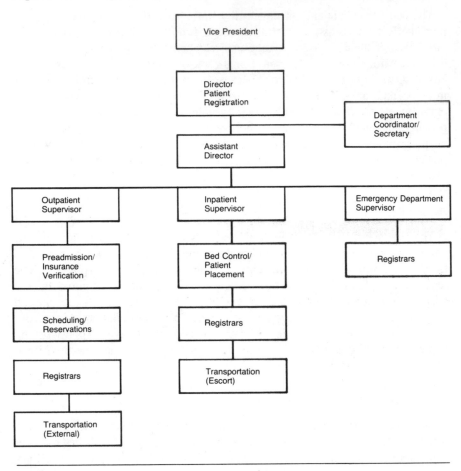

OBTAINING FINANCIAL INFORMATION

Securing Hospital's Financial Stability

Securing the financial stability of the hospital should be a major objective of the hospital admitting department regardless of its aligned position on the organizational chart. Because of the natural access to all points where patients are entered into the system, the admitting department has an opportunity to exercise control over this entry and work as an extension of the financial services department to determine in advance of, or at the time of admission, whether the hospital will be reimbursed and how it will be reimbursed.

An automated admissions system makes the task much easier, and the dependability on the human element of third party payer expertise is lessened; however, although a manual system does not prohibit the system from being effective, it may require more time to make manual references.

Monitoring Reimbursement

The admitting office takes the "edge" by monitoring reimbursement at points of entry as follows:

The reservation or scheduling operation working in conjunction with and in close physical proximity to the preadmissions section should always, when taking a bed reservation, request "type of insurance" along with other pertinent data. This enables the reservation clerk to help physicians or their office staff determine, for example, whether a prior authorization number is needed, whether a second opinion should be considered, or whether this particular case should be handled on an outpatient basis.

When reservation information is passed along and the preadmission registrar contacts the patient, sometimes information totally different from that received from the physician or staff begins to surface. If at this time it is discovered that the third party payer falls into a category that needs special attention, it is then returned to the reservation clerk to be referred to the admitting physician's office for follow-up.

The bed control/patient placement area, which is a point of entry for emergency or same day admissions, also requires a third party reimbursement expert in attendance or accessible because timing is so important in this area. Special attention must be given to the reimbursement method of patients transferring from other hospitals. Sometimes patients who have been taken from an accident scene to the city or county hospital prefer for one reason or another to be in a different hospital. These cases should be considered individually and carefully.

Personnel at other points of entry (i.e., outpatient, inpatient, and emergency department registrars) monitor all reimbursement methods and refer any that are questionable.

Maximizing Available Resources

Using all available resources to the maximum is a major stride toward achieving a goal based on the financial stability of the institution.

Preadmissions is the means by which patients can be expedited through the admission process, or at least this was the "necessity" for which preadmissions was "invented." Since that day preadmissions has helped to spread the workload to facilitate more effective staffing. When used to its maximum, preadmissions can also be a good foundation on which to build strong financial security. In these times when hospital census is down across the nation, it is even more important to be sure that the beds that are occupied are not *all* filled with patients who already have open accounts, bad debts, and/or no visible means of resolving a financial obligation to the hospital.

Drafting a Preadmission Questionnaire

The preadmission questionnaire can be whatever one wants it to be. It is not a legal document nor a part of the medical record, nor is it a part of the financial record. It is a basis from which information is taken to complete these two documents. It can contain information other ancillary departments require for home health agencies, nursing home placement, pulling old medical records, marketing, completing uniform billing (UB-82) forms, checking open accounts, bad debts, and so on.

Developing a preadmission questionnaire should be a joint effort between the admitting department and any other hospital department that needs information on preadmission. A memorandum sent to all department managers requesting input may start the thinking process, and a follow-up meeting of those who may have questions to include will probably prove the importance of this one document. Chances are that one question will serve more than one department. For example, smoking/nonsmoking accommodations is a question relevant to patient placement and respiratory therapy.

Although meetings with ancillary departments are taking place, meetings with just the financial services department for their input are valuable. As a result of these meetings, the questionnaire can be drafted.

Drafting the questionnaire to match the admission form or summary sheet is never good advice unless the information on the summary sheet is separated into sections where questions are relative. It is much easier to teach the preadmission registrar to "pick" the information from a questionnaire than to have a bewildered patient never complete the form because it is too confusing.

Clarifying Given Information

Interviewing patients can be difficult because of the stress and/or anxiety level at admission time.

For example, in order to get all the information onto an admission set and for certain information to be contained in special sections, the questions on an admission set went like this: "last name, first, middle," "room number," "patient type," "hospital service," and so on, and at the end of the first line of questions was "father's name." The second line of questions began with "address" in order to keep the name together with the address in a special section of the summary sheet. The registrar is going through the routine questions and gets to "father's name." The patient is an adult and answers "deceased." The registrar shows concern, apologizes, but still requests "father's name" for means of identifying medical records. The name is given and the registrar moves on to "address." The patient then started giving an address that seemed strange to the registrar who is trying now to clear up this problem, only to discover the patient is giving a name and plot number of a local cemetery where the father is buried. For this reason preadmission questionnaires should be well thought out and as simple and uncomplicated as possible.

Verifying Reimbursement

The best time to verify the means of reimbursement is at the time the preadmission is completed. This can be done in the admitting department or the business office, but timing is important. Many persons do not know their insurance coverage; most know the name of the insurance company but do not understand preexisting clauses, deductibles, or coinsurance, for example. Therefore the hospital should have someone to act as an interpreter (especially in cases where there is a potential problem) and explain insurance coverage to the patient before admission, if at all possible while there may be other options. Patients with nine months' preexisting clauses anticipating elective surgery can reschedule the surgery after the preexisting time period is satisfied.

Ignoring these situations at admissions time only causes problems when patients check out of the hospital and discover that their insurance will not pay and they are now solely responsible for the entire bill. This is quite a surprise to them, and certainly no endearment takes place between the patient and the hospital.

Having enough time to get the money together for patients who must make deposits or partial deposits is another good reason for verifying reimbursement at the time a patient is preadmitted. If time permits, a letter explaining the hospital's deposit requirements and the amount of deposit for this type of hospitalization should be sent to the patient.

Workers' compensation and/or liability cases are sometimes in litigation and can be tied up for months or years. It is good to know about these situations as soon after the reservation is taken as possible so patients can be preadmitted and referred to the financial services department for its involvement.

Priorities should be set with obtaining preadmission information and subsequent verification of reimbursement. Medicare or Medicaid with prior authorization could go into a lower priority while workers' compensation and liability reimbursed admissions would take a high priority. In some instances certain diagnoses (such as those indicating cosmetic surgery) should also be prioritized.

Checking Open Accounts and Bad Debts

Another potential of the preadmission is the ability to check open accounts or bad debts prior to admission time. Many patients repeatedly use the same hospital. Some institutions have a repeat rate of 50 percent or higher. With a repeat rate of 45 to 50 percent someone should be checking open accounts and bad debts on preadmission. It is much easier for the financial counselor to speak to potential patients or their representatives about the account and make arrangements for payment.

Seeking Help from Financial Counselor

This same procedure, which is followed by most hospitals in this area, is very successful in collecting open accounts or bad debts that have been deemed "uncollectible." The procedure works like this: When the patient is preadmitted the insurance is verified and bad debt/open accounts are checked. If the patient does not have adequate insurance and an open account or bad debt, the financial counselor begins immediately to work the account. If there is insurance and the coverage is good for this hospitalization, the financial counselor contacts the patient and discusses the previous account and makes arrangements for the patient to pay the account before or at admission time. A note to the registrar to collect the money and write a receipt at admission time is attached to the preadmission information.

Patients are much more cooperative in these matters before they reenter the hospital. Once they are in the hospital they do not feel well enough to talk about finances, and when they are discharged, previous financial patterns begin their cycle once again.

THE FINANCE DEPARTMENT'S VIEW OF ADMITTING

The hospital financial services department often views the admitting department with a critical eye. Spending hours, sometimes, trying to bill insurance or collect bills with incomplete or erroneous information creates an impression that the admitting department is not doing its job well.

Identify Billing Problems

To counteract this impression the admitting department needs to really work to improve this image. A meeting with the business office manager to identify the problems and an assurance that the problems will be addressed with a timetable set up for resolving them will immediately start to improve a bad image.

Understand Billing Problems

A major step toward improvement is communication. Communication is the key to many successful attempts to make departments feel differently about one another. Admitting registrars have little to no idea how a hospital bill is recovered unless they have worked for a time in insurance billing; by the same token, the insurance biller has probably never thought about a patient showing up at the emergency department registration desk without an insurance identification card complete with mailing address. It is very obvious now that there is a link missing in the communication chain. A few hours each day for several days exchanging jobs, or just observing, is one recommendation. Observing in the cashier's office, insurance billing, and credit/collections during orientation is a valuable experience for a new employee. ''Walking a mile'' in another employee's shoes seems to get the message across nicely, as well as building rapport with co-workers in the other department.

Share Billing Information

Another means of communication is a very simple one that is, in fact, so elementary that we forget it exists. Leave a note. Employees should always be encouraged to write notes to each other attached to the billing office copy of the admission set. If insurance information is not available or is scant, leave a note, ''Patient lost insurance ID card'' or ''Patient does not know insurance company's mailing address because he pays premium to Mr. John Doe, agent. No further information.'' This simple task removes the impression that the admitting registrar is not thorough or produces slipshod work.

Registrars should understand the importance of getting complete billing information. One way to understand this is to have admitting registrars think how they would bill the insurance on every registration they process, if they were walking in the insurance biller's shoes.

Photocopy Billing Information

Photocopying all insurance cards (front and back) and then attaching the copies to the business office copy of the admission set is an excellent way to improve relations. A small photocopier in the admitting department will pay for itself in a few months from the time and money saved in insurance billing.

Secure Billing Information

The second notification, or name and telephone number of a relative or neighbor not living at the patient's address, is vital for emergency notification as well as for skip tracing a bad debt. Patients sometimes are reluctant to give more than one telephone number for emergency information, or some think they are only having a minor procedure and no emergency will arise. The admitting registrar may suggest perhaps that the first emergency notification may not be at home or that telephone service sometimes goes out of order: "If we just had the name and telephone number of your neighbor so we could tell them that we're trying to locate your wife."

If the patient still refuses, this should be referred to someone who can watch for the type of reimbursement and the probability of it paying 100 percent, then *write a note*.

Maintain Good Relationship with Billing

The way to build a good relationship with financial services is to work constantly at doing an exceptional job "up front." There is no rule written that the line is drawn and that each department goes halfway and no further. If the admitting image is to be changed in the eyes of the financial services department, the line must be crossed a little.

GUARANTOR: WHO IS RESPONSIBLE?

A guarantor is one who gives a guarantee. Who is responsible? In some states the husband is responsible for the wife's debts; in others, the wife is responsible for the husband's. In most cases if the patient is an employed adult with group insurance, then he or she becomes the responsible party and gives the hospital a guarantee that the account will be paid. If for some reason the insurance company does not pay the hospital within a specified time, then the hospital can look to the guarantor for payment.

Insured Parties

It is important to remember that workers' compensation and personal liability admissions should also list the patient or agent as the guarantor and that a signature on the contract with the hospital as the responsible party is required. In this case the guarantor is giving a guarantee that he or she will be responsible for an obligation in the event of default.

Responsible Party

The responsible party or guarantor on the admission summary (face) sheet should be the same (if at all possible) as the person who signs for financial responsibility. If for some reason this is not possible, the name, address, and telephone number of the person who does sign for responsibility should be included in the business office copy.

Single Custody

In cases in which children are being hospitalized and the parents are divorced, the parent who has custody of the child must sign the consent for treatment. The other parent may be responsible for the child's medical bills. In this case that parent should sign for responsibility or guarantee payment. One parent may insist the registrar locate the other parent for financial information and signatures for responsibility. This is not the registrar's responsibility, and as gracefully as possible, the parent should be informed that this is between the two parents and the hospital will not get involved.

Working Spouses

Third party payers will dictate through coordination of benefits who is responsible in other cases such as when a husband and wife both work and both carry family insurance coverage. Normally the patient's insurance pays first and the spouse's second. In the case of a child, some insurance companies use the father's first and the mother's second; others are reversed. What is important is for the admitting registrars to get correct information so that the billing process will not be delayed following dismissal.

Uniform Billing

Uniform billing (UB-82) was pioneered in Kentucky, Indiana, and Ohio, and it will be nationwide by 1986. This is a compilation of questions that are normally answered by the patient to complete the insurance assignment or coordination of benefits form. Because of the numbers of questions that the insurance companies require, it has become quite lengthy. Most hospitals have had to add from one to three computer screens in order to obtain all the information required. Most of the information can be retrieved by preadmissions to speed up admission time.

Third party payers will not accept this form without complete accident information, physicians' license numbers, and complete mailing address of insurance company.

This detailed form needs good planning before implementation. Once the "bugs" are worked out, UB-82 will prove beneficial to the hospital financially because prompt reimbursement can be expected from all third party payers.

THIRD PARTY PROVIDERS

All through this chapter third party reimbursement has been discussed along with the importance of having experts in various areas throughout the department who are able to monitor admissions and be of assistance to physicians and their office staff sharing this expertise to secure reimbursement for the hospital and the physician. Now those who provide the reimbursement will be discussed.

Medicare/Medicaid

Medicare in many states along with diagnostic related groups (DRGs) now requires a prior authorization number on all elective patients and concurrent review on all emergency and urgent admissions. What this means to admitting is that the physician or his or her representative (who can be an office staff member) has to contact the peer review organization (PRO) health care coordinator when a decision is made to admit a patient to the hospital. Several basic questions must be answered concerning the admission diagnosis and plan for treatment. If the health care coordinator approves the admission, an authorization number is given; if the admission is not approved, the physician may appeal to a physician advisor. When the registration is called in to the scheduling/reservation clerk, the physician's office gives the type of insurance as Medicare. The reservation clerk automatically requests the authorization number. With very few exceptions, reservations should not be taken without an authorization number. Those exceptions should be "flagged" so the reservation can be cancelled if the authorization number is not called in before admission day. If the authorization number does not accompany the admission, the hospital is at risk for reimbursement, or in very simple language, Medicare will not pay the bill. When patients are admitted as urgent or emergency admissions, the hospital-based health care coordinator reviews the admission to determine if the hospitalization is necessary and if indeed it is a legitimate emergency or urgent admission; if either one of these is adversely determined, the hospital again is at risk.

It is smart to have a medical professional in the admitting office to monitor these emergency and urgent admissions and to advise physicians what would or would not be acceptable as an emergency admission by the health care coordinator.

Medicaid is the medical assistance program offered through the social and rehabilitation services in the various states. Many of its regulations vary from state to state, and it is wise to know those of a particular state when working in that state. Many hospitals have a Medicaid clerk who is knowledgeable in these facts. It is important to the hospital that the incoming patient presents a current Medicaid card on admission.

Medicare and Medicaid both require prior authorization numbers and second opinions on certain surgical procedures. Outpatient services are mandatory for certain surgical and medical procedures and/or tests. Medicaid pays a per diem rate, and the length of stay is limited. Should patients require longer periods of hospitalization, the hospital is at risk for reimbursement.

Blue Cross

Blue Cross plans are as varied as the product or service of the corporation that is the company group. Some Blue Cross plans use the same guidelines as Medicare/Medicaid (i.e., mandatory outpatient services for certain procedures or tests, second opinions, and prior authorization). Some plans require preadmission testing, and the requirements are changing daily. Large company groups are changing benefits as contracts are negotiated for their hourly employees. Salaried employee benefits are changing sooner because they are nonunion. Many companies will have two or more plans for hourly, salaried, and management personnel. The differentiation is sometimes only identified by an employee number.

Champus/Champva

Champus and Champva, never to be confused with each other, are acronyms for Civilian Health and Medical Program for the Uniformed Services and Civilian Health and Medical Program for the Veterans Administration. Those eligible for Champus are dependents of active or retired military service persons.

Patients presenting themselves for admission who will be using Champus as their third party payer must present a nonavailability form at the time of admission or Champus will not pay. The nonavailability form is required when the patient lives within certain proximity of a military hospital and the services are either not available or the occupancy at that institution will not allow the patient to be hospitalized at that particular time.

Champva covers dependents of veterans who are totally or permanently disabled as a result of a service-connected injury, who died as the result of a service connected injury, or who died in the line of duty in the active military.

The Champus form is used to bill both Champus and Champva.

Commercial Insurance

Commercial insurance is the collective name of all insurances that are not Medicare, Medicaid, and Blue Cross. Some commercial insurances are Travelers, Aetna, and Metropolitan. Commercial insurances like Blue Cross vary in benefits according to the group plan. Some have fallen in line with Medicare and require prior authorization numbers, second opinions, and mandatory outpatient services. At one point commercial insurances seemed to be overshadowed by Blue Cross, but many have through reputation excelled and surpassed the stigma.

Workers' Compensation

Workers' compensation is the third party reimbursement for the patient who comes into the emergency department for stitches or radiographs, for the patient with major traumatic injuries, or for the patient having elective surgery or treatments. In all cases it is wise to contact the employer for verification of compensation. In the case of the elective admission, the admitting department may require the patient to bring written verification. This saves the insurance verification personnel's time. A signed document is much better than a telephone conversation. Sometimes workers' compensation will be in litigation. These cases must always be referred to the financial counselor immediately because the finance department may require a deposit or a statement from the patient's attorney. These cases should be handled individually.

Personal Liability

Personal liability is used so many times today as the primary insurance (the insurance that pays first). Medicare, Medicaid, Blue Cross, and certain commercial insurances require liability insurance such as automobile no-fault insurance to pay first and then they act as a co-insurance. It is advisable to ask every patient if the condition results from an accident or injury. It is important to remember that an accident is an unexpected and undesirable event when asking the question and to assist the patient in making this determination after hearing the events that lead to the hospitalization. Next the patient's explanation of the accident is entered on the business office copy of the admission set for billing purposes. The terminology used when entering information should not be biased: "Patient felt sharp pain in back when lifting refrigerator while helping neighbor move," not "Neighbor demanded patient move refrigerator full of beer causing dislocated disk."

It is important to remember that most liability insurances have a maximum. If patients present for admission with liability insurance only, it is wise to check the maximum amount and whether or not the patient has been hospitalized at another time, has transferred from another facility, or has expenses that have already been incurred. Do not forget the physicians' bills.

Direct Pay Insurances

Numerous insurances that are widely advertised on television, in newspapers, and through the mail only pay the patient, not the hospital, even though an assignment of benefits to the hospital has been signed.

Preferred Provider Organizations

Preferred provider organizations (PPOs) are cropping up all over the nation and are varied in reimbursement.

A hospital and a large company enter into an agreement whereby the company requires all its employees to be hospitalized in one hospital, and because of the volume, the hospital gives that company a discount on services. Sometimes employees are confused by all this and either go to another hospital by mistake or by preference. These patients need to be aware that if they are not being hospitalized in the employer's PPO it will cost them "out of pocket" expense usually never less than $200 and the range could go to $1,000 or higher.

Health Maintenance Organizations

Health maintenance organizations (HMOs) began years ago. Some of the more famous are the Kaiser Institutes in California. HMOs are becoming more prevalent across the nation, and as their name implies, they practice preventive medicine. Certain hospitals are designated HMO facilities, and patients presenting themselves for admission must have prior authorization or the hospital will once again be at risk for reimbursement. The only exception to this rule is emergency or trauma situations when authorization is requested by emergency department registrars.

OBLIGATIONS AND REFERRALS

The Hill-Burton Act

Hill-Burton funds are available at hospitals that used Hill-Burton funding in their building projects. These funds are available to patients who meet certain income guidelines. Hill-Burton funds may be started and stopped by the month or the year. At the time the funds are stopped, however, a notice must be posted stating the hospital's Hill-Burton obligation has been fulfilled for the month or the year.

Charitable Organizations

Local, state, and national agencies are available for assisting patients with reimbursement. A few of these are the State Vocational Rehabilitation Agency, the Lions Club, Crippled Children's Agency, and the Shriners. A list of these agencies and their locations, as well as guidelines, is available in hospital social service departments.

CONCLUSION

The admitting clerk of 30 years ago was just that—a clerk typist, operating the switchboard, the posting machine, and the front door (after hours on a buzzer system). This employee was also the information desk clerk and the cashier. A former clerk once said she wore out four pairs of rollers on her chair in one year moving from desk to desk to cover all the duties.

Patient summary sheets required little more than name and address, but that was before Medicare, Medicaid, and prior authorization numbers. In fact, the third party payers numbered in the single digits and insurance billing was no problem. As long as they could afford it, new mothers could stay an extra day to rest before returning home to family and household chores. Some patients even became permanent residents by their own choice; that was before DRGs. Government regulations had not yet crept into hospital business affairs.

With the advent of automated systems, UB-82, DRGs, Medicare, Medicaid, and ever-changing third party payer regulations, the admitting clerk of 30 years ago has from necessity become a professional. The admitting department has evolved into an integral part of the hospital with responsibilities that touch and overlap those of other departments with no regard for the appointed place on the organizational chart.

Admitting managers have the edge because of an inherent ability to keep a finger on the financial pulse beat of the hospital.

Chapter 11

Legal Aspects of Admitting

James M. Perez

The admissions and registration department of a hospital plays a vital role in developing a certain bond and trust between the patient and the health care team. However, in recent years, that bond and trust has diminished with increased technology and costs. Admission personnel must now deal not only with patients who are emotionally and physically upset but also with individuals who are aware of their rights and what is expected of those who provide health care and services.

The information presented here can be used to assist the admitting professional in understanding how the law impacts in admitting and how one can be better prepared to handle daily situations that may have potential legal actions. This chapter is not intended to be an official legal handbook nor a substitute for legal counsel when the need arises.

Court decisions and laws at different levels of the government are made every days. Therefore, it would not only be difficult to keep abreast of all the changes but also what impact a new law may have in a particular state or region. The basic definition of law and what impact it has on health care will be reviewed first. The admission record and its legal application will be covered along with what patient information should be released. The types of consents used in hospitals and which one is generally used in the admitting department will also be discussed. The role of admitting in the proper disposal of a body after death along with the safekeeping of patient valuables will be examined. Finally, eligibility of patients into the hospital will be considered.

BASIC ELEMENTS OF LAW

The System of Law

In order to review the legal aspects of admissions, one must have a general understanding of what the law is by definition and how it affects health care professionals.

The law is a system in which general rules of conduct are established and enforced by a society. It is a way in which two parties can resolve a dispute without force. Because it is a human system, the law is ever changing. Issues are being challenged in today's court that have no precedence.

The Variety of Law

Laws that are found at various levels of the government, whether they be federal, state, county, or municipal, may be classified as either private or public. Private law deals with the relationship between two individuals or parties. Public law governs the relationship between a private party or individual and a government no matter at what level. It is not important here to determine how the two differ but that the law is divided into two categories, which at times are interwoven.

Because each state issues statutes (laws enacted by Congress) according to their area, laws will vary from one part of the country to the next. Court decisions based on these laws vary or may not have an impact on other states. A California law regarding the disclosure of patient information may be different from the one that is enacted in Kansas.

The Health Care of Law

Most suits brought against the hospital and their staff fall into the area of private law. The most common actions under private law that have an impact on health care professionals are tort and contract. A tort action asserts that there is a wrongful act against a person or party in which compensation is sought. A tort may fall into one of two categories, intentional and negligence. An intentional tort is, as the name indicates, an intended wrongful act. This action includes assault and battery, defamation, false imprisonment, invasion of privacy, and intentional infliction of emotional distress. A negligence tort is committed when a wrongful act is a result of negligence or failure to exercise due care.

The Landmark Case of Hospital Law

A majority of today's malpractice suits are based on negligence. A landmark decision that had an impact on hospital liability for negligence was the case of *Darling v. Charleston Community Memorial Hospital*.[1] In this case an 18-year-old football player was injured during a game and taken to a community hospital emergency department. A physician, who was a general practitioner, was on duty at the time. Radiographs were taken of the leg, which revealed a fractured tibia and fibula. The physician treated the fracture and applied a cast from the patient's groin to the toe. Shortly thereafter, the patient was admitted to the hospital where the general practitioner continued his care. The patient continued to complain about his pain to the physician and nursing personnel. After two weeks, the patient was then transferred to a larger hospital where he came under the care of an orthopedic physician. The specialist soon discovered dead tissue in the fracture. After two months of trying to save the leg, the specialist then had to amputate the leg below the knee.

The father then sued the general practitioner and the community hospital. A decision against the defendants was reached by a jury, using as evidence documents outlining the standard of care, Joint Commission on Accreditation of Hospitals (JCAH), and the by-laws and regulations of Charleston Community Memorial Hospital. As a result of the case, hospitals no longer enjoyed charitable immunity from lawsuits as they had since 1876. Now, under what is known as the doctrine of respondeat superior, a hospital as an employer is held liable for the negligence of its employees whether they be admissions staff or nursing personnel.

ADMITTING FORMS AS LEGAL DOCUMENTS

The Admitting Form As Part of the Medical Record

The admitting form, as a rule, contains a patient's personal and financial information. The data collected are generally the demographics of the patient, the reason for admission, what physician is admitting the patient, the person to notify in case of an emergency, and enough employment and insurance information for billing purposes.

The admitting form becomes part of the medical record, which is used to document the care and treatment of a patient. The JCAH highly endorses a standard that a medical record should be initiated and maintained for every person who is treated within a hospital: "An adequate medical record shall be maintained for every individual who is evaluated or treated as an inpatient, ambulatory care patient, or emergency patient, or who receives patient services in a hospital-administered home care program."[2]

The Medical Record As Evidence

A medical record is generally admissible as evidence in a court of law. Therefore, it is essential that every medical record, which includes the admitting form, be accurate, complete, and updated when applicable. Failure to do so may have an adverse impact on any suits brought against the hospital. In *Hiatt v. Groce*,[3] a young woman was admitted to Bethany Hospital to give birth to her second child. The medical record showed that a physician who happened to walk by was called on to deliver the baby. Evidence that was entered into the trial revealed that the nurse was the actual person who delivered the child, a clear discrepancy between what really happened and what was recorded. Therefore, if one part of the record was in error, then the whole record could be considered invalid.

Errors and Formats

Because the admitting department is the initiator of the medical record by generating the admission form, it is important that when training appropriate personnel, emphasis be placed on an error-free form. A misspelling of a diagnosis or the name of the patient may undermine the accuracy of the medical record, thereby questioning its validity if it were ever entered as evidence in a court of law. Also, policies and procedures should exist on the methods of correcting errors and who is eligible to correct errors on the admitting form.

The format of an admitting form is generally based on the needs of the hospital. The content or information required may vary according to the hospital licensing regulations established in each state. Hospitals that are involved with federal reimbursement programs must meet the following minimum requirements for standard contents[4]:

> The medical record contains sufficient information to justify the diag-
> nosis and warrant the treatment and end results. The medical record
> contains the following information: identification data; chief complaint;
> present illness; past history; family history; physical examination; pro-
> visional diagnosis; clinical laboratory reports; x-ray reports; consulta-
> tions; treatment, medical and surgical; tissue report; progress notes;
> final diagnosis; discharge summary; autopsy findings.

RELEASE OF PATIENT INFORMATION

Information As Property

Since the beginning of medicine, there has been an ongoing struggle between what information should or should not be released. Because of this, it is important that hospitals establish a policy regarding the release of patient information.

A basic guideline to follow in the admitting department is that all records are the property of the hospital and the information from the same may not be released without proper authorization by the patient and/or the courts. However, in cases like drug and alcohol abuse patients, there are strict federal regulations that must be adhered to by the hospitals. Under the Public Health Code of Federal Regulations (vol. 42, part 2), it is outlined that no information may be released about the treatment of a drug or alcohol abuse patient unless the patient signs a specific consent as outlined in the regulations. The generic release of information form that is generally signed at the time of admission is considered insufficient for the release.

Because we now live in a world of electronic communication, admitting departments with computer terminals must have procedures for access to patient information as well as security clearance. Today, computers give us the capability of storing and immediate retrieval of files on patients, physicians, and employees of a hospital. Access and misuse of the information from these files could have potential legal actions.

Related Legal Action

The two possible areas of tort action that would involve the improper release or use of patient information by an admitting staff member may be defamation of character and invasion of privacy. Defamation is defined as a written or oral communication to a third party with the intention of bringing harm to a person's reputation,[5] and in this case, the patient's reputation. Written communication under defamation is known as libel, while the oral form of this tort is known as slander. No proof of damage is needed for a libel action suit. However, in the case of slander, damages must be proven by the person who is filing the suit. Although cases involving defamation of character are difficult to prove in a court of law, it must be noted that they exist. The unauthorized release of information that was intended to cause harm is the underlying theme for a defamation action suit against a hospital and its employees.

The Disclosure of Information

The invasion of privacy is defined as a wrong that invades the right of a person to personal privacy.[6] Admitting personnel who orally disclose information on patients who request no release of information may be subject to this tort action. A person's right of privacy is recognized by the law. Hospitals and their employees must be aware that they are held liable if they intrude or allow others to invade one's privacy. Therefore, it is vital that admitting personnel be trained in the proper procedures for releasing patient information. In general, an admitting department may release the patient's name, room number, and telephone, if available, to visitors. Requests for additional information on a patient should be reviewed by one department, preferably medical records.

Admitting personnel must be trained on how to handle news media's request for information on VIPs, prisoners, or individuals who wish to classify their information. By following protocol in dealing with the media, this will ensure that pertinent parties' information will not be released with resultant potential legal action. Generally, the hospital should designate a spokesperson to work with the press in providing information about a patient. Also, any detailed questions about the condition of the patient should be answered by the physician with the consent of the patient or family.

THE MATTER OF CONSENTS

The Reason for Consents

It is a standard procedure that a health care provider obtain a patient's consent before any examination or treatment is performed, unless it is an emergency. The principal reason is that any intentional touching of the patient without the patient's consent constitutes tort action of assault and battery even if no harm comes to the patient. Once the wrongful act has been committed, the patient then has the opportunity to sue for damages.

Types of Consent Forms

In order to protect themselves, a majority of hospitals have been advised to use two separate consent forms for all inpatients. The first is a general consent form that is obtained at the time the patient enters the hospital, and a second is a specific consent form to be used when surgery or a special diagnostic procedure is performed.

The general consent form should be in simple language that is easily understood by the patient. It should state the patient's consent to all routine radiographic examinations, laboratory procedures, and treatments as ordered by the attending physician. Furthermore, it should outline the hospital's relationship with the physician (independent contractor or employee of the hospital) and describe the nursing care provided. Because the practice of medicine is not an exact science, the general consent form should also recite that there are no guarantees as to the results from the patient's care and treatment at the hospital.

Along with the general consent for treatment, it is advisable to include the hospital's policy on personal valuables, release of information, and the agreement to pay for services. A typical admission consent form is seen in Exhibit 11–1.

The Responsibility of Admitting

Admitting personnel, because of their position with the hospital, are held accountable for explaining the general consent (condition) of admissions as well as obtaining the proper signatures at the time of admission. If a special procedure or

Exhibit 11–1 Admission Consent Form

Admission Record

GENERAL CONDITIONS OF ADMISSION

1. CONSENT: The undersigned consents to x-ray examinations, laboratory procedures, anesthesia, medical or surgery treatment, or other hospital services rendered the patient under general and special instructions of the attending physician or consulting physician. The patient is under the control of his attending physicians, their assistants or designees, who are in charge of the care and treatment of the patient. The Hospital is not responsible for acts of care and treatment ordered by the physician which are properly performed pursuant to his instructions. The undersigned understands that all doctors furnishing services to the patient, including the radiologist, pathologist, anesthesiologist, and the like, are independent contractors and are not employees or agents of the Hospital. The undersigned further acknowledges that the patient's admission and discharge are arranged by the attending physician and that the patient is obligated to leave the Hospital upon his release by his physician.

2. GENERAL DUTY NURSING: The Hospital provides general duty nursing care. Under this system nurses are called to the bedside of the patient by a signal system. If the patient is in such condition as to need continuous or special duty nursing care, it is agreed that such must be arranged by the patient, or his legal representative, or his physicians, and the Hospital shall in no way be responsible to provide such care.

3. HOSPITAL SERVICES: The undersigned recognizes that the practice of medicine and surgery is not an exact science, and acknowledges that no guarantees have been made as to the results which may be obtained from hospital care and treatment and the rendition of medical services by the attending physician.

4. PERSONAL VALUABLES: It is understood and agreed that the hospital maintains a safety deposit box area for the safekeeping of money and valuables. Valuables must not be kept in your room. They must either be sent home promptly upon your admission to the hospital or they must be placed in the safety deposit box area for safekeeping. Such articles include, but are not limited to, money, jewelry, rings, glasses, documents, furs, fur coats and garments, radios, or other articles of value. The hospital shall not be liable for loss or damage to any of your personal property and cannot guarantee you against loss of such valuables. If you place them in the safety deposit area, we can provide you some protection in accordance with an agreement and receipt for the storage of personal property which will be signed by you. The hospital also provides denture cups for use by patients requiring them. Please take special precautions to be sure your dentures are properly kept and cared for and keep them in the denture cup at all times when you are not using them. The hospital cannot and will not accept responsibility for their loss.

5. RELEASE OF INFORMATION: It is agreed that all records concerning the patient's hospitalization remain the property of the Hospital. The Hospital, pursuant to proper authorization or court order, may disclose all or any part of the patient's record to any person or corporation which is or may be liable to the Hospital, to the patient, or to a family member or employer of the patient for all or part of the Hospital charges.

6. ASSIGNMENT OF INSURANCE BENEFITS: In the event the patient or the undersigned is entitled to benefits arising out of any policy of insurance insuring the patient, those benefits are hereby assigned to the Hospital for application on the patient's bill.

7. AGREEMENT TO PAY FOR SERVICES: The undersigned agrees, whether he signs as agent or as patient, that in consideration of services to be rendered to the patient, he hereby individually obligates himself to pay the charges of the Hospital in accordance with its regular rates and terms.

The undersigned certifies that he has read and understands the foregoing, and is the patient, or is duly authorized by the patient as the patient's general agent to execute the above and accept its terms.

_____	_____
(Date)	(Patient Signature or Authorized Signature)
_____ ☐ A.M. ☐ P.M.	_____
(Time)	(Relationship to Patient)
_____	_____
(Witness)	(Address)
	_____
	(Address)

(When a patient is a minor, or incompetent to give consent, then consent is secured from parent, guardian, spouse, closest relative, or other person with relationship or authority.)

Source: Courtesy of St. Francis Regional Medical Center, Wichita, Kansas.

treatment is required, then a special consent must be signed by the patient or the patient's representative. The attending physician is responsible for obtaining these special consents. No one from the admitting staff should be permitted to obtain signatures on special consents nor should the admissions consent form be an alternative to the special consent form. Both forms should be required.

Patients or their legal representatives not only must be informed what they are signing but also understand the contents of the consent form. For example, if the form is used to help identify who is to pay for services, the person who is signing the form must understand the agreement to pay. If the patient is blind, or unable to read the consent form, it is generally a good practice to read the conditions to the patient in front of a witness. In areas where other languages prevail, the consent forms should be available in that particular language. If not available, an interpreter should be obtained.

Consents and Emergencies

In an emergency case, when a patient presents to the hospital, no general consent form is immediately necessary. When a patient seeks emergency medical care from a hospital, this would be considered an implied consent for treatment. One example would be a mother in active labor who arrives at the front counter of the admitting department. Completion of an admission consent form would not be of great significance because of the patient's preoccupation with her labor pains. Priority must be the care of the patient in this particular case.

Consents and Minors

A consent to treat minors should be obtained from the parents or legal guardians. However, because the definition of minor or legal age varies from state to state, it is difficult to define the exceptions to this practice.

As an example, in Kansas a minor is defined as any male or female eighteen years of age or under. However, for medical treatment, some of the exceptions are the following:

- K.S.A. 38–123: An unmarried pregnant minor, when no parent or guardian is available, may give consent to the furnishing of hospital, medical, and surgical care related to her pregnancy, and such consent shall not be neglect to disaffirmance because of minority.
- K.S.A. 38–123b: Any minor 16 years of age or over, when no parent or guardian is immediately available, may give consent to the performance and furnishing of hospital medical or surgical treatment or procedures, and such consent shall not be neglect to disaffirmance because of minority.

As a rule, treatment may be given to a minor if it is an emergency situation. Consent may be obtained through the courts or by the patient if he or she is not under the control of or supported by parents. This is defined as emancipation.

In a situation in which the minor's life is in immediate danger, the hospital may act and then later seek consent for treatment. If there is a question whether the consent would be approved, a court order should be obtained. In most emergency cases, every effort must be made to obtain a special consent prior to treatment.

Minors who are allowed to give consent for their own treatment are known as emancipated minors. They are individuals who are living on their own and are not controlled by their parents. Also included in this category are individuals who are seeking treatment for alcoholism, venereal disease, or drug abuse in some states. Because the laws vary from state to state, it would be advisable to review each state's statues on who can consent for treatment.

DEATH AND THE LAW

The Definition of Death

Death is the ending of life. However, because we now live in a society that has the technology to sustain life, the final determination of death is no longer the sole decision of a physician but of the legal-medical profession. Various states have enacted statutes that outline the definition of death. It is this reason that hospital personnel should become familiar with their own state's death law, although all hospital personnel will not be directly involved in the handling of a dead body. It is important that admitting personnel understand the legal implications of a duty not performed in order to avoid a liability suit against the hospital.

The Responsibility of the Hospital

It is the responsibility of the hospital to notify the appropriate person (member of the family) of a patient's death. Any wrong information given out may result in the hospital being held liable. There have been cases were cadavers were mistagged, resulting in emotional harm to the family.

Once the family has been notified of the patient's death, the body may be released in accordance with each state's law. Any delays or refusals in releasing the body by the hospital may result in liability. If the patient has no relation or next of kin, the hospital may dispose of the body in accordance with state and local laws.

Autopsies may be performed if consent is obtained from the person who has the right to possession of the body by the courts. State laws will vary as to who can give consent and how the consent may be given. A general guideline that is followed in obtaining consent is as follows: (1) the spouse, (2) sons and daughters, and (3) parents of the deceased. It is generally understood that the surviving adult children have an equal right to give consent.

VALUABLES: HOW SAFE IS SAFE?

The Policy on Patients' Valuables

Every effort should be made to discourage patients from bringing valuables into a hospital. If a patient's valuables are lost or stolen, the hospital may become liable for the missing articles. The patient then has an opportunity to bring suit against the hospital for compensation.

The policy regarding a patient's valuables and the hospital's liability should be stated in an admission information booklet as well as on the admissions form of the medical record that is signed by the patient. It is recommended that admitting personnel, and in some cases emergency department personnel, inform patients of the hospital's policy on valuables and encourage them to send their valuables home with their family.

The Procedure for Valuables

Patient's valuables that are unable to be sent home must be stored in a locked area provided by the hospital. If the patient refuses to store the valuables within a locked area, a release form should be signed by the patient noting this refusal to send the valuables home or release them to the hospital for safekeeping.

Transactions that involve valuables to be stored must be recorded on an agreement and receipt for valuables form signed by the patient or authorized representative and a hospital employee. At least two copies of the agreement should be required, one being the original given to the patient and the other a copy for the hospital. Later, if the stored articles are missing, then the hospital must compensate for the loss and the employee possibly charged with theft. An example of this form is found in Exhibit 11–2.

The listing of valuables on the agreement form is very important. Cash, credit cards, checks, jewelry, and other items must be counted and identified. The transaction should be witnessed and signed by the patient and by at least two employees of the hospital. Some hospitals take an additional step by bonding their employees who receive valuables for storage.

The Release of Valuables

The release of valuables is as important as accepting them for storage. Valuables may be released to the patient or legal representative if the patient is

Exhibit 11–2 Valuables Storage and Release Form

▲ St. Francis Regional Medical Center
929 N. St. Francis / Wichita, Kansas / 67214

DEPARTMENT OF ADMISSIONS/REGISTRATION
AGREEMENT AND RECEIPT FOR STORAGE OF PERSONAL PROPERTY

Date _____

Unit # _____

Case # _____

The undersigned requests that St. Francis Regional Medical Center, Wichita, Kansas (herein called the Medical Center) provide space to the undersigned on the premises of the Medical Center for the storage of the items or parcels listed below.

In consideration of our providing storage space for such items and our not imposing a charge for the same, the undersigned agrees that:

(1) The sole duty of the Medical Center is to provide the undersigned with storage space for such items as a gratuitous bailee;

(2) In the event of loss, destruction, or damage of or to the items of personal property the Medical Center, under no circumstances, shall be responsible to the undersigned for a greater sum than twenty-five dollars ($25.00);

(3) The parcel(s) or items may be opened or withdrawn only upon presentation of a copy of this Agreement by the undersigned in person or by his or her duly authorized attorney-in-fact;

(4) The Medical Center shall have the exclusive right to fix the hours during which the storage area of the Medical Center shall be accessible to the undersigned and such hours may be changed from time to time by the Medical Center without notice;

(5) It is understood and agreed that items left for storage are to be picked up no later than ten (10) days after dismissal date of the patient; and

(6) The Medical Center may terminate this Agreement and require the vacation and surrender of the storage area and of the key thereto at any time with or without cause by delivery to the undersigned or mailing to the undersigned, at the last known address on the Medical Center's records, notice of such termination.

NURSING SERVICE REP. (if applicable): _____

ACCEPTED:
ST. FRANCIS REGIONAL MEDICAL CENTER

BY: _____
    Signature

Received By Medical Center

Date	Article

Initials of Adm. Personnel _____

Name of Patient: _____

Signature of Depositor: _____

Address: _____

Returned to Patient or Authorized Individual:

Date	Article	Initials of Adm. Personnel	Signature of Recepient

If additional space is required to list transactions, please use reverse side.

White Copy-Patient   Pink Copy-Department

Rev. 12/83

incompetent upon the presentation of the agreement and receipt of valuables form. As before, the transaction should be witnessed by the patient or legal guardian and a hospital employee. It is important to remember that caution must be taken when an individual claims to be a legal representative of an incompetent patient. If there is some uncertainty about the representation, the hospital legal counsel should be consulted.

Valuables may also be released to immediate family members who have written authorization from the owner. The authorization should be specific as to what articles should be released and to whom.

When a patient dies in the hospital leaving valuables locked up in storage, it is advised that no articles be released to anyone except the legal representative of the estate. In some states, the immediate spouse is eligible to receive the property. If there is no legal spouse, then the only other person who may claim valuables must have court-appointed certification indicating executor or administrator of the deceased patient's estate. If no estate is to be probated, a legal indemnifying statement will be required and the hospital's legal counsel should be consulted.

Valuables of a deceased patient who has no next of kin or a will should be released to the administrator of the county where the patient last lived.

RESTRICTED ADMISSIONS

Laws Affecting Admissions

It is the general assertion that a nonemergency patient does not have a right to be admitted to a hospital. However, if hospitals were to pursue this common rule to the letter, it could possibly raise legal questions that might result in a libel suit against the hospital.

The federal government has enacted several pieces of legislation that have either a direct or indirect impact on admission policies. The first is the Hill-Burton Act, which requires an institution that receives federal monies for building to establish a program to aid those patients who are unable to pay for medical services. Second is Title VI of the Civil Rights Act, which forbids discrimination on the basis of race, color, or national origin in a facility that receives Medicare, Medicaid, or any other federal assistance. The third is the Rehabilitation Act of 1973, which includes handicaps as a basis of discrimination for institutions receiving federal monies. Although these statutes do not give a patient the right to be admitted, it does pose some legal risks for a hospital if they are not admitted.

There are, however, situations in which a patient does have the right to be admitted into a hospital. Two situations are as follows:

1. If a hospital enters into a contract with another party (organization) to provide medical services, then the patient has a right. An example would be

a hospital agreeing to provide health services (physicians, emergency, outpatient, and inpatient) for a particular company and its employees.
2. Hospitals whose main function is to provide health services to a designated population within a defined region. An example of this would be the government hospitals (federal, state, county, and city).

The Denial of Admissions

Although a patient may have a right to be admitted to a hospital under the above guidelines, there are several circumstances in which a nonemergency patient may still be denied admission:

- if the hospital is not equipped to treat the patient adequately. An example would be a patient requiring surgery trying to enter a psychiatric hospital.
- if the reason for admission is not medically necessary as determined by the physician
- if space is not available to accommodate the patient
- if occupancy levels require the rescheduling of patients

In emergency cases, it is a general rule in most states that if a hospital has emergency services, then a patient with an actual emergency has the right to be treated.

The rights of the patients and hospital in any given area with regard to admission for treatment should be spelled out in policies and procedures. Any questionable cases that may arise should be handled by the appropriate medical and administrative staff.

THE ADMITTING MANAGER AS WITNESS

There may be an occasion when an admitting manager may be asked to testify regarding a case affecting the hospital. Most suits, prior to going to trial, may require a deposition. A deposition is when a witness is called (subpoenaed) to give a testimony in a given place and time before a court reporter. Attorneys will question the manager about his or her education and other activities that they believe are pertinent to the case. The manager should review any notes and charts prior to the actual testimony. This is a good method of refreshing his or her memory about the case.

When called to testify, it is important to tell the truth, understand the question that is being presented, and be brief when answering. It is also important that one does not speculate on or exaggerate the incident or situation in question. Only information that is asked for should be given.

CONCLUSION

In recent years, the health care field has been faced with a growing number of legal issues and will continue to do so under the prospective payment system. The admitting manager and staff must be able to identify potential legal situations and prevent them from occurring. An incident that may happen today may go to court in the future. This chapter was written not as a concise legal guide for the admitting department but as a source of information to assist the manager in developing or revising policies and procedures. We live in a world of changes. What may not be law today may very well become law tomorrow.

NOTES

1. *Northeast Reporter* (33 Ill., 2d 326, 211 N.E. 2d 253) (St. Paul: West Publishing Company, 1965).

2. Joint Commission on Accreditation of Hospitals, *Accreditation Manual for Hospitals* (Chicago: American Hospital Association, 1985), 63.

3. *Pacific Reporter* (215 Kan. 14 523 P. 2d 320).

4. Office of the Register, National Archives and Record Service, General Services Administration, *Code of Federal Regulations, Public Health* (Washington, D.C.: National Archives and Record Service, 1983), vol. 42, 405.1026.

5. William L. Prosser, *Handbook of The Law of Torts* (St. Paul: West Publishing Company, 1971), 727–744.

6. Ibid., 802–806.

Chapter 12

Admitting and the Regulatory Environment

Miriam Ross and John E. Jacoby

There are many facets to the modern day admitting department. The admitting manager must be concerned with how to manage the department while choosing appropriate staff. The admitting manager must also be concerned with the computerization of the department and how it serves the financial concerns of the hospital. The admitting department, as a whole, is important to every element of hospital administration. This chapter addresses how admitting is not only a tool within the hospital setting but also a tool for the regulatory agencies that are partners in the rendering of health care services throughout the country.

MEDICARE AND ADMITTING

The Beginnings

Historically, the admitting department was the first place the patient reported to when being admitted to the hospital. A clerk would ask for the patient's information, check and record the Blue Cross number, make up a chart, and transport the patient to the nursing unit. It was assumed that the information was correct and all the necessary departments were notified of the patient's arrival. The chart had a face sheet, a ledger card for the billing department, a card for the information desk, and the various slips for the laboratory. The admitting department's role was simple. Then, in 1965, Congress enacted the Social Security Act, Title XVIII. This was a three-part program with the first part of the program to go into effect on July 1, 1966. This act was referred to as the "hospital insurance benefits for the aged" or basic hospital insurance or Medicare. With the introduction of Medicare, the health care field would be revolutionized.

The Impact

The impact of the Medicare law on the hospital sector was tremendous. Not only did the new Medicare law now give hospital coverage to a group whose earnings were decreasing and health needs increasing, it gave the individual the right to be seen by a private physician and seek admission to a hospital as a first-class citizen instead of going to a clinic. Hospitals were no longer places to serve the sick. They were to become a business, an industry with a gross national product of 10.2 percent of the total for 1982. Prior to 1966, voluntary hospitals were institutions that predicated their budgets on what their costs were the year before. They would add a percentage factor for the following year, present it to their board of trustees and, with possibly a few modifications, have it accepted. Income came from third party payers, self-pay patients, and endowments. The government on the federal level had very little involvement with health care other than with special groups such as those in the armed services, veterans, and the American Indians. Psychiatric hospitals were funded by the state.

The Program Parts

There were two parts to the medical care for the aged program. Part A or the hospital insurance benefits was to be financed by the Federal Insurance Contributions and Self-Employment Act (FICA) through taxes paid by employers, employees, and the self-employed. Railroad workers, employers, and railroad employee representatives would pay hospital insurance tax under the Railroad Retirement Tax Act.

Part B, the second part of the program, was referred to officially as the Supplementary Medical Insurance Benefits for the Aged and concerned itself with physician benefits. It covered in part the cost of the physician and such items and services not covered by the basic program. The financing of the program was by the enrollee with deductions from the individual's Social Security check on a monthly basis. These deductions were then matched by the federal government. There would also be a cash deductible that had to be met by the recipient when services were rendered. An example of the rising costs of health care is noted when one realizes that it was a $40 deductible in 1966 and a $356 deductible in 1984.

The Role of Admitting

Now with the federal government involved with Medicare, all attention began to be focused on from where all the information was going to be obtained. Since the admitting department is the first point of entry to the hospital, it became its responsibility to secure as much sociologic, demographic, and financial information as possible. From a very simple admitting procedure, the focus was on how much more information the admitting department would be able to obtain from the patient over age 65. In the initial interview, the following steps were to be taken.

First, the clerk would request the patient's health insurance card with the familiar red, white, and blue border. The number appearing on this card would then be recorded on the admission form. This number was generally the patient's social security number with a suffix attached to it. Finally, the Medicare notice of admission would be completed. In conjunction with this form, the patient would be asked if he or she had been in another health care facility 60 days prior to the current admission. Finally, this notice of admission, form SSA-1453, would be submitted by the admitting department to an intermediary agency. In New York, this agency was the Associated Hospital Services, better known as Blue Cross.

MEDICAID AND ADMITTING

The Program

The Social Security Act of 1965 also provided a third program to provide medical assistance to the poor in a joint federal, state, and city program. This group included all welfare recipients as well as the elderly who were receiving supplemental income (SSI) and who were unable to pay for medical care, drugs, and other medical services that were necessary but not covered under Medicare. This part of the act was to be known as Medicaid or Title XIX and was to go into effect in 1967.

The Role of Admitting

The admitting department found itself involved in still another procedure. This time, it was the admission of a Medicaid patient. A procedure similar to the Medicare admission, but requiring more information, was implemented in admitting departments across the country. In addition to requesting a Medicaid card from the patient, admitting personnel now had to check for diagnoses that required a preadmission certification.

Preadmission certification would be needed for specific surgical procedures that required a second opinion by another surgeon. These would require a special form, later referred to as a "204" form. Admitting would be responsible for making sure the physician made these arrangements before the admission was completed. A notation was made on the reservation card stating that either the 204 form had already been filed or was going to be. It was also the department's responsibility to make sure that once requested, the form would be available for the patient's chart prior to the day of admission. The utilization department would take responsibility for the 204 form.

The admitting department would also be concerned with the issue of Medicaid validity. Admitting personnel would be responsible, when admitting a patient, for checking the signature on the Medicaid card and the chart. Two copies of the Medicaid card were also required, with these being sent to the billing department and the financial department of the hospital. Also, if a patient being admitted did not have Medicaid, the physician would deem it a necessary admission. It was then admitting's responsibility to refer the patient or family to the hospital's financial investigation department for a Medicaid application, referred to as a "515."

The Impact on Admitting

Aside from the new procedures implemented as a result of these programs, admitting managers and their departments were also affected in numerous other ways. One of the first noticeable signs in the admitting department was an increase in admissions. As a result, waiting lists became an accepted part of the admitting department. Also, the length of stay of each patient increased. As a result, elective surgery cases had to be booked weeks in advance. Finally, costs were rising significantly.

With the advent of most hospitals receiving funds from federal, state, and city programs, it was only a matter of time before someone would begin watching how these funds were being spent. Along these same lines, the quality of patient care would also be a new area of concern. Finally, length of stay and appropriateness of the admission would have to be monitored. All of these concerns would have to be addressed with the creation of still another program and another agency to regulate the health care environment.

PSRO AND UTILIZATION REVIEW

Professional Standards Review Organization

The federal government in 1972 introduced the professional standards review organization, most popularly referred to as the PSRO. This agency would do the monitoring for the federal government's dollars being spent for health care services.

The Social Security Act of 1972, Part B of Title XI, mandated that a PSRO be established. Its purpose was to ensure that health care services and items for which payment may be made in whole or in part under Medicare, Medicaid, maternal and child health, and crippled children's programs were the following:

- medically necessary
- conforming to appropriate professional standards
- delivered in the most efficient and economical manner possible

With the purpose established, the next step was to organize a group of practicing physicians approved by the Secretary of Health, Education and Welfare. This organization would monitor and control the medical care under the federal health programs. Five criteria would be used to ensure that the care being paid for was as follows:

- high quality
- cost effective
- medically necessary
- conformed to professional standards of care
- based on the above standards with the patient admitted to an appropriate facility for that level of care

Regarding the payment of such services, claims for payment would be processed by a PSRO using parameter screens of professionally determined criteria. Claims not conforming to the criteria would be referred for physician review to determine justification for payment. Data from this procedure would then be used to develop patient, physician, and institution profiles of performance. The data were to be fed back to providers to bring about indicated charges.

Utilization Review

In order to meet the demands of the mandated PSRO, a utilization review program had to be established. At a hospital, the board of trustees delegated authority and accountability to the organized medical staff. In turn, the medical staff, in accordance with its bylaws, appointed the utilization review committee and designated a chairperson and vice-chairperson. It was also recommended that nursing and all allied health professionals be represented on the committee. The utilization review committee was responsible for the management of the entire utilization review program. It was accountable to the board through the executive committee of the medical staff, the vice-president for medical affairs, and the chief executive officer of the hospital.

Generally, a registered nurse was named as a coordinator for the program and was to report to the chairperson of the committee. The liaison between admitting and utilization had to be a very close one. An understanding that had to be clearly spelled out in the organizational structure was the relationship between these two departments.

The role of the utilization review coordinator was to ensure the need for a patient's admission and the continued stay for each patient in the hospital. The admitting director was to be informed of any new criteria by the coordinator. The admitting department was to provide the coordinator with daily lists of admissions, discharges, transfers, and any information as might be necessary in compliance with PSRO regulations. In addition, the department would supply the coordinator with a copy of the admitted patient's face sheet of the admitting form with diagnosis as well as sociologic information. When second opinions were necessary, the forms were sent by the physician requesting admission to the utilization review coordinator. The coordinator in turn would send the approval to the admitting department or the denial to the physician. The coordinator would approve the length of stay, getting this information from the professional activity study, a computerized information system.

Staff members of the utilization review committee would read the patient charts on the nursing unit. They would visit with the patient, and the coordinator would consult with the head nurse. If the patient had developed complications, the coordinator would have to give additional days and certify this on the chart. These reviews are referred to as "concurrent reviews." It was hoped they would eliminate unnecessary days or what are known as "carve out" days.

QUALITY ASSURANCE

The Program

In addition to the federal government mandates to keep costs down, the JCAH, in 1973, was fearful that containing costs would compromise the quality of care being delivered. It mandated that all institutions develop a quality assurance program.

By this time, admitting departments across the country were expected to know much more about a patient's admission than just a date of admission and the physician on the case. The criteria for quality assurance were very much like those for the PSRO, and although the quality of care was to be measured, the program would also monitor for appropriateness as well. These reviews were to be for all inpatients, not just for Medicare and Medicaid patients in the hospital.

The Physicians

Until the quality assurance program and PSRO, physicians had little accountability for behavior in treating a patient. They did not have to give any reasons for the admission or the type of tests to be performed. Now, they would have to explain their actions when the utilization review committee had any questions.

They would also have to get involved in discharge planning. Could the physician know where the patient would go after the acute stage of an illness was over? The responsibility of planning ahead to shorten the length of stay became more of the physician's role. All of this accountability was the result of the mandates previously mentioned.

The Discharge Planning Program

In 1974, with the PSRO firmly installed in the hospital system, another mandate came about that stated the need for discharge planning. Discharge planning would include both the preparation of the patient for the next level of care after discharge from the hospital and the arrangement for the placement of the patient in the appropriate care setting. Seven items of information were needed for the discharge planning process to begin:

1. prior health care status of the patient (i.e., was the patient receiving care at home or in some type of long-term facility or other hospital)
2. current level of care needed
3. projected level of care needed
4. projected time frame for moving patient to next level of care
5. therapy and teaching that must be accomplished prior to hospital discharge
6. available resources for post-hospital care
7. mechanism for facilitating transfer to other levels of care

The Role of Admitting

The role of the admitting department through all of these new requirements was relatively low key. There were many forms that had to be filled out by the various departments other than admitting, but the information used was essentially supplied by the admitting department. The face sheet was very important, not only to the utilization review coordinator but also to the social work service department, the medical records department, and the billing department as well. It was used as a follow-up for social service. They work together with the utilization review coordinator and the discharge planning committee to anticipate and take care of potential problems. If it were anticipated that there would be a delay in a discharge, a referral could be made at the beginning of the admission, not several days after. The information on the patient face sheet was also most essential for home care planning, a service provided for Medicaid as well as Medicare patients.

JCAH Role

After the PSRO mandate of a discharge planning program in 1974, the JCAH mandated much of the same kind of program by stating that the utilization review plan must describe methods for providing discharge planning. It was believed that discharge planning should be started as soon as the need for it was determined. This would facilitate discharge at a time when acute care was no longer required. Furthermore, the JCAH did not believe discharge planning should be limited to long-term care facilities. Any service that would maintain the patient's healthy status after discharge was eligible for consideration.

THE PROSPECTIVE PAYMENT SYSTEM

The Need

With all of the mandates by the federal government to hold costs down and with all the requirements by the PSRO and the JCAH, the reality was that the cost of health care in the United States was still soaring. In 1982, it had spiralled to $322 billion, with an inflation factor of 12.5 percent. This meant that the government was spending $1,400 per person a year for health care. Certainly, this could not continue. There had to be more of an incentive for hospitals to do better than they were doing to keep costs down. In 1982, an announcement was made that would change the hospital industry once again, this time changing it to a competitive one. Hospitals, instead of being paid "on cost," would be paid on a unit of service type of reimbursement.

The Action

Finally, in 1983, the Social Security Amendment Act of 1983 (P.L. 98–21) established the prospective payment system. There was to be a change in the Medicare payment for inpatient hospital services. This amendment came about through the Tax Equity and Fiscal Responsibility Act of 1982 (P.L. 97–248) or what is now known as TEFRA.

This act would accomplish the following five motives:

1. limit costs per discharge adjusted to reflect the hospital's case mix of patients
2. place a limit on the yearly rate of increase of total costs per discharge
3. provide an incentive payment mechanism
4. stop reimbursement made on a retrospective basis
5. allow payment on a prospective basis and on a rate set up prior to services rendered and on the diagnosis class and volume of patients in that category

An amendment would follow this decision (Title I, subtitle C of TEFRA), which was the Social Security Amendment of 1983. This would establish further monitoring by utilization and quality assurance. It also established a new group over and above the old PSRO originally created in 1972 and was to be known as the peer review organization (PRO) program. Its purpose was to enhance the cost effectiveness of the program of peer review under Medicare.

There would also be a final piece in the new TEFRA regulations. As with all of the previous mandates, the government realized that although the hospital industry had complied with all the demands for monitoring, the hospitals were not able to keep costs down. The government also realized that they could no longer wait for the hospital sector to submit any kind of cost-containment program. Given this concern the federal government brought about another change known as the diagnostic related group (DRG) payment system.

PAYMENT SYSTEMS IN THE PAST

Previous Payment Systems

The three basic payment systems for hospitals have been (1) no-pay or global budget, (2) per diem payment, and (3) charges. Hospitals such as municipal hospitals that relied extensively on a no-pay system existed with an outside payment source, and the care they rendered was paid by a global budget system. Veterans Administration hospitals, army hospitals today, and hospitals in most of the world that have government-run medical care systems operate on this global system.

The majority of the acute care hospitals in the United States operate on a per diem and fixed charges system. Here rates are set and charged based on either previous budgetary expenditures or anticipated costs for the area of service. Some areas of hospitals charge more than they actually cost while others charge less than actual cost.

There are many laws in various states that limit the amounts hospitals can charge and regulate charges very closely. Hospitals are usually limited to charging those amounts of money to cover the actual shown costs for those services. There is no allowance in general for coverage of the payments that are not collected for various reasons.

Problems in the Hospital Payment System

The gradual change from a no-pay system to a per diem and charges system of hospital payment seemed to work for several decades. The Medicaid and Medicare programs were organized to fit in with these systems along with the Blue Cross, private insurers, and other payment plans. Increases in costs of hospitalization have led insurance companies to be very careful about services for which they would pay or not pay. For instance, the Medicare program generally covers the elderly who do not use maternity services, nursery, or pediatric services, and so Medicare auditors were careful to exclude from their portion of the payment any services connected with capital and operational functioning of labor and delivery suites. This is but one example. In general, the costs of hospitalization rose very rapidly, with more elderly patients, new technology, and other factors making hospitalization extremely expensive.

All of the previously discussed payment systems were designed to pay hospitals for services rendered. The more bed-days a hospital could get, the more services in its various areas, the more revenue a hospital could expect. Economists argued that there were no incentives in this system not to use the services. All incentives were based on maximizing the utilization of the various aspects of hospital care. This lack of incentive to economize was combined with good insurance coverage in which the patient was shielded from the economic effects of health care decisions. Since most medical care decisions are made by physicians, the patients have little knowledge or choice but to go along with a physician's recommendation.

What was needed was a system whereby a health care "market place" could be established and there would be an incentive toward efficiency in provision of health services and rewards for those who were able to cut costs and save money. There would be penalties for those who were inefficient in providing   appropriate or   necessary care.

THE DRG SYSTEM

What Is the Rationale?

Surgeons have always been paid on a per case payment system. Essentially, they charge a fee based on the type of surgery and are paid regardless of how long the patient remains in the hospital. In the payment to the hospitals, it was thought to offer some benefits if hospitals could be paid on a per case basis. This would allow the hospitals to expand whatever resources were necessary for the patient in the most efficient manner. One problem with paying on a per case basis is the different types of cases that different hospitals had and different types of cases within the same hospital. The basis of payment of the case is the diagnosis that the patient has, just as in surgery the basis of the payment is the type of surgery the patient has. Thus, for all patients with the same diagnosis, the hospital would receive the same fee regardless of the length of stay or the amount of ancillary services used. Certain patients within each diagnosis with unusual circumstances are "outliers," and per diem payments would still be made. There is a breakdown for the age of the patient, whether or not the patient had surgery, and whether the patient had more than one condition. This is thought to make the classification of the patient equitable.

What Is the DRG?

A DRG is a system of classifying patients into groups who have the same or very similar diagnosis and also use in general the same types of hospital services. DRGs were developed at Yale University as a method of classifying patients for use in a per case payment system. The classification of patients has evolved over the past few years with some slight changes in the exact system in use.

The current system in use by the federal government contains 467 different DRGs. The previous system in use in New Jersey for instance had 383 DRGs. The principles of each classification are essentially the same. Patients are classified into an individual DRG category based on the diagnosis, age, whether they had surgery, and whether they had secondary diagnosis. The age breakdown for several of the major categories is different, and this is based on whether an actual fact analysis of large number of hospital discharges reveals different patterns of costs. Not only are the age cutoff points different in different categories, but also in some categories, the other factors are not necessary to be used. So in some cases, patients with and without surgery are grouped together. Some other cases have patients with and without secondary diagnosis grouped together. The assignment of the DRG is based on the discharge diagnosis not the admission diagnosis, and the major category is based on the principal discharge diagnosis.

ASSIGNMENT AND MANAGEMENT OF DRG SYSTEM

The Patients

Let's take a typical patient that comes into a hospital and see how a DRG would be assigned to her. A 39-year-old woman enters the hospital for treatment of a lump in her left breast. The lump is removed and found to be benign. She spends two nights in the hospital. She has no other diagnosis. How would this case be assigned to a DRG?

First, her diagnosis would fall under the major diagnostic category ICDM-9, diseases of the skin, soft tissue, and breast. There are 23 major diagnostic categories (MDCs). The next determination is whether or not the patient had a surgical procedure (in this case, yes) and so we go into the surgical branch of the MDC. There are five possible categories of surgical procedures. This patient had a breast procedure. The next branch is whether or not there was a diagnosis of malignancy. The answer is no, and the next decision branch is whether there was a biopsy and local excision. The answer is yes, and so this patient falls into DRG category 262. Once a DRG has been assigned to a patient, this will determine the payment that the hospital receives. Hospitals are paid a fixed rate for each DRG, with adjustment factors for whether or not it is a teaching institution and for labor costs.

The Management Goals

Management goals of providing good patient care will continue. Management goals of having a clean, well-run, and efficient hospital will also continue, but under a DRG system certain new factors will take on added importance to the institution:

- selection of patients
- efficient, rapid management of each case
- thorough and accurate diagnosis of patients
- on-line information for management as to the type of cases in house and the length of stay as well as the use of ancillary services

Management goals in these areas will be designed toward formulating an efficient operation so patients can be cared for as rapidly as possible and with as economic an approach as possible. Patients will be selected as much as possible by management without affecting their health, on the basis of the potential for expeditious management.

CONCURRENT MANAGEMENT

The Requirement

Admitting managers will no longer be able to sit back and analyze data on a post-hoc basis to see what sort of patients have been discharged from their hospitals. Managers will have to know on a daily basis who is actually in the hospital, which patients are on track for a prompt discharge, and which patients have manifested a potential to stay too long or consume too many resources for their diagnosis so corrective action can be taken immediately. The elements of this concurrent management of hospitals are as follows:

- overall coordination of this system
- responsibility of physicians to keep track of their activities and the need for the hospital to be aware of their activities
- the responsibility of the medical records department for a thorough and accurate review of the medical records
- accurate data in the aggregate so the hospital can see how it's doing
- a sophisticated computer system for analysis of the diagnostic data as well as aggregate management information data

An aggressive admitting department will initiate this entire system. Looking at the overall management system, it is very important that the many elements of the hospital learn to work well together. The various specialties within a hospital have in the past been content to "sow their seeds and harvest their own crop" in their own areas. With the DRG system and the need to become efficient, hospitals will have to work together as members of the same team toward achieving the goal of efficiency.

The Physician's Role

What about physicians? Physicians have a crucial role in working with the hospitals. Hospitals must pay more attention toward educating physicians into the DRG system. They must cooperate with physicians so that the physicians do not feel that hospital administrators are trying to use their patients as raw material for economic gain. If the physicians see this, and see to it that there is cooperation, they will then be able to use the system to the best advantage of all parties. Admitting patients and then promptly discharging those patients that are doing well will be the physician's role. From experience, it is not the patient who has a long stay who needs to be looked at and discharged earlier. Rather, it is the patient who probably could go home a day sooner than he or she does, which would save the hospital money and resources. It is the patient with no complications who will not suffer by an earlier discharge. Physicians will cooperate when they are taught the value of being parsimonious in the use of tests. Many tests that are ordered are superfluous and even have the potential of causing harm to the patient.

The Computer

Ongoing printouts and reports of data will be necessary to manage the system. In addition, the best hospitals will be totally on-line as far as their tracking of each patient from the time the case is booked until the time the annual data are reviewed. There will be no room for errors in keeping track of patients. By having an integrated system, it will save entering the patient several times into the same system. The patient's name, number, and various other information will have to be available to all elements of the hospital on an ongoing basis. Of course, there will be issues relating to patients' confidentiality, and these will have to be dealt with by having secret access codes to get into this hospital system. Nevertheless, staff from all areas of the hospital will have access to this patient information system, which would include laboratory, admitting, medical records, radiology, utilization review, and financial department.

DRGs AND THE ADMITTING DEPARTMENT

The admitting department should be totally aware of the patients who are yet to be admitted, of the patients that are in the hospital, and of the patients that have been discharged from the hospital. The admitting department forms the connection of the patient with the system. The patient is entered into the system through the admitting department. Once entered into the system, the way is paved for payment, assigning of beds, surgical scheduling, discharge scheduling, the recording of the medical records data, and the transmitting of the necessary medical records data to various payment authorities and to various governmental agencies. If this process works smoothly, the whole hospitalization is facilitated. Hospitals not only should have computerized admitting lists, but they also should have discharge lists. The preparation of the discharge list should not occur after patients are discharged but should be an ongoing system in which patients are assigned a discharge date even prior to their admission. The assigned discharge date would be based on norms or on specific information for each case that may be reserved at the time the patient reservation to the hospital is made. Thus, if a patient fails to meet this discharge date, action can be taken.

DRGs AND THE FUTURE

The Moral Question

In some hospitals, there will be pressure to categorize patients and accept certain patients based on the ability to pay and to fit into the needs and goals of the hospital. This is a serious moral question, but it will be the role of the admitting department to be aware of policy and to try and enforce it in a fair manner and to feed back to administration any reason why there are problems with this issue. It is important for hospitals to be recognized and continue to be the force for help and a moral force in the community that they have been since they were founded as charitable institutions. The true manager will be aware of the moral as well as fiscal issues and can highlight the free care given to the community at a time when funds are needed to fulfill the mandates of the hospital. Moral issues must be faced squarely. A hospital must know when it is performing a charitable function or when it is being reimbursed, and the admitting department can assist the hospital in being aware of which type of patients it is serving.

The Importance of Diagnosis

If a discharge date is postponed for various reasons, such as changing diagnosis, action is taken. The admitting department takes the admission diagnosis for the patient. It is now more important that the admitting diagnosis be as accurate as possible, and hospitals should take steps to know their level of awareness of admitting diagnosis and agreement with the final discharge diagnosis. Since payment is made on the basis of the final diagnosis, an awareness of changes in the admitting diagnosis should be an ongoing process and not await discharge of the patient. The patient should thus be carried as a certain diagnosis and assigned a DRG at the time of admission in an ideal system. A length of stay and other norms could then be assigned, and the system could keep track if the patient is fulfilling the expectations of the diagnosis or some explanation could be found.

The Prospect of Better Management and Reimbursement

A system such as the one discussed would not only ensure better management and better reimbursement for the hospital but would also be a key in risk management, prevention of errors, and improving patient care. If the patient were found to have a change in diagnosis or delay in discharge or have complications, medical as well as managerial expertise could be brought to bear on the case to find out why and to help the patient achieve a better recovery. The role of the admitting department is essential in all of these facets.

CONCLUSION

As a summary on how the admitting department has been affected by the regulatory agencies, it must be stated that admitting managers have become professionals. The change from a simple admitting sheet with a few pertinent questions to a 14-part form with an in-depth interview in all cases except an emergency has become a reality. It is no longer acceptable by admitting policy to note only the demographic information. It is now mandatory that admitting personnel adhere to an established system such as a follow-up initial interview for information that might not have been available at the time of admission; a supervisory staff to keep abreast of new requirements that are so essential for reimbursement; or a supervisory staff monitoring data on a daily basis.

Although the admitting department has never been thought of as a vital department, the requirements of the regulatory agencies pointed out the reality that it is the admitting department where it all begins.

Chapter 13

Quality Assurance in the Admitting Department

Marion P. Tanner

The preceding chapters of this handbook have helped to define and clarify many of the components of a successful admitting department. These components include proper organization, physical design and layout, staffing, computers, preadmissions, bed assignment, financial responsibilities, laws, and regulations. Although each component is essential, it represents only one element of the admitting department. The measurement and success of all the elements is determined by quality assurance.

HISTORY OF QUALITY ASSURANCE

In 1979, the Joint Commission for Accreditation of Hospitals (JCAH) adopted the term *quality assurance*. This term initially referred to an "umbrella standard" of quality that was expected in all the other standards.[1] This was revised and expanded in 1980. "There shall be a well-defined, organized, ongoing QA effort designed to demonstrate improvement in patient care."[2] JCAH left this new standard, quality assurance, open for individual hospital interpretation within four guidelines[3]:

1. integration and coordination of all quality assurance activities
2. a written plan that clearly defines program organization and management
3. a problem-focused approach to quality assurance
4. an annual reassessment of program effectiveness

In the next two years hospitals experimented with various quality assurance plans and programs. By 1982 more specific guidelines/elements of a quality assurance program were identified[4]:

- organizational chart
- quality assurance definitions
- organization and authority
- purpose and intent
- goals and objectives
- problem-focused approach to quality assurance
- quality assurance reports
- quality assurance responsibilities: medical staff
- quality assurance responsibilities: hospital services
- annual appraisal/evaluation of system
- appendix:
  quality assurance function flow chart
  minimal hospital service responsibilities
  individual departmental quality assurance plans

RESPONSIBILITY FOR QUALITY ASSURANCE

JCAH is responsible to enforce their quality assurance standards by granting or withholding hospital accreditation. The individual hospitals have the responsibility to organize and implement a viable quality assurance plan in order to maintain their accreditation. To comply with a hospitalwide quality assurance program, individual departments must be responsible to develop and carry out their own departmental quality assurance plans. The department responsibilities may rest on the department manager; however, the manager should involve all members of the department.

The original intent of a quality assurance plan was to focus on problem identification and problem solving. This chapter will discuss quality assurance in the admitting department as an integrated plan for examining the routine operations as well as specific problems.

The department plan is subject to individual interpretation just as it is for the hospitalwide plan. Therefore this chapter will not propose a standard quality assurance plan. However, each plan should follow four guidelines:

1. department standards
2. employee standards
3. assessment of results
4. monitoring for quality

These guidelines will be presented with specific examples. They can all be remembered with an acronym—TEAM.

Department Standards

This first team concept will be explained by examining the need and process for establishing standards.

Need for Standards

The success of every organization, department, and employee depends on setting and achieving standards. Each unit needs to identify its mission (its primary purpose for existing) and then identify the functions and standards that are consistent with the mission. Allen explains the importance of objectives as follows, ''Productivity increases as the work performed is directed toward understood and accepted objectives.''[5]

Terminology

The terminology in this section may have a variety of meanings and uses. To avoid confusion the terms will be listed, defined, and their relationships shown in a diagram (Figure 13–1).

- mission—the purpose and essential characteristics of an organized unit; also considered as the key objective of an organization
- functions—the performance areas that are most vital to the accomplishment of the mission; also considered as the critical objective
- standards—the conditions that will indicate when the functions are performed properly; specific standards should accompany each function
- needs—a problem or a condition that indicates that a standard has not been achieved
- goals—a desired action/plan that will satisfy an existing need and standard; also considered specific objectives
- policies and procedures—steps and methods used to accomplish repetitive activities

Establishing Standards

The diagram in Figure 13–1 shows there is a cascading relationship from the mission to the functions to the standards to the needs and to the goals. Before standards can be established the preceding levels need to be identified.

The mission statement should contain an overview of the purpose, service, client, scope, and functions of the organized unit. The mission of the hospital is provided by the administrator, and the related missions of the departments are provided by the department managers. The statement generally is constant and ongoing for the duration of the organization.

Figure 13–1 Relationships of Mission, Functions, Standards, and Goals

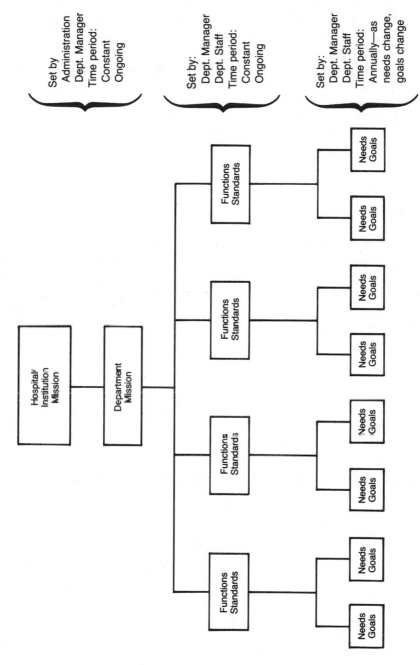

The department functions refer to the performance areas that are essential to the accomplishment of the mission. The functions may be determined by the department manager with input from the department staff. These functions are constant and ongoing in the department.

The standards represent the performance units that are needed to fulfill the functions. They should be described in terms that can be measured and quantified. The standards should be established with input from those personnel who are responsible for performing the work. Deegan and O'Donovan state that "participative decision making at each step is a major ingredient for a successful program."[6]

An example of the mission, functions, and standards for an admitting department is shown in Exhibit 13–1.

Employee Standards

The second of the TEAM concepts is employee standards. Employees constitute one of the major resources of most industries—the human resource. The effective management and utilization of this resource has become a major concern. The concern for employees is aimed at increasing or improving their job performance. A manager's interaction with the employees can be analyzed by examining the process of appraising employees and the principles of motivating and developing employees.

Process of Appraising Employees

Those department managers who view employee appraisals as a one-time event during the year may be in the 90 percent group of businesses that claim that the appraisals are ineffective or even detrimental. The successful 10 percent group may view employee appraisals as a year-round process. The objective of the process is to "induce behavioral change and thus lead to productivity improvement."[7] The critical part of the process is the employee. The human nature in all of us often causes a natural defensive or resistant reaction to change, especially behavioral changes. The defensiveness and resistance can be minimized by involving the employee in an appraisal process that is integrated into the work cycle. "Participative performance-oriented appraisal programs represent a promising marriage of current behavioral science research and theory with practical business objectives. . . . The program is built around a continuing work-planning and progress-review process between the supervisor and his individual subordinates."[8]

The appraisal process consists of four tasks or steps (Figure 13–2): (1) interpersonal contract, (2) helping relationship, (3) appraisal interview, and (4) goal setting.

Exhibit 13–1 Admitting Department Standards

I. Mission

To perform the admitting/communications work in a manner to promote positive relationships with patients, physicians, hospital departments, and visitors. These activities will
be measured periodically and reported to administration, the quality assurance committee,
and the governing board.

II. Functions and Standards

A. Preadmission: to prepare as much as possible for the patient's admission to the hospital
two days prior to arrival.

1. Elective patients are called to confirm admitting information, to be given an
appointment time, and to be reminded to bring in insurance cards.
2. Complete and accurate information is entered on the admission record prior to the
patient's arrival.

B. Preadmission testing: to provide for patients to receive laboratory, radiology, or other
studies prior to admission to the hospital.

1. Signatures are obtained on medical and financial documents.
2. Test results, physician's records, and medical and financial consents are retained
until time of admission.

C. Admitting: to complete the admitting process in a manner that is convenient and timely
for the patient, family, and nursing personnel.

1. Elective patients are admitted at private admitting desk and non-elective patients are
admitted at bedside.
2. Complete and accurate information is entered on the admission record.
3. Signatures are obtained on medical and financial documents.
4. Identification bands are prepared and placed on the patient.
5. Patient valuables are properly recorded and deposited.

D. Escorting patients: to ensure the proper routing of patients and admission records to the
appropriate service areas.

1. The nursing station is called before the patient is escorted to the assigned room.
2. Elective patients are walked either to the service areas when physician's orders are
present or to the nursing station.
3. Nonelective patients are placed in a wheelchair and taken to the nursing station.

E. Operating the telephone system: to process telephone communications in an efficient,
courteous manner for patients, physicians, general public, and hospital staff.

1. Priorities are used by acknowledging all calls as soon as possible and returning to
answer operator level calls and then outside hospital calls.
2. All paging is done in a clear, distinct, audible voice.

F. Preparing reports: to compile and distribute information to the appropriate individuals/
departments when requested.

1. The information on reports and lists is accurate and legible.

G. Maintaining security systems: to ensure the safety of all concerned parties associated
with the alarm systems.

1. The alarm signals are answered by promptly calling the proper authorities.
2. The keys are controlled by maintaining a log.

Exhibit 13–1 continued

H. Training: to provide for the ongoing development of knowledge and skills for all department personnel.

1. Hospitalwide policies and procedures, safety and disaster plans, and the quality assurance program are followed by the department personnel.
2. Departmental meetings are attended monthly to present and/or exchange pertinent information.
3. Individual meetings are held periodically to discuss performance and other relevant matters.

Source: Courtesy of Providence Hospital, Medford, Oregon.

Figure 13–2 Appraisal Process

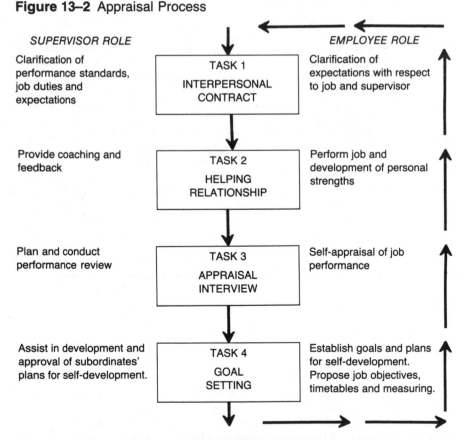

SUPERVISOR ROLE		EMPLOYEE ROLE
Clarification of performance standards, job duties and expectations	**TASK 1** INTERPERSONAL CONTRACT	Clarification of expectations with respect to job and supervisor
Provide coaching and feedback	**TASK 2** HELPING RELATIONSHIP	Perform job and development of personal strengths
Plan and conduct performance review	**TASK 3** APPRAISAL INTERVIEW	Self-appraisal of job performance
Assist in development and approval of subordinates' plans for self-development.	**TASK 4** GOAL SETTING	Establish goals and plans for self-development. Propose job objectives, timetables and measuring.

Source: Reprinted from the October 1975 issue of *The Personnel Administrator,* © 1975, with permission of the American Society for Personnel Administration, 606 North Washington Street, Alexandria, Va.

Interpersonal Contract. This initial step of interpersonal contract does not require any signed agreements. However, the agreements should be verbalized between the manager and the employee about the performance standards and job expectations. The standards of performance are the criteria for assessing satisfactory performance, which will be done in the appraisal interview. Allen states ''it is only against understood and accepted performance standards that we can legitimately evaluate performance.''[9] To facilitate the agreements, the standards and expectations should be developed with input from the manager and the employee:

> Improvement in job performance can be accomplished most effectively if the employee participates directly in establishing the achievement measures for his job. . . . Criteria of job performance should be related to the job itself. . . . While personal qualities such as honesty, loyalty, integrity, and conscientiousness are presumed to be prerequisites for any job, they need not be enumerated.[10]

Helping Relationship. According to Rogers, a helping relationship is ''one in which at least one of the parties has the intent of promoting the growth, development, maturity, improved functions, improved coping with life of the other.''[11] To develop this relationship between the manager and the employee, the exchange of information such as questions, answers, and feedback should be provided regularly. The manager should make notes of the employee's observed performance to be used in the appraisal interview.

Appraisal Interview. The interview date is set in advance so that both the manager and employee can prepare their notes. A private room should be arranged where both parties can sit on the same side of a table or desk. The communication should be relaxed and open for both parties to review the employee's performance.

The results of the review are recorded on a performance appraisal form. The term *performance appraisal* is often interchangeable with the term *job evaluation*. A more precise definition of performance appraisal is ''a systematic review of an individual employee's performance on his job to evaluate the effectiveness or adequacy of his work.''[12]

Many uses have been identified for performance appraisals:[13]

- for salary administration (to determine individual salary treatment)
- to provide a basis for supervisor–employee communications
- to help supervisors to know their workers better
- to identify training needs
- to identify employees for layoff or recall
- to assist in placement
- to validate the selection process and evaluate other personnel activities, such as training programs and psychological tests

- to improve departmental employee effectiveness
- to determine special talents
- to determine the need for disciplinary action
- to determine progress at the end of probationary periods
- to furnish inputs to other personnel programs, such as manpower and succession planning
- to supply information for use in grievance interviews

The variety of uses above may be achieved with a variety of appraisal techniques.

- essay appraisal: The evaluator writes the strong and weak points of the employee's performance in narrative form.
- graphic rating scale: The evaluator selects from a scale a descriptive word and point value that corresponds to the employee's performance.
- critical incident technique: The evaluator observes and records the critical incidents of success or failure as they occur.
- forced choice: The evaluator selects items that are most applicable to the employee from a preestablished list of behaviors.
- weighted checklist: The evaluator reviews a set of descriptive statements that are assigned a number value from poor to excellent. Only the applicable statements are checked.
- management by objectives (MBO): The evaluator and employee jointly set the objectives in advance. The objectives are stated in quantitative terms, and the performance is measured against them.
- behaviorally anchored rating scales (BARS): The evaluator establishes the possible behaviors that may be expected from specific jobs. The performance is measured by selecting the applicable behaviors.
- ranking: The evaluator rates all of the employees from highest to lowest on each job criteria.
- paired comparison: The evaluator compares each employee against all other employees on job criteria. This develops an index of the number of preferences compared with the number of employees being evaluated.
- forced distribution: The evaluator grades all of the employees on a curve by placing them in percentage groups from the top ten percent to the bottom ten percent.

The selection of the appraisal technique will depend on its uses (Table 13–1). After the technique is selected a corresponding form should be designed with

Table 13–1 Comparison of Performance Appraisal Techniques

Criterion	Graphic Rating Scale	Forced Choice	MBO	Essay	Critical Incident	Weighted Checklist	BARS	Ranking	Paired Comparison	Forced Distribution
Cost of developing instrument	Moderate	High	Moderate	Low	Moderate	Moderate	High	Low	Low	Low
Cost of using method	Low	Low	High	High Supervisory Costs	High	Low	Low	Low	Low	Low
Ease/difficulty of use by evaluators	Easy	Moderately difficult	Moderate	Difficult	Difficult	Easy	Easy	Easy	Easy	Easy
Ease of understanding by employees	Easy	Difficult	Moderate	Easy	Easy	Easy	Moderate	Easy	Easy	Easy
Useful in making promotional decisions	Yes	Yes	Yes	Not very	Yes	Moderately	Yes	Yes	Yes	Yes
Useful in making compensation decisions	Yes	Moderately	Yes	Not very	Yes	Moderately	Yes	Not very	Not very	Yes
Useful for counseling and employee development	Moderately	Moderately	Yes	Yes	Yes	Moderately	Yes	No	No	No

Source: Reprinted from *Handbook of Performance Evaluation Programs* by S.E. Parnes with permission of the Bureau of Law & Business, Inc., 64 Wall St., Madison, Ct., © 1981.

performance standards. This form may be used initially as a job description and subsequently for employee appraisals. Examples using a form of management by objective technique can be seen in Exhibits 13–2 through 13–4.

Goal Setting. In a separate session the manager and the employee review the deficiencies/needs that were identified in the appraisal interview. The employee should be encouraged to establish goals and plans to meet the specific needs and standards. "If performance is to be improved or maintained, specific needs must be identified and a nonthreatening environment provided in which the employee can be motivated to change both his behavior and his attitude."[14] The goals should be recorded along with a time frame for implementation. Forms for goals and improvement plans are shown in Exhibits 13–5 and 13–6. When the goal setting is completed the appraisal process returns to the first step of interpersonal contract.

The process for appraising employees requires some paper work but, more importantly, good management skills.

Looking for a perfect appraisal form—for a checklist or rating scale that will produce a "foolproof" appraisal—can only lead to frustration and failure. Why? Because no form or set of forms, no matter how well designed, can by itself create a successful appraisal interview. It can facilitate the interview, but only the manager or supervisor can make the interview work. Another reason is that no checklist, rating scale, or other written appraisal device can come to grips with all the complexities of human interaction that go into the appraisal interview. The tension, the concern, the anxiety—these are only a few of the emotions that must be contended with in almost every appraisal. No form in the world can help a manager deal with these feelings. Training and human relations skills are the only possible answers.[15]

Principles for Motivating and Developing Employees

According to Allen, motivation is "an unfulfilled need or desire that causes a person to act."[16] The manager's challenge is to assist in filling the needs that will more fully use the abilities of each employee.

Understanding . . . motivation begins with a recognition of the fact that a business can buy with money only some of a person's physical and mental energies. A business cannot buy, however, the individual's mental or emotional commitment to do the best job he or she can. It is partly up to each manager to inspire the employees in his or her charge to give of these things.[17]

Exhibit 13–2 Job Description and Performance Record

PROVIDENCE HOSPITAL
Medford, Oregon

JOB TITLE: Admitting Representative

RESPONSIBLE TO: Admitting Manager

PRINCIPAL DUTIES AND PERFORMANCE STANDARDS:

1. Interpersonal relationships: relates well with hospital staff, medical staff and public.
2. Attitude: positive and cooperative outlook toward his/her position, the hospital and fellow employees.
3. Attendance: reports on time and avoids unnecessary absences.
4. Complies with hospital's general policies and procedures.

SCHEDULING ADMISSIONS

5. Enters patient information from the surgery scheduling book, and physicians' office calls into the reservation log as far in advance as possible.
6. Updates the daily reservation log from the daily surgery schedule.

PREADMITTING

7. Contacts elective patient to confirm admitting information, assigns appointment time, and reminds patient to bring in insurance cards.
8. Enters complete and accurate information on the admission record prior to the patient's arrival.

PREADMISSION TESTING

9. Obtains signatures for medical and financial documents.
10. Retains test results, physician's records, and medical and financial consents until time of admission.

ADMITTING

11. Admits patients at private admitting desks and nonelective patients at bedside.
12. Enters complete and accurate information on the admission record.
13. Obtains signatures on medical and financial documents.
14. Prepares and places identification bands on the patient.
15. Records and deposits patient valuables properly.

ESCORTING PATIENTS

16. Contacts nursing station before the patient is escorted to the assigned room.
17. Escorts by walking elective patients to either the service areas when physician's orders are present or to the nursing station.
18. Places nonelective patients in wheel chairs and takes them to the nursing station.

TRAINING

19. Complies with hospitalwide policies and procedures, safety and disaster plans, and the quality assurance program.

Exhibit 13–2 continued

	Meets Standards	Needs To Improve
20. Attends monthly departmental meetings to present/exchange pertinent information.		
21. Discusses performance and other relevant matters in individual meetings.		
22. Assists with the hospital's disaster, safety and fire prevention programs.		
23. Performs other related tasks assigned by the director.		

QUALIFICATIONS

    High School graduate or equivalent. Clerical experience is required. Hospital experience is preferred.

Performance Review Only

Name _____ Type of Review _____ Due Date _____

APPROVALS: _____ DATE _____

               _____ DATE _____

Source: Courtesy of Providence Hospital, Medford, Oregon.

Employees' commitment and actions relate to what they are thinking, feeling, and needing.

    Every supervisor concerned about his or her job and subordinates must try to know his or her people well enough to answer the following questions about each of them:

1. What are his or her immediate goals?
2. What are his or her immediate needs?
3. What are his or her unique attitudes about me, his or her job, and our company?
4. Why does he or she hold these attitudes?

    The answers to these four questions will help you determine what your subordinates' current needs are and what will motivate them at a given time. This knowledge will allow you to provide some incentives that might trigger a greater effort and contribution from each subordinate, and that will assist that person and your department to achieve a greater output.[18]

Exhibit 13–3 Example of Evaluation Form

UNIVERSITY OF CALIFORNIA -- LOS ANGELES

PERFORMANCE EVALUATION

(For Use in Designated Classifications Only)

Employee Name	Department	Division

Payroll Title	UC Hire Date	Length of time in present job	Period covered by this evaluation:
	/ /	Yrs Mos	FROM: / / TO: / /

Supervisor's Name	Supervisor's Payroll Title	Length of time you have supervised this employee:
		Yrs _____ Mos _____

Check One: Exceeds Expectations ---------------

Meets Expectations---------------

Does Not Meet Expectations ----------

SECTION ONE

Primary Job Functions for Period of Evaluation	Supervisor's Performance Expectations	(Col. 3)	Comments
(Column 1)	(Column 2)		(Column 4)

Source: Courtesy of University of California, Los Angeles, California.

Exhibit 13–4 Evaluation of Performance for Admitting Officers

EVALUATION OF PERFORMANCE FOR ADMITTING OFFICERS
(OFFICE USE ONLY)

EMPLOYEE: _____

POSITION: _____   ANNIVERSARY DATE: _____

1. Most of the time
2. Sometimes
3. Infrequently

	Evaluation 1			Evaluation 2			Evaluation 3		
	1	2	3	1	2	3	1	2	3

RELIABILITY

- Reports to work on time/and/or early enough to start work at assigned time.
- Takes responsibility for knowing and keeping work schedule.
- Adheres to lunch schedule – leaves and returns promptly.
- Notifies supervisor, well in advance, of requests for scheduling changes.
- Is neat and clean in appearance and appropriately dressed for business office.

COOPERATION

- Recognizes need for changes in daily routine; willingly alters lunch schedule, completes assignments before leaving, gives more than eight hours when workload dictates.
- Demonstrates willingness to adjust work schedule due to illness, etc.
- Treats every patient and employee with courtesy, respect, and concern.

INITIATIVE

- Maintains adequate supplies and when necessary orders new ones.
- Assumes responsibility for maintaining clean and orderly work area, (i.e., eats only in designated areas, keeps rugs & walls clean, etc.).

RESPONSIBILITY

- Recognizes and resolves financial problems.

- Oversees and supervises Admitting office personnel in absence of immediate supervisor.

- Discerns and reports to appropriate supervisor problems requiring their attention.

- Follows through to completion assignments and projects.

- Maintains accurate bed list and count of medical admissions.

- Knows nursing divisions, room locations, and accommodations.

- Utilizes available beds (Urgent Book, Psychiatry Book, etc.) and properly assigns patient according to hospital procedure, etc.

- Places correct, complete, and appropriate information on patients' flyers.

- Makes sure patient's papers are properly completed (i.e., correct signatures, correct plates, Medicare forms, etc.).

- Acquires pertinent information regarding emergency admissions (i.e., if patient is being transferred, from where, is insurance coverage adequate, is patient re-entry, will patient come through Emergency Room or Admitting Office).

- Demonstrates willingness to train and support new employees.

- Plans ahead (i.e., arranges for adequate messengers and notifies Housekeeping for needs of cribs, etc.).

- Keeps room status accurately.

Exhibit 13–4 continued

EVALUATION OF PERFORMANCE FOR ADMITTING OFFICERS

(OFFICE USE ONLY)

EMPLOYEE: _____

POSITION: _____   ANNIVERSARY DATE: _____

1. Most of the time
2. Sometimes
3. Frequently

	Evaluation 1			Evaluation 2			Evaluation 3		
	1	2	3	1	2	3	1	2	3

COMMUNICATION

- Places appropriate people on move card.

- Gives accurate and thorough report.

- Maintains inter and intra-departmental working relationships.

- Alerts necessary people of computer/x-ray shutdowns.

- Is diplomatic in dealing with financial problems, department errors.

1st Evaluation Date - Supervisor's Comments:

Employee's Comments:

Employee's Signature:

2nd Evaluation Date - Supervisor's Comments:

Employee's Comments:

Employee's Signature:

3rd Evaluation Date - Supervisor's Comments:

Employee's Comments:

Employee's Signature

Source: Courtesy of Barnes Hospital, St. Louis, Missouri.

Exhibit 13–5 Example of Form for Planning Improvement

ACTION TO BE TAKEN BY SUPERVISOR TO ASSIST EMPLOYEE IN IMPROVING PERFORMANCE (Indicate Time Frame)
ACTION TO BE TAKEN BY EMPLOYEE TOWARDS IMPROVING OWN PERFORMANCE (Indicate Time Frame)
SECTION FIVE – Employee Comments
SECTION SIX – Signatures

This employee has been under my supervision for_____months.

＊ Employee's Signature: _____

Supervisor's Signature: _____ Date: _____

Department Head Signature: _____ Date: _____

Date: _____

＊ Your signature indicates neither agreement nor disagreement with this evaluation, but it does indicate the evaluation has been reviewed by you.
   RETENTION PERIOD: 0-5 YRS. AFTER SEPARATION

Source: Courtesy of University of California, Los Angeles, California.

The relationships of the employee, manager, needs, and performance are shown in Figure 13–3. An employee may start out with the desire to achieve the performance standards. However the work may be temporarily stopped at a barrier/need such as the preadmission telephone caller with laryngitis. The manager's influence may be used to practice the principle of team building by rotating the preadmission person with the person sending mail or filing. This temporary assignment may result in cross training and achievement of the performance standards. "Without reasonable integration of personal and enterprise objectives, sustained motivation is impossible."[19]

Exhibit 13–6 Example of Form for Planning Improvement

EMPLOYEE PERFORMANCE IMPROVEMENT PLANS		
Standard No.	Goal/Action for improvement	When

Employee comments	Supervisor comments
Signature _____ Date _____	Signature _____ Date _____ Administrative Review _____

Source: Courtesy of Providence Hospital, Medford, Oregon.

The role of the manager in motivation and development is similar to the role of a coach. "Coaching is a process of instructing and inspiring another individual to perform or achieve at a higher level."[20] The coaching duties include identifying needs and applying correct principles.

The most common and accepted list of human needs has been provided by Maslow and includes physical needs, safety needs, social needs, esteem needs, and self-realization needs (Figure 13–4).

The first duty in the coaching role is to know each employee's needs.

> It is more important to know people's thoughts and to anticipate their reactions than to draw up a semantically correct manifesto of the firm's aims and regulations . . . Every human act can be understood if we know all the pertinent facts . . . How can we be of greater service to people than by detecting their emotional disturbances, quietly learning the cause and instilling confidence while helping toward good adjustment? When you help someone to be right you are satisfying one of his greatest needs.[21]

Figure 13–3 Model for Motivating and Developing Employees

```
                                              ┌─────────────────┐
                                              │  PERFORMANCE    │
                                              │  STANDARDS      │
                                              └─────────────────┘
                                                       ▲
                                                       │
┌─────────────┐         ◇◇◇◇◇◇         ┌─────────────┐
│ Barriers/Needs│       ◇        ◇      │ Barriers/Needs│
│  Identified  │  ──▶  ◇ Manager's ◇ ──▶│  Satisfied by │
│ Personal     │        ◇ Influence ◇   │  applying     │
│   related    │         ◇        ◇     │  specific prin-│
│ Job          │          ◇◇◇◇◇◇        │  ciples to    │
│   related    │                        │  specific needs│
└─────────────┘                         └─────────────┘
       ▲
       │
┌─────────────┐
│             │
│  EMPLOYEE   │
│             │
└─────────────┘
```

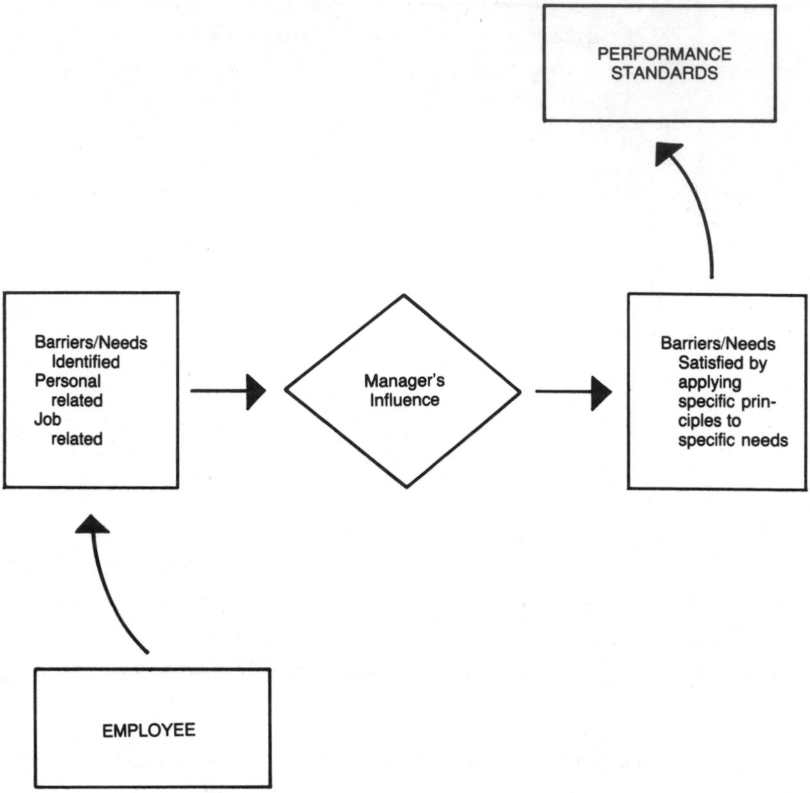

When the needs have been identified and understood the coach/manager can now apply the appropriate principles to motivate and develop employees.

> Successful human relations are essentially the results of a complicated interplay of these virtues and principles, but every person must play the game within his own particular environment and according to his own personal qualities and ideals.[22]

The principles that are most applicable to motivating and developing employees are listed and explained below.

Figure 13–4 Hierarchy of Needs

SELF-REALIZATION NEEDS	Job-related satisfiers
Reaching your potential Independence Creativity Self-expression	Involvement in planning your work Freedom to make decisions affecting work Creative work to perform Opportunities for growth and development

ESTEEM NEEDS	Job-related satisfiers
Responsibility Self-respect Recognition Sense of accomplishment	Status symbols Merit awards Challenging work Sharing in decisions Opportunity for advancement

SOCIAL NEEDS	Job-related satisfiers
Companionship Acceptance Love and affection Group membership	Opportunities for interaction with others Team spirit Friendly co-workers

SAFETY NEEDS	Job-related satisfiers
Security for self and possessions Avoidance of risks Avoidance of harm Avoidance of pain	Safe working conditions Seniority Fringe benefits Proper supervision Sound company policies, programs, and practices

PHYSICAL NEEDS	Job-related satisfiers
Food Clothing Shelter Comfort Self-preservation	Pleasant working conditions Adequate wage or salary Rest periods Labor-saving devices Efficient work methods

Source: Based on Hierarchy of Needs in *Motivation and Personality*, 2nd edition, by Abraham H. Maslow. Copyright © 1970 by Abraham H. Maslow. By permission of Harper & Row, Publishers, Inc.

Principle of Communicating. Communication may come through all five senses: sight, sound, touch, smell, and taste. Prerequisites to good communication are the skills of asking and listening. Both the body language and choice of words convey messages. Athos emphasized the importance of words when he stated,

"Hard drives out soft." The language of success can be recognized from the following word groups.[23]

Hard	Soft
Win/lose	Win/win
Hard on people	Soft on people
Hard on problems	Soft on problems
Strong position	Changing position
Personal interests	"What's best"
Threats	Offers
Conditional rewards	Earned rewards
Demands	Agreements
Negotiations	Consensus
Tell	Consult/join
I accept	We accept
Adversaries	Friends
Manipulate	Disclose
Problem givers	Problem solvers
Logic	Wisdom
Distrust	Trust
Position based	Interest based
Single solutions	Multiple solutions
Drive solutions	Test solutions
Content	Process
Practical considerations	Symbolic considerations
Short range	Long range
Fixed	Ad hoc
Results	Group welfare
Structural	Behavioral
Few decisions	Multiple decisions
Hindsight	Insight

Principle of Building Self-esteem. Individuals tend to respond outwardly based on their inner feelings of self-worth. The manager should look for ways to build up the value and importance of each employee. "Motivation to accomplish results tends to increase as people are given recognition for their contribution to those results."[24]

Principle of Team Building. Employees can be more productive as they understand how each duty/position relates to all the other duties/positions to help accomplish the department's mission. This awareness can be done by cross training and rotating positions and shifts, thereby developing a respect and appreciation for each other. "Motivation to accomplish results tends to increase as people are given opportunity to participate in the decisions affecting those results."[25]

Principle of Delegating. The saying that "many hands make light work" is still true. Sharing work responsibility and authority increases the self-esteem in individuals and the effectiveness of team building. "Motivation to accomplish results tends to increase as people are given authority to make decisions affecting those results."[26]

Principle of Observing. The manager's response to employee needs is determined by his or her observation and perception of the needs. Accurate observations and notes of daily performance can assist in an accurate performance appraisal. Misjudgments can be prevented by avoiding the following errors:

- stereotyping. Judgment is due to apparent membership in a particular category of people (e.g., race, religion, sex, age).
- halo effect. A skill or characteristic influences the manager to view all skills the same way (all good or all bad).
- contrast. The person is compared with another without regard to performance.
- projection. The manager allows his or her own values to be superimposed on the employee without prior discussion.
- fixed impression. An observation of one behavior is allowed to form a judgment for future behaviors.
- recency or primary effect. Behaviors that were done early or late in the observation period are the basis for final judgment.
- effects on time. Positive and negative observations that occur at different times may lead the manager to make a judgment based on the stronger impression.

Each of the principles when properly applied can instill the power to change and improve performance. This power is evident in the spontaneous effect on other principles as well as on other individuals. In an address by Bussey delivered at the 1983 NAHAM convention in Denver, Colorado, the power of listening was emphasized as follows:

Listening to employee's problems builds acceptance.
  Acceptance becomes credibility.
    Credibility becomes trust.
      Trust leads to mutual trust.
        Mutual trust leads to harmony.

In the admitting department this power/influence may carry from the manager to the staff to the patient. A discharged patient sent a letter of praise to the hospital in which he stated, "the attitudes displayed by staff . . . reflect the staff's perception of administration attitudes. You and the supervisory people have done a very good (service) for the patients who come to you."

Assessment of Results

The third TEAM concept, assessment of results, is the general term for any program that measures the quality of services provided against established criteria.[27] The program consists of action to be taken after the department standards and employee standards have been implemented. The department performance needs to be evaluated just as the employee performances need to be evaluated. The department performance represents the accumulation of the employee performances. "The measurement of individual performance is an essential component of the measurement of organizational performance."[28] Even though the standards may be well stated and the personnel may be competent this does not guarantee quality results. "As important as credentials are, they are at best a partial criterion for measuring quality. . . . Even the most highly credentialed professionals cannot deliver quality care without a comprehensive support system."[29] The quality of the support system can be determined by using appropriate assessment methods and by recording the assessment information.

Many different assessment methods are used to accomplish a variety of purposes. Each purpose or standard should be examined using the method that is the most applicable to the situation. A summary of the methods is listed by title and author in Exhibit 13–7. This list may be helpful in selecting the methods and/or being familiar with available alternatives for identifying problems and collecting data.

The assessment information can be recorded on the Admitting Department Quality Assurance and Goal Index (Exhibit 13–8). Each column will be explained in sequence.

Problems and Goals

In the first column the terms *problems* and *goals* are closely related, as was shown in Figure 13–1. When a problem/need has been identified, then a goal can be stated that will solve the problem. The problems and goals refer to all aspects of the department operation. The department goals that were traditionally prepared as a separate document for the beginning of each year can now be totally integrated with the department quality assurance and goal index. The specific goals will help "to improve job performance or the services delivered by any individual or department."[30]

Problem identification consists of a general overview of the department activities. The methods used to obtain this information can be grouped in five categories: (1) identifying problems through data analysis, (2) identifying problems through review mechanisms, (3) identifying problems through needs assessments, (4) identifying problems through creative thinking techniques, and (5) identifying problems through external organizations.[31]

Exhibit 13–7 Taxonomy of Methods

Title	Author
1. ABNA: Achievable Benefit Not Achieved	John W. Williamson
2. Age–Sex Register	Eugene S. Farley
3. Ambulatory Care Quality Assurance Project (ACQAP)	Nicole White
4. Autopsy Findings	Jack Hasson
5. Brainstorming	Allen D. Spiegel
6. Computer-Stored Ambulatory Record System (COSTAR)	G. Octo Barnett, U.S. Congress
7. Concurrent Quality Assurance	Paul J. Sanazaro
8. Cost–Benefit Analysis	Carol Weiss, Allen Spiegel, Lyle Bootman
9. Criteria Mapping System (MAPS)	UCLA: Sheldon, Greenfield, Linda Worthman
10. Delphi Technique	A. Spiegel, A. Delbecq
11. Diagnostic Index-E-Book	Jack Froom
12. Edge-Notched Cards	A.C. Foskett
13. Generic Screening	Samuel R. Sherman, CMA/CHA
14. Goal Analysis	Robert F. Mager
15. Health Accounting System	Williamson, Anderson, Cunningham, Schropp
16. Hospital Support Services	Sidney W. Vanloh
17. Index of Sentinel Health Events	David D. Rutstein
18. Medical Care Evaluation Study Process	Health Standards & Quality Bureau
19. Nominal Group Process	Delbecq, Williamson & Spiegel
20. Occurrence Screening System	Interqual
21. Problem Definition and Prioritization Process	American Hospital Association
22. Problem-Oriented Medical Information System (PROMIS)	U.S. Congress
23. Profiles of Physician Morbidity Data	Eugene S. Farley, Jack Froom
24. Program Planning Model (PPM)	Andre L. Delbecq
25. Quality Assurance Monitor	Commission on Professional & Hospital Activities
26. Quality Assurance Program	Paul B. Batalden
27. Sampling, Accidental	Festinger, Kerlinger, Patton, & Selltiz
28. Sampling, Cluster	Festinger, Kerlinger, Selltiz
29. Sampling, Purposive	Festinger, Kerlinger, Selltiz, & Patton
30. Sampling, Quota	Same as above
31. Sampling, Simple Random	Same as above
32. Sampling, Stratified	Same as above
33. Sampling, Systematic	Same as above
34. Sickness Impact Profile	Marilyn Bergner, Betty S. Gilson
35. Special Reviews: Blood Utilization, Respiratory Therapy, Surgical Cases	American Hospital Association

Exhibit 13–7 continued

Title	Author
36. Staging	Interqual, Joseph S. Gonnella
37. Staging II	Interqual
38. Technicon Medical Information	U.S. Congress
39. Tracers	Kessner, Olin, Smith, Novick
40. WOTS UP Analysis	George A. Steiner

Source: Reprinted with permission from *Quality, Trending, and Management for the 80's,* copyright 1981 by the American Hospital Association,© 1981.

Exhibit 13–8 Admitting Department Quality Assurance and Goal Index

				Year _____
1	2	3	4	5
Problems and Goals	Priority and QA Study #/Month	Personnel Responsible	Action Plan (from QA Study)	Follow-up/Date

Identifying Problems through Data Analysis. Several data sources contain information pertinent to the admitting department:

- medical records chart
- financial/billing data
- operating room schedule
- admission report
- transfer report
- budget report
- department checklist

A department checklist could be designed to incorporate some of the data sources. Periodic examination of the data may help identify problems or inconsistencies. See Exhibit 13–9.

Identifying Problems through Review Mechanisms. In the admitting department the following reviews are usually performed daily:

- the admission schedule log to verify names from the surgery schedule and preadmission work
- the medical staff suspension list to prevent admissions by a physician whose medical charts are incomplete
- the physician record files (history and physical and orders) to ensure timely delivery to the proper nursing station
- the admission records to ensure the correct number for distribution

Problems discovered through review mechanisms may be itemized and evaluated by using method No. 13, "generic screening," an ongoing process for identifying problems based on generic criteria (see Exhibit 13–7).

Identifying Problems through Needs Assessment. Some needs may become apparent through input from patients, physicians, hospital personnel, and the general public. This input may be received in several forms:

- Suggestions from patients/family
- Suggestions from employees/staff
- Feedback from department heads
- Patient questionnaires/surveys
- Employee exit interviews
- Appraisal interviews
- Observation of hospital activities

Method No. 26, Quality Assurance Program, can be used to collect and compile data from the above sources (see Exhibit 13–7).

Exhibit 13–9 QA Check List

SIGN IN SHEET #_____

Did patient get his room preference? ____ ____
                                    (yes) (no)
_____ Room Ready ____ ____
(no preference)   (yes) (no)

PATIENT'S NAME

If no, what is hold up? _____
                       (no room at this time)

ADMITTING: _____
          (IN)   (OUT)
X-RAY: _____
          (IN)   (OUT)

_____ _____ _____
(not clean)   (not vacated)   (transfer)

NURSING STATION: _____
                              (IN)

(other, explain)

ROOM NUMBER: _____

Hold up explained to patient? ____ ____
                              (yes) (no)
Patient told what type of room? ____ ____
                                (yes) (no)

Patient pre-admitted? ____ ____
                      (yes) (no)
If yes _____ _____
       (accurate) (re-typed)
If retyped: _____ _____
            (int.) (# typos)

All blanks completed? ____ ____
                      (yes) (no)
If no, explain _____
_____

Personal Property
   Consent Signed ____ ____ If no, why? ____
                  (yes) (no)

_____

_____ _____ _____
(Signed)   (Witnessed) (Date)

INSURANCE INFORMATION
Blue Cross
   CoB Completed ____ ____
                 (yes) (no)
   Claim Form ____ ____
              (yes) (no)
Medicare
   Form Signed ____ ____
               (yes) (no)
   KPRO Typed ____ ____
              (yes) (no)
Medicaid
   Hill-Burton 1&2 Completed ____ ____
                             (yes) (no)
   KPRO Typed ____ ____
              (yes) (no)

Patient Information Packet Given and Explained:

____ ____
(yes) (no)

Hill Burton #1 Completed? ____ ____
                          (yes) (no)

Hill Burton 1&2 Completed? ____ ____
                           (yes) (no)

Any Problems Concerning Patient Or His Admission?

_____

Exhibit 13–9 continued

Commercial Insurance
    Policy #s ___ ___
              (yes) (no)
    Mailing Address ___ ___
              (yes) (no)
    Assignment Signed ___ ___
              (yes) (no)
    Social Security # ___ ___
              (yes) (no)
 	
Insurance Cards Xeroxed? ___ ___
              (yes) (no)
	_____
	_____
	_____
	
	Date _____
	
	_____
	Signature, Admitting Representative

Source: Courtesy of Jewish Hospital, Louisville, Kentucky.

An example of a survey for admitting personnel is shown in Exhibit 13–10. Questions 1 through 7 concern the admitter's attitude toward the patient. Questions 8 through 15 concern how others treat the admitter. Questions 16 through 20 concern the admitter's perception of his or her own skills.

Examples of patient questionnaires are included in Exhibits 13–11 and 13–12. The questions and format can be designed to obtain general or specific responses. In Exhibit 13–11 the general responses that affect the admitting department are contained in the first three statements. In Exhibit 13–12 the specific responses that may affect the admitting department are after questions 3, 6, and 9.

Identifying Problems through Creative Thinking Techniques. Some needs/problems may be found through group discussion and interaction. The combined insights and personal knowledge in a group are often more effective than a single individual at assessing standards. In the admitting department the group input can be accomplished through department meetings or special goal-setting meetings. Methods for gathering group information (see Exhibit 13–7) include the following:

- Method No. 19, Nominal Group Process, allows group members to generate ideas individually and then discuss them one at a time.
- Method No. 5, Brainstorming, allows a group to generate ideas spontaneously.
- Method No. 10, Delphi Technique, allows individual responders to remain anonymous.

Exhibit 13–10 Admitting Personnel Survey

ADMITTING PERSONNEL SURVEY

Directions: Circle one choice: SA = Strongly Agree, A = Agree
SD = Strongly Disagree, D = Disagree

SA	A	D	SD	1.	The presence of newly arrived patients is always acknowledged within a minute of his/her arrival.
SA	A	D	SD	2.	I show warmth and concern for the patients I admit.
SA	A	D	SD	3.	I am never so "business like" to be considered "cool" to patients.
SA	A	D	SD	4.	I am never so casual that I am considered rude.
SA	A	D	SD	5.	I always explain to patients why I ask the questions I do.
SA	A	D	SD	6.	I feel awkward when I ask patients for money.
SA	A	D	SD	7.	Paperwork seems more important than people in this job.
SA	A	D	SD	8.	The admitters in our department really work as a team (stay late if needed, help each other, etc.)
SA	A	D	SD	9.	Admitters are treated well by nursing.
SA	A	D	SD	10.	There is a high level of stress and tension in my work area.
SA	A	D	SD	11.	I work well under normal pressures.
SA	A	D	SD	12.	I am seen by our administration as important to our organization.
SA	A	D	SD	13.	My opinions are valued by up-line management.
SA	A	D	SD	14.	We receive compliments from the Business Office whenever they are deserved.
SA	A	D	SD	15.	Most complaints about our department are justified.
SA	A	D	SD	16.	My knowledge and spelling of medical terms needs improvement.
SA	A	D	SD	17.	My typing skills are sufficient for my job.
SA	A	D	SD	18.	I rarely repeat the same type of error in completing an admission.
SA	A	D	SD	19.	I respond well to a change in department routine.
SA	A	D	SD	20.	I can function effectively even when the computer is down.

© The Barbazette Training Clinic, 1981 (reprint permission allowed when this source is acknowledged)

Source: Courtesy of Barbazette Training Clinic, Seal Beach, California.

Identifying Problems through External Organizations. The most common external organizations impacting hospitals are government agencies (city, county, state, and federal). Changes in government regulations often create problems in meeting the new regulations. The admitting department must comply with directives from the following organizations:

- professional standards review organizations
- Medicare (Title XVIII)
- Medicaid (Title XIX)
- fiscal intermediary groups (e.g., Blue Cross)
- commercial insurance carriers

Exhibit 13–11 Patient Questionnaire

PROVIDENCE HOSPITAL
Medford, Oregon

I was a patient on:

☐ 1st Floor   ☐ 3rd Floor East
☐ 2nd Floor East   ☐ 3rd Floor West
☐ 2nd Floor West   ☐ ICU-CCU

INSTRUCTIONS:

Here are some statements with which you may strongly agree, agree, disagree or strongly disagree. For each statement, indicate your reaction by checking in the appropriate space at the right.

PLEASE ANSWER EVERY STATEMENT	STRONGLY AGREE	AGREE	DISAGREE	STRONGLY DISAGREE	PLEASE ANSWER EVERY STATEMENT	STRONGLY AGREE	AGREE	DISAGREE	STRONGLY DISAGREE
1. The preadmission form I received was easy to understand.					12. The spiritual support offered was adequate for my needs.				
2. The admitting clerk was helpful in explaining the paper I signed.					13. I was treated well by laboratory personnel.				
3. The admitting personnel were pleasant and courteous.					14. The x-ray people were careful and considerate.				
4. The nurses explained nursing care and procedures in a manner I could understand.					15. The x-ray people explained procedures in a manner I could understand.				
5. The nurses were pleasant and courteous.					16. The physical therapy I received was helpful to my recovery.				
6. The nurses seemed interested in me and my welfare.					17. The physical therapy personnel were pleasant and courteous.				
7. I received as much nursing care as I needed.					18. The purpose of the physical therapy treatments was explained to me in a manner I could understand.				
8. Nurses were prompt in responding to my requests.					19. I received adequate instructions about my respiratory therapy treatments from the therapists.				
9. While receiving treatments my privacy was respected.					20. Respiratory therapy personnel were professional in their performance.				
10. My room was free of disturbing noise.					21. Considering my diet, the food was tasty.				
11. At discharge, I was given sufficient self care instructions.									

Exhibit 13-11 continued

PLEASE ANSWER EVERY STATEMENT	STRONGLY AGREE	AGREE	DISAGREE	STRONGLY DISAGREE	PLEASE ANSWER EVERY STATEMENT	STRONGLY AGREE	AGREE	DISAGREE	STRONGLY DISAGREE
22. The hot food was hot and the cold food was cold.					29. The volunteers were thoughtful and helpful.				
23. I always received the food I ordered.					30. My room was properly lighted and ventilated.				
24. The dietitians were courteous and helpful.					31. My doctor discussed progress with me.				
25. Social service helped me with my practical needs.					32. I received courteous attention from the business office.				
26. Social service helped me with my emotional concerns.					33. Business office personnel answered my questions promptly and clearly.				
27. My room was kept clean.					34. In general, I had very good hospital care.				
28. Housekeeping personnel were pleasant and courteous.									

COMMENTS: _____

_____

_____

Signature _____

Source: Courtesy of Providence Hospital, Medford, Oregon.

Column No. 2, Priority and QA Study #/Month

Column No. 2 is used to rank all of the problem areas from the most significant effect on patient care to the least significant. "Priorities shall be related to the degree of impact on patient care that can be expected if the problem remains unresolved."[32] The prioritizing should be done according to the following criteria:[33]

- impact on effectiveness of outcome
- impact on efficiency of care
- frequency of occurrence
- impact on cost effectiveness

Exhibit 13–12 Patient Questionnaire

PROVIDENCE HOSPITAL
PATIENT QUESTIONNAIRE

1. How would you describe the care and attention you received from the staff on your floor?

    _____

2. Are there any comments you would like to make regarding your room's cleanliness, comfort, quietness, etc.? _____

3. Were there any nurses, staff, or volunteers who were particularly helpful to you? _____

    _____

4. Aside from any dietary restrictions you may have had, what comments do you have regarding the food and service provided to you? _____

    _____

5. Were there any occasions when a nurse or staff member was slow in responding to your requests? _____

    _____

6. Were the forms you signed for medical, financial, and surgical consents explained to you in a manner you could understand? _____

7. Do you have any comments regarding the care and attention provided by your physician?

    _____

8. Many patients use the services of the laboratory, radiology, and physical therapy departments. Do you have any comments regarding the personnel in these departments? _____

    _____

9. Are there any other comments you wish to make concerning your stay at Providence Hospital? _____

    _____

My room number was _____

Please fold and seal this form and place it on your bedside table as you leave the hospital. You may also mail the form if you so desire. Thank you for your assistance.

Signature (optional) _____

Source: Courtesy of Providence Hospital, Medford, Oregon.

The following methods may be helpful in establishing priorities (see Exhibit 13–7):

- Method No. 24, Program Planning Model, uses small groups to identify, discuss, and prioritize problems.
- Method No. 21, Problem Definition and Prioritization Process, outlines information about problems and focuses on the degree of adverse impact on patient care.

- Method No. 26, Quality Assurance Program, prioritizes problems according to a group ranking problem.
- Method No. 1, Achievable Benefit Not Achieved, provides a system of weighing problems based on individual/group input.
- Method No. 10, Delphi Technique, provides for anonymous individual prioritizing and discussion to reach a consensus.

When an order of priority has been determined the same order can be used to number the quality assurance studies. The studies should be given on a monthly schedule, and both the number and the month should be entered in column No. 2.

The quality assurance study of an identified problem represents a comprehensive data collection process using the applicable methods described for column No. 1. An example of a quality assurance study form is shown in Exhibit 13–13. The terminology is clarified below:

- Quality Assurance Study No.___: Obtain from Quality Assurance and Goal Index form, column No. 2.
- Original ___ Follow-up___: Check appropriate space for each study.
- Department/Personnel: Obtain from Index form, column No. 3.
- Problem and Goal Identified: Obtain from Index form, column No. 1.
- Methods: Refer to Taxonomy of Methods.
- Size of Study Group: Include number and/or time frame.

  Retrospective—after care has been provided
  Concurrent—while patient is still hospitalized
  Prospective—future hospital care

- Criteria: Develop standards to describe performance.

  Structural—focus on organization and resources
  Process—focus on technique and skill
  Outcome—focus on the results of the activity

- Findings: Summarize data.
- Action plan: Add to Index, column No. 4.

Column No. 3, Personnel Responsible

In column No. 3 the personnel should be listed who have an interest or a need to improve in the problem area to be studied. Those interested may use this quality assurance study as an educational opportunity. This knowledge and experience may also lead to career advancement.

Exhibit 13–13 Example of a Quality Assurance Study Form

```
QUALITY ASSURANCE STUDY # _____     Date Started _____
ORIGINAL _____FOLLOW-UP _____     Date Completed _____
═══════════════════════════════════════════════════════════════════

Department/personnel responsible: _____
_____

Problem and goal identified: _____
_____
_____

Methods applied to gather data: _____
_____

Size of study group: _____
_____

Criteria: _____
_____
_____

Findings: _____
_____
_____

Action plan: _____
_____
_____
```

Those personnel who need to improve in the problem area may have been identified in the employee appraisal process. The manager should "involve staff early. . . . People are interested in their own discoveries and respond better to their discoveries than to those of others. Change will occur more frequently if those required to change have been involved in determining that the change is necessary."[34]

Column No. 4, Action Plan

Column No. 4 contains the details that are stated in the action plan of the quality assurance study. An effective plan depends on an accurate evaluation of the findings, specific recommendations, and an implementation schedule.

The evaluation of the findings is necessary to define the specific problems. The nature of most problems may be found in three categories: (1) knowledge, (2) performance, and (3) systems.[35]

- knowledge problems: relate to technical or procedural requirements
- performance problems: relate to behaviors, skills, and abilities
- systems problems: relate to the organization, structure, and environment

The specific recommendations are the measures/steps to achieve the goals stated in column No. 1, Problems and Goals. An applicable assessment method is No. 40, Wots-Up, which itemizes the weaknesses, opportunities, threats, and strengths (see Exhibit 13–7). The improvement measures are intended to bring about change. The change strategies vary with the nature of the problems.

- change strategies for knowledge problems:
    inservice meetings
    workshops
    continuing education programs

- change strategies for performance problems:
    counseling
    application of principles for motivating and developing (see Figure 13–3)

- change strategies for systems problems:
    new or revised policies/procedures
    staffing changes
    reorganization
    equipment/physical plant changes

The implementation schedule should include measurable actions, personnel responsible, time frame, and expected results.

Monitoring for Quality

The fourth TEAM concept, monitoring for quality, is the culmination of the quality assurance program. The process that began with the department standards, employee standards, and assessment of results now requires specific actions that will maintain the desired quality. "Quality is inherently a relative concept. It may be deemed excellent, good, or poor only when it is measured against some valid standard or bench mark of performance."[36] Actions for monitoring quality include follow-up and reporting.

Follow-up

The term *follow-up* may also be considered as a reassessment. "An essential part of any quality assurance activity, reassessment is the method by which one determines and documents the extent of problem resolution. Reassessment is vital to the overall success of quality assurance activities."[37] Follow-up activities not only determine the resolution of problems but also reinforce further employee participation.

It is essential to resolve issues and concerns that are identified through the audit process. One of the most devastating organizational dynamics that can take place is for the feeling to exist among employees that issues and concerns cannot or do not get resolved. This could lead to organizational apathy, conflict, and confrontation. For this reason, an administrative system for monitoring progress in achieving recommended corrective action must be established to ensure timely closure to all pertinent issues and concerns.[38]

Since the follow-up areas are the same as the original study areas the same form can be used (see Exhibit 13–13).

- Quality assurance study no.___: The number should be the same as in the original study.
- Type of study: The space after follow-up should be checked.
- Date started _____: The follow-up should start after allowing sufficient time for the action plan to be implemented.
- Personnel responsible: The follow-up personnel should be different than those performing the original study.
- Problem and goal identified: These should be the same as those on the original study.
- Methods: They may be the same or different than those used in the original study.
- Size of study group: The size may be smaller than the original study but large enough to be a representative sample.
- Criteria: The follow-up may focus on one or more of the standards stated in the original study.
- Findings: These should be summarized and recorded.
- Action plan: See outcomes of follow-up studies.

The outcome of follow-up studies may be one of the following types:

- Action plan was successful: When the action plan solves the identified problem then the entry "problem resolved" can be recorded on the quality assurance follow-up study and on the quality assurance and goal index (see Exhibit 13–8).
- Action plan was incomplete: More time may be necessary to bring the desired results. Appropriate notes should be made on the quality assurance study form and the quality assurance index.
- Action plan failed: The failure to solve the identified problem may be due to inaccurate statement of the problem, inappropriate method applied, improper size or type of study group, insufficient criteria, inconclusive summary from findings, or inapplicable action plan. After examining the above items the recommendations should be recorded on the quality assurance study form and the quality assurance index.

Exhibit 13–14 Admitting Department Quality Assurance Reporting Chart

QA Activities	Documentation	Dissemination	Frequency
The Department Standards →	Department Standards (see Exhibit 13–1) →	Hospital QA Coordinator →	As changes occur
Employee Standards →	Job Description (see Exhibit 13–2) →	Employees, Personnel Department →	During initial probationary period
	Performance Evaluation (see Exhibits 13–2 and 13–6) →	Employees, Personnel Department →	Annually near anniversary date
Assessment of Results →	Department QA and Goal Index (see Exhibit 13–8) →	Administration, QA Coordinator, QA Committees →	Annually or as problems are identified
	QA Original Study (see Exhibit 13–13) →	QA Coordinator, QA Committee, Department Personnel →	Monthly or quarterly according to meeting schedules
Monitoring for Quality →	QA Follow-up Study (see Exhibit 13–13) →	QA Coordinator, QA Committee, Department Personnel →	Monthly or quarterly according to meeting schedules

Reporting

The reporting function is intended to provide evidence that quality assurance activities are accomplishing their purpose of resolving problems and improving patient care. This can be achieved through proper documentation and dissemination of quality assurance information (Exhibit 13–14).

The documentation is necessary for all of the quality assurance activities that were discussed in the previous sections. The dissemination of information is intended to keep personnel informed of quality assurance activities. Some of the data may be confidential and should be released only to those who have a "need to know." In addition to the individual level, effective hospitalwide dissemination can be accomplished through committees. The committees may be organized by the quality assurance department coordinator with representatives from all the hospital departments. The purposes of these committees include the following:

- to educate department representatives in quality assurance activities
- to coordinate and integrate quality assurance activities between departments
- to encourage departments in providing quality service (e.g., patient care and support services)
- to assist departments in resolving problems
- to provide recognition for successful quality assurance activities

The frequency of reporting quality assurance activities will depend on each activity. Informal contacts and reviews with employees can occur as a daily routine. Formal meetings may be scheduled annually for employee evaluations, monthly for department meetings, and quarterly for committee meetings.

CONCLUSION

Quality assurance in the health care setting is finally reaching the significance of quality control in the industrial setting.

Private industry has practiced quality control longer than hospitals, so it seems reasonable to look to that experience for guidance. Industry's ultimate quality goal is "zero defects." Industrial quality control systems are designed to monitor production, identify deviations from a standard, and correct deficiencies before they reach the market. When an automobile rolls down the assembly line, quality control professionals can observe defects and use instruments to check tolerances against finite standards.

> The quality of problem care cannot be measured so easily: the standard is not absolute. Every patient is different, and the care received is a complex conglomerate of human and technological services.[39]

The application of "quality" in the hospital does present many unique challenges. In addition to the guidelines from other industries, JCAH advises that quality assurance should be ongoing, involve all departments, and encompass all other control activities.

Quality assurance in the admitting department has been proposed with four guidelines, represented by the acronym TEAM.

1. the Department Standards
2. employee Standards
3. assessment of Results
4. monitoring for Quality

These guidelines will be reviewed as a quality assurance cycle and their impact will be evaluated.

Quality Assurance Cycle

The TEAM concepts are all interrelated, as demonstrated in Figure 13–5. The department standards contain all of the duties of the department. These duties are organized into the different work positions and become the employee standards. As the standards/duties are performed, they reflect the performance of the total department. The evaluation of the department is conducted through the steps outlined in the assessment of results. After the assessment process is completed, follow-up is accomplished by monitoring for quality. The outcomes from monitoring may result in revisions or additions to the department standards.

Each phase of the quality assurance cycle has a common resource—the employee. Employees may become the most valuable and productive asset when they are properly influenced and motivated (see Figure 13–3). Peters made the following observation:

> You can force people by their economic needs to come into work eight hours a day, but you cannot force people to behave in an excellent fashion. This is a voluntary decision.

> The best companies . . . are "voluntary" organizations that encourage their employees to participate on all levels of management and innovation.[40]

Figure 13–5 Quality Assurance Cycle

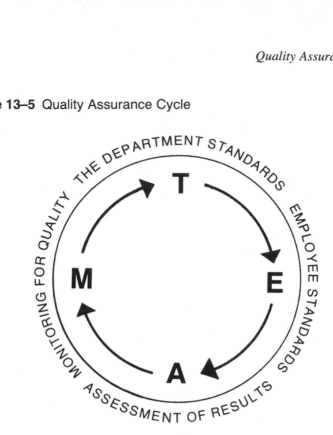

As the manager shows care and concern to employees, the employees in turn improve the quality of care to patients.

> I would say that the central idea is that if you don't care for people properly, you won't cure them. Medicine is not a technology. Medicine is an art depending upon trust, and therefore the caring comes first, because if you don't care for someone then that person cannot trust the provider, and the therapy will not be effective.[41]

Quality Assurance Impact

The impact of quality assurance can be felt in the relationship to hospital costs and marketing the hospital's services.

The government's attempt to control escalating hospital costs has resulted in a prospective payment system. This system authorizes Medicare payments to hospitals based on predetermined amounts for specific diagnostic related groups (DRGs). With limitations on revenues, hospitals have been forced to reduce costs or close their doors.

In the process of reducing costs it is also possible to reduce the quality of services. The control to maintain quality and offset the economic pressures has been the objective of quality assurance programs. Ginzberg believes strongly that "we have the responsibility to make sure that while seeking to slow health care costs quality is not forgotten, because access and quality really are the major factors in health care."[42]

As hospitals compete for patients one of the major factors will be the quality of services. Hospitals that have an effective quality assurance program will have an advantage in providing quality services and attracting patients.

In the admitting department the quality of services can have a positive impact on all of those stated in the department's mission: patients, physicians, hospital departments, and visitors (see Exhibit 13–1). The TEAM concepts can work together just like team members in the department to produce quality services.

NOTES

1. Patrice L. Spath, *Contemporary Issues In Quality Assurance* (Portland, Oreg.: Brown–Spath & Associates Health Care, 1982), 5.

2. Arthur X. Deegan II and Thomas R. O'Donovan, *Management by Objectives for Hospitals* (Rockville, Md.: Aspen Systems Corporation, 1982), 253.

3. Spath, *Contemporary Issues In Quality Assurance*, 10.

4. Ibid., 17.

5. Louis A. Allen, *Position Charter* (Palo Alto, Calif.: Louis A. Allen Associates, Inc., 1975), 26.

6. Deegan and O'Donovan, *Management by Objectives for Hospitals*, 259.

7. John D. Colby and Ronald L. Wallace, "Performance Appraisal: Help or Hindrance to Employee Productivity? *The Personnel Administrator* (October 1975): 37-39.

8. Dale Yoder and Herbert G. Heneman, Jr., *ASPA Handbook of Personnel and Industrial Relations*, Vol. 1, *Staffing Policies and Strategies* (Washington, D.C.: The Bureau of National Affairs, Inc., 1974): 4–170, 4–172.

9. Louis A. Allen, *Developing People* (Palo Alto, Calif.: Louis A. Allen Associates, Inc., 1975), 37.

10. Yoder and Heneman, *ASPA Handbook*, 4–171.

11. Colby and Wallace, *Performance Appraisal*, 39.

12. Yoder and Heneman, *ASPA Handbook*, 4–161.

13. Ibid., 4–163.

14. Yoder and Heneman, *ASPA Handbook*, 4–170.

15. S.E. Parnes, *Handbook of Performance Evaluation Programs* (Stanford, Conn.: Bureau of Law & Business, Inc., 1981): 48.

16. Louis A. Allen, *Motivating* (Palo Alto, Calif.: Louis A. Allen Associates, Inc., 1975): 40.

17. W. Richard Plunkett, *Supervision: The Direction of People at Work* (Dubuque: Brown, 1975): 122.

18. Ibid., 177.

19. Allen, *Motivating*, 41.

20. Roger Tunks, *Managing Excellence* (Portland, Ore.: Richard-Rogers Group, 1982): 35.

21. The Royal Bank of Canada Monthly Letter, "Strategy in Working With People" (Montreal, Canada, February 1977), vol. 58, no. 2:1.

22. Ibid., p. 4.

23. Tunks, *Managing Excellence*, 13.

24. Allen, *Motivating*, 22.

25. Ibid., 21.

26. Ibid.

27. Deegan and O'Donovan, *Management by Objectives for Hospitals*, 259.

28. Yoder and Heneman, *ASPA Handbook*, 4–170.

29. Joyce W. Craddick and Barry S. Bader, *Medical Management Analysis*, Vol. I, *An Introduction*, 4 (Auburn, Calif.: Joyce W. Craddick, 1983).

30. Deegan and O'Donovan, *Management by Objectives for Hospitals*, 259.

31. Judy M. Gustafson, Susan C. Kopher, and Marguerite M. Terze, *Quality, Trending, and Management for the 80's* (Chicago: American Hospital Association, 1981): 1–5.

32. Ibid., 6.

33. Spath, *Contemporary Issues in Quality Assurance*, 24.

34. Karen Orloff Kaplan and Julie M. Hopkins, *The QA Guide: A Resource for Hospital Quality Assurance* (Chicago: Joint Commission on Accreditation of Hospitals, 1980), 122.

35. Ibid., 119, 120.

36. Craddick and Bader, *Medical Management Analysis*, 3.

37. Kaplan and Hopkins, *The QA Guide*, 125.

38. Deegan and O'Donovan, *Management by Objectives for Hospitals*, 261.

39. Craddick and Bader, *Medical Management Analysis*, 4–5.

40. Thomas J. Peters, "How To Put Excellence into Operation," *Hospital Forum* (July/August 1984): 35.

41. Eli Ginzberg, "Ginzberg Prescribes a Diet to Shrink the Industry," *Hospital Forum* (July/August 1984): 31.

42. Ibid.

Chapter 14

Ambulatory Care and Emergency Services

Edsel A. Cotter

A key person in the ambulatory and emergency services areas of a hospital is the admitting manager. Whatever other title this person may have, this individual is involved in the initial entry point of a patient into the health care facility.

One of the primary responsibilities for these departments is to provide well-trained personnel with interpersonal skills that make patients comfortable while under stress and pain. Personnel who also can accurately obtain demographic, third party, and diagnostic information are essential.

Admitting managers must be flexible in the daily activities of these departments and creative in initiating new procedures and protocols to meet administrative philosophies, governmental, and third party regulations. The manager must also organize disaster procedures that expedite the patient registration and diagnostic process at a moment's notice. Most of all, the manager must learn how to expedite the registration procedures for all patients.

DEFINITIONS

Ambulatory care can be defined as the provision of health care services to outpatients and to other patients who do not require admission to the hospital as inpatients.[1] Similar to this, an *ambulatory care center* is defined as a facility with an organized professional staff that provides various medical and health-related services to patients who do not require admission to a hospital as inpatients.[2]

On the other hand, *emergency services* in a hospital setting can be defined as a service providing immediate initial evaluation and treatment of acutely ill or injured patients on a 24-hour basis.[3]

TYPES OF AMBULATORY CARE FACILITIES

Basically, there are three types of ambulatory care situations: (1) free-standing facility, (2) hospital outpatient clinic, and (3) hospital emergency department.

256

Other ambulatory care facilities exist as well. These may include skilled nursing homes and hospice facilities, which are considered by the American Hospital Association as ambulatory care facilities.

Free-Standing Facility

A free-standing outpatient facility can be located in a high traffic area of the city. Marketing studies have been conducted that indicate that a location such as this would be convenient to the clientele served. It can also be a facility located in a city where there is no hospital. Free-standing outpatient facilities go under a variety of names. The center may be called a clinic, urgent care center, or a satellite clinic of a larger hospital. The center may be owned and operated by a professional practice group, an insurance company such as a health maintenance organization (HMO), a hospital, or a proprietary chain such as Humana or Hospital Corporation of America. Support services are available such as pharmacy, radiology, and laboratory. A main responsibility for the admitting manager is to organize a staff that will register the patients into the facility.

Outpatient Clinic Facility

An outpatient clinic facility is operated by a hospital and located within the physical structure of that hospital. There are other instances in which the facility is a separate building within itself adjacent to or near the main hospital. Sometimes this type of facility goes under the name of a medical professional facility where private practitioners have offices and support services available.

Emergency Services Department

The emergency services department is usually located within a hospital. It is open 24 hours a day, seven days a week. This operation has the capability to support professionally and diagnostically the acutely ill or injured patient, including the availability of all necessary supportive and ancillary services. Names for these facilities are listed in Table 14–1.

SEPARATE OR TOGETHER?

Advantages and Disadvantages

Which works best, the integrated emergency and outpatient clinic or separate areas within a hospital or separate facilities? This issue really should be addressed from the viewpoint of efficiency and duplication of services if they are combined

Table 14–1 Types of Ambulatory Care Facilities

Free-Standing Facility	Hospital Facility
Emergent/Urgent Care Center	Urgent Care Division
Outpatient Clinic	Emergency Department
Medical Services Building	Outpatient Clinic
Skilled Nursing Home	Ambulatory Surgery Division/Center
Day Care Center	Extended Care Division/Center
Extended Care Facility	
Ambulatory Surgery Center	
Hospice Center	

or separated. There are really no clear-cut answers. The variables are many, however, depending on the particular situation presented to the admitting director. The advantages and disadvantages of both a separated facility and an integrated facility are shown in Table 14–2.

The Conditions of Choice

The admitting manager may work in a setting in which the volume of patient visits and size of the facility allow one to integrate emergency and ambulatory care services. This can work rather well because it maximizes the use of the professional and support staff. It is cost effective usage of equipment, and it maximizes the return in dollars on the direct and indirect expenses.

There are conditions or situations in larger hospitals in which the volume of patient visits dictates separate physical facilities for ambulatory outpatient care and emergency service. A case in point is Ohio State University Hospitals, which has 241,000 outpatient clinic visits and 34,000 emergency department visits. If this is the case, then the emergency department in such a facility is usually located in an area convenient for patient transport in the way of ambulance and squad access. The ambulatory outpatient clinic can be located on an upper floor or a wing of the hospital. It may also be located in a separate facility. The support services offered should be kept in close proximity to each other for patient and practitioner effectiveness and convenience. Many inefficiencies are created when the outpatient services are separated, such as laboratories on the second floor, radiology on the third floor, and electrocardiography on the fifth floor. It creates more telephone calls for results and requests. This loss of time will mean loss of dollars and productivity. In some facilities patients may have to move from one outpatient clinical area to another, which could be from floor to floor, building to building, without escort.

Table 14–2 Advantages and Disadvantages of Separate and Integrated Facilities

	Advantages	*Disadvantages*
Separate Facility	Decentralizes volume Supports a localized geographical market Separates inpatients and outpatients Reduces patient travel internally Can reduce cost to patients due to reduced indirect expenses	Adds staff Adds equipment (duplication) Reduces physician efficiency Can increase cost of operation
Integrated Facility	Maximizes use of equipment Maximizes use of staff Reduces travel time for staff and patients Can reduce cost to patient	Increases volume and confusion Decreases efficiency of staff Creates patient delays and waiting for use of support equipment

WHO SHOULD MANAGE?

Who should manage the outpatient and ambulatory care clinic and the emergency department? This will depend on the administrative philosophy of the hospital or corporate leaders. One perspective is predicated on the fact that both areas have a common primary function. This function is to register patients. This presents a valid case for the manager of these departments to be the admitting manager.

Depending on the size of the hospital or facility, one could have an admitting manager who is responsible for the inpatient and outpatient registration areas. One may have a large volume of patients that dictates separate locations of services. The admitting director may be responsible for inpatient admissions only. The outpatient areas such as emergency services and clinic are then managed by another director, manager, supervisor, or assistant director of admitting.

As an example, Ohio State University Hospitals admits 30,000 inpatients and registers 241,000 outpatients annually in a separate private practice clinic building. The emergency department, located in the main hospital building, registers 34,000 patients annually. The hospital has a director and an assistant director of admitting responsible for inpatient registration. The office manager supervisor is responsible for the emergency department and an area coordinator is responsible for the outpatient registration areas. All four of these management persons are responsible to the same administrator, which facilitates interaction that produces continuity of management. Figure 14–1 shows the reporting relationships of these individuals.

The continuity of decision making occurs expediently when the management team works and creates together under similar leadership. This example of standardized information gathering and registration forms represents a team consensus of management that produces results. In this case, the outpatient registration form is used not only in the outpatient clinic but also in the emergency department. An example of this form is seen in Exhibit 14–1. Similarities of information collected can be seen with this form and the inpatient admitting form shown in Exhibit 14–2. The inpatient admitting form is an original plus three copies, while the outpatient form is an original and one copy. The goal of Ohio State University Hospitals is really the goal of any admitting manager assigned to these departments. It is to have a single form. Exceptions as to information required may be there, but they are few. In addition, the admitting manager, along with the administrative team, should develop an ambulatory care manual that can be used by the department and the physicians. An example of a shortened version of the manual used at Ohio State University Hospitals is seen in Appendix 14–A.

Figure 14–1 Organizational Chart for Ambulatory Care and Emergency Services

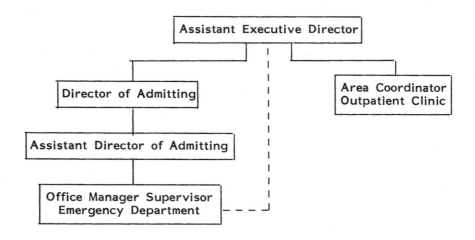

Source: Courtesy of Ohio State University Hospitals, Columbus, Ohio.

Exhibit 14–1 Outpatient Registration Form

OUTPATIENT REGISTRATION		OSU	The Ohio State University Hospitals
Please Print			Columbus, Ohio 43210

Patients Name: Last | First | MI | Maiden Name or Former Name | Date | Medical Records No.

Street Address | Attending Physician

City | State | Zip | County

Telephone No. Area | Sex M. F. | Race | Marital Status | Birthdate | Age | Social Security No.

Birthplace | If Born at OSU Mother's First Name

Referring Physician | Address

Next of Kin | Relationship | Telephone No.

Street Address | City | Area State | Zip

Responsible Party | Street Address | Relationship

City | State | Zip

Occupation | Social Security No. | Telephone No. | Employer

Employer's Address | City | State | Zip

Insurance Coverage

Medicare — Subscriber's Name | Medical Effective Date | Claim No.

Blue Cross — Address • City • State • Zip on Blue Cross Card | Major Medical Yes ☐ No ☐

Subscriber's Name | Relationship | Certificate No. | Group No. | Plan Code

Workmen's Compensation — Claim No. | Date of Injury | Employers Name & Address at Time of Injury | Effective Date

Welfare — Category | Case Name | Case No. | ADC. No. | County

Other Hospital Insurance — Name of Insurance | Subscriber's Name | Relationship | Certificate No. | Group No.

Insurance Company Address: Street | City | State | Zip

Additional Hospital Insurance — Name of Insurance | Subscriber's Name | Certificate No. | Group No.

Insurance Company Address: Street | City | State | Zip

Memos

Medical Records

The Ohio State University
Form 5261—Rev. 6/83

Source: Courtesy of Ohio State University Hospitals, Columbus, Ohio.

Exhibit 14–2 Inpatient Admitting Form

ADMITTING				OSU		The Ohio State University Hospitals Columbus, Ohio 43210		

NAME:	LAST	FIRST	M.I.	MAIDEN NAME	ROOM NO.	ADM. NO.		MED. REC. NO.
STREET ADDRESS					HOW LONG			OWN/RENT/UNKN
CITY		STATE	ZIP		COUNTY		INFO. BY	CLERK
TELEPHONE NO.		SEX	RACE	MARITAL STATUS	BIRTHDATE		AGE	SMOKER
SOCIAL SECURITY #		RELIGION		BIRTHPLACE	VALUABLES			DCP
ADM. DATE	ADM. TIME	ADM. TYPE		DISCH. DATE	DISCH. TIME		DISCH. TO:	
ATTENDING PHYS.		SERVICE	REASON FOR ADMISSION		PREV. ADM. DATE		INSTITUTION	DISCH. DATE
TRANS. TO O.S.U.H.		CODE #	FACILITY NAME			ADDRESS		
REFERRING PHYSICIAN				ADDRESS				
FAMILY PHYSICIAN				ADDRESS				
NEXT OF KIN				RELATIONSHIP			TELEPHONE NUMBER	
STREET ADDRESS				CITY		STATE		ZIP
PRIMARY GUARANTOR			RELATIONSHIP TO PT.		OCCUPATION		SOCIAL SECURITY #	
STREET ADDRESS				CITY		STATE		ZIP
EMPLOYER			ADDRESS		CITY		STATE	ZIP
EMPLOYER TELEPHONE			HOW LONG					
SECONDARY GUARANTOR			RELATIONSHIP TO PT.		OCCUPATION		SOCIAL SECURITY #	
EMPLOYER			ADDRESS		CITY		STATE	ZIP
EMPLOYER TELEPHONE			HOW LONG					

			INSURANCE COVERAGE				
AGENCY		INSURANCE COMPANY				SUBSCRIBER NAME	
INSURANCE COMPANY ADDRESS			CITY	STATE		ZIP	
MEDICARE NO.		POLICY NO.	CERTIFICATE NO.	GROUP NO.		TYPE CODE	
CASE NAME		CASE NO.	A.D.C. NO.	COUNTY	VOID DATE	REFERRAL DATE	
CODE	EFFECTIVE DATE	NUMBER OF DAYS	AMOUNT PER DAY	MISCELLANEOUS AMOUNT		DAYS USED	CLAIM FORM
ASSIGNED	CO-INSURANCE	DEDUCTIBLE	NON-COVERAGE	MAJOR MEDICAL COVERAGE			

			ADDITIONAL INSURANCE COVERAGE				
AGENCY		INSURANCE COMPANY				SUBSCRIBER NAME	
INSURANCE COMPANY ADDRESS			CITY	STATE		ZIP	
MEDICARE NO.		POLICY NO.	CERTIFICATE NO.	GROUP NO.		TYPE CODE	
CASE NAME		CASE NO.	A.D.C. NO.	COUNTY	VOID DATE	REFERRAL DATE	
CODE	EFFECTIVE DATE	NUMBER OF DAYS	AMOUNT PER DAY	MISCELLANEOUS AMOUNT	DAYS USED		CLAIM FORM
ASSIGNED	CO-INSURANCE	DEDUCTIBLE	NON-COVERAGE	MAJOR MEDICAL COVERAGE			

Exhibit 14–2 continued

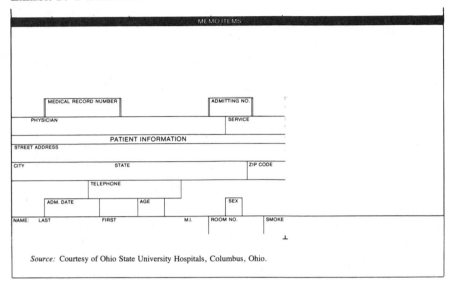

MEMO ITEMS

MEDICAL RECORD NUMBER | ADMITTING NO.

PHYSICIAN | SERVICE

PATIENT INFORMATION

STREET ADDRESS

CITY | STATE | ZIP CODE

TELEPHONE

ADM. DATE | AGE | SEX

NAME: LAST | FIRST | M.I. | ROOM NO. | SMOKE

Source: Courtesy of Ohio State University Hospitals, Columbus, Ohio.

PERSONNEL

Title and Function

Personnel are the key ingredients as to how well the facility provides services. They will be the public relations builders. They will be the lasting image that will remain with many patients. The manager must be selective when interviewing for staff. Personnel must have many skills, such as typing and computer terminal operation, with the most important being a pleasant personality. They must be able to smile, work well under pressure, and have a desire to help and serve people.

Individuals working in these departments can go under a variety of job titles. Some of these titles can be receptionist, secretary, preadmission coordinator, and ambulatory surgery unit coordinator. Appropriate job descriptions should also accompany these titles for the departments. Three typical job descriptions used at Ohio State University Hospitals in the ambulatory care and emergency services departments can be seen in Exhibits 14–3 through 14-5.

Staffing Ambulatory Care

Staffing the emergency services department and the ambulatory care department has its own challenges and problems based on the erratic activity in these

Exhibit 14–3 Job Description for Ward Clerk Position

OSU Position Description

See reverse side for instructions

1 General Information

Action:
☐ New position
☐ Vacant position replacing (name): _____

Category:
☐ Administrative &
  Professional monthly
☐ Classified biweekly
☐ Specials monthly
☐ Wages

Personnel Services use only
☐ Principal Administrative Officers, Senior Administrative & Professional Staff
☐ Unclassified Professional Staff
☐ Classified Staff
☐ Exempt
☐ Non-exempt

Name of incumbent	Position title: Ward Clerk, Clerk II
College or office	Department: University Hospital
Departmental area	Department number: 600 / Salary range number
Supervisor's title	Name of supervisor

☐ Reclassification ☐ Type 1
☐ Request for audit ☐ Type 2
  100 % FTE

2 Supervisory responsibility

Number	Title	Title

Personnel Services use only:

Approval by
Office of Personnel Services

Date _____ (_____)

3 Overall responsibilities & specific duties

% of time / Degree of supervision (see instruction for Item 3A on reverse side)

50% Greets patients arriving at reception desk; checks patients in by verifying information and appointment on doctor's list; imprints flow sheets and directs patients to physicians' offices or waiting area; may escort patients to exam area; coordinates registration procedure for ambulance and wheelchair patients with nursing staff and reception desk; verifies hospital number with Medical Records and/or CRT terminals; observes patients and secures immediate help depending on patient needs; uses CRT terminal for verifying patient information, making and cancelling appointments, and scheduling doctors' times; verifies charge forms for hospital visits. Checks hospital chart and replaces needed forms; stamps and dates forms for accurate identification; calls Medical Records

for accurate identification; calls Medical Records for old and missing charts; transcribes doctors' orders for lab work, special procedures, and gives instructions to patients for special tests; coordinates patient scheduling with various diagnostic and treatment areas.

47% Performs receptionist duties; answers telephone, takes and relays messages; pages personnel as directed; answers questions from patients, visitors, and staff; orients new personnel to ward clerk duties; compiles data as required; orders unit supplies; maintains physical environment in a neat and orderly manner; maintains doctors' appointment books in good order.

3% Performs other related duties as assigned.

(Use additional sheets as needed)

4 Contacts

Patients, doctors, personnel from medical complex, general public, various levels of nursing personnel, and students.

(Use additional sheets as needed)

5 Minimum qualifications

Two years clerical or office work experience; one year of college can be substituted for one year office work; or two years on nursing unit.

(Use additional sheets as needed)

6 Signatures

Incumbent	Date	Dept. head/supervisor	Date	Dean/Vice President	Date

Source: Courtesy of Ohio State University Hospitals, Columbus, Ohio.

Exhibit 14–4 Job Description for Registration Clerk

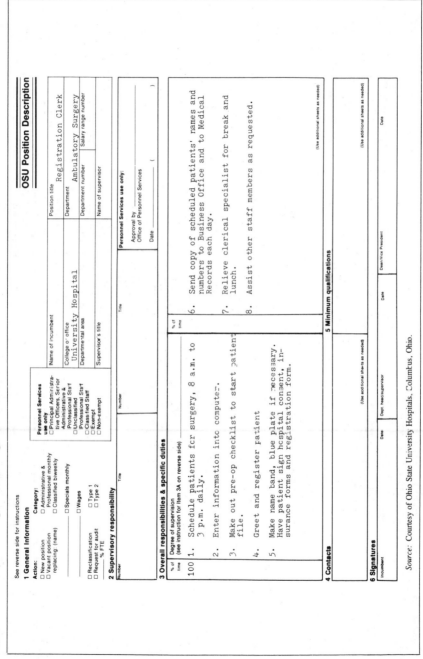

OSU Position Description

1 General Information

Action:
- ☐ New position
- ☐ Vacant position replacing (name)
- ☐ Reclassification
- ☐ Request for audit
- % FTE

Category:
- ☐ Administrative & Professional monthly
- ☐ Classified biweekly
- ☐ Specials monthly
- ☐ Wages

Personnel Services use only
- ☐ Principal Administrative Officers, Senior Administrative & Professional Staff
- ☐ Unclassified
- ☐ Administrative & Professional Staff
- ☐ Classified Staff
- ☐ Exempt
- ☐ Non-exempt
- ☐ Type 1
- ☐ Type 2

Position title: Registration Clerk

Name of incumbent

College or office: University Hospital

Department: Ambulatory Surgery

Departmental area

Department number

Salary range number

Supervisor's title

Name of supervisor

2 Supervisory responsibility

Number

Title

Number

Title

Personnel Services use only:

Approval by
Office of Personnel Services

Date _____ ( )

3 Overall responsibilities & specific duties

% of time — Degree of supervision (see instruction for Item 3A on reverse side)

100

1. Schedule patients for surgery, 8 a.m. to 3 p.m. daily.

2. Enter information into computer.

3. Make out pre-op checklist to start patient file.

4. Greet and register patient

5. Make name band, blue plate if necessary. Have patient sign hospital consent, insurance forms and registration form.

% of time

6. Send copy of scheduled patients' names and numbers to Business Office and to Medical Records each day.

7. Relieve clerical specialist for break and lunch.

8. Assist other staff members as requested.

(Use additional sheets as needed)

4 Contacts

(Use additional sheets as needed)

5 Minimum qualifications

(Use additional sheets as needed)

6 Signatures

Incumbent — Date

Dept. head/supervisor — Date

Dean/Vice President — Date

Source: Courtesy of Ohio State University Hospitals, Columbus, Ohio.

Exhibit 14–5 Job Description for Clerical Specialist Position

OSU Position Description

See reverse side for instructions

1 General Information

Action:
☐ New position
☐ Vacant position replacing: (name)

☐ Reclassification
☐ Request for audit
100 % FTE

Category:
☐ Administrative &
☐ Professional monthly
☐ Classified biweekly

_____
☐ Wages

☐ Type 1
☐ Type 2

Personnel Services use only
☐ Principal Administrative Officers, Senior Administrative & Professional Staff
☐ Unclassified Professional Staff
☐ Classified Staff
☐ Exempt
☐ Non-exempt

Name of incumbent	Position title Clerical Specialist
College or office University Hospital	Department Clerical Emergency Dept. Services
Departmental area	Department number 6000 Salary range number
Supervisor's title	Name of supervisor

Personnel Services use only:

Title   Number

2 Supervisory responsibility

Number   Title

Approval by
Office of Personnel Services

Date _____ (____)

3 Overall responsibilities & specific duties

% of time

Degree of supervision
(see instruction for Item 3A on reverse side)

60–70 Registers and interviews patients entering Emergency Department; sends, receives and directs telephone calls and other messages; serves as liaison person in communication network in ED (e.g. deals with families, friends of ED patients, provides public information; promotes good public relations, aids in handling of complaints and potentially unpleasant situations); orders medical records, x-rays, etc.; channels calls, information mail to proper person. Operates CRT and pneumatic tube, light typing. Discharges patients, gives referral information, schedules appointments, obtains billing information, bills charts, accepts cash payments, balances cash drawer, maintains daily logs of patients, specific lab tests, transfers, deaths, etc.,

30–40 mails referrals, files and other related clerical duties.

Assists with management of clerical staff activities under supervision of Business Services Officer. Manages office records and verifies charges in coordination with the Business Office and Business Services Officer. Gathers, organizes and summarizes data for department management reports. Searches and follows through on requests for lab results, clothing, etc. Maintains and orders office and provides backup in ordering storeroom supplies as needed. Types forms and orders. May assist with special projects as assigned by supervisor.

(Use additional sheets as needed)

4 Contacts

Police and Fire Departments, ambulances, nursing and physician personnel. Ancillary departments serving the E.D.

(Use additional sheets as needed)

5 Minimum qualifications

Mature person preferred. High school graduate; E.D. experience essential. Some typing, knowledge of office machines. Remains calm under stress.

(Use additional sheets as needed)

6 Signatures

Incumbent	Date	Dept. head/supervisor	Date	Dean/Vice President	Date

Source: Courtesy of Ohio State University Hospitals, Columbus, Ohio.

departments. Yet, good, sound staffing techniques can be calculated to assist in covering these key areas. Staffing for these departments needs to be addressed both quantitatively and philosophically.

The first step is knowing what management's philosophy is concerning the level of service. Do they desire no queuing lines of patients or is a 15 minute wait acceptable? What are the expectations of the physicians? If patients are processed in 15 minutes, is the area organized so that a physician can see the patient immediately? Can patients be scheduled in an outpatient environment, which is one way to control the flow?

Second, a study should be performed to analyze what times of day peak and minimum workloads occur. Peak and slow days can be analyzed. One may do this by listing each hour of the day vertically and each day of the week horizontally, starting with midnight and ending with midnight Sunday through Saturday. The study is performed for a minimum of two months, preferably with months chosen that do not have major holidays. A hash mark is placed between the hour and on the day each time a patient is registered. At the completion of the study, the number of patients by hour each day of the week is added and divided by the number of the day of the week the data were accumulated. This will give an average for that particular time and day of the week. Exhibit 14–6 is an example of such a study when averaged.

The data can be analyzed as follows:

1. Total the number of registrations per shift week.
2. Divide this total by seven days, which will give the average registration per shift day.
3. Divide this total by the number of registrations one full-time employee can complete during the shift. The final total will be the number of full-time employees required on this shift per day.

The calculations and sample figures are as follows:

1. 11 P.M. to 7 A.M. = 212 registrations
   7 A.M. to 3 P.M. = 787 registrations
   3 P.M. to 11 P.M. = 304 registrations
2. 212 ÷ 7 =   30.28 average per shift
   787 ÷ 7 = 112.42 average per shift
   304 ÷ 7 =   43.42 average per shift
3.   30.28 ÷ 32 = 0.94 (1.0) full-time employee required
   112.42 ÷ 32 = 3.51 (3.5) full-time employees required
     43.42 ÷ 32 = 1.35 (1.4) full-time employees required

Exhibit 14–6 Patient Admissions by Hour

	Sun	Mon	Tue	Wed	Thurs	Fri	Sat
12MN–1	7	3	0	2	4	10	11
1–2	8	0	1	0	2	0	3
2–3	8	5	7	1	4	0	2
3–4	9	5	0	0	1	0	1
4–5	10	0	3	2	1	1	4
5–6	5	6	3	4	2	3	2
6–7	11	4	9	7	8	12	13
7–8	10	12	14	16	17	19	22
8–9	17	10	18	23	22	14	17
9–10	11	8	12	14	9	7	8
10–11	12	13	15	14	18	14	19
11–12Noon	14	15	15	13	12	11	12
12–1	10	13	19	18	12	16	14
1–2	13	15	17	15	11	13	19
2–3	12	12	9	11	13	12	16
3–4	11	11	12	13	19	17	14
4–5	11	7	8	10	6	7	9
5–6	4	6	8	7	3	5	6
6–7	9	4	7	6	4	9	5
7–8	2	3	4	3	0	1	3
8–9	3	2	2	3	4	5	2
9–10	2	1	3	0	1	2	4
10–11	4	0	1	2	5	3	1
11–12MN	0	1	2	0	1	0	4

As can be seen, the 11 P.M. to 7 A.M. shift requires one full-time employee; the 7 A.M. to 3 P.M. shift requires 3.5 full-time employees; and the 3 P.M. to 11 P.M. shift requires 1.4 full-time employees.

Another factor that must be taken into account is that during the second and third shifts part-time employees will be needed to cover the peak hours on the shift. The 0.5 and 0.4 × 8 hours needed on this shift are used to cover the peak workload. Example: 0.5 × 8 = 4 hours and 0.4 × 8 = 3 hours and 12 minutes.

Remember, one should staff for the average and not allow the peaks to become the staffing criteria. If this is done the department will be overstaffed.

ISSUES IN AMBULATORY CARE

Ambulatory care outpatient visits are on the increase. Diagnostic related groups (DRGs) will be established by the federal and state governmental health care agencies for outpatient services. Private insurance carriers are expected to follow suit. Less highly publicized than DRGs is the natural extension of this idea into the outpatient area. Outpatient DRGs, known as ambulatory patient related groups (APGs), were developed at Yale University to serve the same role in the outpatient area that DRGs play in the inpatient area.[4]

The prospective reimbursement system demands that the facility be cost effective or it will lose money, and no one operates a business that loses money. One must start now to increase productivity without adding staff. The staff may need to be reduced after the present productivity of each area of responsibility is evaluated.

Another issue in conjunction with this is how much work can be expected from an employee? After a decision is made regarding the function of an employee, what can be measured as a performance standard must be decided. It could be the number of reservations taken daily, the number of admissions, the number of telephone calls, the number of discharges, and so on. Once these standards are established, staff requirements can be decided on and adjusted immediately. Staffing budget expenses are a major factor in whether the facility loses or gains financially with DRGs.

It is important to be creative and do some strategic planning because the facility is in competition with other facilities for patients. Some useful programs and suggestions an admitting manager can offer are the following:

- evening clinics such as obstetrics/gynecology, arthritis, geriatrics, and diagnostic
- "walk-in" clinic in the emergency department
- urgent care divisions

- weight loss clinic program
- Lamaze classes
- twenty-four hour/seven days per week operation
- adjacent parking facilities
- simpler registration systems and forms
- demand billing systems
- marketing programs for services provided in newspapers, television, and radio
- ZIP code studies to know where the catchment area of patients is coming from
- physician staff listing and telephone numbers provided to facilities for referral of patients
- referral telephone number hot-line service

The services an admitting manager renders will be scrutinized severely by the health care consumers who are more price conscious. The HMOs and the preferred provider organizations (PPOs) are rapidly and actively controlling the market place. Will the facility be a PPO for some company or industry? It is the responsibility of the admitting manager in charge of ambulatory care and emergency services to become well versed in all aspects of the present programs and the revolutionary health care programs that are on the horizon. The admitting manager is a key management person in determining a hospital's future.

ISSUES IN EMERGENCY SERVICES

Urgent care centers are here to stay. They meet the needs of the health care consumer at lower costs than most hospitals because they are free-standing facilities with lower overhead expenses. Their purpose is to provide immediate access to health care in a localized, geographical area of a town or a city. Hospital emergency departments will need to establish similar outpatient services in their departments at competitive rates. The admitting manager's expertise is needed to organize a triage procedure that separates the acutely ill from the minor injury. The clerical process must be condensed and the patient moved expeditiously through an urgent care procedure.

The admitting manager will need to initiate a financial interview process and procedure that obtains the information required to bill the patients immediately on discharge from the facility. Producing a patient's bill at the time of discharge allows increased cash collections when there is no third party coverage. The more information and money that can be collected at the time of discharge, the possibility increases 100 percent that the institution's accounts receivables will decrease.

DISASTER AND THE ROLE OF ADMITTING

When discussing potential disasters, the key phrase is "be prepared." A disaster can be announced when one least expects it. The admitting manager should prepare a written departmental plan that is distributed to all employees. The plan should be concise, and it should support the hospital's overall disaster plan.

The department's goal, during a disaster, is to register (admit) patients with minimal primary demographic information and diagnosis. The department is responsible for immediate bed assignments. Therefore, the manager must know instantly where the empty beds are located. The plan must include the names and telephone numbers where the staff can be reached if additional assistance is needed. Group lists are organized with the first person listed in each group calling those in his or her group once notified that the hospital disaster plan has been initiated. The staff should be organized to support the entry area for patients so they can be registered. Someone is assigned to answer the office telephone, to assign beds as needed, and to call the nursing units for empty bed verification and potential discharges. An example of a disaster plan can be found in Appendix 14-B.

CONCLUSION

This chapter has been devoted to a discussion of experiences, observations, and reference information applicable to ambulatory care and emergency services in an admitting context. The admitting manager of a registration department in a hospital, an outpatient clinic, or other facility situation has a primary responsibility to manage a staff that provides the initial services rendered to the patients that receive health care at that facility or institution. Established written procedures are mandatory.

Admitting managers must have a staff sufficient to meet the service demand that has an "I care" attitude. Productivity and staffing requirements go hand in hand. Productivity standards must be established, and the manager must also be creative with new ideas for marketing services offered at the facility because the competition is trying to acquire its share of the marketplace. The admitting manager must be a cost-effective manager or the facility will not survive financially. Finally, an admitting manager with responsibility for emergency services must be prepared for a disaster with a written procedure guide.

The suggestions and recommendations contained in this chapter are not the ultimate solution. They are intended to stimulate thinking and possibly provide a starting point and a direction. The important thing is to learn an idea; enhance, elaborate, and adapt it to a specific setting; and use it to solve problems. Only procedures or systems that benefit the patient and the facility should be created. Finally, the manager must be prepared for the future.

NOTES

1. American Hospital Association, *Hospital Administration Terminology* (Chicago: American Hospital Association, ANA No. 001110): 2, 13.

2. Ibid.

3. Ibid.

4. Robert E. Knapp, "The Development of Outpatient Diagnostic Related Groups," *The Journal of Ambulatory Care Management* (May 1983): 3.

Appendix 14–A

Ambulatory Surgery Manual

INTRODUCTION TO AMBULATORY SURGERY

What is Ambulatory Surgery?

Ambulatory surgery is the completion of a surgical procedure on the same-day basis without anticipation of an overnight hospitalization. It is applicable to carefully selected patients who are healthy except for the complaint that necessitates elective surgery and in whom serious complications are highly unlikely.

What Are the Advantages of Ambulatory Surgery?

1. High quality surgical care is conveniently and safely provided to patients at less cost than is required for similar services requiring overnight hospitalization.
2. Government and commercial medical insurance agencies encourage the appropriate use of ambulatory surgery facilities.
3. A more effective use of hospital beds is provided by eliminating the need for hospital admission.
4. Patients can be discharged by 5 P.M. the same day of surgery and convalesce in the familiar surroundings of their home.
5. Postoperative care is minimal and simple, with a patient's normal level of activity altered for only a few days.

Source: Courtesy of Ohio State University Hospitals, Columbus, Ohio.

GENERAL POLICIES*

A. *Surgery Selection*

    1. Elective procedures (see list at the end of this section):
The surgical operations listed form a basic outline of appropriate ambulatory surgery procedures. The list is not all inclusive. Procedures not appearing on this list may be most appropriately performed in an ambulatory setting under certain circumstances. By the same token, procedures listed may require inpatient management under other circumstances. Decisions regarding the mechanism of health care delivery remain the prerogative of the attending physician and are based on data and experience only available to him or her. Documentation may be required to support these decisions in some instances.

    2. Inappropriate procedures:
       a. Operative duration greater than two hours
       b. Recovery duration greater than four hours expected
       c. Blood transfusion requirement anticipated
       d. Septic or "dirty" cases
       e. Admission anticipated

SUITABLE PROCEDURES FOR AMBULATORY SURGERY
may include, but are NOT limited to, the following:

Abscess, I & D
Adhesions of clitoris, lysis
Amniocentesis
Arthroscopy

Bartholin Cystectomy
Biopsy of bone
Biopsy of breast
Biopsy — cervix, vagina, vulva
Biopsy of ear canal
Biopsy or excision of skin or
    subcutaneous tissue
Biopsy of oral cavity, tongue and lip
Blepharoplasty
Bronchoscopy with or without biopsy

Caldwell-Luc with biopsy
Cataract extraction
Cerclage
Cervical amputation
Circumcision
Closed reduction of nasal fracture
Closure of septal perforation
Cold knife conization
Colostomy, revision
Colposcopy
Colpotomy
Cryotherapy — cervix, vagina, vulva
Culdocentesis
Culdoscopy

---

*Note: All exceptions to these policies will require consultation with the attending surgeon, anesthesiologists, and, in some instances, nursing personnel.

Cyst excision — cervix, vagina, perineum

Cystoscopy

Dilatation and curettage

Drainage of peritonsillar abscess

Electrocautery — cervix, vagina, vulva

Eiosiotomy

Esophagoscopy with or without biopsy

Examination under anesthesia

Excision of benign or small malignant tumor of the oral cavity, tongue or lip

Excision of cervical note

Excision of lesion of tendon sheath or soft tissue

Excision of skin lesions with local flaps

Exploratory tympantomy

Extraocular muscle surgery

Fetoscopy

Fiberoptic internal examination

Flap delays

Foreign body excision

Full thickness skin graft

Hymenotomy

Hysteroscopy — diagnostic or surgical

Hysterosalpingogram

Incision and drainage of postauricular abscess

Intranasal polypectomy

Laparoscopy — diagnostic, sterilization, surgical

Laryngoscopy with or without biopsy

Laser therapy

Lymph node biopsy

Marsupilization, Bartholin's gland

Maxillary sinusotomy with irrigation

Mini Laparotomy — sterilization

Myringoplasty

Myringotomy with or without tube insertion

Nasal septoplasty

Otoplasty

Outfracture and cautery of the inferior turbinates

Paracentesis

Perineorrhaphy

Polypectomy — cervical, uterine

Release of carpal tunnel

Removal of arch bars

Removal of foreign body from ear

Removal of salivary stone

Rhinoplasty

Rhytidoplasty

Rhymoplasty

Scar revisions

Septoplasty

Sigmoidoscopy

Simple lymphadenectomy

Skin grafts, minor

Submucous resection of the inferior turbinates

Submucous resection of the nasal septum

Tarsorrhaphy (permanent or temporary)

Takedown of tissue flaps

Urethral dilatation

Vaginal stenosis, release

Vaginoplasty

Vasectomy

Vocal Restorative Surgery (Tracheal-Esophageal shunt)

Z-plasty

B. *Patient Selection*

American Society of Anesthesiologists (ASA) Class I and Class II patients with anesthesia consultation will generally be those selected for ambulatory surgery.

A Class I patient is one who has no organic, physiological, biochemical, or psychiatric disturbance. The pathologic process for which the operation is to be performed is localized and not conducive to systemic disturbance. *Example:* An inguinal hernia, D & C, and laparoscopic procedure in an otherwise healthy patient.

A Class II patient is one who has mild to moderate systemic disturbance caused either by the condition to be treated surgically or by other pathophysiologic processes. *Example:* The presence of mild diabetes (treated by pill or diet) or mild essential hypertension, moderate obesity, or chronic bronchitis. For the purposes of this program, also included here are the extremes of age, either the neonate (under one month) or the octogenarian, even though no discernible systemic disease is present.

Other patients may be occasionally considered for Ambulatory Surgery pending consultation with anesthesia.

C. *Preoperative Investigation*

1. History and physical examination
   Completed history and physical examination including preoperative diagnosis and proposed procedure must be available in the Ambulatory Surgery office by noon on the day prior to the scheduled operation except under unusual circumstances.
2. Laboratory Testing
   All laboratory and radiologic tests must be performed within fourteen (14) days of the scheduled procedure. The following tests need to be done for patients receiving general, regional, or local standby anesthesia:
   a. Patients less than 40 years of age to receive a Hemoglobin/Hematocrit or CBC.
   b. Patients 40 years of age or over are to receive:
      —Hemoglobin/Hematocrit or CBC
      —Sodium, potassium
      —Chest x-ray
      —Electrocardiogram
   c. If regional anesthesia is anticipated, patients are to receive:
      —PT
      —PTT
      —Platelet count

    d. Additional tests may be ordered for appropriate conditions, i.e., glucose

    e. Each surgeon will determine preadmission testing for patients scheduled for local anesthesia.

    f. A mechanism will be available for testing on the day of surgery for follow-up investigation.

    g. All preoperative test results must be available in the Ambulatory Surgery Office by noon on the day prior to the scheduled operation except under unusual circumstances.

  3. Lack of laboratory data, deficient history and physical examination, patient noncompliance, or intercurrent illness will result in cancellation.

  4. An attending anesthesiologist will review all patient data on the afternoon prior to surgery, and in consultation with the attending surgeon, correct all deficiencies or reschedule the procedure.

D. *Scheduling Times*

  1. Patients requiring general or regional anesthesia must be scheduled from 8 A.M. with the last patient scheduled at noon. This allows for sufficient recovery time prior to closure of the unit.

  2. Patients receiving local anesthesia may be scheduled after noon with the last patient scheduled in such a manner that he/she will be ready for discharge by 5:30 P.M.

E. *Patient Companion*

Patients must be accompanied by a responsible adult on the day of surgery. Patients are not permitted to leave the hospital alone, and surgery will be postponed if arrangements have not been made for a responsible adult to accompany the patient home.

F. *Informed Consent*

It is the responsibility of the surgeon to counsel the patient concerning the proposed surgical procedure and ambulatory surgery policies and to document this in the medical record.

G. *Discharge Criteria*

An order for discharge from the Ambulatory Surgery Unit must be written by a physician. Criteria for discharge include:

  1. Stable vital signs consistent with pre-operative status
  2. No excess bleeding from wound site
  3. Able to sit up for 5 minutes without dizziness or nausea
  4. Able to take and retain appropriate oral fluids
  5. Able to walk without difficulty or dizziness

H. *Patient Flow through the System*

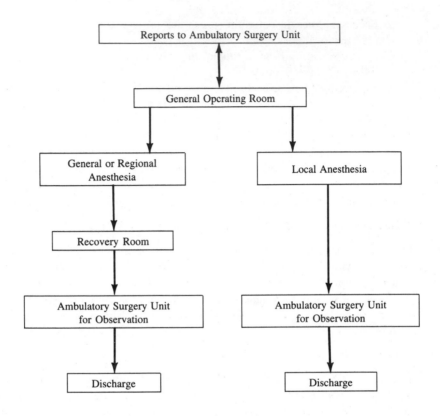

REGISTRATION PROCEDURE

I. Pre-registration

The physician office telephones the Ambulatory Surgery Registration desk to schedule an appointment for surgery. The following information must be provided to the Registration Clerk:

_____ Patient Name (maiden also if applicable)

_____ Address (include county)

_____ Attending Surgeon and First Assistant

_____ Referring Physician

_____ Patient Home Telephone Number

_____ Sex

_____ Race

_____ Date of Birth
_____ Social Security Number
_____ Hospital Number (if on file)
_____ Diagnosis
_____ Exact OR Procedure
_____ Estimated length of procedure
_____ Anesthesia

II. Scheduling OR Time

The Registration Clerk will schedule cases in the designated Ambulatory Surgery Operating Rooms at the time of pre-registration and on a first come, first served basis. The surgery schedule will be closed two working days prior to surgery. Call between the hours of 8 A.M. and 3 P.M. to schedule surgery.

III. Registration in Outpatient Appointment System

The Registration Clerk will enter all pertinent information from the registration form into the Outpatient Registration System. A report of all patients scheduled for Ambulatory Surgery on a given day will be produced at noon the day prior to surgery.

IV. Day of Surgery

On the patient's arrival in the Ambulatory Surgery Staging Area, the Registration Clerk will emboss a patient charge plate (providing no previous clinic visit) and place a patient identification band on the patient's wrist. The Registration Clerk will have the patient sign a Hospital Consent form and an Assignment of Benefits form if applicable or collect the deposit. Deposits will be immediately forwarded to the Inpatient Business Office.

FINANCIAL INTERVIEW

A financial interview must be completed and a clearance given to all patients before ambulatory surgery will be provided. The Referral Clearance Form (Exhibit 14–A1) will be used for that purpose. Patients should be referred to the Business Office to complete a financial interview prior to preadmission testing and surgery. The patient information brochure can be used to advise patients of their financial responsibility.

If the patient is in a physician's office within the Hospital or in the Clinic on the day of pre-registration, the patient should report to the Outpatient Business Office for financial clearance.

If a patient is not located within the Hospital on the day of pre-registration, the Outpatient Business Office will contact the patient by phone to determine third party coverage. If there is none, an appointment will be made for that patient to come to the Business Office and complete a financial interview.

Exhibit 14–A1 Ambulatory Surgery Referral Clearance Form

Date _____

PATIENT'S NAME   _____
PATIENT'S ADDRESS   _____
                        _____
                        _____
TYPE OF PROCEDURE   _____
DATE OF PROCEDURE   _____

BUSINESS OFFICE USE *ONLY*

CLEARANCE   _____ APPROVED   _____ DISAPPROVED

DATE OF CLEARANCE   _____
SIGNATURE   _____

It is important to note that the Business Office *should* interview the patient the same day they are in the physician's office to schedule the surgery. However, if for any reason the patient cannot come into the Business Office on that day, the patient *must* be interviewed prior to receiving the presurgical testing.

The interview will consist of the following steps:

1. If a patient has full pay third party coverage (verified), he or she will be cleared for presurgical testing and surgery. Coverage will be verified by calling the insurance company or the employer unless Medicare or Medicaid is involved. If one or both of these agencies are used, we must have a copy of the card. If Medicaid is going to be used, the card must show the current effective date for coverage for the month in which surgery is performed.
2. If the third party coverage pays 75 percent or more, a deposit should be required to cover the remaining percent. If the patient does not have the required deposit, a financial interview will be completed and a promissory note required before clearance will be given.
3. When a patient does not have third party coverage, a full deposit will be required.
4. If a patient does not have third party coverage and does not have the required deposit, a financial interview is required. Based on the financial evaluation, a deposit of 50 percent will be required and a promissory note for payment of the balance due upon receipt of the bill will also be required.

5. A patient who is unable to pay a deposit and may qualify for welfare will be referred to the social worker in the Clinic for assistance and must be sent to the Welfare Department to complete the application. The surgery will be postponed until Welfare determines eligibility.

6. After having completed the financial interview, in person or by phone, the person who conducted the interview will date and sign the Referral Clearance Form. Each patient interviewed in person will be given the Referral Clearance Form, which will be stamped "Cleared" by the Business Office. *The patient must present the cleared form to the Preadmission Testing Area at the time of arrival.* If no preadmission testing is to be done, the Outpatient Business Office will forward the form to Ambulatory Surgery Unit.

7. If the Referral Clearance Form cannot be approved, the patient will be informed that the procedure cannot be performed, unless it is an emergency, and the referring physician will be notified by the Outpatient Business Office.

8. It must be understood that all patients must be cleared by the Business Office prior to surgery and testing. If a patient is cleared on the basis of a deposit and shows up for surgery without the deposit, the surgery will be postponed until the deposit is paid.

PREADMISSION TESTING (P.A.T.) PROCEDURES

Appointment Scheduling

1. Physician's office schedules presurgery testing through P.A.T.
2. Appointments may be scheduled Monday through Friday during the hours 8:00 A.M. to 4:30 P.M.
3. Appointment times will be determined by the number of tests required/ordered as well as date/time of scheduled surgery.
   —Patients scheduled for a Monday surgery time must be tested before the previous Thursday.
   —The maximum interval between P.A.T. and date of surgery cannot exceed 14 calendar days.
4. Physician's office gives the following information to P.A.T. nurse:

   1. Patient's name (maiden if married female)
   2. Patient's address
   3. Telephone numbers: business/home
   4. Social Security number
   5. Hospital number (if on file)
   6. Date of birth/age

7. Surgeon's name/office phone number
8. Date and time of surgery
9. Operative procedure
10. Anesthesia
11. Lab tests and physician orders
12. Financial clearance
13. Interview scheduled _____

Patient Instructions/Information

1. Physician's office will instruct patient to:

   —Complete financial clearance prior to P.A.T.
   —Report to lobby information desk (information desk receptionist will notify P.A.T. nurse that patient has arrived).
   —Plan to spend at least two hours (three hours if financial clearance necessary just prior to P.A.T.) in the P.A.T. area.
2. Information desk receptionist will direct patient to room where tests will be initiated.
3. P.A.T. nurse will not proceed with preadmission testing until patient's approved financial clearance form has been received.

P.A.T. Nurse Responsibilities

1. Determine and record appointment times in scheduling book according to date of scheduled surgery.
2. Contact master file to obtain/verify patient hospital numbers (use information from flow sheet).
3. Prepare folder and plate for scheduled patient.
4. Prepare daily lists of scheduled patients for lab, x-rays, and clerical staff.
5. When patient arrives at P.A.T., verify financial clearance and check patient information for accuracy.
6. Take height, weight, B.P./T.P.R. and record on P.A.T. flow sheet.
7. Send patient to lab, X-ray, ECG as indicated.
8. Review with patient instructions regarding date and time of surgery; answer any questions patient may have.
9. Correlate reports and charge documents as they are received from clinic lab and delivered from X-ray and ECG.
10. Deliver patient P.A.T. folder to Ambulatory Surgery Unit reception area (at least 24 hours prior to scheduled surgery).

Exhibit 14–A2 Patient Discharge Instructions

Patient _____ Date _____ Time _____
Call Office _____ To Make Appointment for _____
To see Dr. _____ ☐ Clinic Appointment _____
Medications _____ ☐ No Medicines for 24 Hours

_____

Activity _____ ☐ No Restrictions
Diet _____ ☐ No Restrictions
Care of Operative Area _____

_____
_____ ☐ Keep Clean and Dry
Special Instructions _____

_____

☐ Do not drink alcoholic beverages, drive a car, or operate hazardous machinery for
   24 hours. Call your physician or the Ambulatory Surgery Unit if you have any problems
   or questions.

_____   _____
Physician's Signature   Nurse's Signature

COMPLETE IN DUPLICATE

SURGERY DAY

A. When To Report
   Patients should plan to arrive at the hospital one and one-half hours before the
   scheduled time for the operation (one hour for local anesthesia patients).

B. Where To Report
   The Ambulatory Surgery Unit is located on the fifth floor. Patients should take
   the public elevators to the fifth floor, and walk through the atrium to the
   registration clerk's desk. The patient's companion or escort responsible for
   transporting the patient home should report to the Ambulatory Surgery Unit
   with the patient. The registration clerk will ask the patient to complete and sign
   a hospital consent form, an outpatient registration form, and assignment of
   insurance benefits form.

C. Parking

The medical center parking ramp is available for visitor parking.

D. Waiting Area

During surgery the patient's escort should wait in the surgery lounge located in the lobby. This is the location where he or she will be notified by a hospital volunteer when surgery is finished. If the escort wishes to leave the hospital during the operation, a telephone number must be left with the Ambulatory Surgery Unit nurse.

E. Discharge Instructions

1. A responsible adult must be available to accompany the patient home or he or she will not be discharged. The patient is financially responsible for any extended stay due to the absence of an escort. A patient may not drive or go alone by taxi.

2. Written discharge instructions will be given to all patients (Exhibit 14–A2).

Appendix 14–B

Example of a Disaster Plan

ADMITTING DEPARTMENT

DISASTER PLAN

Administration will notify the Admitting Department of a disaster in the area. The person in charge of the department will call persons shown in the "Disaster Call List" Group A. These persons will call the employees assigned to their group.

Group A

Director	
Assistant Director	(B)
Office Manager	(C)
Supervisor, Evenings	
Supervisor, Weekends	(D)
Secretary	

See Disaster Call List for Telephone Numbers.

These may be called from the office, or from home, whichever place you may be at the time. Tell them, "there is a disaster, come to the office as quickly as possible, and be sure to have your I.D. card with you." Make a checklist of your calls and give it to the supervisor in charge.

The supervisor in charge will assign employees on their arrival as shown in the "Employee Location List."

Employees who drive must enter from the 12th Avenue entrance (North of the Dental Building) and park in B lot, Polo Field, or the Parking Ramp. Enter the Hospital via the back doors of the North Wing.

Source: Courtesy of Ohio State University Hospitals, Columbus, Ohio.

Casualties will enter the Emergency Room (Triage Area). Doctors will direct the patients to the proper area as shown in the "Employees Location List."

Control Center phone numbers are 8197, 8446, 8649, 8148; this is located in the Administration Offices, 104 Doan Hall. Questions that cannot be answered by the supervisor in charge should be directed to the Control Center.

The important points in any disaster are few but very necessary. Do your utmost to respond when you are called. Do exactly what you are told to do. Be sure you understand your instructions completely. Do a complete job and *do not* leave one section out regardless of how small it may seem.

Supervisor in Charge of Duties:

1. Notify "Disaster Call List A" and advise of disaster and tell them to make their calls.
2. Obtain from Control Center (8197, 8446, 8649, 8148)
   A. Type of Disaster
   B. Location
   C. Time
   D. Expected Casualties
3. Advise Control Center
   A. Usable beds in all buildings by the following categories:
      1. Burn Room
      2. Med/Surg
      3. ICU (SICU, MICU, SSD, MSD)
      4. CCU
      5. Total for Dodd—Upham
      6. OB and NB
      7. Possible Discharges
         a) Number of Clean Beds
         b) Number of Dirty Beds
4. Advise Housekeeping of all dirty beds by room number.
5. Assign employees as they arrive.
6. Send all scheduled admissions to a holding area in the East side of Rhodes Hall Lobby. A Hospital representative must be assigned to stay with each group and await further instructions.
7. Make a new bed board showing all usable beds in all buildings and list all expected discharges as the nursing units call them in.
8. Assign one employee to walk the floors and pick up discharges and transfers from the nursing stations in University Hospital and Rhodes Hall. The Admitting Office will constantly keep the Control Center informed of bed availability. If additional beds are needed, the same procedure will be initiated in Dodd and Upham Halls.

9. Assign casualties to beds as done under normal conditions.
10. Discharges and transfers are to be reported to the Control Center via the Information Desk as soon as possible.
11. Prepare report as follows:
    A. Number of employees available
    B. Length of time between events
    C. Any unusual events
    D. Evaluation
    E. Suggested changes
12. Routine admissions will be delayed until further notice, except *Emergency Room* and *OB Patients*.
13. The Admitting Office supervisor will contact the Control Center to request auxilliary help at 8197, 8446, 8649, 8148.

INSTRUCTIONS FOR COMPLETING THE "DISASTER TAG"

The Disaster Tag is a three-part form. It will be placed on the patient's arm by the medical records department. The yellow copy is for Admitting, the white copy is for the Emergency Room desk, and the hard copy remains on the patient. Below is a sample of the form and the X's indicate what we must complete. When you have completed the form, tear off the Admitting and Emergency Room copy. Bring the Admitting copy to the main office for a bed assignment and take the white copy to the Emergency Room Front Desk.

NOTE: Admitting personnel will return all hard copies of Disaster Tags when patients are released from check areas to the Admitting Supervisor.

PRINT ALL   ATTACH TAG
INFORMATION   SECURELY TO PATIENT

Family Name		First	Initial	Tag No.
X				123
Address				Phone
X				X
Date	A.M. P.M.	Age-Yrs.	Sex M-F	Religion
X	X		X	X

Notify in Case of Emergency	Relationship
X	X
Address	Phone

Tentative Diagnosis: If injury, state when, where, how incurred

Priority:	urgent	less urgent	least urgent
Surgery:	major	minor	first aid

Family Name	First	Initial	Tag No.
X			123

COPY FOR ADMITTING DEPARTMENT

Please use a hard surface when completing the form so all copies will be legible.

EMPLOYEE LOCATION LIST

PLACE	*NUMBER*	*DUTIES*
1. Emergency Room (Triage)	3 (Or What is Needed)	Place all the necessary information on the Disaster Tag
2. Main Office	As Assigned	As Directed
3. Upham Hall	As Assigned	As Directed
4. Dodd Hall	As Assigned	As Directed

Chapter 15

Interdepartmental
Relationships

Donald E. Hancock

When one thinks of the admitting department and its relationship to other hospital departments, it is important to first understand the peculiar characteristics of that particular admitting department. Some admitting departments play a major role in the operation of the hospital, being responsible for many different facets of the patient business operation. This would include preadmission, admission registration, insurance verification, financial counseling, discharge planning, cashiering, billing, and collections. Depending on the size of the hospital, the governance of the hospital, and the location of the hospital, admitting departments can take on many different appearances. Most admitting departments in large hospitals tend to be quite specialized, for example, concentrating solely on patient registration or financial arrangements, whereas admitting departments in smaller hospitals tend to be very general, encompassing several areas of responsibility (e.g., billing, collections, cashiering). Some admitting departments may be totally automated with the most up-to-date, state-of-the-art technology, whereas others may be totally manual in their operations. Admitting departments in for-profit hospitals and most not-for-profit hospitals generally have a stronger financial orientation than do admitting offices in government hospitals, county hospitals, and other not-for-profit hospitals. Some admitting offices are full-fledged departments, while others are a division of a larger unit and may include the billing and collection function, medical records function, or finance and accounting. In general, admitting departments are very interdisciplinary in their role in the hospital since they bridge several areas of responsibility.

Note: Contributing to this chapter were Andrea Brinsko, Admitting Supervisor, North Florida Regional Hospital, Gainesville, Florida; Margaret Holtsclaw, A.A.M., Supervisor, Inpatient Relations, University Community Hospital, Tampa, Florida; and Ruth Mathis, A.A.M., Supervisor of Reservations, University Community Hospital, Tampa, Florida.

When one mentions the admitting department, rarely will the term have the same meaning to individuals from different hospitals. Although these differences are numerous and significant, there are several basic responsibilities every admitting department carries out:

- It is the mechanism for a physician to get a patient into the hospital.
- It is the initial contact point with the hospital for most patients and/or their families.
- It is the initial repository of critical information about the patient and, subsequently, becomes the central distribution point of this information.

Each of these roles carries with it a relationship with one or more critical members of the health care team. This is illustrated in Figure 15–1.

The relationship between the admitting department and the actual process of scheduling the admission primarily deals with coordination of resources necessary to take care of the patient. This includes the physician's time, the nurse's time, available operating room time, laboratory, radiology, and other ancillary resources. Once the patient arrives at the hospital, the admitting department then becomes that of an accommodator of the patient and the family, with admitting personnel soliciting the necessary information required by the hospital. The assignment of the patient's bed is basically a coordinated effort between the physician and the nursing staff and the admitting department to locate the most appropriate bed given the patient's condition and the desires of the physician and nursing staff. The relationship between the admitting department and the information systems is critical in that it is a patient data base from which the admitting department begins most of its data gathering efforts. All of this information is, at some point, passed to the departments listed under data distribution in Figure 15–1. For the most part, these departments depend very heavily on the accuracy and timeliness of the information provided by the admitting department. Although most of the relationships are of a service nature, it takes a particular amount of political savvy and sensitivity to carry out these roles effectively. Many of these departments have their own priorities and needs, some of which conflict with those of the admitting department. The manager of the admitting office must recognize the sensitivity of these issues from the standpoint of those departments and work in a manner that meets everyone's needs. An example of this is when a prominent physician wishes to admit a patient with very questionable financial resources. The admitting manager certainly knows the policies of the hospital with respect to financial arrangements but also understands the status of that particular physician on the hospital's medical staff. It is in this context that the admitting department and its relationship to other departments in the hospital is viewed.

Figure 15–1 Admitting's Relationship to Other Departments

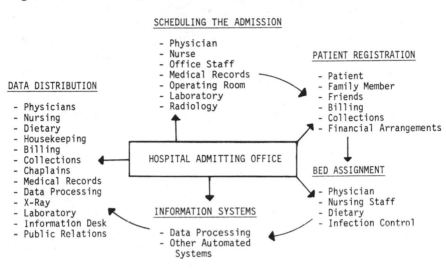

THE MEDICAL STAFF

The relationship with the hospital's medical staff is perhaps the most critical for any admitting department. Regardless of the size or the complexity of the hospital, the interaction between the physician and the admitting department is basically the same—the physician or a member of the physician's staff arranges for the admission and the admitting office then processes that transaction in accordance with the hospital's policies and procedures. Although this scenario is straightforward and very simple, there are many variables that affect the relationship of the admitting department staff with the medical staff.

Classification of the Patient

Many hospital admission policies require that each admission be classified as either an elective, urgent, or emergency admission. This classification generally determines the priorities for processing the patient through the admitting department. Although elective admissions are generally worked in as the patients arrive at the hospital, obviously the emergencies and sometimes the urgent admissions take priority. These patients are generally processed through the admitting department first, take priority in the assignment of the patient's bed, and take priority in getting all of the necessary paperwork to the appropriate inpatient unit. In order for this system to work efficiently, it is imperative that the admission policies of the hospital clearly define the criteria used for classifying these patients. If the hospital census is very high, it may be an old game to classify patients as urgent or emergency to take advantage of getting the patient into the hospital over any elective admissions that may be scheduled for that day. Admitting managers play an important role in working with hospital administration and the members of the medical staff to develop medical criteria used for classifying incoming admissions. Once these medical criteria have been developed, then the priority for processing admissions should also be defined with the help of the members of the medical staff and hospital administration.

The Financial Condition of the Patient

Aside from the physical condition of the patient, the financial status of the patient is also a very important issue in medical staff relationships. Obviously, hospitals have to implement thorough financial screening of all admissions, particularly the elective admissions, in order to survive. Although most physicians' offices conduct financial screenings of their patients, hospital admitting departments generally go into much more thorough detail and are dealing with a larger financial strain on the patient and the family. Most physicians are very cognizant of the hospital's financial policies regarding admissions and are very cooperative in honoring those conditions of admission. However, there are often times when a patient's physical condition and the necessity to be admitted to a particular hospital override all financial considerations. The admitting manager should work very closely with the admitting physician to make sure these patients are handled in a very objective and expeditious manner, in accordance with the hospital's admission policies. Obviously, there is little choice but to admit the patient in an emergency situation, regardless of the financial arrangements, but sometimes this means of entry into the hospital can be abused by the admitting physician. The hospital admitting policies should be very clear in addressing these types of patients. If the hospital has clearly defined criteria for classifying admissions and efforts are made to secure adequate financing of the patient's care, then generally any conflicts with members of the medical staff can be solved to everyone's satisfaction.

Availability of Beds

Once the decision to admit the patient has been made by the physician and cleared by the admitting department, finding an available bed on a suitable admission date is the next issue. The admission date must not only accommodate the patient but also be satisfactory to the physician. Also, the appropriate resources, including operating room time, must also be available. Utilization review issues also play on this decision since patients cannot be admitted too far in advance of any scheduled procedures (e.g., being admitted on Friday for a Monday surgery date). The availability of the patient, the physician, and operating room time must all be coordinated before a suitable admission date can be scheduled. This is not always the easiest task to accomplish, particularly if the hospital census is running very high.

Priority of Teaching Cases

Many hospitals that maintain resident teaching programs will see patients whose condition constitutes a significant teaching case for its house staff. Physicians treating these patients want the patient to be admitted regardless of any financial problems the patient may have paying for the care. Most hospitals that maintain such teaching programs have policies that address teaching cases and how to handle them from a financial standpoint. Generally, such cases are referred to the admitting manager directly by the admitting physician with all the appropriate justification for admitting the patient accompanying such requests. In some cases it may be necessary to involve the hospital's chief of staff. The admitting department must interpret and carry out the hospital's policies and procedures with respect to these variables in order to maintain an effective relationship with the medical staff.

Most admission scheduling systems prioritize the patients based on the urgency of the admission, whether or not the patient is scheduled for surgery, the date and time the admission was called in, and the financial classification of the patient. Since each of these issues affects the way a physician can schedule an admission, it is wise for the admitting manager to solicit the input from the medical staff in writing policies and procedures that address this system. Physicians should have direct input into defining the categories of admission and establishing the criteria for an elective, urgent, or an emergency admission. In addition, the physician, along with the director of the operating room, should define clearly the procedures necessary to schedule patients for surgery. Many admitting departments use a common telephone number to schedule both the admission date and the operating room date. It is the responsibility of the admitting department to make sure that members of the medical staff are aware of the relevant procedures regarding this issue and schedule their patients accordingly. Although most physicians become aware of the admitting policies on their appointment to the medical staff, many procedures may be forgotten and others may change. The successful admitting manager always maintains good communications with both the physicians and their clerical staff to update them on current admission policies. Such communications may consist of periodic meetings with members of the medical staff, hosting a luncheon for the clerical staff of the physicians, or printing a brochure on the current admission policies and procedures. Taking the initiative to maintain such communications goes a long way toward establishing a very positive relationship with members of the medical staff. In today's competitive environment, the "name of the game" is to keep the hospital's beds full and that requires an excellent relationship with physicians who admit patients to the hospital. In order to maintain these good relations, it is the responsibility of the admitting manager to be aware of the sensitivities of the above issues with the medical staff and the need to keep them informed of the policies and procedures that deal with the bed assignments.

Patient financial policies and procedures of the hospital also affect the relationship with the medical staff. Most physicians are familiar with the financial policies of the hospital and generally cooperate with admitting personnel in the admission of their patients. However, often financial issues are secondary to the physical problems of the patient. Thus, the admitting department must deal directly with the physician in an attempt to resolve the conflict to the mutual satisfaction of the hospital and the physician. In teaching hospitals, often the clinical issues take precedence over the financial ones owing to the need to maintain a broad-based patient load designed to meet the objectives of the teaching program. Most teaching programs have minimum case loads by specialty that must be met in order to maintain the accreditation of those programs. In these cases, the clinical benefit of the patient to the teaching program certainly overrides any and all financial considerations. The primary physician of a patient's case is generally a faculty member on the staff of the teaching hospital and, thus, must also consider his or her teaching and research responsibilities in addition to the straightforward clinical aspects. This often puts the attending physician in conflict with the admitting manager if the admitting policies and procedures do not adequately account for research and teaching cases. Physicians admitting patients to other private hospitals have little regard for the educational or research benefit of the case and strictly admit the patient on medical and financial considerations. Patients must have adequate financial arrangements in order to be admitted to the private hospital, whereas in teaching hospital settings there is some consideration given to patients who are either medically or financially indigent.

Prior to any physician being formally admitted to the hospital's medical staff, that physician's credentials must be reviewed and approved and privileges granted to that physician. This action is usually done by a medical staff committee and, in essence, assures the hospital (and the patients for that matter) that the physician is capable of providing appropriate and quality medical care. An important part of the credentialing process deals with the physicians' agreements to abide by the by-laws written for the hospital's medical staff. Included in these by-laws are generally administrative "do's" and "don'ts" as well as agreements to participate in administrative/committee matters, appropriateness of care/quality assurance matters, Joint Commission on Accreditation of Hospitals and state licensure matters, and promptness in the completion of all paperwork. The most important paperwork involved is the patient's medical record.

Most hospital/medical staff by-laws have as a condition of appointment the agreement that all operative reports, discharge summaries, and other medical record issues be completed on a timely basis. *Timely* is generally defined specifically in those by-laws. Punitive measures for failure to complete such documents promptly are also spelled out in the by-laws and generally involve the revocation of admitting privileges for that particular physician, until such time all records are complete. The revocation of these privileges generally comes about when such incompleteness is flagrant and little or no effort is made by the physician to complete the records. As one might guess, this is an extremely important and sensitive issue in the relationship between members of the medical staff and hospital administration. The responsibility to invoke this revocation is generally the responsibility of the hospital's chief of staff and the admitting manager. This puts a tremendous amount of pressure on the admitting manager in any dealings with the physician in question. In order to minimize all long-lasting conflicts between the physician and the admitting manager, it is advisable that the hospital's by-laws and policies and procedures clearly establish the procedure for enforcing this decision and involve members of the administrative staff in resolving the problem. Again, when one considers the era of competition, hospitals can only thrive on an efficient medical staff that abides by all of the hospital's policies. Although the revocation of such privileges is a drastic measure, it is effective in ensuring the prompt completeness of all medical documents.

The prospective payment system will create a whole new environment in which the admitting physicians and admitting managers will interact. Most hospitals will have very sophisticated case-mix management software packages that can profile its admitting physicians with respect to length of stays, profitability, utilization of ancillary resources, and other critical factors regarding reimbursement. Although most of these issues will be handled by members of the financial management team, it will be the responsibility of the admitting manager to review admissions from these physicians from a more critical standpoint. Admitting diagnoses, estimated length of stays, and utilization of operating rooms and other ancillaries will all be intensely reviewed from the standpoint of prospective reimbursement.

The last important factor in the relationship between hospital admitting and the medical staff is the admitting department's ability to treat the patient with respect, reverence, and dignity. As everyone knows, the patient's first impression of the hospital and its services is generally formed by the way he or she is treated during the admission process. Not only does this affect the hospital's relationship with the patient, but it also affects the patient's relationship with the physician since it is on the physician's recommendation that the patient is coming to that particular hospital in the first place. A pleasant waiting room, an efficient interviewing process with private quarters, a pleasant staff, and a bed assignment that meets the patient's needs all affect this relationship issue. The admitting department must protect the interests of the hospital, and it must do so in a conciliatory fashion with the members of the medical staff.

NURSING SERVICES

The primary relationship with nursing services centers around the assignment of beds in the hospital. Although most bed assignments are made by admitting personnel, little can be done without the direct input of the nursing staff on the appropriate inpatient unit. Issues critical to this relationship include the following.

Admitting Diagnosis

The severity of illness with respect to the assignment of the bed determines the location on the floor where the patient may be assigned, the necessity for an isolation case, whether or not a private versus a semiprivate room would be appropriate, whether a bed in the intensive care unit is necessary, or whether any special nursing requirements are needed on the part of the patient. Although the bed control area in the admitting department may show several beds open on a particular unit, there may be only one that would fit all the necessary requirements of a patient with a particular illness. Such assignments can only be made with the input of the nursing staff.

Infection and Isolation

Again, the patient's condition may require an isolation situation, isolating either the patient from visitors or the visitors from the patient. Treating these patients may require special logistics from part of the nursing staff in terms of access, appropriate attire, and so on, and it is advisable to rely very heavily on the nursing staff to assist in the assignment of beds for isolation patients.

Smoking

Incoming patients typically are asked if they smoke by the admitting representative, and generally smokers are housed together. Of course, any oxygen in use in the patient's room or any other safety conditions may preclude the patient from being able to smoke during his or her hospital stay.

Preoperative and Postoperative Condition

Many hospitals with high census have to assign incoming patients a bed on a floor different from what they would ordinarily be admitted to. Such an assignment is strictly to accommodate the patient, considering that there may be very few other beds available in the hospital. Generally those patients who go to the operating room are not able to return to their initial bed assignment, primarily owing to the lack of experience on the part of the nursing staff in treating patients with certain postoperative problems. Thus, the patients may have to be transferred to an appropriate inpatient floor with staff who are experienced in the particular surgical issue or yet may be admitted to an appropriate intensive care unit after release from the recovery room. In general, preoperative bed assignments are fairly easy to make with little restrictions involved. Postoperative bed assignments are certainly more complex when one considers the appropriate skills of the nursing staff.

Roommate Compatibility

In hospitals with patient representatives or formal social work departments, in many cases roommate incompatibilities can be picked up fairly early in the patient's hospital stay. In addition, there may also be some problems with the patient's family or visitors and, by all means, such issues should be considered either in the initial bed assignment or subsequent in-house transfers.

For many reasons, known and unknown, it seems that patients always end up being transferred several times before they are discharged from the hospital. Many of these transfers are necessitated by changes in medical condition and others to accommodate incoming admissions during periods of high census. For whatever reasons transfers occur, it is always extremely frustrating and an inconvenience to the patient. Not only does the patient have to become reoriented to a new room and a new roommate but also runs a risk of losing valuables and personal effects. Transfers initiated due to changes in a patient's medical condition are usually initiated by the nursing staff. Transfers initiated to accommodate incoming admissions are, obviously, initiated by the admissions department. Such transfers cause additional work for the nursing staff and also cost the hospital several hundred dollars in terms of the housekeeping effort, changes in the computer system of the patient's location, changes in the dietary system, and other information systems that have to be updated to reflect the change. Friction often occurs between the nursing staff and the admitting department if adequate reasons are not given for this transfer.

Patient Discharges

It is well known in the admitting field that an effective system for communicating and effecting patient discharges has a direct relation to an efficient admissions system. In other words, prior notification of all pending and final discharges allows the admitting department to schedule incoming admissions at a certain time of the day. This provides adequate time for housekeeping and other necessary services to prepare the room for the incoming admission. This prompt notification also initiates other various discharge functions, including the release of patient valuables, the finalization of financial arrangements, the discharge cashiering function, and, perhaps most importantly, the arrangements for the patient's transportation home. In addition, prompt notification can also preclude any late dietary trays from being delivered to the room after the patient has been discharged and also can minimize any delays in take-home prescriptions from the pharmacy.

ADMINISTRATION

The key to an effective admitting system is well-defined and detailed policies and procedures. These policies must thoroughly address all admitting issues from the time the patient is admitted to the hospital through discharge. The role of the administration in this process cannot be underestimated, since it is its ultimate responsibility to develop policies and procedures with input from the medical staff, nursing services, and admitting personnel. It is through these policies and procedures that administration is carrying out the duties and responsibilities as delegated by the hospital's governing board. Other administrative inputs to this relationship are as follows:

- ensuring that members of the medical staff are familiar with the hospital's admitting policies and procedures
- making sure that the hospital has a well-designed and comfortable admitting department
- resolving disputes and complaints regarding the admission and/or financial policies
- providing support for the enforcement of hospital admitting policies
- providing an outlet for admitting personnel considering exceptions to these policies.

As noted in the diagram at the beginning of this chapter, admissions is basically the hub of many different activities that go on regarding the patient's stay in the hospital. Many different departments are involved in this scenario, and it is administration's responsibility to ensure that all of these services are coordinated in such a manner that all resources are used most effectively. Administration is generally involved in any disputes between the admitting department and other departments whether it be notification to housekeeping or dietary services or documentation of accurate information for the billing and collections function. Hospital administration provides a broad, general direction with respect to the overall admitting process. Admitting managers should work very closely with their administrators to ensure that all aspects of the admissions process are followed correctly, that exceptions to any admission policies meet the approval of administration, and that the system that has been developed meets the needs of the physicians, the patients, and the hospital's staff, as well as providing a comfortable environment for all who use the admitting department.

BUSINESS OFFICE

The closeness of the relationship between the admitting department and the business office can best be illustrated by the fact that in some hospitals these two departmental titles are, in essence, synonymous. It is very difficult, in some instances, to draw a line that would separate the functions of the admitting department with those of the business office. Typically, admitting involves the scheduling of the admission and the completion of the socioeconomic information about the patient. Preliminary financial information is also gathered. The business office depends totally on the information gathered at the time of admission to further complete the detailed financial profile on the patient. On a continuum, this would involve the identification of any third party insurances, verification of such information, the collection of hospital-based charges, the generation of a hospital bill, the discharge cashiering function, and the credit and collections effort. Each of these business office functions may place special demands on various aspects of the admissions process. Input from the business office on the admitting process may involve whether or not the patient's diagnosis is a covered service by the appropriate insurer, the verification of any third party coverages, the resolution of any outstanding accounts of the patient, or the collection of any cash deposits. In an era of prospective reimbursement, the relationship with the business office can take on a whole new personality. "Case-mix management" is the current buzz word with respect to hospital financial management. Most hospitals are aggressively pursuing software packages that would allow them to profile all of their admissions from the standpoint of the attending physician, the length of stay, the utilization of ancillary resources, the projected hospital bill, and quality and appropriateness of care. The well-run admitting department should have up-to-date and accurate information regarding the case-mix profile of the patient and be able to identify immediately those patients that may be exceptions to unacceptable patient profiles. Issues that must be reviewed include the number of days the patient will be hospitalized before any planned surgery has been scheduled; the use of multiple diagnosis, in particular the identification of any primary versus secondary diagnosis; any unusual or unnecessary tests ordered by the physician (unnecessary as defined by the hospital utilization review program); and any patient that can be identified as an "outlier."

All of these crucial steps require a close working relationship between the hospital admitting department, the business office, and the controller's office. Hospital administration must make the initial effort to inform all admitting physicians as to what patient profiles can be considered acceptable and, thus, allow the admitting function to progress smoothly within this framework. In addition to the role of administration, the hospital's chief of staff will also play a critical role in resolving any issues between the admitting physician and any business-related problem that may crop up during the admitting process. Quality and appropriateness of care, which includes the utilization review process, plays an extremely important role in allowing the hospital to manage its case mix effectively. The information provided by both the admitting department and the business office must flow quickly and accurately to the quality assurance/utilization review function in order that any problems or needs regarding discharge planning can be identified as early in the patient's stay as possible. Under the cost-based reimbursement system, the physician determines all of the resources the patient would require during this hospital stay. This would he in terms of operating room time, laboratory tests, radiographic tests, physical therapy, respiratory therapy, and so on. Reimbursement is based on the standing hospital charge for such services. Today, reimbursement is derived solely by the patient's primary and secondary diagnoses, regardless of the amount of resources consumed during the hospital stay. Thus, the reimbursement would depend on the quality of the information gathered in the admitting department, the identification and verification of any and all third party coverages by the business office, and the accurate and prompt coding of all diagnostic information by the medical record abstract personnel. Thus, the prospective reimbursement system places a much greater importance on the relationship between the admitting department, the business office, and the medical records department.

MEDICAL RECORDS

The relationship with medical records primarily deals with the patient identification system and the patient's medical record. Although medical records is usually the custodian of the patient identification numbering system, the success of this system depends on the accuracy of the patient information generated by the admitting department. Failure to secure accurate information generally results in the hospital issuing duplicate patient identification numbers, which in turn results in duplicate medical records, duplicate patient accounts, and lost charges. Although some of these problems may be eliminated with an automated registration system, the departments are not relieved of their responsibility to generate and maintain accurate patient demographic information. With the advent of the hospital information systems, more of this responsibility is now being placed on the hospital admitting department. In a manual system, most all of these records are maintained by medical records and are subject to review and approval by the patient identification clerk in the medical records department. With an automated system, this information is maintained in the hospital data files and it is only the admitting clerk who updates this information. Granted that most automated systems have checks and balances for errors in the patient information, it is critical that admitting clerks realize their responsibility to enter in and update these files with accurate patient information.

As mentioned in the section regarding the medical staff, many hospitals suspend admitting privileges of certain members of medical staff if the number of delinquent charts exceeds a certain level. In these cases, it is the responsibility of the admitting department, based on input from medical records and the hospital's chief of staff, to enforce these policies. Members of the medical staff are generally given several opportunities to complete their delinquent charts before admitting privileges are suspended, and some members of the medical staff may even complete such charts immediately in order to not have these privileges suspended. In order to make these sanctions effective and not create any embarrassment on the part of admission personnel, it is critical that any information regarding delinquent charts be communicated immediately to the admitting office, primarily the admitting manager. The most effective way of communicating this information is through an automated information system, whereby such admitting physicians' names can be flagged in the system as having delinquent charts and would be immediately called to the attention of the admitting clerks when they are processing the information into the system. Telephone calls, memoranda, and verbal communication are not always the most accurate, up to date, and reliable in communicating this critical information.

In those admitting departments responsible for billing and collection functions, it is generally their responsibility to also code the records for the discharge diagnosis and procedures. As mentioned above, such coding becomes much more important when the hospital's reimbursement rate depends directly on the accurate coding of all primary and secondary diagnoses. Many hospitals are expanding their admissions staff with medical records personnel in order to ensure accurate interpretation of physician notes and the subsequent coding for reimbursement purposes. Such personnel may be stationed on each inpatient unit, with their primary responsibility being a day-to-day review of all charts on that particular unit. If the "chart analyst" identifies any delinquent documentation in the chart, then it is much easier to call it to the attention of the admitting physician at that particular time rather than waiting for the patient to be discharged and trying to track down the admitting physician after the fact. Following this information on a daily basis also allows the billing function to bill the account to the appropriate third party immediately after discharge rather than having to wait for the delinquent chart to be completed by the admitting physician. Such analysts are well worth the additional costs when one considers the stakes involved in terms of reimbursement based on the accurate coding of the diagnosis and procedures.

HOUSEKEEPING

The primary relationship between admitting and housekeeping is the coordination of the cleaning of rooms on a patient's discharge for an incoming admission. Quick turn-around time of such rooms is contingent on notification from the nursing staff on the inpatient unit to the admitting department of the patient's discharge and an efficient communication system between the admitting office and the housekeeping staff once the room has been cleaned. Such communication should take into consideration isolation cases, special equipment needs, sleeper chairs, bassinets, cribs, and so on, to meet the patient's needs. An example of such a communication system is as follows.

If the hospital is still using manual systems, then the unit clerk at the appropriate nursing station should document on a log sheet all patient rooms that have been vacated and are awaiting housekeeping. Generally, the supervisor of housekeeping on that floor checks the rooms according to any priority ordered. Once the room has been cleaned by the custodian, that person can telephone the bed control function directly from the patient's room, informing them that the bed is clean and ready for the next admission. The housekeeping supervisor should randomly check patient rooms to ensure that all cleaning standards have been followed.

If the hospital is using an automated information system, then this communication method is much easier. Once the patient's discharge has been communicated to the admitting department, the bed control screen in the system can be updated to reflect the patient's discharge. Pending discharges can also be entered into the bed control screen as soon as these are known, either the night prior to discharge or early on the morning of the discharge. A printout of all pending and actual discharges can be scheduled to print in the housekeeping supervisor's office and from the information on this sheet, the supervisor can then assign the custodians to clean the rooms as necessary. One of the benefits of notifying the admitting department of all ''pending discharges'' is that housekeeping can schedule the allocation of custodians to each inpatient unit based on the anticipated workload for that day. Once the custodian has cleaned the bed, he or she can telephone the bed control function directly from the patient telephone in the room. Given the large volume of transactions that usually occur on the hospital information system terminals at the nursing station, it is generally not advisable to allow the house-keepers to update the discharge screens directly on the terminal. In many larger hospitals, trying to access the bed control function can be frustrated by the number of busy signals one might receive. If the housekeeper calls the bed control function to alert them of a cleaned patient unit and gets a busy signal, then it can be very easy to forget to place that call again. Many admitting departments have installed telephone answering services on a certain telephone number that would allow the housekeeper to leave a message as to which patient bed has been cleaned. It is the responsibility of the bed control clerk to monitor this tape periodically to update the status of the bed.

DIETARY SERVICES

The admissions relationship with the dietary department is one of notification of new admissions, patient transfers, and discharges in order for the dietitian to serve

Exhibit 15–1 New Patient Meal Ticket

```
                                                    Ticket No. _____

Department of Food & Nutrition Services
Hospital Name                              Patient's Name _____
NEW PATIENT MEAL TICKET                    Hospital Number _____

This meal ticket replaces ONE PATIENT MEAL Area _____
served to the room. It may NOT be used for Date _____ Meal _____
snacks or family. Please note the amount of Purchase Limits --- Circle one
purchase allowed.
Other items may be purchased for cash.     Breakfast — $2.00
                                           Adult Lunch/Dinner — $3.25
Issued by _____  Pediatric Lunch/Dinner — $2.75

                                           Amount of Purchase_____
Title _____
                                           Patient's Signature _____

                                           Accepted by _____
                                                                  (Cashier)
```

Source: Courtesy of Shands Teaching Hospital, Gainesville, Florida.

the appropriate meals to the right patients. These services may also include requests for gourmet meals, fruit trays, or any other specialty items usually reserved for VIP admissions or employees of the hospital being admitted. Patients awaiting room assignments for prolonged periods of time or over the noon hour may be sent to the cafeteria with a snack or meal ticket that provides them with their selection from the cafeteria items at no charge. Such a program can add a nice touch to the admitting process when it is known that the patients may have to wait for quite some time for an appropriate bed to become available. An example of such a ticket is shown in Exhibit 15–1.

In addition to these tickets, the admitting department may also store soft drinks or milk or formula for patients waiting for a room to become available. Discretion must be used in offering such snacks to these patients if they are waiting in a general waiting room space. Many hospitals have special waiting rooms for parents with children, and such surroundings lend themselves well to providing snacks while they are waiting for the bed.

CHAPLAIN SERVICES

One of the primary sources of information regarding a patient's religious preference comes from information collected during the admitting process. This information is usually provided to chaplain services by way of a manual or automated report and is used by the hospital's chaplains or any visiting clergy. Although most patients do not have any second thoughts about disclosing their religious preference, some patients may be offended by being asked to declare a certain religion. This can be overcome by training the admitting clerks to be sensitive to this issue and to ask the patient if he or she would prefer to declare any religious preference on the registration form.

DATA PROCESSING

The extent of the relationship with data processing is dependent on the scope of automated systems available in the hospital. The design, maintenance, and utilization of these systems requires a close working relationship between admitting and data processing in order to meet the various policy and procedure requirements of the hospital. Even though the actual admitting process may be the manual use of typewriters, the data processing personnel still have to keypunch this information into the appropriate format for submission to the automated census system. It is usually the responsibility of data processing to assist in the training of the admitting clerks as to the necessity for accurate and clear information that is submitted to the keypunch operators. Totally automated admission functions usually receive most of their training from data processing personnel as well as working with them on any additions or deletions to any of the admissions screens on the system.

OTHER RELATIONSHIPS

Depending on the size of the hospital, the hours of the admitting department, and the philosophy of administration, many admitting departments have a variety of other responsibilities that result in unique relationships with various other internal and external operations.

Internal Operations

Deceased Patients

Many admitting offices are responsible for all aspects of records, personal effects, and release of bodies on patients who have died in the hospital. Owing to their 24 hour a day, seven days a week operation, most hospitals find it very convenient to place this responsibility in the admitting department. These duties include the processing of the burial transit permit, the death certificate, and the release of any personal valuables to funeral home directors and/or the family. In addition, the coordination of any autopsies with the pathology department, along with coordinating the obtaining of the autopsy permit, generally is within the realm of admitting's responsibility. If the death qualifies as a coroner's case, usually it is the admitting department's responsibility to notify the proper authorities.

Patient Television Sets and Telephones

Most hospitals provide patient television sets and telephones free of charge (included in the hospital's room rates), but other hospitals charge incrementally for such services. Usually, it is the admitting department's responsibility to inform the patient of whatever arrangements exist at the hospital and to collect the necessary money to provide television sets and telephones to the patients.

Hospital Information Desk

Since the admitting department is generally located in the front of the hospital, many of these offices are also responsible for the hospital's information desk. This could include staffing this information desk outright, sharing the staffing with the hospital's volunteer services, or coordinating with the volunteers who may staff the desk all the time.

Volunteer Services

In addition to working with the volunteers on the hospital's information desk, many admitting departments coordinate volunteer efforts with regard to distributing patient mail, escorting patients throughout the hospital, or delivering important hospital documents to various offices within the hospital.

Discharge Holding Area

Some admitting departments are also responsible for the discharge function, including the cashier, and for staffing the discharge holding area. Patients who may be waiting for last minute arrangements, including transportation, may be released from their rooms and sent to a common holding area usually staffed by a medically trained professional.

Patient Parking

Many admitting departments are responsible for the coordination of parking and other security arrangements for patients' vehicles while they are in the hospital. This may also include special arrangements to accommodate recreational vehicles brought to the hospital by the patient's family. Many hospitals provide special parking arrangements, including utility hook-ups for these vehicles at a nominal charge per day and collected by the admitting department personnel.

Public Relations

Public relations plays an important role in the admitting process, particularly regarding VIP patients. These patients and other individuals (e.g., victims of crime) usually require special needs in terms of anonymity or other arrangements for their protection and privacy. Usually, admitting information systems have the capability to identify VIP patients and others who require anonymity for these various reasons.

Hospital-to-Hospital Transfers

The reservation clerk in the admitting department is usually responsible for coordinating hospital-to-hospital transfers whether they be by ground transportation or air ambulance. This also includes any special needs the patient may have as well as delivering appropriate patient records to the proper medical personnel.

External Operations

Health Care Alternatives

Because of the prospective reimbursement system and the increased competition among all health care providers, this country has seen a rapid growth in free-standing emergency centers, ambulatory surgery centers, health maintenance organizations (HMOs), preferred provider organizations (PPOs), consolidation of smaller hospitals into multihospital chains, and an increased number of large group practices. All of these providers feed patients into the inpatient hospital setting. Whereas, previously, admitting departments primarily dealt with a clerk in the referring physician's office, all of these new providers must now deal with admitting personnel to coordinate the admission into the hospital as well as any special payment arrangements that have been worked out with any formal contracts between the hospital and the providers such as HMOs and PPOs. Usually these formal arrangements have specific guidelines that qualify patients for admission into the hospital (e.g., appropriate medical diagnoses, required second opinions, elimination of certain elective procedures) and require the admitting manager to be very familiar with the arrangements of these contracts. These new providers usually result in the admitting manager having to deal with a variety of personnel on the front end of the admitting process to meet both the requirements of the hospital and the outside primary provider regarding the patient's admission.

Home Health Care

With the rapid growth of home health care agencies, the admitting manager must be very familiar with the requirements for placing the patient in the home health care environment. Since most admitting departments are responsible for discharge functions, they will get involved in coordinating the discharge planning effort with social services and the utilization review personnel in placing the patient in an appropriate environment for post-hospitalization care.

Health Care Advocacy

Given the tremendous amount of media attention that has been given to the prospective reimbursement system, many consumers are asking a lot of questions regarding health care costs. The admitting manager and admitting personnel play an important role in being knowledgeable of the cost of high technology, utilities, medications, and other "big ticket items" that patients may be asking about. Patients, as well as physicians, are now shopping for the best health care package, much like a consumer shopping for clothes would do. It is important that admitting personnel be knowledgeable of the services and the costs when dealing with patients on these matters. Admitting personnel should be prepared to answer questions regarding the costs of certain medications and why a certain pill costs a certain price. Health care consumers are much more knowledgeable about hospital costs than they were several years ago, and admitting personnel must keep up with this increased awareness of hospital operations.

CONCLUSION

In discussing interdepartmental relationships, the notion comes to mind of a department being the hub of a wheel with the spokes extending out to other areas. The size of the hub depends on the size of the department, and the number of spokes illustrates the number of critical relationships the department is involved in. One can argue that the admitting department is the hub of patient activity given its relationship with the medical, nursing, and other staffs as well as external primary care providers referring patients into the hospital. All of these relationships require a certain type of communication. The most efficient admitting system is only as strong as the weakest link in this entire communication process. Admitting managers must be very knowledgeable of all of the increasing number of changes in the communications field such as stand-alone mini-computers, personal computers, word processing networks, and other high technology options. Given the tremendous amount of attention on cost containment, many suppliers to the health care field know that an efficient office communications system can reduce the number of staff required in the admitting process. Admitting managers should take every opportunity to further their own education regarding state-of-the-art communications.

Admitting managers can be proud of the growth of the admitting profession over the past ten years. The profession has come a long way, largely owing to the respect and degree of professionalism its personnel have demonstrated in their day-to-day dealings with other members of the health care team. It was not too long ago that the admitting function was performed by one or two employees in either the medical records department or the business office. Given the increased attention to cost containment, medical-legal matters, computers, and information systems, it is not a surprise that the admitting field has developed into the profession that it is today.

Chapter 16

The Human Dimension of Admitting

Kevin D. Blanchet

The health care environment is in a period of flux. There are concerns and questions, and problems and solutions seem either too many or too few. There has been a dramatic change in emphasis. Issues such as financial feasibility, professional staff relations, and creative methods of health care delivery are just some of the areas delved into by hospital administrators. A new language is now heard in hospitals of all sizes. Buzz words such as competition, marketing, diagnostic related groups (DRGs), preferred provider organizations (PPOs), and prospective payment are no longer confined to intimate users of the system. Today, it is everybody's business to know everything about the business of health care. Change is no longer on the horizon. We are breathing change. We are working with change. We are trying to survive change.

Prior to the current status in health care, admitting as a hospital department was rather a static and standard, if not routine, area of the hospital. Responsibilities were limited and clearly defined. Individuals with good manners and of average intelligence could find steady work in the department. Admitting managers more often than not were simply seasoned veterans of the department. They worked their way up from the ranks; the directorship was their reward. The change that did occur was change the admitting manager could handle. Admitting was really a good place to be in the hospital.

Today, many professional admitting managers would not agree with the above statement. Of all the departments in the hospital, the admitting department has seen such a quantity and complex quality of change that many admitting managers now understand what being put to the test is all about. The admitting department has become a pivotal entry point into the hospital system for patient and professional alike. Managers of admitting departments are thinking of only one thing— whatever their administrators are thinking about at any given moment. Admitting and administration are coupled in a union of strength, weathering the current health care crisis. As a result, a principal perspective needs to be emphasized once again. It is a perspective especially important for the admitting manager.

The health care field has always been dynamic, possessing an attractiveness other professions still yearn for today. The factor responsible for this dynamic nature is hidden inside the degree of change hospital admitting personnel are experiencing. This factor is the real product of current marketing efforts. It is the reason for such fervor and competition. It is also the same reason for basic humanitarian values remaining prime motivators in young persons considering careers in health care. The constant is the patient. The objective is interpersonal relations. The challenge is communication. Change has not altered the one chief responsibility of hospital admitting managers and personnel—to understand and relate to the patient, their peers, and themselves.

ADMITTING AS AN INTERPERSONAL AND COMMUNICATIVE DISCIPLINE

The Hospital Is Introduced

The hospital admitting department is a rich center for interpersonal behavior and the accompanying communication that forms an integral part of that behavior. Admitting is not unique in possessing such a nature and human dimension. Most persons are very familiar with the more traditional areas of the hospital serving as centers of human behavior and communication. Ironically, many of these centers such as the nursing units and the physician staff have been criticized for not paying more close attention to these critical areas of patient relations. Yet, the case for admitting as a principal area of interpersonal behavior and communication is strong indeed.

Admitting serves as the introductory link in the complex chain of health care events a patient will experience during the stay in the hospital. The hospital admitting environment serves, to a large extent, as a sizing up area for patients and professionals. People learn about each other for the first time. Intimate facts are shared. Emotions are sometimes expressed. Future perceptions are concretely shaped. Impressions are developed. In short, in the admitting department the most complex forms of communication and human relations take place.

The Patient Is Understood

What are some of the issues facing the hospital admitting manager with regard to interpersonal behavior and communication as it pertains to the patient being admitted? Certainly, an essential element for any admitting manager is to understand the psychological nature of the patient confronting the department and its personnel. All patients entering the health care system share certain common denominators in composing a patient profile. Each patient also brings a set of complex variables that makes him or her unique. It is out of these characteristics admitting professionals try to understand the human dimension of a patient. As one undertakes this, issues of loss and grief become of paramount importance. These concepts, along with the concept of empathy, require careful analysis and understanding in order for one to communicate effectively with any patient arriving in admitting on any given day.

The Information Is Shared

It is from these first fundamentals about the patient that forms of communication can be developed to assist in the information gathering objective of the admitting function. Development of certain skills connected with the interpersonal behavior makes it easier to perform the tasks at hand in the department while allowing the patient to ease into the system with a minimum of difficulty. After this understanding has taken place, admitting managers can then begin the process of evaluating this often vague and abstract element of admitting from a more objective position. Finally, the admitting manager can then begin to educate subordinates about the lessons learned in this important area. The resulting systems and programs can then be implemented and put into place for future evaluation, action, and administration of quality service.

The Professional Interacts

Up until this point, patients have been emphasized as a primary reason for admitting managers to develop good interpersonal and communication skills in their daily responsibilities as managers of complex hospital departments. This is rightfully so because the bottom line of health care, outside the financial connotation this term takes on today, is the patient. Hence, it is not only normal but simply good business to make the patient the prime motivator and reason in all areas of admitting management.

There is a second reason, however, that makes the importance of interpersonal and communication skills twice as critical to the success of any admitting department than the patient alone. By virtue of health care dynamics, admitting managers must relate to a variety of professionals in the field and develop outstanding relationships with their subordinates. As such, what is true of interpersonal relations for the patient is the same for the persons with whom the manager works on a daily basis. It also applies to a critical task of the admitting supervisor. This is the task of problem solving. Finally, whatever the manager learns about patients and employees can surely be adapted and used in his or her personal life.

In short, these areas of interpersonal behavior and communication are really inescapable for any admitting manager. Since they pervade the atmosphere of admitting so heavily, it is vitally important to know something about them. The word communication comes from the Latin word *communicare,* meaning "sharing." A direct result of sharing eventually is caring. Communication also means sharing knowledge and responsibility as a modern admitting manager.

PROFILE OF A PATIENT

An Unwanted Situation

Any attempt to discuss and understand the psychological profile of a patient entering the admitting department must begin by realizing a basic premise. No one chooses to be admitted. Granted, there may be some situations in which that individual wants to go into the hospital for elective surgery such as a face lift or other cosmetic reason. Yet, even in these situations, the choice on the part of the patient is limited. Some unpleasant condition still exists in the patient that warrants the patient to undergo such a procedure. Regardless of the situation, circumstance, or diagnosis, all patients will, at some point, undergo very similar emotions and events. Hence, the admitting professional like any other health care professional is placed in the awkward position of dealing with a person in a very unwanted situation. It is imperative for those involved in hospital admitting to understand what a patient feels before, during, and after the admitting process. By having this basic understanding, the admitting professional can deliver a higher quality of service based on the insight from such an understanding.

A Process Called Hospitalization

A question that needs to be asked at the onset is just when does a patient's hospitalization begin? At first glance, one would readily answer with the reasoning that it begins when the patient arrives at the hospital. If one views the term *hospitalization* on the same level as *stay,* this definition would be most appropriate.

Hospitalization is not, however, something that begins when the patient steps into the main hospital lobby en route to admitting. Likewise, it is not something that starts up when the patient is placed in bed or in the room. This type of understanding would seem to indicate that the only health team members are physicians, nurses, and technicians.[1] Hospitalization must be viewed as a process. It is a process that is ongoing and begins long before one enters the hospital. It is a process of many stages and with each stage comes unexpected feelings and emotions. Some persons begin the process unknowingly when they enter the physician's office. It is at the juncture in time when patient and physician agree to the hospital stay that the hospitalization process begins and the emotional state of the patient needs to be considered. Ironically, the point of hospitalization begins with a choice, but a limited one. The choice is the consent of the patient. It is in this regard that obtaining hospital consents by admitting personnel can prove to be one of the most stressful moments in the patient's process of hospitalization. It is the sum of the experiences of the patient (and the family) from the point outlined above (physician–patient agreement) that the admitting staff will have to deal with on the day of admission.

The Patient Gives Up Control

The point at which the hospitalization begins will not be the last opportunity for the patient to exercise choice. The admitting department, and more specifically the patient interviewing cubicle, becomes the site of the last valid opportunity for choice, free will, freedom, and control. Patients, when they are in the admitting department, are more vulnerable than they are at any other time in their hospital stay. They are at their most threatened point in that part of the psychological process called hospitalization.[2] The point that is critical to any patient in terms of the psychological makeup of the patient is at the point of consent and the required signatures.

Up until this point in time, patients have retained a very important human vanguard. This is their control. They have said yes to their physician, yet they are still in control of their life and life style. They have answered all preadmission questions over the telephone or in person during the preliminary interview but still they are in control. The request by the admitting representative to sign a formal consent to allow hospitalization and treatment is really a request to relinquish control from the patients. The "we want to take care of you" attitude may very well be interpreted as "we want to take control over you." The admitting representative wields great power when requesting consent signatures for chances are patients have already undergone the process of admission prior to this point. Patients may feel pressured to make this decision to enter the hospital because they have gone this far. Surely, they would not want to turn back now after all this trouble. Yet, this is really the only opportune time for patients to change their minds. It is second thoughts time. This is the last time when the patients can bolt and run. Once they are in pajamas, it is not so easy to leave. Now, they still can run.[3] It is vitally important for admitting managers to make their employees aware of this critical moment in the admitting process. No patient, at this most vulnerable of times, should be pressured or convinced to sign any form. Also, this stage in the admitting interview should not be treated as simply a "formality." All patients have the right to understand what it is that they are signing to the best of their ability. The admitting professional needs to uphold the patients' rights in this regard as well as other rights such as privacy and confidentiality so that this moment of choice is just that—an informed choice. Giving up control is no easy matter for anyone to do freely. Admitting representatives can be the facilitators to this process. In turn, admitting and the ensuing process of hospitalization can become less traumatic and more understood by the patients and their families.

The Patient Is Atypical

There is one other note that should be given here. Admissions personnel are no longer seeing the basic, routine cases of years past. Outpatient services, same-day surgery programs, and the focus on preventive medicine have eliminated many minor surgeries, treatments, and diagnoses. In all likelihood, the type of patient a modern-day admitting department staff member sees is a patient with a life-threatening disease and/or major operative procedure. Cancer and heart disease are just two of the major problems admitting department personnel now see as "routine" diagnoses on admitting forms. As such, patients are coming to admitting departments with large attendant anxieties and other emotional states managers need to be aware of if they are to handle them effectively.

THE STRESS AND EMOTIONS OF THE ADMITTING PROCESS

An Emotional Profile

As admitting professionals, admitting managers may be the last individuals in the admitting department and hospital with whom the patient has contact and who will not do anything to the patient. Every encounter with a provider of medical care is terrifying whether it is in the physician's office, the hospital, the clinic, or the emergency department.[4] The patient comes into the admitting department with a number of emotions. Although every emotional profile of a patient being admitted is as unique as each patient, several basic emotions and feelings seem to be predominant. An understanding of the associated stresses and emotions that accompany illness and the hospital stay is crucial to the success of an admitting department and the satisfaction of patients with the hospital from which they are seeking care for their problem.

Fear and Anxiety

Probably the two biggest emotions experienced by a patient pending hospitalization are fear and anxiety. It is important to discuss these two emotions as a pair for very legitimate reasons. The two emotions are closely related. It is a difficult task to distinguish them in a patient being admitted to a hospital.

Fear

In terms of any order in which these two emotions are experienced by a patient, fear probably comes before anxiety. Generally speaking, fear appears to be a reaction to a specific stimulus and to have a "right now" quality about it.[5] It is probably the overriding emotion present during the admitting interview, although in some patients the fear may have been worked out or channeled into anxiety or other expressive emotions such as anger. The specific stimulus in this case is the hospital and the emotion of fear may begin at the thought or sight of the hospital building. As the process of hospitalization progresses, new challenges of fear present themselves to the patient that produce new levels of this emotion. So, the fear becomes more prevalent with each answer to every question, with the signing of the consent, with the attaching of the identification bracelet, with the elevator ride up to the room, and on and on. The distinguishing quality of each state of fear the patient experiences lies in the object of the fear presenting itself to the patient at a particular time.

Anxiety

Anxiety is one of the most powerful of emotions and has far-reaching effects on behavior. Unlike fear, anxiety is a vague, unpleasant feeling accompanied by a premonition that something undesirable is about to happen.[6] Anxiety does not focus itself on the present situation but rather on the future and on occurrences that may happen somewhere in time. As an example, take a patient being admitted for a cancer operation. The patient is fearful of the operation, which he or she knows will occur in the hospital. Yet, the patient is anxious about what the surgeon will find during the operation. The patient feels this lingering doom that he or she has cancer even though it has not yet been verified. This is anxiety, and the patient is feeling this as he or she sits in front of the admitting representative during the interview. Anxiety is really the fear of the unknown.

Physical Signs of Anxiety. Admitting professionals need to understand the physiological effects of anxiety on patients in the admitting department so they know these responses are normal for the patient in this situation. Many patients feel heart palpitations and feel out of breath on their arrival into the admitting cubicle. The admitting representative may see the patient shaking or unable to hold the pen steady enough for signatures. In addition to the above and to tingling sensations of the skin, the patient probably has sweaty palms. This is readily apparent during an introductory handshake if one is used. This is the galvanic skin reflex. All of these physiological responses to the emotion of anxiety (and fear) are, of course, produced by the release of adrenalin in the patient's blood.

The Patient's Mood

As any admitting professional can attest, patients can have very dramatic swings of mood during their admitting process. Everyone has a story of the patient who took a swing at or yelled at him or her. Perhaps an admitting manager has seen a patient become extremely jovial, bursting out in laughter and hysterics. Perhaps a patient may come into the admitting department in one emotional state and leave in another.

Another word to describe feeling anxious is "jumpy." Although this word is as vague as the other words used to describe anxious feelings, it is particularly appropriate because the person who is in the grip of anxiety has a lowered threshold for other kinds of emotional responses. The patient is likely to be quite irritable and quickly moved to anger. On the other hand, the individual may also overreact to pleasurable stimuli. The person tends to have wide swings of mood with often unpredictable behavior. One of the first sites this unpredictability can manifest itself is in the admitting department, and one of the first objects of an unpredictable emotion can be the admitting representative.

It may be a help to understand a patient's emotional state on a whole if one considers the accompanying stress of an illness. Every person is faced, when growing older, with the temporary stress of an operative procedure or a brief and acute illness. Older individuals face the prospects of a more permanent stress brought about by the potential of a chronic illness or debilitating condition. The uniqueness of patient emotional states can sometimes be explained on the basis of the diagnosis or the body part involved.

Surgery as a Threat

A frequent cause for hospital admission is the necessity for surgery. The location on the body where the surgical procedure will take place determines the degree of stress that a patient may be experiencing. Eye operations, with the threat of blindness and the necessity for postoperative bandaging with its consequent darkness and isolation, are particularly anxiety provoking.[7]

Women entering the hospital for a hysterectomy present with a considerable amount of stress. Removal of the uterus is a direct assault on a woman's femininity since it represents this concept so clearly. The same holds true for breast removal and for the removal of the testicles in men with a malignancy. Many factors are involved in the stress associated with surgical operations. The fear of mutilation and death, the symbolic significance of a particular body organ, the fear of emotional and financial dependency, and similar factors may lead to temporary psychological disorganization.[8]

Grief and Loss

One of the greatest emotions experienced by a patient is one most persons would not readily recognize or apply to a patient about to undergo the process of hospitalization. In fact, it is an emotion many give little attention to in their lives. It is the emotion of grief and the concept of loss. For most individuals, grief is associated with only one type of loss, that experienced through death. Yet, anything we personally lose, whether it be our freedom, self-esteem or some object we cherish or need, is a stressor that produces the emotion of grief. Since a patient undergoing hospitalization has so much to lose, grief is very much a normal and necessary emotion to feel at such a time.

A patient's entire hospital stay can be described as a sequence of losses of varying degrees and significance. The diagnosis itself represents a major loss, particularly if it denotes future death or disability. Significant loss in self-respect and esteem occur as the result of behaviors extended to patients by the health care team. Some patients may even lose a hospital valuable that should have been locked up in the safe but that represented for the patient a sense of worth and accomplishment. Loss in hospitals is common. It is, in fact, the cause of many of the behaviors manifested by patients, families of patients, and hospital professionals themselves.[9]

Other losses for patients are not uncommon. Impersonal admitting procedures and the removal of the patient's clothing creates a loss in identity as the patient blends in with the general look of a patient. Patients may even experience a loss of respect if they are being admitted by a specialist who only views them as the disease being treated as opposed to the whole person. Patients may lose trust in the nursing staff if they are suddenly moved to another floor or from an intensive care unit into the wards. Many of the same reactions at the emotional level experienced during fear and anxiety are also felt during these losses and this response is called grief.

The Value to Admitting

Obviously, admitting personnel do not need to be counselors. Likewise, they should not be expected to know everything about human behavior or diagnose every patient they see as to what psychological state the patient is in at the moment. Everyone in admitting should, however, have a basic understanding of a patient's emotional state in general. By knowing this they can respond favorably to that patient and make the admitting process easier for the patient and themselves as well. Admitting after all is a system of human beings admitting other human beings. Admitting personnel can at least understand themselves, understand the patient, and better both parties for doing so.

INTERPERSONAL ADMITTING

What exactly does one mean when talking about something in "interpersonal terms?" Basically, the term *interpersonal* means "between persons." Of course, this definition can be expanded to include groups of individuals as well. If one looks at the central role of hospital admitting, one can readily see just how important knowledge and understanding of the interpersonal processes within this department are critical for its success. The main objective in admitting is to gather preliminary information on every patient. This information gathering invariably occurs between two individuals: the admitting representative and the patient being admitted. Unless future trends dictate that patients will be admitted into the hospital by a talking computer, interpersonal behavior skills and communication will remain topics of interest for admitting managers to understand, use, and evaluate in their respective departments.

Interpersonal Behavior

What is interpersonal behavior? Really, here the only definition needed is for the term *behavior*. Behavior is how a person acts, either alone or with others. It basically is what another individual says or does. Since admitting and the health professions deal with one-on-one behavior between two persons, the behavior admitting professionals should be interested in is how a patient acts, behaves, and relates to persons coming in contact with them in the admitting department. Obviously, how the admitting professional behaves and acts influences how the behavior of the patient will turn out. Behaviors will be dependent on the other behavior involved. It is in this way that the term *interpersonal behavior* is an apt description as to what takes place between patient and admitting professional in this coupled communicative effect.

The Value

Fortunately, enough research into the methods of human behavior as it relates to communication has provided much valuable insight into skills that can enhance or take away from interpersonal behavior. These interpersonal skills create a more positive interaction between individuals. Admitting professionals need to cultivate these skills in order to develop a rapport between themselves and the patient. Interpersonal skills are not limited to professional–patient interaction in the admitting department. Equally so, they are extremely valuable for successful relations between the admitting manager and the administrative team.

An admitting clerk may be very knowledgeable about what type of demographic information is required from a patient. Each piece of information may be covered thoroughly and completely. Yet, if the admitting representative does not couple certain interpersonal skills with this questioning, such as warmth and active listening, the patient may develop an angry or frustrated attitude toward that interviewer, the admitting department, and ultimately the entire hospital. Aside from this ripple effect taking place, the patient may, in the end, respond incorrectly or incompletely to questioning, making the admitting representative's task even more difficult. Of course, other health care professionals such as physicians and nursing personnel need to develop extensive interpersonal skills in order to take effective medical histories and examinations. Nevertheless, the significance is there for persons working in the admitting profession to cultivate a variety of interpersonal skills to make their job-related tasks easier, to make the patient's introduction to the hospitalization process easy and efficient, and to form a positive impact within the patients about the hospital services they are about to receive and about the deliverers ready to deliver those services.

Communication

One could easily discover many varied definitions of what exactly is communication. One definition is the exchange or transfer of an idea, thought, or feeling from one person to another.[10] On a more technical level, communication can be the process of sharing meaning through an intentional or unintentional sending and receiving of messages.[11] The central theme that unites all definitions of communication centers around meaning. If meaning is received from a person or whatever is being dealt with, then it was communicated.

In admitting departments, personnel usually do not sit back to receive meaning from a modern piece of artwork hanging on their office wall. They want to receive meaning from persons and specifically the patients they deal with on a daily basis. This form of communication so integral to successful admitting departments is called interpersonal communication. An excellent definition of interpersonal communication that can be offered and that lends itself well to situations encountered in the admitting department is as follows: Interpersonal communication occurs in relatively informal social situations in which persons in face-to-face encounters maintain a focused interaction through the reciprocal exchange of verbal and nonverbal cues.[12]

If one takes the admitting department and the interactions that occur within it, the above definition serves well what actually occurs between patient and admitting representative. Communicating with patients might be said to be a process within the process of hospitalization. Meaning must be shared in an encounter because the patient needs to understand some basic fundamentals about entering the hospital. By the same token, the representative needs to understand the basic demographic information about the patient in order for any additional interaction of a more complex nature (diagnosis and treatment) to take place. Both the patient and the admitting representative take on the dual roles of receiver and sender of information. But the most important element in this definition centers around the intentional versus the unintentional sending or receiving of these messages. It is here that most of the problems associated with admitting a patient take place owing to confusion as to interpretation or unawareness. Thus, one can see how admitting lends itself well to this and other definitions of communication of an interpersonal nature.

The Connection

Understanding how a definition of interpersonal communication can have relevance to an admitting department does not produce the full importance implicated in the desire for admitting managers to develop effective interpersonal skills. A perspective based on patient satisfaction in the admitting department and the dependency of that satisfaction on the performance and interaction of personnel may drive the point home more dramatically. It is with this in mind that every hospital admitting manager would agree that the quality of experiences between the patient and all hospital personnel bears a strong relationship to the good and bad feelings that each patient develops while being treated and those attitudes that remain after discharge.[13]

Patients meet many individuals during their recovery in the hospital. Aside from personnel who tend to patients during an unconscious state such as surgery, almost all of these meetings are of a very intense personal nature. When patients finally do leave the hospital, they take with them a collective impression of that hospital based on their previous interactions with the health care team. Nevertheless, first impressions have been proven to be very effective in shaping attitudes in human beings. It is the admitting department employees who provide patients not only with their initial impressions but also whose initial contact has a potential effect on how the patient may evaluate subsequent experiences with nursing and ancillary personnel.[14] A theory has been suggested that patients may use their experiences of mistreatment by admitting and patient accounts personnel as a rationalization and justification for not paying their self-pay portion of the bill.

The above description illustrates for every admitting manager the importance of admitting personnel being cognizant of their manner in which they admit patients. The manner in which the admitting clerk deals with a patient and the family will cause stress to diminish or to increase, depending on how the patient views the clerk's communicative efforts. It is not important how the clerk intends to be understood; what is important is how the clerk is understood.[15] It takes a skillful admitting representative to accomplish the major objective of obtaining correct information. It takes an admitting representative skillful in interpersonal communication techniques to create a positive impression for that patient involved with this partnership called interpersonal behavior.

COMMUNICATION THEORY AND ADMITTING

As in any other aspect of human behavior, there are several theories that help to explain interpersonal behavior. One thing that unifies them all centers around communication as a process. Communication is ongoing and continuous and, as such, has no beginning or ending; yet there are various distinct events and actions that make up this process.[16]

The communication theory of interpersonal communication involves several states and several distinct processes. This theory will be examined here in the context of a patient interview inside the admitting department.

The Process

The first event in this process centers around message formation on the part of the source or sender. In the case of admitting, the source or sender would be the admitting interviewers. As an example, the admitting representative might want to learn the Blue Cross number of the patient.

Next comes the process of encoding the idea into a message that is in an adequate form to be sent to the receiving party. The message formed is probably a question such as, "May I have your Blue Cross number please?" The receiver, of course, is the patient being interviewed. The message is then transmitted to the receiver by way of a channel or medium. In this case it is the spoken word in the form of a question put to the patient.

The receiver or patient then hears the question from the admitting interviewer and message reception takes place. After this, the patient must translate what it is that was just heard. This is called decoding of the message received. In this particular instance, the patient understands that the interviewer wants to know his or her Blue Cross identification number. It is at this level that both the message sent and the message received should be the same. Often, however, it is not. Finally, the patient provides the proper feedback to the interviewer by responding with the number either verbally or by presenting the card to the interviewer. The admitting interviewer receives this information and knows that the message initially formed was sent correctly and was received correctly from the receiver.

The Ways of Information Relay

A variety of problems can arise in the admitting department, especially during the interviewing situation. Admitting representatives relay messages to patients by a variety of ways. An important way is through speech, which is essential to a successful interview situation. Yet, there are two additional ways in which an admitting representative relays information to a patient, and it is these two areas that are least understood or realized by that individual. One is the tone of the voice and how questions are said to the patient during the interview. The other centers around nonverbal language such as the interviewer's expression during the interview or the way the body is positioned throughout the time with the patient.

Admitting is an apt place to see how the three major interpersonal problems health professionals have to deal with present themselves in the department. In each situation, one or both parties involved plays a role in which the problem becomes a personal one.

One situation is when there is a problem that is upsetting the patient and preventing proper focusing on a task. In admitting, practically all patients have the problem of illness or disease that prevents them from concentrating on the tasks being performed in the admitting department.

Along the same lines, another problem centers around both the admitting interviewer and the patient working together to complete the interviewing process. Here, communication plays a vital role in ensuring successful completion of this task.

Finally, there is the instance in admitting when the admitting department employee has a problem in responding to the patient's behavior. This especially holds true for admitting personnel working in the emergency department where patients are under tremendous stress. It is in this environment that the admitting clerk may come across a patient who is crying, who is angry, who is hysterical, or who is in a state of shock. The problem of course is when the admitting clerk does not know how to handle such occurrences when they arise.

Fortunately, there are a variety of skills individuals in admitting can use to solve many of the interpersonal problems encountered in the admitting department. Although the patient interview has been focused on here, other situations dealing with fellow employees and visitors can call for these skills. Knowing how to handle patients in the admitting department will be equally beneficial in other encounters both inside and outside the hospital.

EMPATHY

The essence of all successful communication is empathy.[17] This is a pretty strong statement to make about a skill in communication, but it serves the point in developing a positive climate to foster communication between patient and admitting personnel in the department. Many admitting personnel already display empathy toward their patients without even being aware of it. Yet, empathy is a poorly understood communication skill, which if properly used, can do a great deal to foster clear and positive communication in the entire department.

Empathy Defined

Probably a good way to understand empathy is to illustrate a very nonempathetic statement, such as the popular "I'm glad I'm not in your shoes." Understanding what it is like to be in the other person's shoes is really what empathy is all about. It is the art of understanding the other person's point of view, the ability to put oneself into the other person's frame of reference and look at a situation or idea through his or her accumulation of experiences, values, and attitudes.[18] Empathy really has two elements in its definition. The first deals with recognition. A person who has empathy for another has the ability to detect and identify the immediate affective state of another.[19] The second aspect of empathy involves sensitivity of response, the way a person shows the degree of empathy he or she has. So, being able to detect and identify the immediate affective state of another and responding in an appropriate manner is the process of empathy.[20]

Empathy has a habit of being confused with sympathy, although the two may be present together to form a positive communicative climate in the admitting department. Sympathy is the process of feeling the way another person feels. It is possible however, to empathize—to understand the other person's viewpoint—without sharing it, accepting it, or even approving of it.[21]

Incorporating Empathy in the Admitting Office

There is much one can do to become more skilled at empathy with patients in the admitting department. It is always important to remember that patients have a right to a different interpretation of what is going on based on their own background and experiences. Once recognition of this takes place, the climate for empathetic behavior becomes more fertile. Next is to accept the fact that patients will probably have different viewpoints and that this is all right. Finally, the ability to understand the patients' feelings and the desire to do just that, and only that, will do much to enhance the empathetic response. It will not be necessary to express this verbally since it will be revealed by expressions and tone of voice.

Empathy can be practiced using a variety of educational techniques in the admitting department as inservices. It can also be practiced by the individual as he or she approaches the patients contacted throughout the day. Whatever the case, empathy is a key communication skill to have in one's repertoire whether one is dealing with patients or fellow employees. It is a skill always in demand and always appreciated by those who receive it from you.

FACILITATION SKILLS IN THE ADMITTING DEPARTMENT

Using a wide range of facilitation skills can do much to assist a patient who is having a problem in the admitting department. In essence, all patients in the admitting department have a problem, that problem being the process of hospitalization. Any of these skills can be transferred to other situations persons find themselves in either in daily life or in dealing with others in the hospital environment. If admitting personnel realize that their interaction with a patient is really a microcosm of larger dealings they have with people, they will feel more secure in using techniques learned from these outside dealings.

Encouraging Questions

It is important when interviewing a patient or when the receptionist greets a patient who is entering the admitting department that the patient feel encouraged to ask questions and request anything he or she feels a need for at that moment. Everyone is familiar with the attendant fear of asking questions that makes one appear stupid. Chances are every patient has questions he or she would like answered either by the manager or other professionals in the hospital. Every patient should be encouraged to ask questions and be knowledgeable about hospital services and activity. This makes the admitting department serve a very important liaison and information service function, which is a very effective public relations tool and an excellent way to promote patient satisfaction from the very beginning.

Providing Answers

Akin to promoting requests from patients is the art of responding with information to these requests. Of course, admitting personnel are not in a position to provide all the answers to patients, especially when it comes to diagnostic information. Admitting personnel are in a position, however, to provide the patient answers to questions about hospital services, their location, and any policies and procedures that affect a patient during the hospital stay. Admitting personnel do answer questions when they refer the patient to an appropriate source. It cannot be overstated that these two types of facilitation skills are very important and very much appreciated by patients entering the admitting department. They can be used to advantage to promote a trusting relationship right from the start.

Providing Assistance

Everyone has heard the saying "actions speak louder than words" and to a patient this still holds a lot of weight. Patients in admitting departments sometimes have unusual requests or requests admitting personnel believe it is not their duty to perform. These might include pushing a wheelchair, getting a drink of water for the patient, providing some reading material, helping him or her out of a chair, and so on. All admitting personnel should be prepared to deliver these minor amenities just as a good hotel would cater to its clientele. Once again, this type of facilitation skill does much to enhance the public relations image of the hospital and the admitting department.

Warmth

Warmth is another facilitation skill so useful in the admitting department. A lot has been centered around this skill in other areas of the hospital such as the telecommunications department where operators are requested to answer the calls with their first name. Basically, warmth is displayed in the form of a friendly attitude to the patient. This can be done by calling the patient by name, extending the hand for a handshake or other friendly gesture, smiling, and generally being attentive to the patient.

Active Listening

The final facilitation skill is active listening. Another name for this is empathy. The patient needs to know that the admitting representative understands how he or she is currently feeling.

As one reviews the list of five facilitation skills, admitting personnel reactions might be something like, ''I already do this.'' Probably this is true. Understanding the importance of these skills means using them to greater potential and more often. Patients all have the needs to be understood, to be cared for, to be informed, and to receive action when requested. Resolving these needs in the admitting department creates the first step to total patient care, to total satisfaction, and to making the hospital in question the only hospital the patient will ever go to again.

CONCLUSION

Health care is indeed in a period of transition. The admitting department is feeling the effects of change sweeping across every area in the industry. Admitting managers, who are experiencing their own personal and professional transformations as a result of this change, are looking for some stability and basic meaning to their profession. Many are losing sight of their own personal incentives for entering and staying involved in the profession.

It is reassuring to know that the patient is still the primary emphasis in health care today. Admitting managers and their employees can be proud to know their department and function are very patient oriented in a special way. Never losing sight of the patient's needs can be a tremendous comfort during these times of turbulence.

Admitting representatives can set the tone for subsequent interactions by each patient with the nursing staff, the physician, and other members of the health care team. This important role deserves adequate understanding about the complexities of human behavior and communication.

Perhaps the new role of admitting during these uncertain times should be further enlightenment of others with regard to the importance of the patient. The hospital has a lot to learn from admitting. And admitting has a great deal to teach it.

NOTES

1. Warren R. Althaus, "The Psychology of the Admitting Process," *Journal of Hospital Admitting Management* 6 (Summer 1980): 5.

2. Murray Rimmer, "An Administrator Views Admitting and the Role of the Admitting Manager," *Journal for Hospital Admitting Management* 2 (December 1976): 2.

3. Ibid., 3.

4. Murray Rimmer, "Admitting Manager: What Does Your Administration Expect of You?" *Journal for Hospital Admitting Management* 18 (Autumn 1982): 8.

5. Jerome Kagan and Ernest Havemann, *Psychology: An Introduction* (New York: Harcourt Brace Jovanovich, 1972): 320.

6. Ibid., 320.

7. George W. Kisker, *The Disorganized Personality* (New York: McGraw-Hill, 1972): 195.

8. Ibid., 195.

9. William J. Jones, "Loss in a Hospital Setting: Implications for Counseling," *The Personnel and Guidance Journal* (February 1981): 360.

10. James W. Newman, "If All Else Fails . . . Communicate!" *Leadership* (March 1980): 9.

11 Kathleen S. Verderber and Rudolph F. Verderber, *Inter-Act: Using Interpersonal Communication Skills* (Belmont, Calif.: Wadsworth Publishing, 1977). 4.

12. Dean C. Barnlund, *Interpersonal Communication: Survey and Studies* (Boston: Houghton Mifflin, 1968): 10.

13. Richard L. Moore, "How Hospital Business Office Personnel Can Become Patient Oriented," *Patient Accounts* (February 1983): 2.

14. Ibid., 2.

15. Althaus, "Psychology of the Admitting Process," 6.

16. Verderber and Verderber, *Inter-Act,* 4.

17. Arthur P. Bochner and Clifford W. Kelly, "Interpersonal Competence: Rationale, Philosophy, and Implementation of a Conceptual Framework," *Speech Teacher* 23 (November 1974): 289.

18. Newman, "If All Else Fails," 11.

19. Verderber and Verderber, *Inter-Act,* 39.

20. Ibid.

21. Newman, "If All Else Fails," 11.

Chapter 17

Public Relations and Marketing in Admitting

William A. Giwertz

With the advent of all the innovations in health care delivery systems, operations, and financing during the past few years, the needs of the patient population and the physicians in the hospital make public relations and marketing vital priorities. Indeed, it is a situation in which it is totally inappropriate to ask whose responsibility these items are. Rather, one should proclaim that this responsibility is a shared, hospitalwide one. It is a responsibility of seeing to it that appropriate standards of performance as it relates to public relations and marketing are present in all service areas of the medical center.

Those who work in today's health care environment are only too aware of the competition between hospitals for an even smaller number of patients. This is particularly true with the current trend of outpatient surgery units and third party payers who mandate alternate approaches to the handling of certain diagnoses and procedures in settings outside the inpatient environment. One must begin to examine new and different approaches to matching the standards and special needs of patients and physicians to the services that medical centers offer.

Clearly, there is no other single department in the medical center that is in a better position to handle the public relations and marketing responsibilities than admitting. Often called the "gateway to the medical center" or the "hub of the hospital," admissions and registration is the first contact setting that can truly "make or break" the lasting first impression both physicians and patients make of medical centers and hospitals.

PUBLIC RELATIONS IN A HOSPITAL SETTING

The American Hospital Association defines public relations as "a planned program of policies and performance that, when properly communicated, will build public confidence and increase public understanding and support."[1] One component of a hospital public relations program is publicity. Publicity involves communicating messages about the hospital's actions and activities. Hospital admitting managers may see a variety of examples of positive publicity emanating from the public relations department. Public relations directors may assist admitting managers in framing documents that announce new and existing service features of an admitting department. In addition to the usual press releases and memoranda coming from the public relations department, this office may help, for example, to explain a new telephone system that has been implemented. Admitting managers would be wise to use the public relations experts in the hospital for assistance in implementing admitting public relations programs while at the same time maximizing their own expertise in the admissions field.

MARKETING IN A HOSPITAL SETTING

Marketing refers to all business activity involved in the moving of goods and services from the producer to the consumer. This may include selling, advertising, and packaging these goods and services to that consumer.

Marketing in a medical center or a hospital involves recognizing who are the real users of that institution's health care services. It is also creating impressions as a result of this recognition so that positive relationships are erected between these key user groups and the medical center or hospital staff. In the case of the admitting department, the main user groups are physicians and patients. It is through a variety of marketing efforts with public relations efforts that one can attempt to motivate these user groups positively concerning the available services.

A SYSTEMS APPROACH INVOLVING ADMITTING

A systems approach to public relations and marketing recognizes that there must be a corporate commitment to excellence stemming from the very top of the organization. One must accept and deal from a basic fact. Admitting and registration areas, along with the medical center as a whole, create a complex blending of an incredible number of systems and countervailing forces. All of these systems have a common goal. The goal is the best possible patient care while maintaining a healthy financial position. The management style of admitting managers and the operations of admitting departments must allow for this systems approach. The political position of an admitting department will be enhanced by making admitting a key service area that is dependable and available.

Patient Perceptions

The patient's perception of the hospital is key to that patient's use of the facility. It is also directly linked to the positive or negative feedback the patient will share with attending and consulting physicians. This sharing will have the ripple effect of influencing future admissions.

Public relations and marketing means many things to hospitals and medical centers. It is often accomplished by a variety of techniques and programs. The same concepts, specific techniques, and options used by public relations personnel can also be used by admitting managers to maximize their own positive public relations and marketing position in the department. Admitting managers not only can accomplish positive goals for their own operation but also can accomplish these for the medical center and the given community it serves as well.

HOSPITAL PUBLIC RELATIONS PROGRAMS

Understanding Needs and Trends

Today's issues and concerns in health care are many. They include an ever-growing criticism of rising health care costs, quality of care, and the efficiency of administration in hospitals. Another issue is the increasing amount of government influence in the consideration of the finances of health care costs. All of these issues and concerns create a distinct need for a public relations awareness. Public opinion ebbs and flows in accordance with available information. The same holds true for the admitting department: the various publics served by the department know only what information is available to them. These trends indicate that, both internally and externally, good public relations programs and personal skills have never been of greater importance. It is important that the admitting manager establish a close working relationship with the director of public relations since both are in positions of mutual benefit in understanding trends, issues, and concerns.

UNDERSTANDING PUBLIC RELATIONS RESPONSIBILITY

Most hospital public relations programs have basic elements and responsibilities. They assess the current situation, define the problem areas, and identify the pertinent publics served. Public relations departments also establish goals, implement programs, and periodically evaluate the implemented programs using creative and innovative methods. The department will often coordinate research, publicity, speaker bureau activities, special events, and liaison with the community at large.

Understanding Specific Programs

At times, public relations will take on a broad or narrow focus for a given project or program. Inasmuch as each patient potentially influences opinion, hospitalwide patient sensitivity campaigns are conducted. These "We Care" types of campaigns are helpful over a short period of time. However, lack of sustained contact, information, and interest often make these attempts short lived.

The newest trend in hospitalwide programs is the guest relations program. It is a multifaceted program that structures education and information housewide while tailored to different populations at different times. First, there are meetings with the administrative team to get the necessary commitment. Then, an all-staff workshop takes place to relate the corporate commitment and philosophies of guest relations. There are numerous components to such programs, such as telephone standards and training, patient relations films, brainstorming sessions on how the medical center can work both more efficiently and effectively, and so on. With such programs, however, it is important to remember that, unless treated as a whole, none of the single pieces is effective in achieving the goal of an environment in which all interactions between people (e.g., staff, physicians, patients, visitors, and all others) are mutually positive, supportive, and beneficial.

Other activities of the public relations department may include luncheons for auxiliary and volunteers and dinners for board members. The public relations department also serves as the chief liaison with the media on all appropriate issues, especially relative to the increasing costs of health care.

Understanding the Admitting Manager's Contribution

The admitting manager can use the already established reputation as an effective professional to recommend to hospital administration suggestions about sensitivity programs. The admitting manager should suggest that the only sensitivity program to be supported should be a multiple year, long-range corporate plan and not a cut and paste, short-term, button-wearing program forgotten almost before the first flyer is inserted into the payroll check envelope. Carefully planned and effectively run public relations sensitivity programs that allow for meaningful feedback within a structured time frame are indeed most valuable. They do, however, require a great deal of time, effort, and commitment. Each of these criteria and values must be reflected in the framework from which one draws and exercises the program.

HOSPITAL MARKETING PROGRAMS

The Incentive

Marketing or selling medical center services to targeted publics still feels a bit unusual to many hospital professionals. Many still shudder when they experience television or radio advertisements detailing the services available from their area medical centers. There are too many hospitals in our metropolitan areas. Therefore, marketing hospitals to survive the competition that exists at this time and for the foreseeable future is essential.

The Strategic Plan

Many public relations and marketing departments have incorporated or led the way for the initiation of a strategic planning and marketing department. This department is involved in the process of analyzing, reanalyzing, statistically searching targeted publics, and making recommendations to administrators and boards of directors. The recommendations center around what really needs to be done in order to keep the fair share of the health care market. There are many strategic planning directors who insist they have little idea as to what services will really be in demand. The reason, they say, is because of the incredibly dynamic nature of the health care delivery system. As a result of this uncertainty there are ongoing efforts to apply more and more computerized methods of market research so that the planning directors' own facilities will indeed attempt to be competitive with the passage of time and the development of technology.

The Admitting Manager

It is important that hospital admitting managers understand the context within which to both analyze and plan for the public relations and marketing efforts to take place in the admissions and registration areas. That is, they must understand the macrocosm of the medical center and the community before they can effectively understand the microcosm of their individual functional departments.

A way to understand the microcosm of the individual admitting department is to perform an informal audit of the present best efforts of this department as they relate to public relations and marketing. Once this is accomplished, techniques, concepts, and options focusing on areas in the department can be used to improve and fine tune these same areas.

ANALYSIS OF ADMISSIONS AND REGISTRATION

As a concerned admitting professional, the admitting manager is aware of the images that admissions and registration areas portray, be they emergency department registration, outpatient registration, bed reservations, preadmissions, or inpatient admissions. It will significantly benefit the manager to conduct an informal study of the quality and effectiveness of the marketing and public relations efforts in the admissions and registration areas at this time. Until this current status is known, it is unlikely that there will be a basis of comparison to measure any progress toward improvement.

This analysis should not be regarded as a heavy, significant, and time-consuming effort. The admitting manager should provide a design for its actual administration. An excellent approach to conducting this study is to involve three of the best administrators, department directors, or physicians who happen to be critics of admitting to conduct an informal audit of their own design. The areas of focus mentioned here are simply a guide and departure point for any enhancement and tailoring to suit a particular medical center, as well as the realities of the hospital's individual admission and registration functional areas. The three major component areas recommended for close and careful review are (1) job functions and staff, (2) overall departmental image, and (3) overall efforts toward enhanced effectiveness.

Job Functions and Staff

Job Descriptions and Tables of Organization

Are there well-written job description cards that clearly and accurately represent the actual jobs performed? Are published and administratively approved tables of organization available to the department?

Interview Techniques and Practices

Are those personnel who are responsible for hiring employees fully trained in the art and skill of appropriate interviewing techniques? Are salary rates competitive with other hospitals in the same general geographic area?

Interviewing and hiring are clearly important issues. Appropriate time and energy must be invested before, during, and after the interview to ensure that the best-qualified personnel enjoy the privilege of working in the hospital's admissions operation.

Orientation and Training

Once hired, do new employees receive appropriate and exhaustive orientation and training? Are expectations, including attendance and punctuality requirements, explained and discussed? Does the training plan suit the department's needs, along with those of the medical center?

Turnover Rate

How many terminations were there in the department last year? When this number is divided by the total staffing complement, the turnover percentage is obtained. Is this an acceptable rate?

Staff Analysis

It is important to determine each staff member's individual strengths and weaknesses in the most objective way possible. This is a major effort that yields great rewards. Do the staff members feel positive about their career decision and choice, and does it show in their daily work performance?

Overall Departmental Image   .

Does the staff consistently wear appropriate professional dress? How would patients describe the department's lobbies, admissions, registration areas, and staff? What are the positive and negative components of the overall image? Is the patient's privacy considered a priority at all times?

Overall Efforts toward Enhanced Effectiveness

The following questions can be asked:

- Are examples of both positive and negative performance noted, observed, counseled, and documented consistently throughout all components of the department's operation?
- Does the admissions operation appear organized and neat, including all employees' desks?
- Is the staff used effectively? Are they cross trained for different areas in order to be of the greatest benefit?
- Are there frequent and regularly scheduled staff meetings that share all updated information for the staff's needs?
- What is the average patient waiting time from arrival in the facility to arriving at the bedside? Is this time reasonable and acceptable?
- What percentages of admissions and registrations are preadmitted or preregistered? Is this the maximum percentage possible?
- Is the quality of the operation all that it should be, consistent with objective standards of excellence established by hotel/hospital positive guest relations programs?

Once the survey is completed, the managers should share the results with their management staff. They may, at their discretion, share it with the rest of the staff as well. Those areas that need the most work should be examined, and the survey should be conducted approximately every six months, comparing the results of different instances of conducting the exercise. The results of the survey can be used in a positive way and as a guide in determining which of the specific activities used as public relations tools in admitting departments would be the best assistance in the current operation.

PUBLIC RELATIONS TECHNIQUES FOR ADMITTING

Preadmission Mail-Out Packets

The preadmissions mail-out packet is a positive marketing and public relations concept that almost any facility can institute, regardless of its size and resources. The packet usually consists of the following items:

- a general letter of welcome from the hospital administrator or director of admissions that indicates to the patient that the department is aware of his or her scheduled admission and provides an overview of the medical center
- the general hospital information booklet outlining financial policy, valuables information, visiting hours, and related issues
- a worksheet of social and demographic information that the patient can complete and mail back in a postage-paid envelope

Enclosure of the social and demographic information worksheet would be done if there is sufficient lead time between the point the packet is mailed and the time it would need to arrive back at the facility to be processed on a timely basis prior to the patient's actual scheduled admission day. If there is insufficient lead time, the patient is instructed to complete the form and await a preadmissions phone interview to be conducted by a member of the staff.

Similar pre-registration packets can be developed for larger outpatient registration operations. These yield the same expedited situation when the patient actually arrives for processing at the facility.

Physician's Office Staff Luncheon

Perhaps the most ambitious project from a public relations standpoint in the admitting department is the physician's office staff luncheon. It may be one of the most time-consuming and expensive concepts, but it also may yield the greatest advantages and rewards. The concept here is to have the medical center, represented in the form of the admitting manager, plan, sponsor, coordinate, and execute a luncheon at the facility or other suitably convenient location, extending an invitation to physicians' nurses, office managers, billers, and all such persons concerned.

First, the reservations staff or data processing department can compile a list of the most frequent admitting physicians to the facility. Although I would certainly encourage inviting all of their office staffs, common sense can rule when it comes to considerations of numbers. At a minimum, invite the top 50 percent by admissions frequency of the hospital's physicians' office staffs.

Formal invitations should be printed especially for the occasion or standard tasteful invitations from a stationery store should be personally addressed. If particular names are known in some of the offices, then they can be used. All invitations should be sent out a minimum of three to five weeks prior to the date, with RSVPs to be handled by phone or mail. This is the key to all future planning. Once RSVPs are returned, how many individuals will actually be attending can be analyzed and a convenient facility capable of accommodating all concerned can be chosen.

Simultaneously, a light but informative speaking agenda for the luncheon is planned. It would be appropriate to have brief remarks from the hospital administrator, reservations/bed control manager and/or supervisor, and admitting manager. Remarks should be limited to three to five minutes in order to make the most impact. The reservations system and preadmissions mail-out packet can be described. Sample documents should be available along with a summary handout that includes detailed instructions as to what types of information are the most important. Also, one might wish to include both the names and direct line phone numbers for those personnel most closely allied with the physicians' office staffs. The participants should be allowed to ask questions and give comments.

A personal thank you note can be sent to all who attended, with follow-up calls to those who did not attend. The latter can be contacted and an attempt made to solicit frank feedback as to why certain areas were not represented. The luncheon can be repeated at least once a year or at any time that admissions policies and procedures significantly change.

The admitting manager will find that the budgeted money and time invested will be well worth the improved communications that will be made with the physicians' staffs, who will undoubtedly influence their physicians to use the facility on a more regular basis if there is an apparent choice between facilities.

The Physicians' Dinner

Slightly more different is the physicians' dinner. In this situation, the managers should involve greater numbers of administrators and board members as potential speakers and participants. Remarks can be a bit more extensive and perhaps more general in scope. However, the admitting manager must be extensively included in the preparation and execution to cover the necessary details of admissions and registration at the facility and to inform the physicians that he or she is concerned about their feedback and preferences as to room assignments. In this situation, a similar amount of time is allowed for questions and comments.

Physician Office Visitations

Another way to improve physician relations is for the admitting manager to visit the offices of the most frequent admitting physicians on a regular basis. In these meetings the manager can solicit meaningful feedback regarding the quality of service being rendered in the admissions areas. In a teaching facility such meetings should be held at least quarterly with all department chairpersons. As for chief residents, such meetings should be held weekly or as necessary.

Other Meaningful Techniques

Hospital and hotel public comfort services are very often compared and contrasted by patients. A variety of public relations techniques can be used in admitting to deal with this issue. Parking, television, overnight rooms, and food service functions are just some of the areas these techniques can address.

Inasmuch as patients are often required to wait for appropriate beds and rooms, such special efforts in waiting and reception suites should include coffee, tea, milk, cold water, and so on. Also, daily newspapers along with current magazines should be conspicuously placed.

If the patient's luggage does not have luggage tags, it is possible to create a luggage tag using the patient plate. Also, some facilities arrange for laminated luggage tags to be made with the patient's business card on one side and the medical center or hospital logo on the other side.

Another related concept and practice is when a flower arrangement or other small gift is sent to the patient if there have been any problems associated with the admission process.

Publishing a booklet of admissions protocol is another excellent marketing and public relations idea. In a handy way it enables physicians and all others concerned to know how admissions, reservations, and financial policies fit together. An excellent example is shown in Appendix 17–A.

MARKETING TECHNIQUES FOR ADMITTING

Patient Feedback Questionnaires

Certainly a concept that has stood the test of time is the patient feedback questionnaire. This form allows patients to give candid feedback about their hospital stay, anonymously if they so choose. An example of a patient feedback questionnaire can be seen in Exhibit 17–1.

Exhibit 17–1 Patient Feedback Questionnaire

PLEASE CHECK ONE

	Excellent	Good	Average	Poor	COMMENTS
1. ACCOMMODATIONS					
a. Comfort	☐	☐	☐	☐	
b. Cleanliness	☐	☐	☐	☐	
c. Lighting	☐	☐	☐	☐	
d. Quietness	☐	☐	☐	☐	
2. FOOD					
a. Appearance	☐	☐	☐	☐	
b. Flavor (within diet limitations)	☐	☐	☐	☐	
c. Quantity	☐	☐	☐	☐	
d. Service	☐	☐	☐	☐	
e. Hot Food *Hot*	☐	☐	☐	☐	
f. Cold Food *Cold*	☐	☐	☐	☐	
3. NURSING STAFF					
a. Efficiency	☐	☐	☐	☐	
b. Promptness	☐	☐	☐	☐	
c. Courtesy	☐	☐	☐	☐	
d. Concern	☐	☐	☐	☐	
4. TREATMENT BY OTHER HOSPITAL PERSONNEL					
a. Interns and Residents	☐	☐	☐	☐	
b. Laboratory Technicians	☐	☐	☐	☐	
c. Inhalation Therapists	☐	☐	☐	☐	
d. X-ray Technicians	☐	☐	☐	☐	
e. Physical Therapists	☐	☐	☐	☐	
f. Explanation of Special Tests or Medical Procedures	☐	☐	☐	☐	
5. ADMITTING OFFICE					
a. Courtesy	☐	☐	☐	☐	
b. Promptness	☐	☐	☐	☐	
c. Explanation of Hospital Policies and Routines	☐	☐	☐	☐	
d. Explanation of Insurance and Financial Arrangements	☐	☐	☐	☐	
6. BUSINESS OFFICE					
a. Courtesy	☐	☐	☐	☐	
b. Helpful	☐	☐	☐	☐	
c. Consideration	☐	☐	☐	☐	
7. GENERAL IMPRESSIONS OF					
a. Hospital	☐	☐	☐	☐	
b. Volunteer Service	☐	☐	☐	☐	
c. Visiting Procedure	☐	☐	☐	☐	
d. Mail Service	☐	☐	☐	☐	
e. Television	☐	☐	☐	☐	
f. Telephone	☐	☐	☐	☐	

8. DID YOU WATCH PATIENT EDUCATION TV ON CHANNEL 6   ☐ Yes   ☐ No

  a. What films did you watch _____

  b. Comments _____

  c. What other patient education topics would you like to see _____

9. WOULD YOU RECOMMEND THIS HOSPITAL?   ☐ Yes   ☐ No

I would like to request that this information be kept confidential   ☐

Room No. _____ Length of Stay _____ Was This Your First Stay With Us? _____

Name _____ Physician _____

Street _____ Phone _____

City _____ State _____ Zip _____

Source: Courtesy of Cedars-Sinai Medical Center, Los Angeles, California.   CEDARS-SINAI MEDICAL CENTER ⒸⓈ

Careful analysis of trends by both department managers and administrators helps to ensure continuous quality control efforts. Often the data processing department can arrange for the completed questionnaires to be keypunched. As a result, a monthly summary report can break down what percentage in any category rated a given service "excellent," "good," and so on. Even the narrative comments are often keypunched for the benefit of all who receive the summary report.

The questionnaire should be kept as a dynamic item. Phrasing should be clear, understandable, and to the point if results are to be meaningful. The working or revised questionnaire can be targeted for a trial period with a limited patient population.

Although percentage of return from patients is not usually exceptional, this process is still a worthwhile effort. Every reasonable effort must be made to hand out the questionnaire either in admissions or by a patient relations representative to the patient or patient's family member. Another way to present the patient this questionnaire is to include it as a perforated final page of a patient information booket, as can be seen in Exhibit 17–2. Of course, as with any survey process, patience and diligence are necessary components for successful implementation. Another recommendation is to develop a physician feedback loop questionnaire. Of course, one cannot anticipate as high a percentage of return on the physician questionnaire as on the patient questionnaire.

The Phantom Patient

Another very effective way to measure the marketability of the services provided in the admitting department is the concept of the "phantom patients."

A member of the hospital's administrative team assumes a fictitious name and an elective admission is scheduled for the "patient" as if everything were real. Then, each interaction that the "patient" has is carefully monitored. These interactions are assessed according to the following three guidelines:

1. How long did the patient have to wait to be admitted?
2. How long did it take to reach the room?
3. How much courtesy, tact, warmth, and diplomacy were present and exhibited by receptionists, volunteers, admissions representatives, escorts, and all concerned?

A similar method is for the manager to call the department when away from the hospital and to ask general information questions, such as directions to the medical center. In this manner the manager can assess the telephone manner and helpfulness of the staff. One final approach is for the admitting manager to join a roving group of patient representatives or advocates who visit inpatient nursing units to solicit feedback. The representatives should be chosen from the ranks of the most respected managers.

Exhibit 17–2 Patient Questionnaire As Part of Admissions Booklet

Your Opinion

Please help us to serve you better by answering these questions about your hospitalization. We would appreciate your completing the questionnaire and returning it to us (no postage necessary). Your opinions and suggestions are of value to us.

	Yes	No
1. Your Admission:		
Were you courteously received?	☐	☐
Was your admission efficiently processed?	☐	☐
2. Your Room:		
Was your room ready at the time of admission?	☐	☐
Was it kept clean to your satisfaction?	☐	☐
Was everything in good repair?	☐	☐
3. Your Meals:		
Were you on a special diet ordered by your physician?	☐	☐
Was your food served at an acceptable temperature?	☐	☐
Was it appetizing?	☐	☐
Was there a sufficient selection on the menu?	☐	☐
Overall, were you satisfied with the food service?	☐	☐
4. Your Nurses:		
Were they courteous and concerned about you?	☐	☐
Were they prompt to respond to your needs or requests?	☐	☐
Do you feel your nurses attempted to make your hospital stay comfortable?	☐	☐
5. Your Doctors:		
Did your doctors explain your treatment?	☐	☐
Did they answer your questions?	☐	☐
Did house staff doctors (interns and residents) provide courteous care?	☐	☐
6. Did other hospital personnel (such as dispatch employes, housekeepers, x-ray technicians) give courteous, satisfactory service?	☐	☐
7. Were hospital volunteers courteous and helpful?	☐	☐

	Yes	No
8. Your Rest:		
Was your care or recovery unnecessarily disturbed, especially between 10:30 at night and 6:30 in the morning?	☐	☐
9. Were your business office contacts regarding your account satisfactory?	☐	☐
10. In general, do you feel that you received good care at Barnes?	☐	☐

Remarks and Comments:

_____

_____

_____

_____

_____

_____

_____

_____

_____

_____

_____

_____

_____

_____

_____

_____

_____

Name_____
　　　　　　　　　　　　optional

Hospital Room No._____

Today's Date _____

Source: Courtesy of Barnes Hospital, St. Louis, Missouri.

CONCLUSION

Marketing and public relations from the admitting department is such a relatively new area that there is only a small body of knowledge on the subject. However, new ground is being broken all the time. Admissions is clearly in the best position to handle public relations and marketing capabilities. It is only with the systems approach described that a successful implementation of a public relations program can take place.

It is not necessary to use all of the suggested specific techniques, concepts, and options described here. In fact, to arbitrarily implement them without assessing their applicability to each specific situation and setting would not be in the best interest of the admitting department. Once the manager is clear which techniques are needed, a consultation group is formed with key members of the administrative team for phased implementation. If the manager decides to do a department audit, it can be repeated on a regular, periodic basis.

Perhaps one of the easiest ways for managers to assess whether the department has been improved is to see if their professional status has been raised. If their salary, span of control, and professional visibility have increased, their public relations and marketing efforts are clearly succeeding.

It is crucial that the manager reads all of the current literature, newspapers, and magazines to stay abreast of current developments. Recently developed seminars and workshops on these subjects should be especially noted. An excellent seminar entitled ''Marketing the Hospital from Admissions'' is available from the California Association of Hospital Admitting Managers.

Marketing a facility today is not a luxurious affectation but rather a competitive technique to be used by all service areas of the hospital, but especially in the department of admissions and registration.

NOTES

1. American Society for Hospital Public Relations, *A Basic Guide to Hospital Public Relations* (Chicago: American Hospital Association, 1973): 2.

Appendix 17–A

Admitting Protocol Booklet

PURPOSE

This protocol summarizes the admission policies of the University of California Davis Medical Center, Sacramento—policies intended to assure equitable access to beds by each department and to assure the most efficient and convenient admission processing for patients.

This protocol will be reviewed periodically for continued applicability and revised when appropriate. Any concerns should be directed to the Director of Admissions or the appropriate clinical department chairperson.

ADMITTING INFORMATION CONTACT PERSONS

Director, Admissions and Registration 453-2986
Manager, Admissions Office 453-2450
Reservations (Future) 453-2450
Bed Assignments, Transfers 453-2456
Patient Location 453-3511
Assistant Director of Finance 453-2518
Director of Finance 453-3591

RESPONSIBILITIES FOR PATIENT ADMISSIONS

The Hospital Admissions Department will be responsible for control and assignment of all hospital beds. Beds will be assigned in accordance with approved policies and the bed allocation schedule. Protocols for placement on inpatient units, except Psychiatric, will be developed jointly between the Director of Admitting, Director of Nursing and Chief of Service.

Source: Reprinted with permission of the Regents of the University of California, © 1981.

340

SCHEDULED ADMISSIONS

A scheduled admission is appropriate when the condition of the patient allows admission at any time facilities are available. Five working days advance notification requested.

UNSCHEDULED ADMISSIONS FROM CLINICS OR OUTSIDE FACILITIES

An unscheduled admission is appropriate when the patient's condition requires inpatient care on the current day or within the next 48 hours and must be cleared through the Admission Manager.

EMERGENCY ADMISSIONS

An emergency admission is appropriate when the patient's condition poses a threat to life or developmental damage unless inpatient care is initiated immediately.

GENERAL POLICIES

1. The UCDMC Admissions Department will schedule admissions throughout the week to maintain the most manageable census level.
2. Bed reservations should be made after arrangements have been secured for major hospital services required during hospitalization, such as surgery, diagnostic and radiological tests, etc.
3. During periods of high census, a patient given private accommodations in a multi-bed room for privacy or isolation purposes, will result in a hold on further elective admissions for the admitting service until allocated beds for that service become available or until other unused services' beds are available.

TRANSFERS TO UCDMC

1. The chief of each clinical department will identify those physicians responsible for accepting transfers and referrals. This information will be shared formally with the Hospital Admissions Department and updated as appropriate.
2. Before transfers from other institutions or referrals for admission are accepted, the responsible physician must contact the UCDMC Admissions Department to determine the availability of an appropriate hospital bed. Priority and access to beds for these patients will be consistent with UCDMC admission policies.
3. Patients being transferred from other facilities will be held until cleared by the Admissions Department.

ARRIVAL TIMES

Arrival times for scheduled admissions will be equally distributed at 15-minute intervals between 12:00 Noon and 2:00 p.m. Monday through Friday, and between 10:00 a.m. and 12:00 Noon Saturday, Sunday and holidays. The Admitting Department will advise the patient of the expected arrival times. The earliest reservations will be used for patients scheduled for invasive procedures the following day.

PRIORITY CONSIDERATIONS

Emergency and Transplant Admissions will be given the highest admission priority.

Priority should be granted to those cases meeting the criteria for isolation.

ADMISSION FROM CLINICS

Ambulatory care patients (seen in clinic facilities) who require admission will be taken to the Emergency Room if the responsible physician believes appropriate care cannot be provided in a clinic setting and a bed is not available. If a bed is available, the patient will be admitted. If the clinic is open and the patient is stable, the patient may remain in the clinic until the bed is available.

PATIENTS ON A PASS

The Hospital Admissions Department shall hold a specific bed for patients on a pass overnight if prior arrangements have been made with the Business Office (reference policy #403).

TRANSFER POLICY (INHOUSE)

The attending physician, Nursing and Bed Control share responsibility for transferring patients between nursing units. Physician transfer requests must be initiated by a written order that is dated, timed, and indicates reason for transfer. During periods of high census or for patient needs, the Nursing Department and Bed Control Department will transfer patients in order to accept incoming patients or to accommodate patients requiring a different level of care. The senior resident will be informed of patient transfers by Bed Control. Bed Control will arrange the transfer of all patients to general care areas upon receipt of requests. Nursing will transfer the patient to the assigned location.

Transfer requests must be made to Bed Control between 8:00 a.m. and 12 Noon. Actual transfer of patients will be accomplished by 1:00 p.m.

Patients will be transferred for the following reasons, listed in order of priority.

1. Transfer from an intensive care unit to create a bed for a more critically ill patient to be admitted to the unit.

2. Transfer from an intensive care unit when intensive care is no longer required.

3. Specific therapeutic and emotional needs.

    a. Isolation patients requiring private rooms for medical precaution or strict isolation as published by the Center for Disease Control. The Infection Control Committee will interpret as necessary.

    b. Combative, hostile or noisy patients potentially harmful to other patients.

c. To accept incoming patients.

d. Patient or other requests for different accommodation and transfers to assigned beds within a service will occur before elective admissions have been assigned.

Exceptions to #3 above must be approved by the Admitting Manager or the Director of Nursing or designee.

SURGICAL PATIENTS

Inpatients undergoing a surgical procedure will be assigned an inpatient bed (either a general care location or intensive care unit location as determined by the surgeon) prior to surgery.

AGE LIMIT

All patients who have not reached their 13th birthday will be admitted to the Pediatric Units on East 7 and North 6. All patients beyond the age of 13 who are considered pediatric patients may be placed on North 6 in designated pediatric beds. When bed availability is exhausted on North 6, these patients will be placed wherever beds exist with notification given. to Pediatric Service.

DEFERRAL OF ADMISSIONS

1. During periods of high census, if determined by the Admissions Department and Nursing Management to be in the best interest of patient care, elective admissions will be restricted for brief periods of time. Priority for admission of elective patients will be given to departments which have the smallest percentage of the departmental allocation of beds filled on that day.

2. When it becomes necessary to defer admissions, the department with the highest percentage of utilization of allocated beds will be responsible for deferring elective admissions. Other services will be responsible for deferring elective admissions as relative percentages of allocation change. The chief resident of the affected service will be responsible to select patients to be deferred and to inform the patients and families. If an insufficient number of beds are available and no elective admissions are scheduled, the same procedure stated above will apply to urgent admissions.

DISCHARGE

1. Patients scheduled for discharge will be prepared to vacate their beds by 10:00 a.m. of the day of discharge.

2. The medical staff shall initiate the order for advanced discharge by 9:00 p.m. the day prior to the anticipated discharge, with the final order for discharge written no later than 9:00 a.m. on the day of discharge. Discharge orders must include time and date. Once the discharge order is written, additional patient orders, other than to cancel the discharge, will not be accepted.

Adherence to these policies is essential for efficient patient admission management. Judgment in the best interest of the patient always will be used in their application.

ADMITTING PROTOCOL SUMMARY

1. Bed assignment is to be provided by service. Patients are to be admitted to primary beds of respective services.

2. To the extent possible, all patients with like diagnoses will be placed in close proximity (i.e., oncology, dermatology, etc.).

3. In the event of an extreme bed shortage, the Director of Admitting, with consultation of the Chief of Service and the Director of Nursing, is authorized to utilize any available bed, including ICU for non-ICU patients until appropriate accommodations are available.

4. Elective admissions by service, by day, are to be adhered to as closely as possible, especially during periods of high census.

5. The Admitting Department will receive advance notice for all elective admissions. It will be the Admitting Department's responsibility to log all elective admissions so as to guarantee a bed for the patient on the day of admission.

6. During high census periods, services exceeding average daily census due to excessive ER/unscheduled admissions must provide beds within that service through patient discharges or elective admission for that service will be deferred until required beds are available. Each service may obtain additional beds for elective admissions from other services if beds are available.

7. Patients and physicians will be contacted 24 hours in advance if the admission is to be delayed due to an unusually high census or ER surge.

8. Control of service beds not utilized for elective admissions by respective services within 72 hours of admission day will defer to the Admissions Department for admissions of all services, if so required.

9. In the event of a surge in ER admissions, elective admissions will be deferred by the service admitting patients through the ER.

10. A block of 11 beds, by various types, will be held each evening to accommodate ER admits (as is the current practice).

11. Pre-admission of elective patients will be accomplished as soon as possible after receipt of the Hospital Admitting Request. In the event a patient cannot be contacted after a reasonable effort has been made or is not financially cleared, the admitting physician will be contacted as far in advance of the admission date as possible.

12. Reports reflecting admitting delays and cancellations of elective admissions by service and cause will be prepared and distributed to the appropriate administrative staff and medical service chairpersons.

Chapter 18

Statistical Uses in Admitting

Dale J. Konrad

When someone mentions the hospital admitting department, the first thought that comes to mind is "those are the people who interview incoming admissions and assign beds to admissions and transfers." As is well known, at some time this was the primary mission of the hospital admitting department. Within the past decade, however, the admitting department in all hospitals has become actively involved with public relations, marketing, quality assurance, and hospital statistics. As government regulations increase and third party payers and review agencies require more data from a health care facility, the admitting department will be relied on for statistical data.

BEGINNING A DATA BASE

The following are certain data elements the admitting manager needs to analyze on a daily basis:

- amount of admissions
- discharges
- transfers
- add-ons (emergency add-ons and nonemergency add-ons)
- cancellations
- no-shows
- starting census
- ending census
- future reservations
- physician availability
- daily usable beds

In order to establish a good data base that shows current trends in the institution, it is recommended to gather this data for at least one year, but preferably two to three years. The admitting manager, along with the management team, should be totally aware of these factors since they have an overwhelming effect on the institution. During the course of a year, if these factors change, the admitting manager should be in a position to be the first to recognize a change and relate this change to the administrative director. This should be a key role for the admitting manager now and in the future. Many of the data elements will be mentioned later in the chapter when discussing establishing a manual or computerized census predictor model and statistical data base.

Admission Statistics

The first statistics that should be collected in establishing a historical data base are the numbers of admissions per day, month, and year. These statistics can be further broken down to reflect average admissions per day of week, month, and year. After obtaining these data on admissions, the manager will see fluctuations and be able to obtain standard deviations for the statistic being gathered. A graph can be set up such as the one seen in Figure 18–1. Once tables are established on this base, the above information should also be done for discharges, transfers, add-ons, and so on. The data should then be shared with the hospital's key administrative directors, central supply, building services, dietary department, medical records, business office, and all other departments in which their activity revolves around the activity of incoming admissions, transfers, and discharges of the health care facility. Creative linear graphs to reflect admissions, and so on, can be quite beneficial when discussing admission statistics.

When meeting with individuals from other departments, the visual aid of the linear graphs makes it easier to relate statistical data and the trends by day of the week or month can be easily seen. Admissions in a hospital admitting department should be further broken down into those prescheduled and those that were added on each day. This is a very important factor as it relates to staffing. Most institutions have developed methods of preadmission interviewing either by telephone or mail registration in advance, thereby cutting out much of the interview time on the day of admission. It is very beneficial for an admitting department to know on a daily basis the approximate amount of add-ons either from the physicians' offices or emergency department that can occur. Those institutions that have a medical center or clinic attached will see that on various days of the week the amount of emergencies and add-ons also will vary based on activity in these centers adjacent to the hospital. The add-on emergencies are also a key factor for the nursing department. Most add-on cases require additional studies, tests, and workups by nursing and other ancillary departments. Patients who are having elective procedures normally have most of their laboratory work done before the admission date. The breakdown, whether from the physicians'

Figure 18–1 Admissions per Month

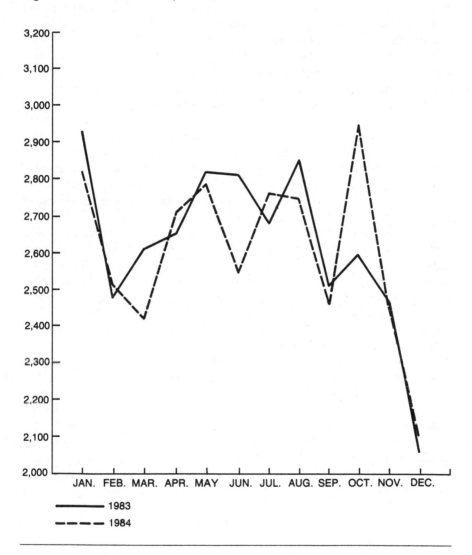

office or emergency department, is also important for the admitting department staffing pattern each day.

Average Daily Census

The average daily census is another very important statistic for the admitting department to provide for its institution. One of the best ways to depict the average daily census is to show this on a linear graph (preferably by quarter) that has on it the same period of time being compared, such as the first quarter of the previous year or the previous two years. Each day the new census is plotted, and then a comparison of how the institution is doing at the present moment versus the same period of time from the past year is done. This type of graph can also indicate what probably will happen in the near future. The cyclical fluctuations repeat themselves, and once these data have been gathered the relationship between peaks and troughs of the week will be seen. One can easily spot a decrease in length of stay if the volume of admissions is as great as the previous year but the census peaks and troughs are much lower. When the daily hospital census graph does not show a similar trend, then what has happened in the hospital must be investigated.

Factors such as physician absences, change in length of stay, and amount of daily beds available will affect the daily hospital census. When gathering data on the hospital census, the effects that holidays have on the institution should also be noted. The holiday factor becomes more significant when a holiday falls on a weekend and the Friday before or Monday after it is celebrated the hospital is closed. As a result, the trough should be much lower than normal. It normally takes two weeks to bring a hospital back to its normal census. By observing the effects of the days of the week when a holiday does occur, the admitting department may be in a position to encourage admissions for the days immediately following a holiday weekend, thereby building up the census as quickly as possible.

It should be noted that prior to investigation of the average daily census, historical data on admissions, discharges, and transfers will definitely help in the analysis. While reviewing the daily hospital admissions, discharges, and transfers retrospectively, the manager can indicate when the holiday occurred in those years that he or she is gathering data. Should the admitting manager and the department realize that a lower than normal census will occur owing to a holiday or another factor such as a physician outage, he or she should relate this to departments that rely on this information. Nursing office, business office, dietary department, and medical records are some examples of the departments that should be notified. These departments should also be notified when an increase in activity or any deviation from the norm is anticipated. The admitting manager, through analysis of past admission and census data, will be able to have a good pulse on the institution's behavior.

Hospital Occupancy Statistics

The hospital occupancy in most institutions will vary by month of the year. Once again, the holiday effect will obviously stand out for certain months of the year (e.g., December, November, May). The admitting manager should further subdivide the hospital occupancy into various special areas in the institution that make up the aggregate bed supply.

A suggested method is to subdivide the total hospital occupancy into the medical surgical area, psychiatric area, pediatric area, and intensive care area. By subdividing the total hospital occupancy by special areas of the institution, the manager will have a better idea on a daily, monthly, or year-to-date basis of each area's utilization. Should the hospital occupancy be either above or below normal for a particular month, often the reason can be easily seen by looking at the various sectors that make up this hospital occupancy. Perhaps the total hospital occupancy was 80 percent rather than 82 percent. In observing special sectors of the hospital, the manager may be able to tell easily that the pediatricians were absent and the low pediatric patient-days and occupancies caused the total hospital occupancy to be lower than normal.

While keeping track of the hospital occupancy, it is essential that the hospital admitting manager keep, on a daily basis, the amount of beds registered per area of the institution. It is not uncommon in the health care environment to go back several years for a particular management study to let a physician know the exact amounts of beds available in certain sections of the hospital. If a daily record is not kept of total beds available by unit or area of the hospital, the trend lines for future projected hospital occupancy rates will never be correct. Previous data on available beds per area of the hospital can also be a significant aid for nursing administration to determine future staffing needs.

During the building of an admitting department statistical data base, it is recommended to have the following format maintained (Table 18–1). In addition to these statistics, the following data elements should also be maintained:

- pediatric patient-days
- pediatric occupancy
- total possible pediatric patient-days
- actual psychiatric patient-days
- psychiatric occupancy
- actual intensive care patient-days
- total possible intensive care patient-days
- intensive care occupancy

If records such as these are not currently kept, time and effort to establish a book containing these data will definitely be an asset in the future. Often, the administrative staff in an institution needs to compare data from previous years with the current year or years. The further back these records are compiled, the more beneficial it will be to the institution.

Table 18–1 Hospital Admission Statistics (Monthly)

YEAR ___1984___

Month	Admissions	Average Admissions Per Day	Actual Hospital Patient-Days	Total Possible Patient-Days	Hospital Occupancy Rate	Length of Stay	Actual Medical-Surgical Patient-Days	Total Possible Medical-Surgical Patient-Days	Medical-Surgical Occupancy Rate	Average Daily Census
January	2,834	91.4	22,860	31,248	73.2%	8.07	18,943	25,358	74.7%	737.4
February	2,510	86.6	23,469	29,232	80.3%	9.35	19,692	23,722	83.0%	809.3
March	2,431	78.4	23,130	31,248	74.0%	9.51	19,021	25,358	75.0%	746.1
April	2,736	91.2	22,420	30,240	74.1%	8.19	18,220	24,540	74.2%	747.3
May	2,783	89.8	23,493	31,248	75.2%	8.44	19,680	25,358	77.6%	757.8
June	2,558	85.3	22,707	30,240	75.1%	8.88	18,608	24,540	75.8%	756.9
July	2,757	88.9	22,876	31,248	73.2%	8.30	18,858	25,358	74.4%	737.9
August	2,738	88.3	23,925	31,248	76.6%	8.74	19,573	25,358	77.2%	771.8
September	2,459	82.0	21,911	30,240	72.5%	8.91	18,205	24,540	74.2%	730.4
October	2,939	94.8	23,882	31,248	76.4%	8.13	19,808	25,358	78.1%	770.4
November										
December										

Source: Courtesy of Cleveland Clinic Foundation, Cleveland, Ohio.

STATISTICAL DEFINITIONS

A variety of definitions are used to describe statistics used frequently in admitting departments. Some of the more common definitions used across the country are the following:

- *inpatient census*: the number of inpatients present at any one time
- *daily inpatient census*: the number of inpatients present at the census taking time each day, plus any patients who are admitted and discharged after the census taking time the previous day. It is normally taken at midnight.
- *total inpatient service days*: the sum of all inpatient service days for the period under consideration (e.g., weekly, monthly, yearly)
- *average daily inpatient census*: the total inpatient service days for a period divided by the total number of days in the period
- *length of stay*: the number of calendar days from admission to discharge. The length of inpatient hospitalization is considered to be one day. If the patient is admitted and discharged the same day or admitted on one day and discharged the next, it is counted as one day. The day of admission is counted as an inpatient day but not the day of discharge from the hospital.
- *total length of stay*: the sum of the day stay of any group of inpatients discharged during a specific period of time
- *average length of stay*: the average length of hospitalization of inpatients discharged during the period under consideration
- *inpatient bed count*: the number of available hospital inpatient beds both occupied and vacant on any given day. This can also be referred to as bed complement or bed capacity.
- *inpatient bed count days*: the sum of inpatient bed count days for each of the days in the period under consideration. This has also been referred to as potential days and maximum patient days.
- *inpatient bed occupancy ratio*: the proportion of inpatient beds occupied is defined as the ratio of inpatient service days to inpatient bed count days in the period under consideration. This ratio is also sometimes described as the ratio of actual days of care to maximum days of care for a period of time. This ratio is usually expressed as a percentage and can be computed at any specified time for any specified day and as a daily average in a period of time.

THE ROLE OF DATA PROCESSING WITH THE ADMITTING DEPARTMENT

The establishment of a good working relationship with the hospital's data processing department is essential for the development of computer reports in the admission area. An important aspect before the admitting department is ready to produce various computer reports is first of all the establishment of a good admission data base. Exhibit 18–1 offers a list of suggested data elements to be collected in the admissions department.

MARKETING STATISTICS INFORMATION

The data elements in the previous section have been expanded over a period of years in order to obtain the type of reports necessary for admitting managers to be able to perform effectively. The following is a list of reports that have been generated through this data base.

- *admission schedules by date sequence*—a listing of reservations in alphabetical order by date for all future reservations
- *admission schedules by name (alphabetical)*—a listing of all reservations in alphabetical order
- *future reservations by service and date*—a listing of all reservations by service for the current day and the next seven days
- *future reservations by physicians*—a listing of all reservations by physicians in date order
- *future reservations by insurance*—a listing of reservations in date order with primary and secondary insurance information
- *preadmission review, advance information*—a listing produced daily of all patients that require preadmission review
- *utilization review, admission list*—a listing, produced daily, of all patients in the hospital that require utilization review
- *schedule changes*—a list produced daily of any patient reservation that was changed from one date to another
- *daily admissions*—a list produced daily of previous day's admissions
- *admissions file cards*—back-up patient demographic cards produced with each admission
- *nursing care work sheet*—a list produced daily for each nursing unit to complete patients' current status at the start of each day
- *daily transfer sheets*—a listing produced daily of all in-house transfers that occurred the previous day
- *daily service charge*—a listing of all patients in-house with current daily bed charge (produced daily)
- *alphabetical census*—an alphabetical listing produced daily of all patients in-house

Exhibit 18–1 Suggested Elements for an Admitting Department Data Base

Name of patient (last, first, middle initial)
Primary physician (code)
Secondary physician (code)
Room preference

RESERVATION INFORMATION

Date reservation taken
Date reservation scheduled
Type of admission (elective, in-and-out, emergency, outpatient, TCI,* regular admit)
Service of primary physician (medical or surgical)
Room number of patient
Primary admitting diagnosis
Secondary admitting diagnosis
Surgical procedure/medical services to be rendered
Anticipated length of stay
Date of surgical procedure
Hospital transfer information

Hospital transfer code
Name of hospital transfer

PATIENT DEMOGRAPHICS

Name (last, first, middle initial, title)
Street address
City
State
ZIP code
Phone number
Religion
Date of birth
Age
Race
Sex
Marital status
Name of spouse
Social Security number
Occupation
Badge number

PATIENT EMPLOYER INFORMATION

Employer
Employer's street address
Employer's city
Employer's state
Employer's ZIP code

EMERGENCY NOTIFICATION INFORMATION

Next of kin information (last name, first name, middle initial)
Telephone number
Relationship

*TCI (*To Come In*)—a patient who is admitted to a bed *after* surgery.

Exhibit 18–1 continued

RESPONSIBLE PARTY INFORMATION	Last name, first name, middle initial Relationship to patient Street address City State ZIP code Employer
INSURANCE INFORMATION*	Hospital insurance code Medical insurance code Assignment indicator Type of insurance indicator Name of insurance company Street address ZIP code Policy number Group number Service codes Medical code of hospital, service code of hospital Name Sex Relationship of patient to contract holder Employment status Name of employer of primary holder Address of employer City of employer State of employer ZIP code of employer
SPOUSE EMPLOYER INFORMATION	Occupation Social Security number Employer Employer's street address Employer's city Employer's state Employer's ZIP code Employer's phone number

*Note: This insurance information is also collected for secondary and tertiary insurances

- *visitor pass alphabetical census*—an alphabetical listing produced daily of all patients in-house for the visitor control desk
- *census summary by nursing station*—a comprehensive list produced daily that has each nursing unit's current census, previous seven-day census, month-to-date census, and year-to-date census

- *census by physician*—a list produced daily for each physician who has patients in-house, indicating patient's name, room number, physicians, and length of stay
- *census summary by service types*—a list produced daily of medical, surgical, psychiatric, and pediatric census (daily, month to date, and year to date)
- *daily dismissal sheets (four-day dismissal)*—a list produced daily for hospital information personnel that has all patients discharged within the past four days
- *admission card*—an index card with patient demographic data produced for each admitting physician
- *census prediction*—a projection of the current day's census plus that for the next 59 days
- *express admission list*—a list of patients scheduled who have been treated within the past six months
- *hospital admissions and patient days by service*—a list produced daily separating admissions and patient-days by age bracket and service for the current day, month to date, and year to date
- *hospital admissions and patient days by physician*—a report produced daily of admissions and patient-days by physician within each service
- *nursing station activity*—a report produced daily indicating the number of admissions, discharges, transfers-on, and transfers-off for each nursing unit
- *insurance audit report*—a report produced daily listing the previous day's admissions and financial data entered in the system for auditing purposes
- *forecast of physicians' absences by department*—a list produced biweekly indicating the projected number of physicians by department to be out for the current month and the following six months
- *off-service patients*—a listing produced daily of all patients not located on appropriate departmentalized floors
- *projected discharges*—a list produced daily indicating the amount of in-house patients expected to be discharged for the current day
- *transfers into service*—a report produced daily indicating the amount of patients that have changed primary service
- *summary of discharge times by service*—a report listing discharge times for all patients discharged the previous day, in nursing station sequence
- *patient care days by room type*—a report produced daily listing patient-days in semiprivate rooms, wards, intensive care units, and so on, by insurance type
- *hospital admissions and care days by financial class*—a report created daily of previous day's admissions and patient-days according to financial class

- *hospital admissions and care days by insurance code*—a report created daily of previous day's admissions and patient-days by primary insurance
- *hospital in-and-out patients*—a report produced daily of previous day's in-and-outs by service along with month-to-date and year-to-date data
- *special room rates*—a listing of all patients in rooms that are not the standard price or indicator for a room

In addition to these daily reports, there are numerous reports that can be requested when necessary:

- *room rate maintenance*—a list produced each time maintenance of room rates occurs
- *room and bed listing*—a list of all beds, current room indicator, and regular and irregular charge for room
- *physician cross reference*—a listing of all physicians who have admitting privileges with their admitting number and service
- *major insurance recipients alphabetical table*—a listing of all insurance companies with their admitting code

ADMITTING REPORTS GENERATED

As an admitting department statistical base is built up over the years, the realization of a multitude of reports on various activities of the institution can be created. One of the first reports that can be generated on a monthly basis is a comparative statistics report (Table 18–2). This report lists admitting department statistics for the current month, the comparative month of the previous two years, and year-to-date statistics. The statistics that are compared each month are the admissions, average admissions per day, hospital patient-days, hospital occupancy rate, length of stay, medical/surgical patient-days, medical/surgical occupancy rate, and average daily census. On the report the statistics for the current month are compared with the previous month of the previous years and also with year-to-date statistics. By looking at admitting statistics on a monthly basis and statistics over the years, administrators, nursing directors, and department heads can see what is happening in the hospital.

There are further subsections of this report that compare, on a monthly basis, the admitting statistics of intensive care, psychiatric, pediatric and other areas of the hospital. Thus the report has served as a base to see if the current month is similar to the same month a year ago; or if there is a difference, what variables in the admitting statistic report indicate a difference. Once this has been determined, a further in-depth analysis of the specialized area(s) of the institution can be looked into.

Table 18–2 Comparative Statistics

	1984 Sept.	1984 YTD	1983 Sept.	1983 YTD	1982 Sept.	1982 YTD
Admissions	2,459	23,806	2,501	24,302	2,779	24,695
Average Admissions Per Day	82.0	86.9	83.4	89.0	92.6	90.5
Hospital Patient-Days	21,911	206,791	23,475	222,194	25,341	230,403
Hospital Occupancy Rate	72.5%	74.9%	77.6%	80.7%	83.8%	83.7%
Length of Stay	8.91	8.69	9.39	9.14	9.12	9.33
Medical/Surgical Patient Days	18,205	170,800	19,820	187,153	21,593	194,262
Medical/Surgical Occupancy Rate	74.2%	76.2%	80.8%	83.8%	88.0%	87.0%
Average Daily Census	730.4	754.7	782.5	813.9	844.7	844.0

Source: Courtesy of Cleveland Clinic Foundation, Cleveland, Ohio.

If the data base includes monthly and year-to-date statistics on the medical/surgical, psychiatric, pediatric, and intensive care sections of the hospital, the admitting manager will be able to see easily what area exceeded its normal occupancy or fell short of the norm. Often the overall occupancy of an institution may increase or decrease because of a particular subsection of the institution. A sample of a monthly report that is used for intensive care areas is seen in Table 18–3. In this report, the special areas in the intensive care unit are listed with their occupancy rate for the month. This gives the intensive care nursing personnel and administrative personnel for this section an opportunity to view the statistics of the intensive care areas on a routine basis. This report has become quite valuable in the allocation of intensive care beds for future use.

Another report that can assist nursing personnel tremendously is the monthly summary of the nursing floor activity (Table 18–4). On this report, there is daily,

Table 18–3 Intensive Care/Special Care Statistical Monthly Report

Intensive Care Unit	Actual Patient-Days	Possible Patient-Days	Occupancy Rate
Cardiac Intensive Care	750	1,050	71.4%
Coronary Intensive Care	237	360	65.8%
Surgical Intensive Care	239	270	88.5%
Neuro-Intensive Care	163	270	60.4%
Medical Intensive Care	259	390	66.4%
Coronary Step Down	119	150	79.3%
Bone Marrow Transplant Unit	91	150	60.7%
Totals	1,858	2,640	70.4%

Table 18-4 Nursing Station Activity

NURSING FLOOR	DESCRIPTION	DAILY TOTALS ADMITS	TRANS-I	TRANS-O	DISCH	MTD TOTALS ADMITS	TRANS-I	TRANS-O	DISCH	YTD TOTALS ADMITS	TRANS-I	TRANS-O	DISCH
MEDICAL/SURGICAL													
H050	UROL/GYN	9	2	0	2	31	3	2	4	31	3	2	4
H051	UROL/GYN/DERM/PLAS	1	0	0	8	14	2	2	12	14	2	2	12
H060	ORTHO/RHEUM	1	2	0	1	16	0	5	7	16	0	5	7
H061	ORTHO/RHEUM	0	3	0	2	5	7	0	2	5	7	0	2
H070	CARDIOVASCULAR	5	0	3	9	14	7	2	10	14	7	2	10
H071	CARDIOVASCULAR	5	4	7	4	11	11	5	8	11	11	5	8
H080	CARDIOLOGY	3	4	0	6	18	8	26	15	18	8	26	15
H081	CARDIOLOGY	6	2	2	4	33	12	10	10	33	12	10	10
M030	GAST/CORS/GENS	1	0	2	2	9	1	2	7	9	1	2	7
M031	GAST/CORS/GENS	1	1	0	2	7	1	2	2	7	1	2	2
MC33	GAST/CORS/GENS	7	3	2	3	32	1	2	2	32	1	2	2
M040	PRIVATE MED/SURG	0	3	1	2	10	3	2	7	10	3	2	7
M041	OTOLARNYNGOLOGY M/S	6	2	1	2	17	4	2	2	17	4	2	2
M043	HEMATOLOGY-ONCOLOGY	5	2	3	2	16	1	3	8	16	1	3	8
M050	NEUROSURGERY	3	2	3	7	14	4	6	3	14	4	6	3
M051	NEUROSURGERY	0	0	0	0	1	1	0	0	1	1	0	0
M052	PRECAUTIONARY CARE	0	0	5	2	0	1	0	0	0	1	0	0
M053	PULM/ENDO/OPHT	4	0	2	3	17	7	7	9	17	7	7	9
M060	PERIPHERAL VASCULAR	0	2	1	0	9	3	5	7	9	3	5	7
P061	INTERNAL MEDICINE	3	1	1	5	13	3	2	8	13	3	2	8
M070	CARDIOLOGY	0	0	0	0	0	0	0	0	0	0	0	0
M071	GEN MED/SURG	1	0	0	4	19	2	2	7	19	2	2	7
M080	HYPERTENSION	1	1	1	0	0	0	1	0	0	0	1	0
P047	DERMATOLOGY/PLASTIC	0	0	0	0	0	0	0	0	0	0	0	0
	SUBTOTALS-->	56	28	31	72	306	75	87	142	306	75	87	142
INTENSIVE CARE													
H020	CARDIOVASC INTENSIVE	0	5	2	0	2	14	11	0	2	14	11	0
H021	CARDIOVASC INTENSIVE	0	5	7	0	2	19	17	0	2	19	17	0
H022	CARDIOVASC INTENSIVE	0	0	5	0	8	0	9	0	8	0	9	0
H023	CORONARY INTENSIVE	1	3	1	0	5	9	9	1	5	9	9	1
H032	MEDICAL INTENSIVE	1	1	1	0	0	3	2	3	0	3	2	3
M042	HEMA/ONC ISOLATION	0	0	0	0	7	0	0	0	7	0	0	0
M063	NEUROSURG INTENSIVE	0	3	2	0	1	7	7	0	1	7	7	0
M064	SURGICAL INTENSIVE	0	4	2	0	1	7	6	0	1	7	6	0
	SUBTOTALS-->	2	21	19	0	19	59	47	4	19	59	47	4

NURSING FLOOR	DESCRIPTION	DAILY TOTALS				MTD TOTALS				YTD TOTALS			
		ADMITS	TRANS-I	TRANS-O	DISCH	ADMITS	TRANS-I	TRANS-O	DISCH	ADMITS	TRANS-I	TRANS-O	DISCH
P E D I A T R I C S													
M072	PEDIATRICS	3	0	0	3	7	4	1	4	7	4	1	4
M073	PEDIATRICS	2	0	0	6	9	1	4	15	9	1	4	15
	SUBTOTALS-->	5	0	0	9	16	5	5	19	16	5	5	19
P S Y C H I A T R Y													
P077	PSYCHIATRY	2	1	0	1	6	1	1	4	6	1	1	4
P078	PSYCHIATRY	1	0	0	3	1	0	0	4	1	0	0	4
	SUBTOTALS-->	3	1	0	4	7	1	1	8	7	1	1	8
	GRAND TOTALS-->	56	50	50	65	348	140	140	173	348	140	140	173

Source: Courtesy of Cleveland Clinic Foundation, Cleveland, Ohio.

monthly, and year-to-date information on the amount of transfers in, transfers off, discharges, and admissions for each nursing unit. At the end of each month this report is sent to the personnel who are concerned with staffing. They are able to see the amount of volume of different patients entering and leaving a nursing unit each month on a one-sheet format. This makes comparisons of one unit to another quite easy. This report can also be shared by the building service personnel, who, based on the amount of transactions (admissions, discharges, and transfers), are able to staff their personnel more efficiently. This report is released on a monthly basis, but some areas of the institution, including laboratory medicine, can gather these data on a daily basis for several months to study the admissions, discharges, and transfers per day of the week. This enables them to utilize staff according to patient activity.

A report that is generated on a monthly basis and incorporates statistics both monthly and year to date compared with the previous year is the inpatient statistics by primary service report (Table 18–5). This report lists all of the medical and surgical departments. The first column has the number of admissions by primary service for the comparative year and the second column has the current monthly admissions by primary service. The third column is the percentage of change from the current year compared with the previous year. This has enabled administrative directors to see on a monthly basis the admissions by service and how they compare with the same month in the previous year. On the same report is the patient-days by month compared with the same month a year ago along with the percentage of change. This report is reviewed closely when there has been an increase or decrease in the patient-days or admissions. By using this report it is quite obvious what service is responsible for the gain or decrease. One can also see tentative trends with the length of stay, whether it has increased or decreased. After the above format is complete, the report is then done for a year-to-date accumulative comparison by service. The same services are compared with their year-to-date admissions and the patient-days with a percentage change column. The year-to-date report is viewed with more intensity, and trends can definitely be seen as the year progresses. These reports can be shared by the board of governors, hospital committee, and chairman of each department of medicine and surgery. Additional data are available on request for a particular department if information on admissions and patient-days by individual physicians in the department is wanted.

A report that has been developed and serves as a synopsis of the current month's activity is the hospital committee report (Table 18–6). This report lists the patient-days, hospital occupancy, admissions, length of stay, medical/surgical occupancy, and average daily census for the current month. These figures are compared with the same period of time in the previous year along with the projected budget for the current month. The budget variance column shows the difference between the actual and the projected budgets.

Table 18–5 Inpatient Statistics by Primary Service

February 1984

In-Patient Statistics
Monthly Comparison

Service	Total Patients						Patient Days					
Medicine	1980 February	1981 February	1982 February	1983 February	1984 February	83/84 % Change	1980 February	1981 February	1982 February	1983 February	1984 February	83/84 % Change
Allergy	4	4	2	13	7	-46%	26	21	7	66	16	-76%
Catheterization	537	494	432	445	513	15%	2417	2131	1986	1864	2138	15%
Clinical Cardiology	167	167	184	175	181	3%	1094	1201	988	1035	1038	0%
Dermatology	28	17	28	17	25	47%	579	313	403	302	371	23%
Endocrinology	17	26	25	26	31	19%	131	263	224	313	261	-17%
Gastroenterology	69	65	61	86	105	22%	869	611	661	802	992	24%
Hematology	131	143	150	111	106	-5%	1225	1276	1452	1086	1091	0%
Hypertension	97	78	83	98	67	-32%	1185	866	912	1181	775	-34%
Infectious Disease	10	8	14	5	14	180%	197	146	343	125	200	60%
Internal Medicine	49	60	63	71	62	-13%	617	771	760	831	838	1%
Neurology	81	91	93	87	100	15%	883	1062	987	960	955	-1%
Pediatrics	93	60	72	86	54	-37%	706	501	458	560	416	-26%
Peripheral Vascular	29	19	39	49	39	-20%	393	296	495	601	602	0%
Primary Health Care	35	26	35	27	23	-15%	221	187	202	158	83	-47%
Psychiatry	37	44	34	47	39	-17%	1303	1389	1341	1247	1261	1%
Pulmonary Disease	69	40	36	37	53	43%	752	655	434	354	590	67%
Rheumatic Disease	44	32	44	68	47	-31%	613	427	529	671	405	-40%
Division Totals	1497	1374	1395	1448	1466	1%	13211	12116	12182	12156	12032	-1%

Table 18-5 continued

Service	Total Patients						Patient Days					
	1980	1981	1982	1983	1984	83/84	1980	1981	1982	1983	1984	83/84
Medicine	February	February	February	February	February	% Change	February	February	February	February	February	% Change
Surgery												
Colon Rectal	64	100	94	86	139	62%	1166	1135	1270	959	1548	61%
General Surgery	132	97	95	93	104	12%	1099	1052	938	844	1026	22%
Gynecology	147	119	131	118	107	-9%	867	847	748	708	643	-9%
Neurosurgery	67	67	82	72	97	35%	947	1052	1241	1024	1095	7%
Ophthalmology	73	85	70	74	57	-23%	309	392	249	292	188	-36%
Orthopedics	142	183	212	194	193	-1%	1680	1895	2000	1651	1719	4%
Otolaryngology	99	104	104	100	93	-7%	712	611	580	623	494	-21%
Plastic Surgery	55	63	66	37	28	-24%	389	444	393	210	160	-24%
Thoracic Surgery	27	27	34	58	44	-24%	3090	2992	2775	3106	2747	-12%
Urology	152	150	151	140	124	-11%	1397	1267	1141	1199	1046	-13%
Vascular Surgery	61	56	75	58	54	-7%	710	791	956	832	726	-13%
Division Totals	1019	1051	1114	1030	1040	1%	12366	12478	12291	11448	11392	-0%
All Other												
Nuclear Medicine	0	0	0	0	0	0%	0	0	0	0	0	0%
Radiation Therapy	0	0	0	0	0	0%	0	0	0	0	0	0%
Radiology	0	0	0	0	0	0%	0	0	0	0	0	0%
Research	10	10	11	6	4	-33%	59	142	89	61	45	-26%
Other Services	0	2	0	0	0	0%	0	15	0	0	0	0%
Subtotal	10	12	11	6	4	-33%	59	157	89	61	45	-26%
Grand total	2526	2437	2520	2484	2510	1%	25636	24751	24562	23635	23469	-1%

Source: Courtesy of Cleveland Clinic Foundation, Cleveland, Ohio.

Table 18–6 Hospital Committee Report

HOSPITAL COMMITTEE
JULY 1984

	MONTHLY				YEAR-TO-DATE			
	1984 ACTUAL	1984 BUDGET	Budget VARIANCE	1984 ACTUAL	1984 ACTUAL	1984 BUDGET	Budget VARIANCE	1983 ACTUAL
Patient-days	22,876	25,788	−2,912	24,676	160,955	175,798	−14,843	173,125
Hospital Occupancy	73.2%	82.5%	−9.3%	79.0%	75.0%	81.9%	−6.9%	81.0%
Admissions	2,757	2,742	+15	2,671	18,609	19,138	−529	18,950
Length of Stay	8.30	9.40	−1.10	9.24	8.65	9.19	−.54	9.14
Medical/Surgical Occupancy	74.4%	85.2%	−10.8%	81.9%	76.3%	85.0%	−8.7%	84.1%
Average Daily Census	737.9	831.9	−94.0	796.0	755.7	825.3	−69.6	816.6

Source: Courtesy of Cleveland Clinic Foundation, Cleveland, Ohio.

HOSPITAL RESERVATIONS

A key predictor of future hospital activity is the future hospital reservations scheduled. A report that has been able to indicate future hospital reservation trends is the future hospital reservations by service report. This report lists all future hospital reservations by service for all future weeks. Once the data base is established, one can compare the amount of future reservations by service on a specific date compared with the same date the previous years. If the manager is comparing future reservations and notices a decrease or increase in reservations, immediate investigation to what service(s) has caused this variance should begin. Physician outage, planned seminars, or changes in   a physician's normal practice of admission patterns will most often be the reason. If observed early enough, the future reservation report can alert other areas of the hospital to a possible downturn in activity for their appropriate action. Should the institution be considering the remodeling of a specific unit, this report can serve as a useful tool to determine the best time for the remodeling to occur. Throughout the United States, future hospital reservations per hospital range from a very few to more than 2,000 reservations. If the amount of future reservations at the institution is above 300, incorporating future hospital reservations into the data base will definitely be of help. Another application derived from future reservations is knowing in advance the type of insurance the future patient has. If the type of insurance is coded in the reservation, statistical reports concerning the future financial makeup of the institution can be produced.

FINANCIAL AND INSURANCE REPORTS

On a monthly basis, patient accounts personnel and third party reimbursement specialists at an institution can be provided with the following reports:

- admissions and patient-days by insurance type
- admissions and patient-days by financial classification
- admissions and patient-days by room accommodation for Medicare patients and other insurance carriers

These reports will aid financial personnel by making them aware of the type of patients that make up the census each month. These reports are produced on a daily basis and reflect daily, monthly, and year-to-date totals.

The admitting department, through the use of this report, can also see trends from third party payers as to what type of insurance(s) may be increasing or decreasing. By breaking down the admissions and patient-days by insurance type, the various patient accounts personnel can also estimate when payment for services should occur. The category of patient-days by type of bed accommoda-

Table 18–7 Patient-Days by Room Type Report

```
                          PATIENT CARE DAYS
                     BY ROOM TYPE FOR :  01/04/35

                    ------DAILY-------   -----MONTHLY------   ------YEARLY------
                    MEDICARE    TOTAL    MEDICARE    TOTAL    MEDICARE    TOTAL
```

	Medicare	Total	Medicare	Total	Medicare	Total
PRIVATE ROOMS *	7	24	45	118	45	118
ISOLATION ROOMS **	5	15	16	52	16	52
TOTAL PRIVATE	12	39	61	170	61	170
SEMI-PRIVATE ROOMS	177	466	628	2,663	628	2,663
WARD ROOMS	0	1	0	14	0	14
TOTAL SEMI-PRIVATE	177	467	628	2,677	628	2,677
TOTAL GENERAL ACCOM	189	506	689	2,847	689	2,847
INTENSIVE/SPECIAL CARE	26	57	99	205	99	205
TOTAL CARE DAYS	215	563	788	3,052	788	3,052

```
*  PRIVATE ROOMS ARE MEDICALLY UNNECESSARY
** ISOLATION ROOMS ARE MEDICALLY NECESSARY
```

Source: Courtesy of Cleveland Clinic Foundation, Cleveland, Ohio.

---

tion has been quite useful, especially since some of the most recent Medicare regulations want to know Medicare patient-days by type of room accommodation. It should be noted that Medicare days and private rooms are also indicated whether they were medically necessary or not. This is illustrated in Table 18–7. The room accommodation report also makes the admitting director aware of utilization of the hospital's private, semiprivate, ward, and intensive care beds. These reports can be quite helpful when contemplating a change in the number of beds.

CENSUS PROJECTION PROGRAM

One of the most advantageous byproducts of a computerized hospital admissions system is the census projection program of possibilities (Table 18–8). One type of census projection can calculate a length of stay for each future reservation and also the expected discharge date. An average length of stay per physician can be used, but one may want to set up this program by using the length of stay given to the admitting department by the physician or average length of stay by admitting diagnosis. Each day the current day's census is projected and the net 60 days' census is tallied.

There are certain historical columns that should be included in the projection model. Average daily add-ons, optimal census parameters, and suggested reservation levels are just some of these. The optimal census is the census that can be

Table 18-8 Census Projection

DAY	DATE	AVAIL ADD-ON	AVG ADD-ON	EXPECTED ADMITS	RECOMENDED QUOTA	AVAIL ADD RES	PROJECTED DISCH	PROJECTED CENSUS-- (LOW)	(MEAN)	(HIGH)	TALLIED AVERAGE	IDEAL VARIANCE	OCCUPANCY RATE
THURSDAY	51	907	30	6	40	34	70	90	111	132	28	3.05%	2.77%
FRIDAY	1 FEB	864	28	3	17	14	80	62	80	98	65	7.12%	6.44%
SATURDAY	2	891	11		11	11	78	33	47	62	20	2.21%	1.98%
SUNDAY	3	834	13	2	40	38	28	65	76	88	14	1.57%	1.39%
MONDAY	4	893	41	16	40	24	30	69	83	97	24	2.69%	2.38%
TUESDAY	5	835	38	11	40	29	60	46	59	72	48	5.27%	4.75%
WEDNESDAY	6	894	35	3	40	37	72	28	37	47	42	4.59%	4.16%
THURSDAY	7	891	30	3	40	37	71	21	29	38	44	4.80%	4.36%
FRIDAY	8	876	28	1	17	16	82	5	12	19	53	5.81%	5.25%
SATURDAY	9	873	11		11	11	79	6	3		33	3.65%	3.27%
SUNDAY	10	833	13	3	40	37	29	28	32	37	15	1.69%	1.49%
MONDAY	11	836	41	8	40	32	30	42	50	58	31	3.47%	3.07%
TUESDAY	12	883	38	3	40	37	61	14	18	23	50	5.49%	4.95%
WEDNESDAY	13	898	35	6	40	34	73	4	9	14	38	4.15%	3.76%
THURSDAY	14	884	30	1	40	39	72	5	6	7	51	5.56%	5.05%
FRIDAY	15	834	28	2	17	15	82	17	13	9	45	4.93%	4.46%
SATURDAY	16	869	11		11	11	80	35	31	27	42	4.65%	4.16%
SUNDAY	17	876	13	1	40	39	29	11	16	21	22	2.47%	2.18%
MONDAY	18	871	41	7	40	33	31	24	30	36	26	2.91%	2.57%
TUESDAY	19	878	38	2	40	38	60	4	4	8	55	6.04%	5.45%
WEDNESDAY	20	893	35	1	40	39	73	24	18	13	38	4.15%	3.76%

Source: Courtesy of Cleveland Clinic Foundation, Cleveland, Ohio.

normally achieved on each day of the week. Before this can be determined, historical data must be gathered concerning the average number of unoccupied beds for the intensive care areas, pediatric areas, and psychiatric areas and the average number of semiprivate beds lost due to isolation or private room requests daily. These figures should be subtracted from the total registered beds of the institution to determine what the actual average capacity of the institution is. The average add-ons per day is another set feature of the program. This is determined by normally looking at the most recent year(s) of add-ons per day of the week.

The expected admission column is calculated by taking the total amount of reservations scheduled minus the ins and outs and minus the scheduled reservations times the cancellation factor. This then gives the expected admissions. The projected discharge column states the total number of patients that should be discharged on each day of the week.

A census predictor model will allow the admitting manager to have a better grasp of current utilization of the hospital and what is expected in the near future. The program can also compile data that would normally take hours to gather. Decisions to expand or contract reservations on a future date can be made with reliable data, and information about future changes in census can be given to the departments where proper staffing is a necessity.

CONCLUSION

In this day of constant change in the health care field, the admitting manager can keep the staff and hospital informed through some of the processes explained in this chapter. Not only can the institution have better information, but the admitting manager will be able to better use the department's personnel and develop cost-saving efficient operations for the admitting department. Through comprehensive data collecting and analysis, the admitting manager will find solutions to the many problems that exist, rather than finding problems in every solution.

Index

Note: Pages appearing in *italics* indicate entries found in artwork.

About the Editors

Kevin D. Blanchet began his commitment to the hospital admitting field in 1975 at Memorial Hospital in Albany, New York, where he specialized in emergency services and outpatient clinic registration. In 1978, he continued his admitting career at St. Luke's Hospital, a 500-bed teaching facility in Cleveland, Ohio, where he was involved in their emergency services department. He began a new specialization in the area of reservations and bed control as reservations officer in 1980. Currently, he is the coordinator of research and development for the Cleveland Health Education Museum in Cleveland, Ohio.

Mr. Blanchet is the author of "Behavioral Decision Making for the Admitting Manager," which appeared in the *Journal for Hospital Admitting Management*. His major areas of interest are the psychology of the admitting process, registration methods in emergency services, policy and procedure development, and organizational behavior as it relates to admitting management.

He received his B.S. degree in biology from the State University of New York at Albany and has done graduate work in basic medical sciences at the Ohio College of Podiatric Medicine and in health care administration at the University of Cincinnati with a specialty in admitting management.

Sister Mary Margaret Switlik, A.A.M., received her Bachelor of Arts degree in business administration from St. Mary of the Plains College in Dodge City, Kansas. She entered the Congregation of the Sisters of St. Joseph of Wichita, Kansas in 1955 and has served in their hospitals. Her admitting career has included positions ranging from office clerk to business manager and accountant to admitting manager.

Sister is a charter member of the National Association of Hospital Admitting Managers, and was among the original group of admitting managers to receive the new designation of "accredited admitting manager." She was the winner of NAHAM's first essay contest held in 1976, and has served as editor of *NAHAM*

Admitting Bulletin and *The Journal for Hospital Admitting Management* for over 7 years. Sister was the recipient of the Marian Blankenship Distinguished Service Award given by NAHAM in 1980, as well as a member of the Task Force which founded the Kansas Association of Hospital Admitting Management and is now an honorary member of KAHAM.

About the Contributors

Edsel A. Cotter, A.A.M., is Assistant Executive Director of the Ohio State University Hospitals where he has responsibility for a number of departments, including outpatient clinics and the emergency department. He began his career in 1969 as Assistant Director of Admitting, becoming Director of Admitting in 1971 and assuming his current responsibilities in 1981. An accredited manager and charter member of the National Association of Hospital Admitting Managers, he served as their secretary for four years. Mr. Cotter is active in the Southwestern Ohio Hospital Admitting Managers Association where he has served as president. In 1984 he was the recipient of the Marian Blankenship Award for distinguished service in the admitting management field.

William A. Giwertz, M.B.A., A.A.M., is Director of Admissions for Cedars-Sinai Medical Center in Los Angeles, California. Prior to this appointment, he was Director of Patient and Information Services for the University of California, San Diego Medical Center. Other affiliations include Manager of Admissions for The Roosevelt Hospital in New York, New York, and Supervisor, Admissions and Business Office for Kaiser Foundation Hospital in Panorama City, California. Mr. Giwertz is a member of the National Association of Hospital Admitting Managers, the Healthcare Financial Management Association, and serves on the board for the California Association of Hospital Admitting Managers.

Donald D. Hamilton, A.A.M., is Admitting Manager for Deaconess Hospital in Cleveland, Ohio. He has led a distinguished career in hospital admitting for the past 25 years. Mr. Hamilton has served as treasurer for the National Association of Hospital Admitting Managers for seven years and is also an active member of the Ohio Hospital Admitting Managers Association.

Donald E. Hancock, M.B.A., A.A.M., is Vice President for Operations, Shands Hospital, Inc., at the University of Florida at Gainesville. Previous to assuming his current responsibilities in 1983, he served as Director of Ancillary Services, Director of Clinical Services, and Director of Admissions/Financial Arrangements. Mr. Hancock is a member of the advisory board of the National Association of Hospital Admitting Managers and served as their secretary from 1978–1980. He is a member of the American College of Hospital Administrators.

Ollivene Hickman, A.A.M., is the Director of Admitting for St. Luke's Episcopal Hospital, Texas Children's Hospital and the Texas Heart Institute hospital complex in Houston, Texas. She has held accreditation status for the past five years and is regional representative for Region VII of the National Association of Hospital Admitting Managers.

Lynn Howard, A.A.M., is Admitting and Communications Manager for North Colorado Medical Center in Greeley, Colorado. She began her career in admitting at Weld County General Hospital, also in Greeley and has held many offices in the Colorado Council of Hospital Admitting Managers and the National Association of Hospital Admitting Managers.

John E. Jacoby, M.D., M.P.H., is a consultant in hospital quality assurance and a principal in METROMED, an immediate medical care office in New York. Prior to this he served as Director of Quality Assurance for Bronx-Lebanon Hospital Center for four years. Dr. Jacoby has also served as Assistant Director for Medical Professional Affairs, New York City office, the New York State Department of Health, Office of Health Systems Management. He is Assistant Professor of Pediatrics, Albert Einstein College of Medicine, and has held faculty appointments at Harvard, Mount Sinai Schools of Medicine, and Columbia University.

Dale J. Konrad, B.A., A.A.M., is Director of Admissions for the 1,008 bed, internationally renown Cleveland Clinic Foundation. A former president of the Northeast Ohio Hospital Admitting Managers Association, Mr. Konrad is a member of the National Association of Hospital Admitting Managers. He is also active with the Ohio Hospital Association and the Center for Health Affairs in Cleveland, Ohio in the areas of admitting, billing, and collection.

A. Laurie Laughner, B.S., A.A.M., is Director of Admitting at New England Baptist Hospital in Boston. She has been involved in admitting management since 1977. Ms. Laughner received the 1980 Achievement Award from the National Association of Hospital Admitting Managers. She is an active member of the Massachusetts Association of Hospital Admitting Managers and has given numerous presentations and authored several papers on the field of admitting.

Lucile LePert is retired after serving 25 years as Admitting Manager of St. Joseph's Hospital and Medical Center in Phoenix, Arizona. An active member of the National Association of Hospital Admitting Managers, the Arizona Chapter Admitting Managers Association, and the California Association of Hospital Admitting Managers, she has conducted numerous seminars and conferences for admitting managers throughout the country and has also developed an admitting orders nurse program.

Michael H. Littmann, B.S., A.A.M., is Director of Admitting for Beth Israel Hospital, Boston, Massachusetts. He designed their admitting computer system, which includes over 100 separate programs. The system has been modified and installed at the Brighams and Womens Hospital of Boston. Mr. Littmann is also Data Base Manager for Clinical Administration at Beth Israel.

Patricia A. Long is an independent health care consultant in Scottsdale, Arizona. Since 1961, she has worked in the fields of admitting and finance in Arizona, New Mexico, and Kansas. At St. Luke's Hospital in Phoenix, Ms. Long served as Supervisor of Patient Registration and as Supervisor of Patient Accounts. She is a member of the National Association of Hospital Admitting Managers and is past president of the Arizona Chapter Admitting Managers Association, now serving on the board of directors.

James M. Perez, B.S., is Director of Admissions for St. Francis Regional Medical Center in Wichita, Kansas. Prior to this position Mr. Perez was Director of Admissions for Kansas Newman College in Wichita where he increased student enrollment by 5 percent each year through a marketing program he developed. He is a past president of the Kansas Association of Hospital Admitting Management and is a member of the National Association of Hospital Admitting Managers.

Betty Powell, A.A.M., is Director of Patient Registration for Jewish Hospital in Louisville, Kentucky. Previously she served as Director of Admissions for St. Anthony Hospital, also in Louisville. Ms. Powell served as president of the National Association of Hospital Admitting Managers in 1982 and is immediate past-president of the Kentucky Hospital Admitting Managers Association.

Murray Rimmer, M.P.A., F.A.C.H.A., is Administrator of the Gracie Square Hospital in New York City. Prior to this he was the Administrator of Hillside Hospital, a division of Long Island Jewish Medical Center, for nine years. He began his career in health care at Long Island Jewish Medical Center as Chief Admitting Officer in 1966. Mr. Rimmer is a fellow of both the American College of Hospital Administrators and the Royal Society of Health and holds a master's degree in public administration with a concentration in health care management from New York University. He received the Marian Blankenship Distinguished Service Award in 1979 in recognition of his significant contribution to the field of hospital admitting.

Miriam Ross, A.A.M., has been a pioneer in the field of hospital admitting management both nationally and in New York. She is Director of Admissions for the Bronx-Lebanon Hospital Center in Bronx, New York. A charter member of the Hospital Admitting Officers Association of New York and the National Association of Hospital Admitting Managers, Ms. Ross was instrumental in getting accredited coursework developed at the State University of New York, Downstate Medical Center.

Marion P. Tanner, M.P.A., A.A.M., is Director of Admitting/Communications for Providence Hospital in Medford, Oregon. Prior to holding this position, he was the Manager of Admission/Discharge Department for Children's Hospital and Health Center, San Diego, California. Mr. Tanner has served as an assistant regional representative for Region IX for the National Association of Hospital Admitting Managers. He has his degree in hospital administration from the University of Southern California.

Annette L. Valenta, Dr.P.H., is director of facility planning and design, Office of Hospital Management Programs, for the American Hospital Association in Chicago, Illinois where she is responsible for the architecturally-affiliated activities of the Association. Prior to joining the A.H.A., Dr. Valenta was a health facility consultant for four years with TriBrook Group, Inc. in Oak Brook, Illinois. Dr. Valenta specializes in the examination of architectural psychology within health care facilities. She is the author of numerous articles dealing with admitting office environments, and a design guide examining the behavioral needs and their architectural implications for staff and patients within the hospital admissions setting.

She received both her M.P.H. degree in health care services and her Dr. P.H. degree in health resources management from the University of Illinois Medical Center, School of Public Health. Dr. Valenta was named an AIA-AHA Fellow in Health Facility Design in 1980.

George E. Woodham, B.A., A.A.M., is Patient Admissions Manager for the Southern Baptist Hospital in New Orleans, Louisiana. Mr. Woodham serves as the editor of the *Journal for Hospital Admitting Management*. He has also been regional representative for Region VII of the National Association of Hospital Admitting Managers.

A